The Kurdish Women's Movement

The Kurdish Women's Movement

History, Theory, Practice

Dilar Dirik

First published 2022 by Pluto Press
New Wing, Somerset House, Strand, London WC2R 1LA

www.plutobooks.com

British Library Cataloguing in Publication Data
A catalogue record for this book is available from the British Library

ISBN   978 0 7453 4194 1   Paperback
ISBN   978 0 7453 4193 4   Hardback
ISBN   978 1 78680 738 0   PDF
ISBN   978 1 78680 739 7   EPUB

Typeset by Stanford DTP Services, Northampton, England

Simultaneously printed in the United Kingdom and United States of America

This book is dedicated to Sakine Cansız, Fidan Doğan, and Leyla Şaylemez, three Kurdish women, who were cold-bloodedly murdered in Paris on 9 January 2013. In their person, I commemorate all women who struggle against all forms of oppression, exploitation, and injustice.

Contents

Figures	ix
Abbreviations and acronyms	xi
Locations in Kurdish	xiv
Map	xv
Acknowledgements	xvi
Preface	xviii

Introduction: The Kurdistan women's revolution – A social history
from below — 1

PART I: HISTORY

1.	Mapping the Kurdistan of women	19
2.	The Kurdistan Revolutionaries	25
3.	Berxwedan Jîyan e! – The Diyarbakır prison resistance	28
4.	Vejîn! – The first bullet	33
5.	Edî bes e! – The dirty war	37
6.	Towards women's autonomy	42
7.	International conspiracy and internal crisis	50
8.	The battle for the PKK's soul	53
9.	Enter Democratic Confederalism	56

PART II: THEORY

10.	'Struggling woman': Ideology and identity	65
11.	Building 'democratic modernity'	69
12.	Jineolojî: 'A science of woman and life'	76

PART III: PRACTICE

13.	Stateless society	83
14.	Öcalan: Leader, prisoner, comrade	90
15.	Revolutionizing love	99
16.	Mothers	112
17.	Self-defence	120
18.	Martyrs	126

19. Prisoners   129
20. Education   134
21. Media   142
22. Ecology   149
23. Mexmûr: From displacement to self-determination   156
24. Bakur: Women against politicide   170
25. Başûr: 'Freedom is more than the absence of dictatorship'   192
26. Rojava: A women's revolution   208
27. Resistance or feminicide: Women against Daesh   241
28. Şengal: From feminicide to women's autonomy   252
29. Kobanê did not fall   275
30. Life after Daesh: Women's solidarity in Manbij   285
31. War and peace   290

PART IV: EMPOWERMENT OR REVOLUTION?

32. Two rivers, two freedom agendas?   301

Notes   315
Bibliography   326
Index   336

Figures

1. YJA Star guerrillas from Rojava and Bakur, building a new camp in the mountains. Xinerê. May 2015 — 43
2. Guerrillas admiring the decoration of the venue for the first Jineolojî conference. Xinerê. May 2015 — 77
3. Newroz celebration in Amed, attended by thousands of people, including international delegations. Amed. March 2015 — 84
4. Ilham (see Chapter 26), member of a *mal a jin* (women's house) in Qamişlo, with a photo of Abdullah Öcalan edited to go with the Kongreya Star logo. Qamişlo. July 2015 — 97
5. YJA Star guerrilla with an Êzîdî child after the protest to commemorate the first anniversary of the genocide. Mount Şengal. August 2015 — 10a
6. Martyr's memorial centre of the Mexmûr Refugee Camp. Mexmûr Refugee Camp. May 2015 — 120
7. A guerrilla bookshelf with translations of international works on history, sociology, and political science, as well as the movement's own literature. Qendîl. April 2015 — 140
8. Kurdish women performing traditional songs with drums (known as *daf* or *erbanê*) as part of the activities to host the World Women's March. Mêrdîn (Mardin). March 2015 — 144
9. Guerrillas taking a break during the first Jineolojî conference in 2015. Xinerê. May 2015 — 155
10. Seventh conference of the People's Assembly of Mexmûr Camp. Mexmûr Refugee Camp. May 2015 — 159
11. Centre of the Revolutionary Youth Movement. Mexmûr Refugee Camp. October 2015 — 165
12. KJA-led 8 March International Women's Day celebration in Amed. Amed. March 2015 — 180
13. The launch of the World Women's March of 2015, with feminist delegates from around the world. Nisêbîn. March 2015 — 190
14. Protest to condemn the Turkish state's violence in the aftermath of the collapsed peace process. Silêmanî. September 2015 — 200
15. Kurdistan and PKK flag alongside each other on top of a PKK institution in Kirkûk, a short drive from territories that were Daesh-held at the time. Kirkûk. September 2015 — 206

16. Photos of Sakine Cansız (Sara), Fidan Doğan (Rojbîn), and Leyla
Şaylemez (Ronahî), and Clara Zetkin and Rosa Luxemburg, above
a statue of Mother Mary, at the Ishtar Women's Academy in Rojava.
Rimelan. July 2015   220

17. Members of the Young Women's Movement in Rojava in one of their
centres. Qamişlo. December 2014   226

18. A group of wounded and disabled YPJ fighters being looked after
by their comrades. Amûdê. December 2014   235

19. Billboard honouring Ivana Hoffmann, a Black German revolutionary
from Germany and the first internationalist, who lost her life in the
fight against Daesh in Rojava. Qamişlo. July 2015   250

20. Martyr's cemetery on Mount Şengal, partially still under construction
at the time. Mount Şengal. July 2015   259

21. Founding conference of the Şengal Women's Assembly. Mount Şengal.
July 2015   262

22. Protest commemorating the first anniversary of the genocide. Mount
Şengal. August 2015   264

23. A YPJ-Şengal fighter among the young women and men guarding the
protest to mark the anniversary of the genocide. Şengal. August 2015 265

24. A makeshift living area at the Newroz Camp, Dêrîk (al-Malikiyah),
Rojava. November 2014   268

25. An HPG guerrilla with Mother Qadifa (mentioned in Chapter 16), an
Êzîdî woman from Rojava and a community organizer at the *mal a jin*
(women's house) in Tirbêspiyê (al-Qahtaniyah). Mount Şengal. August
2015   270

26. Xensê, co-founder of the Şengal Women's Assembly and mother of
Bêrîvan Şengal, sitting next to her son while discussing something
with YJA Star guerrilla fighter Özgür. Mount Şengal. August 2015   274

27. Ruins from the battle of Kobanê, a short walking distance from the
Turkish border. Kobanê. May 2018   277

28. A street sign named after fighters who died fighting against Daesh
on this spot. Kobanê. May 2018   283

29. Members of a women's commune. Kobanê. May 2018   284

30. Guerrillas visited by a Peace Mother, watching an HDP rally ahead
of the general elections in Turkey. Qendîl. June 2015   291

31. View overlooking Sur district of Diyarbakır (Amed). Sur, Amed.
January 2015   294

32. Street art in Rojava, portraying YPJ martyrs Avêsta Xabûr, Barîn
Kobanê, and Arîn Mîrkan. Near Qamişlo. May 2018   312

Abbreviations and acronyms

AANES	Autonomous Administration of North and East Syria
AKP	Adalet ve Kalkınma Partisi (Justice and Development Party)
ARGK	Artêşa Rizgariya Gelê Kurdistan (People's Liberation Army of Kurdistan)
BDP	Barış ve Demokrasi Partisi (Peace and Democracy Party)
CIA	Central Intelligence Agency
DEHAP	Demokratik Halk Partisi (Democratic People's Party)
DÖKH	Demokratik Özgür Kadın Hareketi (Democratic Free Women's Movement)
DTP	Demokratik Toplum Partisi (Democratic Society Party)
ENKS	Encûmena Niştimanî ya Kurdî li Sûriyê – Kurdish National Council in Syria (KNC)
ERNK	Eniya Rizgariya Netewa Kurdistan (National Liberation Front of Kurdistan)
FSA	al-Jaysh as-Sūrī al-Hurr (Free Syrian Army)
HADEP	Halkın Demokrasi Partisi (People's Democracy Party
HDP	Halkların Demokratik Partisi (Peoples' Democratic Party)
HPC	Hêzên Parastina Civakî (Civil Defence Forces)
HPG	Hêzên Parastina Gel (People's Defence/Protection Forces)
HPJ	Hêzên Parastina Jinê (The Women's Defence/Protection Forces)
HRK	Hêzên Rizgariya Kurdistan (Kurdistan Liberation Forces)
ISIS/ISIL	ad-Dawlah al-Islāmiyah (Islamic State (of Iraq & Syria/Levante), referred to as Daesh throughout the text)
JITEM	Jandarma İstihbarat ve Terörle Mücadele (Gendarmerie Intelligence and Counter-Terrorism Organization)
KADEK	Kongreya Azadî û Demokrasiya Kurdistanê (Kurdistan Freedom and Democracy Congress)
KCD/DTK	Kongreya Civaka Demokratîk (Turkish: Demokratik Toplum Kongresi) (Democratic Society Congress)
KCK	Koma Civakên Kurdistan (Kurdistan Communities Union)
KDP/PDK	Partiya Demokrat a Kurdistanê (Kurdistan Democratic Party)
KJA	Kongreya Jinên Azad (Free Women's Congress; later reformed after the ban as Tevgera Jinên Azad TJA (Free Women's Movement))
KJAR	Komelgeya Jinên Azad ên Rojhilatê Kurdistanê (Society of Free Women of Eastern Kurdistan)

KJB   Koma Jinên Bilind (High Women's Council/Union)
KJK   Komalên Jinên Kurdistan (Kurdistan Women's Communities)
KODAR   Komelgeya Demokratîk û Azad a Rojhilatê Kurdistanê (Free and Democratic Society of Eastern Kurdistan)
Kongra-Gel   People's Congress
Kongreya Star   Congress of Star (Ishtar)
KRG   Hikûmeta Herêma Kurdistanê (Kurdistan Regional Government)
MFS   Mawtbo Fulh.oyo Suryoyo (Syriac Military Council)
MGRK   Meclîsa Gel a Rojavayê Kurdistanê (People's Council of Western Kurdistan)
NATO   North Atlantic Treaty Organization
PAJK   Partiya Azadiya Jin a Kurdistan (Kurdistan Women's Freedom/ Liberation Party)
PJA   Partiya Jina Azad (Free Women's Party)
PJAK   Partiya Jiyana Azad a Kurdistanê – Kurdistan Free Life Party
PJKK   Partiya Jinên Karker ên Kurdistanê (Kurdistan Working Women's Party/Kurdistan Women Worker's Party)
PKK   Partiya Karkerên Kurdistan (Kurdistan Workers' Party)
PLO   Palestine Liberation Organization
PUK/YNK   Yekîtiya Nîştîmanî ya Kurdistanê (Patriotic Union of Kurdistan)
PYD   Partiya Yekîtiya Demokrat (Democratic Union Party)
SDF   Hêzên Sûriya Demokratîk (Syrian Democratic Forces)
SNC   al-Majlis al-Wat.anī as-Sūri (Syrian National Council)
TAJK   Tevgera Azadiya Jinên Kurdistan (Kurdistan Women's Liberation/Freedom Movement)
Tev-Dem   Tevgera Cîvaka Demokratîk (Movement for a Democratic Society)
Tevda   Tevgera Demokratîk û Azad a Êzîdiyan (Êzîdî Movement for Democracy and Freedom)
TJA   Tevgera Jinên Azad (Free Women's Movement)
UKO   Ulusal Kurtuluş Ordusu (National Liberation Army)
YAJK   Yekîtiya Azadiya Jinên Kurdistan (Kurdistan Women's Freedom Union)
YBŞ   Yekîneyên Berxwedana Şengalê (Şengal Resistance Units)
YDG-H   Tevgera Ciwanên Welatparêzên Şoreşger (Turkish: Yurtsever Devrimci Gençlik Hareketi) (Homeland-loving Revolutionary Youth Movement)
YJA   Yekîtiya Jinên Azad (Union of Free Women)
YJA Star   Yekîneyên Jinên Azad ên Star (Star (Ishtar) Free Women's Units)
YJŞ   Yekîneyên Jinên Şengalê (Şengal Women's Units)

YJWK	Yêkitîya Jinên Welatparêzên Kurdistanê (Union of Homeland-loving Women of Kurdistan)
YPG	Yekîneyên Parastina Gel (People's Protection/Defence Units)
YPJ	Yekîneyên Parastina Jin (Women's Protection/Defence Units)
YPS/YPS-Jin	Yekîneyên Parastina Sivîl/Yekîneyên Parastina Sivîl a Jin, YPS-Jin (Civil Defence Units and Civil Defence Units – Women)
YRK	Yekîneyên Rojhelatê Kurdistanê (Eastern Kurdistan Units)
YXG	Yekîneyên Xweparastina Gel (People's Self-Defence Units)
RJAK	Rêxistina Jinên Azad a Kurdistanê (Free Women's Organization of Kurdistan)

Locations in Kurdish

Amed – Diyarbakır
Bakurê Kurdistan (Bakur) – northern Kurdistan/Turkey
Başûrê Kurdistan (Başûr) – southern Kurdistan/Iraq
Batman – Êlih
Cizîr – Cizre (Jazeera); (multiple locations)
Colemêrg – Hakkâri
Dêrîk – al-Malikiyah
Dêrsim – Tunceli
Dirbêsiyê –al-Darbasiyah
Erdîş – Erciş
Gewer –Yüksekova
Girê Spî – Tel Abyad
Hesekê – al-Hasakah
Hewlêr – Erbil/Arbil
Kobanê – Ain al-Arab
Mêrdîn – Mardin
Mexmûr –Makhmour
Nisêbîn – Nusaybin
Pirsûs – Suruç
Riha – Urfa
Rojavayê Kurdistan (Rojava) – western Kurdistan/Syria
Rojhelat a Kurdistan (Rojhelat) – eastern Kurdistan/Iran
Qamişlo – al-Qamishly
Şemzînan – Şemdinli
Şengal – Sinjar
Serêkaniyê – Ras al-Ain
Silêmanî – as-Sulaimaniyah
Şirnex – Şırnak
Tirbêspiyê – al-Qahtaniyah
Wan – Van
Wêranşar – Viranşehir

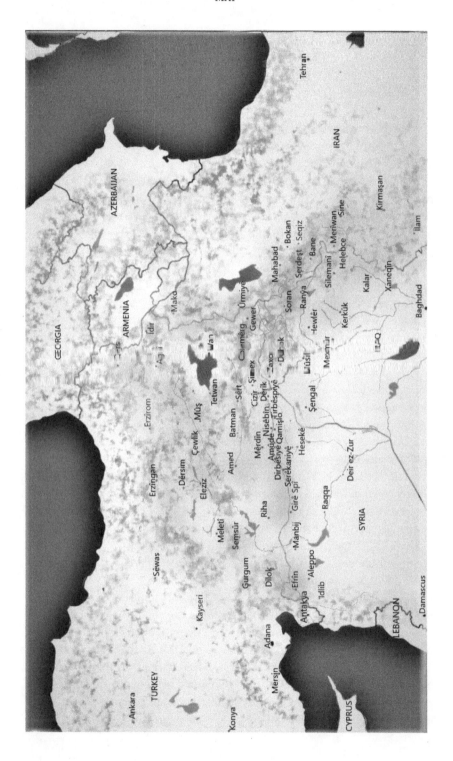

Acknowledgements

Writing this book has been an intense personal and political journey. Nobody knows this better than my family, especially my parents, my sisters Hêlîn and Yelda, my grandmothers, aunts, uncles, cousins, and my friends, housemates, and comrades, all of whom are woven into every sentence of this book. These pages came into being thanks to their love, labour, care, and support for many years. I wish my two grandfathers, one buried by the sea, one buried in the mountain, knew the extent to which their life philosophies towards peace, justice, and co-existence, paved my personal journey. I also commemorate all the revolutionaries I had the honour of meeting as they created freedom, beauty, hope, and meaning during their short lives. This book is a tribute to them.

Many people contributed to the book's argument and perspective, but some requested anonymity. As it is impossible to do justice to everyone who matters, I limit myself to a rather technical acknowledgement here. I will thank my loved ones in my own ways in a more private manner.

This book would not have been possible had it not been for the hundreds of women who let me witness and document their stories. Men's solidarity, too, played a great role in the realization of this project. I am grateful to numerous institutions in Kurdistan, especially REPAK Kurdish Women's Relations Office and Kongreya Star, for facilitating my fieldwork in various ways. My deepest gratitude also goes to Nilüfer Koç, Havîn Güneşer, Mohammed Elnaiem, the Jineolojî Academy in Kurdistan, and my sister Hêlîn for their feedback on different sections of earlier versions of the manuscript. I have fond memories of the creative time with the 'truth-seeker' in Oxford, whose critical comments and 'big picture' perspective shaped this book and my thinking in general.

My doctoral thesis supervisor at Cambridge, Thomas Jeffrey Miley, never refrained from demonstrating his belief in my research process. Many thanks to Alan Roj for arranging meetings with various actors in Rojava and helping me overcome language barriers. I am indebted to Baro for his help in going over the recordings of interviews I had conducted in the Soranî dialect of Kurdish. Like a star, my father spent days helping me transcribe some of the interview recordings in Kurdish and Turkish. I thank Professor Radha D'Souza and the late Professor David Graeber for their critical feeedback on my thesis. Finally, a big thank you to David Shulman, who approached me about writing this book, as well as the team at Pluto Press for their patient and generous support and labour in the publication of this book.

The system we envision is not just limited to Kurdish women or the Middle East. It's like a mirror everyone should be able to see themselves in. Our line of women's autonomy and self-defence is a road map we present. It's a society-building project. Women everywhere can benefit from its programme, philosophy and way of life and adjust it to their own contexts. In different parts of the world, women can paint our proposals with their own colours.

– Meryem Kobanê, YPJ commander in the battle for Kobanê, where women first defeated Daesh, 2015, Tell Mozan, Rojava/Syria

Preface

In 2014, organized Kurdish communities in Syria and Iraq came to be known through their resistance against the so-called Islamic State (hereafter Daesh), a group whose warfare, ideology, and governance systematically employed genocide and sexualized violence as tools of power and domination. Following a history of nearly no representation or visibility, the worldwide fascination with the image of the Kurdish woman fighter rapidly opened up previously non-existing avenues for voicing collective grievances, desires, and demands of the Kurds, whose homeland – Kurdistan – stretches across the borders between Turkey, Iraq, Iran, and Syria. Yet, people who admired this image often remained oblivious to the radical, revolutionary history and meaning of the Kurdish women's liberation struggle.

The following pages present a feminist ethnography of a Middle Eastern, largely lower class-based mass women's movement. They focus on the evolving history, theory, and practice of the revolutionary Kurdish women's liberation movement, an organized, autonomous women's struggle that developed within the socialist Kurdistan Workers' Party (PKK). This struggle is entangled with a broader, more than 40-year-old social movement, hereafter referred to as 'Kurdistan freedom movement', which evolved around the ideological guidance of the imprisoned leader and PKK co-founder Abdullah Öcalan (nicknamed: 'Apo') and mobilized millions of people across different parts of the Middle East and in the diaspora. This multifront, popular, transborder and internationalist movement ideologically and organizationally unites genocide survivors, guerrillas, prisoners, workers, politicians, refugees, intellectuals, artists, and youth, who organize through local and regional bottom-up assemblies, communes, cooperatives, academies, and congresses. Since one major component of this movement is its armed struggle against NATO member Turkey, its structures are largely criminalized as 'terrorist' by most Western countries. The most radical aspect of this meticulously organized movement is its self-understanding as a 'women's paradigm'. One core tenet that permeates its anti-capitalist and anti-state ideology is that patriarchy is a 5,000 year-old system that can and must be abolished, not through reform, but in a 'women's revolution', and that the liberation of all of society is impossible otherwise. In the perspective of the movement, in a patriarchal world, women's autonomous organization in all spheres of life, from knowledge production to armed self-defence, is a paradigmatic stance and precondition for true democracy.

This book has its origins in years of research for my doctoral degree at the University of Cambridge and my postdoctoral research at the University of Oxford. It is written for a general, non-specialist audience interested not only in the history and current practice of the revolutionary Kurdish women's movement, but also in the possibility of political action, including the meaning of revolution today more broadly. It is by no means an exhaustive account of the ongoing struggle of millions of people. Many of the aspects in this account merit further elaboration. My primary aim here is to introduce the scope and scale of the revolutionary Kurdish women's liberation movement's political vision and practice from its own viewpoint, with the hope of building bridges between struggles for liberation.

One glaring gap in this book is a discussion of the situation of women in Rojhelat (eastern Kurdistan/Iran). This is the only part of Kurdistan I was not able to travel to and it is also the region that the Kurdistan freedom movement is the least organized on the ground. Compared to the other parts of Kurdistan, the PKK reached Rojhelat relatively late. Young people began to join the guerrilla especially in the aftermath of protests against Öcalan's capture in 1999. My shortcoming on this front should not be read as an indication of an absence of Kurdish and other women's resistance against patriarchy and other forms of oppression in Iran. Despite repression and criminalization, and at great risk to their lives, Kurdish people there engage in grassroots activities against imprisonment, death penalty, torture, cultural assimilation, censorship, economic exploitation (including security forces' systematic killing of the *kolbar*, traders who carry goods across borders to make ends meet), and environmental destruction.

My research and relationship to the movement are entangled with my personal background: I grew up in the political environment of the Kurdistan freedom movement in Europe after my family sought asylum upon leaving Turkey in my childhood, and this intimate relationship naturally shapes my perspective and approach to the struggle and its actors. I was in my early 20s, when in the context of the war against Daesh, suddenly countless journalists, researchers, activists, and even agents squeezed themselves through the doors of the collectively criminalized, working-class political diaspora community I had grown up in. In the middle of my university research on what was at the time an esoteric topic, high-speed news cycles created a voyeuristic atmosphere in which Kurdish women's resistances and vulnerabilities were reduced to the battlefield and framed in Western-centric ways for mass consumption. Their militant uniforms were turned into fashion items, and their sexual lives were publicly interrogated, all while the political alternatives they develop are terror-labelled and attacked. In a time in which terms like feminism and women's empowerment increasingly entered mainstream spaces around the world, the protagonists of this book were sanitized by outsiders at the same time as they were systematically isolated, censored, imprisoned, tortured, forcibly displaced, stigmatized, and killed. This publication comes several years after the initial 'hype' that often represented the Kurdish women's struggle in highly depoliticized and fetishized manners, detached from its socialist roots. In fact, it arrives at a time when the Kurdistan freedom movement and its achievements face existential risks. Some of my interlocutors have been killed by Western-made drones and weapons, others are currently in prison or exile. Many of the places mentioned here have recently been bombed or are currently under occupation. In light of this, the book defends the perspective that it is not possible to appreciate the resistance of Kurdish women without reference to the violence of colonialism, capitalism, imperialism, authoritarianism, and militarism.

In an age of rapid news and disinformation cycles, political struggles are frequently misrepresented while powerful symbols are emptied of their meaning and turned into clichés. To resist the tendency of media and academia to analyze justice movements by way of quick, snapshot-like impressions and to counter male-dominated, Eurocentric, and state-centric accounts of a highly ideological, radical political struggle, I offer in this book a 'women's resistance history from below'. The chapters, divided into three main parts, offer a view of the slow, 'social revolution' led by women in Kurdistan through a largely suppressed radical social history. I particularly emphasize the social relations, shared values, and long-term processes that sustain and reproduce the Kurdistan freedom movement. Alongside the stories of fighters and politicians, the chapters centre the accounts and perspectives of actors that are often overlooked by others, such as refugees, elderly home-makers, or prisoners. While braiding people, events, and issues to each other to describe the movement's overarching 'moral-political culture', I tried to centre experiences and accounts of people participating in the struggle, including their concepts and analyses of the world.

In the hope to strengthen the hand of radical feminist history-writing and theorizing, I tried to do several things at once: to help de-tabooize intellectual engagement by writing as though this movement (or aspects of it) were not terror-labelled in the Western world; to centre the collective stories of actors who have historically been footnoted and to footnote those who are usually at the centre of analysis; to privilege tales of possibility and resistance over instances of defeat when describing untold political and social histories of marginalized communities. While making the connections between the Kurdish women's movement and other Middle Eastern and North African women's struggles would have enriched the book, the remaining gap in knowledge production on Kurdish women necessitated focus. Overall, since mainstream information on political conflicts abound in the age of internet and media, this book does not aim to give a 'neutral' or 'full' picture of the so-called Kurdish issue; rather, it documents a suppressed, radical history with the aim of inspiring hope and action for mine and future generations.

Throughout, I did my best to amplify and privilege other Kurdish women's work, to de-individualize the book's authorship by textually representing at least some of my indebtedness to the collective thinking and theorizing of women, most of which happens in the midst of hands-on struggle.[1] I chose such citational practice also to protest an ongoing tendency among male Kurdish authors or non-Kurdish feminists to ignore or dismiss Kurdish women's intellectual contributions even when writing about them. Although I focus on a specific, organized revolutionary movement in Kurdistan, I acknowledge that despite dangerous risks, women challenge societal norms on individual and collective bases through personal resilience, political activism, social work, research, education, art, literature, and cultural critique all over Kurdistan and the diaspora.[2] These many women's struggles are not separated, but mutually complementary. My analysis is indebted not only to millions of resisting Kurdish and Middle Eastern women, but also to generations of Third World feminists, socialist feminists, indigenous and Black feminists, who argue that no individual liberation from patriarchy is possible without struggles against colonialism, state terror, racism, capitalism, and ecocide.

In radical traditions, feminism is not about visibility or representation inside an unjust world; in fact, feminism should never be compatible with the dominant power-based system and its liberal discourses. I align with those who see feminism as a constantly evolving, critical, and self-critical resistance movement for justice and liberation, a method of radicalizing society's freedom consciousness to organize the world differently. Chandra Talpade Mohanty (2003) refers to 'anticapitalist transnational feminist practice' as a way of building 'noncolonizing' bridges across particular and universal struggle contexts. As it is not a classical national liberation struggle, but a mass movement with a claim to a more universal struggle against dominant systems of power, the revolutionary Kurdish women's movement's experience and analyses are valuable to anyone interested in anti-colonial and anti-capitalist politics, feminism from below, revolutionary social change, climate justice, system-critical theory, and democracy without the state. In this sense, unconcerned with exceptionalizing Kurdish women, I hope that this book can be one of the many efforts to build transnational alliances for peace and justice against the systems that colonize, devalue, and destroy life.

Introduction
The Kurdistan women's revolution –
A social history from below

Women are half the society. You cannot have a revolution without women. You cannot have democracy without women. You cannot have equality without women. You can't have anything without women. – Nawal El Saadawi

In my utopia, you must struggle for freedom all your life. In a liberated Kurdistan, the struggle must be glorious. – Sakine Cansız

Patriarchy is one of the most normalized power systems in the world. It is an organizing principle for domination and hierarchy that reaches from the deeply personal to the global. On any given day, each one of us is likely to walk past several survivors of some form of patriarchal terror, from psychological abuse to sexual violence and harassment. Due to this near universal manifestation of male domination, in particular its widely accepted role in structuring the most intimate relations in society, it often passes as the general will of all. This does not mean, however, that people do not resist. In fact, people have fought back for millennia, increasingly more collectively, often at great risk to their own lives. The countless instances in which people refused to accept violence and control over them may be impossible to account for, but they are a long and living legacy of freedom. Tragically, the normalized role of patriarchy in society, combined with the often-intimate nature of patriarchal abuse, can render resistance not only invisible, but often also impossible or ineffective. Dependency and violence lead to atomization, which silences or fragments demands and objections, making it hard to believe that a world without violence will ever be possible. At best, so we are often told, one might aspire to change laws of individual states towards equality and increased safety. Even that is perceived as a distant dream, only available to a privileged few. Liberation from patriarchy becomes a utopia, a wish, but never a tangible reality.

Even if its forms vary in different contexts, patriarchy is produced and reproduced on a world scale via ideology, class, race, education, religion, science, and media in a statist and capitalist world-system, which was established through patriarchal methods and systems of domination like slavery, militarism, colonialism, and imperialism. Throughout history and around the world, patriarchal violence often served to control society and to repress resistance;

1

framing it as culture or human nature normalizes violence as a 'natural' part of life. Colonialism reorganized social relations in gendered ways. Patriarchy also broke class solidarity among the poor. Women were often able to see their own domination by their partners, families, or societies mirrored in other forms of systemic violence. No surprise then that early organized women's struggles (with all their problems that have widely been critiqued) evolved in interaction with causes such as socialism, anarchism, anti-colonialism, anti-racism, and the abolition of slavery. Whether or not they defined themselves as feminists, throughout history women actively participated in struggles that claimed to fight for change and equality in their societies, and against war, militarism, and ecocide committed in the name of their nations. Resistance deepened and radicalized over decades especially from the twentieth century onward, as Third World revolutionaries, socialists, and Black feminists argued that no individual liberation is possible without liberation from colonialism, state terror, racism/White supremacy, and capitalism. Decades before state armies began recruiting women as soldiers, women were already fighting in resistance movements. In different parts of Europe, women took part in anti-fascist resistance. In places like Algeria, Palestine, Nicaragua, South Africa, Philippines, Colombia, India, Sri Lanka (and more), women participated in guerrilla struggles against colonization, apartheid, and occupation and for sovereignty and national liberation.

Recent years have seen a global rise in local and transnational women's and queer struggles that demand radical system change in a world that rewards sexism, rape culture, homophobia, transphobia, and feminicide,[1] the systematic killing of women. In many spaces, self-identifying as 'feminist' is no longer a taboo. In fact, today, 'This is what a feminist looks like' is a statement mass printed on clothes and accessories available on Amazon, often produced by the exploited labour of women, and sometimes children, in sweatshops; increasingly, feminist causes and arguments are watered down and integrated into the neoliberal order to be made compatible with agendas of business and states; 'women's empowerment' has even become a way to justify war and occupation. Are these positive developments? What does it mean if a radical oppositional movement is at risk of no longer being perceived as a threat to power?

*　*　*

The title of this book mentions three phenomena that have historically been repressed: Kurds, women, and movements. The history of the Kurds is conventionally narrated as that of a 'people without a state'. This state-centric framing of social life echoes civilizational discourses that helped build and legitimize the power-based organization of the world today. Such privileging of the history of the state, in particular the nation-state, naturalizes power and violence in the minds, restricts the possibility for a fuller view of the human experience and suffocates other visions and paths. In the aftermath of state violence, knowledge production on wounded geographies fails to reassemble the remnants of past social worlds; it becomes impossible to fully grasp and account for people's grief over irreversible losses that devastated ecologies and communities. And yet knowledge production matters for questions around justice and truth. In her book *Decolonizing Methodologies: Research and Indigenous Peoples*, Māori feminist scholar Linda Tuhiwai Smith (1999) writes:

> It is not simply about giving an oral account or a genealogical naming of the land and the events that raged over it, but a very powerful need to give testimony to and restore a spirit, to bring back into existence a world fragmented and dying. The sense of history conveyed by these approaches is not the same thing as the discipline of history, and so our accounts collide, crash into each other.

Histories of the state and state systems are entangled with patriarchy. However, patriarchy's historical trajectories are less straightforwardly documented compared to other systems of power, because patriarchal power manifests to a large extent in the realm of the social and interpersonal. Feminist perspectives were among the first radical critiques of the relationship between power and knowledge. These argued that erasing women from the historical view renders the experience of entire social worlds as marginal or irrelevant to our understanding of human societies. Centring our worldviews around the perspective of able-bodied, bourgeois, and white men as representing universal humanity also obscures the true scale of the violence of systems of power and of the power of violence in society. Ideas of history as a linear march towards progress are Eurocentric, male-centric, and state-centric myths or dogmas. Perspectives of the historically oppressed and 'othered' show that the inclusion of some marginalized people into spheres of power does not translate to change in the lives of oppressed people more broadly. For example, countless reports on feminicide, rape, intimate partner and family violence, poverty, harassment, and ill health show that reality is violent, precarious, and ruthless for many women in the world. In the words of feminist activist and scholar Rita Segato (2016):

> There have never been more protective laws for women's rights, training sessions for security forces, more published literature in circulation about women's rights, more prizes and recognitions for accomplishments in the field of women's rights, and yet we women continue dying. Our bodies were never before so vulnerable to lethal aggression at home, and torture until death never existed as it does in contemporary informal wars. Our bodies

never received more medical intervention seeking the shape of compulsory happiness or beauty, and we were never surveilled so closely regarding abortion as we are now.

As in other places, women in Kurdistan are subjected to multiple interlocking systems of violence. The similarities and differences in the lives of Kurds in the four nation-states who together claim all of Kurdistan within their borders (Turkey, Iraq, Iran, and Syria) have shaped Kurdish people's knowledge of the state and of violence. For Kurdish women this also meant exposure to specific patriarchal formations and a destructive continuum of gendered violence. Politically conditioned episodes of large-scale state violence, forced displacement, dispossession, and deprivation interacted with socio-economic and cultural factors like class, religion, feudalism, and tribalism, shaping and reproducing patriarchy in Kurdistan in different ways. From the domestic to the international sphere, Kurdish masculinity often entered alliances with oppressive systems against women. In addition to lacking access to education, work, and social independence, Kurdish women's lives are devastated on a daily basis by domestic abuse, so-called 'honour killings', harassment, trafficking, rape, sexual assault, forced and child marriage, and in some regions even female genital mutilation (FGM). In the context of political conflict, hypermasculinist ideas about nation, land, and power, often systematically excluded women from the means of politics, economy, and knowledge production. Trajectories of genocide and feminicide have historically been entangled.

Feminist activists and scholars note that ideological and physical battles over power and hegemony often play out in specifically gendered ways in the lives of women. Patriarchal mentalities often view women's conduct and bodies as representations of culture and territory. Controlling these becomes a way of publicly coding the permissible and the taboo, the traditional and the modern, especially in times of crisis, chaos, and change. After episodes of war and political unrest, traditional gender roles often push women back into the 'domestic' sphere to assert a sense of normalcy according to conservative ideals. Often drawing on their own experiences in organizing, women have long theorized the tendency of social and political struggles to defer the so-called 'women's question' to some future 'after' the revolution – after decolonization, after the fall of empire, after capitalism, after the war or after elections. Experiences of gendered backlash are crucial episodes in memories of collective struggle. They illustrate the ways in which different forms of oppression are entangled. However, narrativizing them into academic platitudes can have a depoliticizing and pacifying effect. The claim that 'women always get sent back to the home once the show is over' actually reproduces ideas around the naturalness of patriarchy and offers no solution.

Considering that revolution is a term that is largely associated with masculine acts and aesthetics, what would a 'women's revolution' look like? This question matters also in light of contemporary global trends. Parallel to the rising visibility of issues around gender equality, the emergence of new mass movements around the world in the social media-shaped 2010s – from anti-government revolts to youth-led climate justice movements, including mass women's strikes and marches – animated new discussions about the term 'revolution' in the twenty-first century. In a time in which even small reforms or short-lived coalition-based protest movements are celebrated as radical, what are the prospects for sustainable social transformation in a time of war, feminicide, and climate catastrophe? What is the meaning of revolutionary politics in an age in which theories of change mushroom in offices of state power, in which activism becomes a skill that can be acquired in trainings sponsored by institutions with links to states?

Against liberal notions of change that are compatible with existing systems of power, system-critical social movements, especially those at the margins of the nation-state system view the state as a colonizing institution that does not protect but attack society. They often develop politics with alternative methods and mentalities to dismantle, rather than seize power. Feminist movements are at the forefront of thinking – concretely but also imaginatively – about revolution, not reform, by arguing that breaking the patriarchal solidarity that connects violence and domination from the households to world politics means thinking about the possibility and sustainability of meaningful social and political change, from personal relations to the organization of the world economy. Drawing on such legacies, as well as on the theory and practice of the Kurdish women's movement, this book relates to the idea of 'women's revolution' – not as abstract utopia but through lived realities and efforts organized in the here and now. One aim of this book is to contribute to ongoing debates around revolution with a proposal a) to move beyond traditional state/male-centric associations, often shaped by authoritarian fantasies of taking power and b) to break cognitively, spiritually, and emotionally with hegemonic liberal feminisms and their energy-consuming conservative and reformist ideologies. Inspired by different intellectual traditions that emerged within political struggle, one of the main positions of this book is that due to the intimate ways in which patriarchy manifests itself in society, women cannot expect to achieve liberation on their own terms if they do not become a collective and autonomous force in wider struggles for justice. In turn, if social justice campaigns genuinely seek to transform social relations, then women's liberation needs to be foregrounded as a central site of struggle. This approach is related to the recent rise in mainstream discourses that present individual women's achievements (especially in the realm of government and economics) as though these were indicators of a transformation of power relations. Such trends package new forms of elite formation in the language of the oppressed when in reality women's growing participation in structures of state and capital is a trend in the neoliberal system. Celebrating the 'first-women-to' moreover reproduces traditional masculinist ideas around individualist heroism and therefore disengages a key dynamic of women's history: power in collectivity.

Studying the Kurdish women's liberation movement, a popular, terror-labelled Middle Eastern movement, which proposes stateless democracy and women's autonomy, offers an opportunity to analyze urgent contemporary questions about political possibility and revolution. This emphasis of the need to lead the anti-patriarchal struggle as also a fight against the state echoes the politics of many feminist movements around the world, who formulate rich and radical perspectives around autonomy in theory and practice. In such contexts, the realm of the political materially and spiritually extends to all spheres of life.

Understanding the relationship between social movements and knowledge production on social movements is key to making sense of such politics. That global audiences first heard about the struggle of women in Kurdistan from 2014 onward due to the fight against the so-called Islamic State (Daesh) lent itself to ideologically charged portrayals across the political spectrum. The tendency of academic or political accounts to not only frame but also fragment knowledge and understanding meant that although the Kurdistan freedom movement encompasses a diverse ecology of struggle sites, the relationships between these have often been misrepresented. In an environment that is already ideologically hostile to revolutionary politics, the ability of radical political communities to tell their stories is often compromised. Because its history has often been repressed or distorted, and because its view of revolution is anti-statist and focuses on the social realm as the privileged sphere for long-term radical transformation, I believe that what I call a 'radical history from below' or 'social resistance histories' is a useful methodology to understand this and similar movements.[2]

FEMINIZING REVOLUTION

The Kurdistan Workers' Party (PKK) was formed as a Marxist-Leninist party organization in 1978 and started guerrilla warfare against the Turkish state in 1984, with the aim of establishing a state to liberate all of colonized Kurdistan. In 1999, its leader Abdullah Öcalan was abducted to Turkey in a NATO-led operation. He has since been held captive on the prison island of Imralı in the Marmara Sea. As early as the mid-1990s, the movement began to discuss, critique, and abandon the idea of establishing an independent Kurdish nation-state and ever since embarked on a journey to theorize and realize non-state forms of self-determination. In 2005, Öcalan declared, from

6

prison, his proposal to build 'Democratic Confederalism', a system based on autonomous self-organization, realized through communes, assemblies, cooperatives, academies, and congresses, a model outside, against and despite the nation-state framework. The organized and coordinated struggle to build along these ideas – Öcalan's 'democratic, ecological and women's liberationist paradigm' – is hereafter referred to as the 'Kurdistan freedom movement'. Democratic Confederalism is currently being built up in different parts of the Middle East and the diaspora; however, it is a project not only for the Kurds but offered for discussion to peoples and movements around the world. Parallel to enshrining women's liberation in all spheres of the struggle, the movement builds an autonomous women's system from the bottom up, towards the horizon of a 'World Democratic Women's Confederalism' as a way of organizing a twenty-first century internationalism against patriarchal and statist power.

At its heart, the Kurdistan freedom movement is a secular, socialist mass movement that attracts people from different regions, ethnicities, religions, and class backgrounds. The presence of youth, women, religious minorities, and the poor across the different sites is particularly noticeable. A large number of professional revolutionaries (cadres), civilian organizers, and casual sympathizers survived forced migration, state violence, and some sort of trauma. Often, entire families are mobilized, which makes this a highly intergenerational struggle. At its core, it is led by a decades-old, revolutionary party with devoted, militant cadres. It is one of the last remaining guerrilla movements claiming to fight against capitalism. It organizes, in a highly structured way, myriads of cultural, social, political, and military institutions to realize the ideas it articulates in volumes of regular publications. Although the movement has transformed itself ideologically and organizationally, many of its ways are characterized by a partisan mode of organizing familiar from twentieth century socialist and anti-colonial movements: the central role of leadership and ideology and an unapologetic attitude towards political violence ('self-defence'), to name a few. As several chapters of this book explain, the movement's ideology and corresponding political practice offer the main ground for its claims to legitimacy. Instead of speaking in the abstract on behalf of 'the people', the movement is able to refer to thousands of grassroots self-organized revolutionary structures that it helped build over years and across territories to represent collective and organized political will. On one hand, its globally oriented political vision appeals to the new era of planetary justice struggles beyond nationalism or the nation-state; on the other hand, its focus on ideology and ground-up organizing among largely lower-class communities are very much in the fashion of old revolutionary movements. Perhaps this combination of the strengths of different left traditions is what continues to draw diverse political constituencies to the movement, such as local communities and radical social movements, within and beyond the Middle East.

The Kurdish women's liberation movement defines revolution not as a disruptive single 'day in the calendar', but as a long-term struggle to dismantle all forms of domination in society, to therefore enable liberated social relations. The revolution is framed as being about democratizing everyday relations of life, between groups inside society, between societies, and between human societies and nature. In the movement's literature, forceful criticisms are directed towards the authoritarian character of historical socialist projects. Criticizing older socialist schools' fascination with modernity and the state, the movement claims to lead 'a paradigmatic struggle against capitalist modernity', i.e. the ideological, cultural, and social project that dominates and colonizes contemporary human imagination. Instead of aspiring to establish new, power-centric regimes, revolutionary institutions and perspectives should create conditions to restore moral-political reflexes that society lost to state, capitalism, and patriarchy. Organization is key to this. Protest and resistance are seen as insufficient to break the systematic wars waged against women, peoples, and nature. Formless, erratic rebellion, as well as critique that is not backed by organizational capacity, are both seen as expressions of defeatism. Instead of becoming secondary 'wings' of the larger struggles, those who are the most oppressed must become the radicalizing force that pulls the rest along. Because the 5,000-year-old domination of women is seen as the oldest and most profound form of oppression, and intrinsically linked to the institutionalization of all other injustices in human society, the movement views women's liberation not only as an end in itself, but also as a central method to society's liberation as a whole. The active invigoration of women, their history, agency, politics, and interests, has been upheld as a revolutionary ideal especially following the movement's paradigm shift in the early twenty-first century: the respectability of women ought not to rely on their role as mothers or fighters as may have been the case in earlier stages of the struggle. Rather, women, the original owners of economy and organizers of society, must be valued per se, by virtue of hosting within themselves the possibility to be the creators of 'free life'. In other words, the internal colony's own objectified internal colony must become the main subject of the revolution; they are the most radical revolutionaries within the revolution. Practically, women and all oppressed sections in society must organize autonomously in all spheres of life and break free from oppressive social expectations. The movement also claims to be a struggle for men's liberation from the violent templates imposed on all of society under patriarchy. 'Killing dominant masculinity' is regarded as a strategic objective in the movement's works, as manifested in its activities in education, culture, and media. Spread over a long period, and across different sites and spaces, the privileging of women's liberation on the agenda also functions as a rehabilitating antidote to destigmatize men's relationship to emotionality, empathy, and care.

In this sense, the Kurdistan freedom movement claims to struggle against several layers of colonization. At stake is not merely Kurdistan's liberation from specific states. Rather, life must be decolonized from power. When framed as a mobilizational identity, grounded and fluid – like life itself, womanhood can be a platform to struggle against structures of violence and domination. It can create spaces for the formation of more complex personhoods, diverse identities, and more liberationist relations. It can lead the path towards a world in which gender will no longer serve as an organizing principle for power and hierarchy. Seen in this way, 'woman' not only stands for the material ways in which 'half of society' has historically been usurped, degraded, humiliated, brutalized, burned, stoned, raped, marginalized, minoritized, and silenced, but, by virtue of being the 'first colony', also represents all other forms of domination and violence. Turning the 'Housewifized' object (to borrow from Maria Mies, 1986) into the primary subject of the revolution echoes the decades-old feminist slogan that 'the personal is political'. This conception of revolution is simultaneously concerned with the micropolitics of everyday life as well as the large-scale systems and structures that organize world politics.

WHY RADICAL SOCIAL HISTORIES FROM BELOW?

Before the fight against Daesh, it was a murder case that was one of the first occasions to bring the Kurdish women's liberation struggle to the attention of global audiences. After a 68-day long hunger strike of thousands of Kurdish political prisoners in about 40 jails in Turkey, and a phase of escalated war that lasted until 2012, a peace process was to be initiated between the Turkish state and the PKK, represented by imprisoned leader Abdullah Öcalan, to end the decades-old conflict. The fragile prospect of peace was soon struck a major blow when on 9 January 2013, three Kurdish women, Sakine Cansız, Fidan Doğan, and Leyla Şaylemez, were assassinated in the Kurdistan Information Office in 147 Rue Lafayette, Paris.

Tens of thousands of people across Europe immediately rushed to the French capital, a furious sea of Kurdish rage, unseen in the European diaspora since the capture of Öcalan in 1999. Sakine Cansız, *nom de guerre* Sara, one of the co-founders of the PKK, had already become a legend in her lifetime due to her role in the Diyarbakır prison resistance in the early 1980s under the Turkish military coup regime. As a revolutionary, political prisoner, and guerrilla, and as a Kurd, Alevi, and woman, her life story in many ways mirrored the history of the Kurdish women's movement.[3] Of a younger generation than Cansız, Fidan Doğan (Rojbîn) and Leyla Şaylemez (Ronahî) were cadres organizing in

9

the Kurdish movement in Europe, at that time working in the diplomatic and youth spheres, respectively. Although the Turkish intelligence service (MIT) was suspected from the start to be linked to the murder, efforts to seek justice and truth continue to this day. As can be seen from documents revealed by WikiLeaks among others, Sakine Cansız' movements in Europe were long closely monitored by European states in coordination with the Turkish state. What did French authorities know ahead of this triple feminicide?

Half a year before the Paris murders, in July 2012, a conflict-ridden region in northern Syria, which the Kurds call 'Rojavayê Kurdistanê' (western Kurdistan) or simply Rojava, had declared revolution in the context of the regional 'Arab Spring' uprisings. There, ever since the Kurdistan freedom movement started implementing Öcalan's radical political vision, a relatively stable and largely self-reliant non-state system not only actively protected, fed, and educated millions of people in the midst of the Syrian war, but has been claiming to do so based on egalitarian principles. The slogan 'The Revolution of Rojava is a women's revolution' has now been on billboards, graffiti, and community buildings across large swathes of territory in northern Syria for a decade. In Rojava, the three revolutionaries killed in Paris are 'immortalized' in 8 March International Women's Day celebrations, on street walls and on curricula in dozens of autonomous women's academies.

The majority of the people who organized the revolution in Rojava, among them the first to lose their lives fighting against Jabhat al-Nusra, Daesh, and similar groups since the early stages of the war in Syria, were part of a decades-old political community, supportive of the PKK, whose leader and headquarters had been located between Lebanon and Syria from 1979 until 1998. Thousands of young women had grown up with images of PKK guerrillas and stories of martyrs in their family homes. Just as thousands of youth from Rojava had crossed borders to fight against the Turkish state since the mid-1980s, young women and men from these other parts of Kurdistan went to defend Rojava decades later. The experiences of democratic autonomy in Bakur (Turkey) and the self-organized Mexmûr Refugee Camp in Başûr (Iraq) constituted a wealth of experience to draw on when the Rojava Revolution was declared in 2012.[4] Meryem Kobanê, one of the women who commanded the famous battle for Kobanê against Daesh in 2014, told me several months after the end of the battle:

> When the Kurdish people's leader Apo [Öcalan's nickname] came to Rojava, it was as though a new seed had arrived, one that would take roots in this soil. The yeast of the Kurdistan freedom movement matured in Rojava. Its leading cadres, its early system all developed in this smallest part of Kurdistan. When Rojava declared revolution in 2012, it was based on this social legacy.

In the decade that has passed since the Rojava Revolution was declared, countless researchers and journalists interacted mainly with political or military leaders or diaspora-based activists. On the whole, this produced a narrative that excluded the stories of the larger working-class society that had made the movement for decades. Social media users, who learned about the Kurds through the anti-Daesh fight, often fetishized them in a global context of anti-Arab racism and Islamophobia. Although many Kurdish activists and organizations used the momentum to draw attention to the ways in which the US and European states have been inciting war and violence in the region under the guise of the so-called 'war on terror', powerful states, think tanks, and media institutions maintained the upper hand in framing the anti-Daesh war, ultimately turning the Kurds into the posterchildren for US military presence in Syria and beyond. Regardless of intentions, Kurdish references to the 'fight against terrorism' discursively contributed to the legitimation of imperialist and militarist agendas, the consequences of which we are yet to grasp. The near exclusive focus on the military battles in mainstream representations also led suspicious outsiders, who may otherwise be sympathetic, to view the Kurdistan freedom movement's pronouncements around radical democracy, women's liberation, and ecology as mere propaganda.

The instant popularity gained through the anti-Daesh war in Rojava rendered many people oblivious of the scale to which the Kurdistan freedom movement has otherwise been targeted, stigmatized, and criminalized in the West for decades. The PKK's official labelling as a terror organization criminalizes all activities that are broadly associated with the ideas of Abdullah Öcalan. In the hands of Turkey's Western allies, the terror-listing is like a joker card that can be used to discipline and control both Turkey and the PKK. For people wanting to produce knowledge on the movement without handing information to states, this often creates difficult ethical dilemmas. How to write about the relationships between legal political parties inside Turkey's borders and the guerrilla war or the revolutionary processes in Rojava, if such knowledge can be taken as evidence by states and be used to jail people or launch military operations? A social history of the movement, I believe, can connect legal to revolutionary politics, which are otherwise separated in the shadow of criminalization.[5] Thereby shifting the gaze towards state violence can be a form of intellectual resistance.

By accounting for a women's social history from below, this book aims among other things to counter decontextualized Hollywood trope narratives about Kurdish women having resorted to weapons because they experienced violence from a rapist group like Daesh – and not because they had collectively been engaged in revolutionary organizing against NATO for decades. The final sections of the book offer preliminary thoughts on why women's histories – if not actively protected by feminist political consciousness – run the risk of being reduced to 'inspiring' chapters in the otherwise violent story of the oppressors.

On a different but related note, taking initiative in documenting anti-system resistance histories helps equip people against ideological perception manage-ment in the era of digital media and communication. Just as system-feminism consistently fails to protect against the fascistic ideologies that normalize wars on feminine and queer bodies, protest movements that present themselves as leaderless and horizontal are limited in their ability to radically change condi-tions in today's world. This is not least because systems of power frequently frame their interests and design methods of warfare around statements about reform. This impacts revolutionary politics on an international scale. There are well-connected global knowledge communities (think tanks, research institutes, media networks, academic departments, etc.) that gravitate suspiciously close to the intelligence centres of empire and routinely champion or whitewash political blocs – including reactionary groupings – along the lines of Western state interests. Tragically, authoritarian regimes capitalize on this situation to widely repress, jail, or exile political activists by painting any resistance against injustice and unfreedom as foreign conspiracy. As a result, independent liberationist struggles with few resources get diluted or pacified along the way. A similar dynamic is playing out in the capitalist core. As middle-class, 'non-governmental', reformist organizations and movements around equality or environmentalism emerge, the visions and tactics of radicals in the same places – anti-capitalists, socialists, anti-fascists, and anarchists – become targets of stigmatization and criminalization.[6] Radical social histories help de-universalize the colonizer and de-provincialize the colonized by distinguishing between states and the societies that inhabit them, and acknowledging that politics and history are not the property of the powerful. Oppressed peoples are often put in a position of having to appeal to powerful states for protection and political leverage, and so competition for Western state attention often actively harms potential solidarity fronts in the South.

In a time in which words like 'change', 'resistance', and 'revolution' are used in the propaganda of states and fascist and reactionary groups and in advertising slogans, testimonies of liberationist anti-system resistance have enormous pedagogical value. My observations as someone with exposure to both social movements and academia have led me to believe that it is politically important to archive rebellious moments, even if these might evaporate or get wiped out. This is not to romanticize the complex world of politics from below, but to acknowledge that it matters what words were spoken by whom on what soil, to say 'this stance, this politics, this belief, too, has existed. These things, too, are said, believed, and done. There are countless, unnamed people, who do believe that another life is possible and they are willing to die for it.'

In this sense, counter-hegemonic histories are sources for internationalist horizons. Similar to critical threads within Black, indigenous or Palestine studies, knowledge production on freedom quests in Kurdistan can become an epistemic site for the critique of colonization, liberalism, and the nation-state system, and to develop theories of radical democracy, autonomy, and liberation beyond the immediate geography. Likewise, breaking with the Eurocentric construction of women's resistance histories in terms of 'feminist waves' within the Euro-American realm, by centring, taking seriously, and engaging directly with theory and knowledge produced by revolutionary movements and validating anti-system feminisms in all their diversity of tactics is part of the effort of decolonizing the history of resistance against patriarchy. To quote lifelong revolutionary Nilüfer Koç: 'All the heroic people in the world who contributed to the freedom of humanity ... their soul and spirit lives in Kurdistan. There, they just look different.'

* * *

Transparency in knowledge production is a decades-old feminist value. My 'access' to the field is inseparable from my upbringing around the Kurdistan freedom movement's culture since childhood. People trusted me with their stories and knowledge as they politically perceived me as 'one of us' – a 'child of the movement' or a *heval* (comrade). I have done my best to handle this trust with utmost care and sensitivity, while aiming to produce conscientious work. While this proximity opened many doors, it also closed others. This influenced my writing style. My sociological knowledge of the topic in this sense stems not only from systematic research, including one year of ethnographic fieldwork in different regions of Kurdistan,[7] but also from first-hand exposure to the relations, cultures, ideas, people, and values that made the movement over time. Growing up in an environment where people collectively reproduce the love they feel towards ideas like revolution, socialism, and freedom contributed to my own wholehearted belief in the possibility of a women's revolution through protracted, organized struggle, one that must involve all of society. As an activist I have promoted many of the ideas I mention in this book. The years leading up to its publication were also marked by grief over people, including friends, who lost their lives in the war. At the same time, I am in a position of relative power and privilege compared to people who appear in these pages, whose lives are at risk in war zones and under state violence and persecution. I wrote this book in the spirit of women's self-defence. Nevertheless, I do not want my own biases, interests, and limitations to circumscribe the literature and I look forward to critical engagement.

13

Having said that, my positionality and ability to move between different sites of socialization were sources of insight into questions around power, representation, and the role of knowledge production for political horizons. Informed about my background, my interlocutors did not have to breathlessly give me 'the basics' of the struggle, like they did in the avalanche of rapid encounters with other journalists and researchers from 2014 onward. Nobody had to tell me that mass movements attract all sorts of people and have serious problems and contradictions. I knew that principle and reality do not neatly overlap and that political struggle and community-building take time and energy. As such, I was able to ask different questions. Throughout the book, I tried to recreate a sense of the aura that affects people's belief in change: working-class values like solidarity, mutual aid, and respect for labour and sacrifice, or the rehabilitating role that political organizing can have in the aftermath of trauma, displacement, and dispossession. Apart from describing events and structures, the book aims to give an account of the slow, invisible processes within social relations over long periods of time. Some sections describe in detail the technical aspects of the movement's organizing to communicate the labour spent by revolutionaries in its diversity. Other sections convey the movement's spiritual and cultural world by highlighting the role of comradeship, sacrifice, and revolutionary discipline. My strategic omissions relate to the primary ethical concern that prevented me from exploring some issues in more depth (for example, the European diaspora), namely, the shadow of state violence and criminalization that looms over anti-system political activities.

My emphasis on the movement's own terminologies is partly a result of my dissatisfaction with common academic approaches that squeeze movements into catalogues of 'case studies' and try to 'measure' their achievements often based on decades-old positivistic theories. Despite decades of criticism from women in the South, Eurocentrism and liberal ideologies in feminist scholarship continue to treat other women's struggle concepts and theories not as knowledge but as data or objects of inquiry. Having been inspired by feminist theory and practice since my teenage years, I was disappointed with the superficiality of the levels of engagement with the women whose political struggles had animated a rebellious spirituality for my generation. Observing feminist academics' reflexes to police Kurdish women's joyful self-representations and to act as gatekeepers for what constitutes feminist knowledge taught me to view liberal feminism as a global class issue, and to find strength in the knowledge that people 'get' struggle concepts and radical visions especially outside the university and outside the Euro-American realm. Theory and critique are meaningful, but papers written years after struggles, in increasingly marketized university environments, are not the most important site of knowledge production in global times of war, feminicide, and climate catastrophe. The intellectual works of the Kurdish women's movement, collectively developed over decades outside academia, inside struggle, is mainly written in Kurdish and Turkish. However, with more of its resources being translated into Arabic and Farsi, as well as languages from outside the region, engagement with these experiences can be a valuable resource for revolutionaries in different contexts.

These are some of the reasons why this book consciously centres stories of resistance and victory. Not because things are perfect, but because things are possible – through faith and struggle.

I hope that the following pages will encourage readers to resist disciplining *academistic* gazes and to instead think generously about freedom struggles – still critically, but with political awareness – and with genuine care to learn from anti-system movements, in the spirit of *hevaltî*. Above all, I hope that by the end of the book, the reader will appreciate why so many of the women, who died in the battles against Daesh and against a NATO army, take up Sara, Rojbîn, or Ronahî as their *noms de guerre*.

PART I

History

1

Mapping the Kurdistan of women

Understanding and describing the situation of women in Kurdish society means considering and grasping all development processes of human history, to expose all the ways in which sociability has been annihilated; and how this achievement is embodied in the cultural genocide of a nation. – Sakine Cansız, Europe, 2012[1]

Introductions to the Kurds, a native community of western Asia (Middle East), often begin with a state-centric, negative definition: 'the Kurds are the largest nation without a state'. The 'lack' of a Kurdish state is attributed to the division of the Middle East by European powers in the first quarter of the twentieth century after the collapse of the Ottoman Empire. In a world-system of nation-states whose borders have largely been shaped by colonial legacies and interests, the Kurds, living across modern day Turkey, Iraq, Iran, and Syria, have been subjected to all sorts of violence and oppression to the point of genocide over the course of a century. Their rightlessness and thus, exposure to harm is related to their lack of any internationally recognized collective political status as a people. Even the very existence of the Kurds has often been called into question. Forty million is the contested but most common estimate of the Kurdish population in the world today. There are different dialects of the Kurdish language and while the majority of Kurds are Sunni Muslims, there are also Shi'ite Muslims, as well as many other Kurdish-speaking faith communities that are Alevi, Êzîdî, Yarsan/Kaka'i, Christian, and Jewish. Like all other social and cultural identities, Kurdish identity has diverse meanings and is dynamically interpreted and shaped by different people in different ways. As in other contexts of genocide, assimilation, and denial, insistence on identity has often been a springboard for more widely angled political struggles against injustice.

Kurdistan is a culturally diverse region embraced by the Zagros and the Taurus mountains, a geography that overlaps with much of Upper Mesopotamia. The origins of the term 'Kurd' are subject to debate. An early reference to 'Kordestan', a term younger than 'Kurd', described a twelfth century administrative unit under the Seljuk Empire. The 1639 post-war Qasr-e Shirin Treaty between the Ottoman and Safavid empires settled disputes over the shared border, creating a divide between the Kurds in modern day Iran and the rest. Kurdish desires for independence are often dated to begin around the late nineteenth century.

Rebellions were diverse, with varying regional, religious, or tribal characteristics. In 1916, diplomats Mark Sykes and François Georges-Picot signed a secret agreement on behalf of Britain and France to mark their respective spheres of influence in the region's post-Ottoman Empire. As the empire collapsed, the Young Turks movement, influenced by European nationalisms, aimed to modernize the country and expel foreign forces. To establish a uniform state, the Young Turks committed genocidal ethnic cleansing campaigns against the Armenians, Assyrians, Syriacs, Chaldeans, and Greeks in the empire's last years. Kurdish tribes were recruited to participate in the massacres and forced displacement of their Christian neighbours.[2] These genocides were at the same time catastrophic episodes of systematic feminicide.[3] After WWI, the signed Treaty of Sèvres of 1920 included possible Kurdish territories. The treaty was nullified with the Turkish War of Independence against the allied forces. Mustafa Kemal (later granted the last name 'Atatürk', *Father of the Turks*), the founder of the Turkish Republic, who had courted Kurdish notables such as later executed Şêx Seîd (Sheikh Said) for military support, later backtracked on the issue of Kurdish autonomy. The Treaty of Lausanne, signed in 1923, defined the borders of the Turkish Republic and constituted the final international division of Kurdistan. The new order turned the Kurds into minorities in the shortly after established nation-states of Turkey, Iraq, and Syria.

Kurdish-led armed rebellions against central rule took place from the late nineteenth century onward, but proliferated in the first half of the twentieth century in the aftermath of Ottoman collapse. In the early 1920s, the British mandate rule brutally suppressed, with aerial bombardment, the Kurdish rebellions in Iraq, led by Şêx Mehmûd Berzencî (Sheikh Mahmoud Barzanji). After the Şêx Seîd uprising of 1925 ended in a massacre by the Turkish forces, thousands of Kurds fled from Turkey to Syria; among them leaders who retreated to reorganize their activities. By then, urban intellectuals articulated claims for Kurdish self-determination in a modern sense.[4] While in Turkey, massacres against the Kurds launched a republic, in which the mere existence of the Kurds was systematically removed from official records, the early decades of independence in Iraq and Syria took several coups and transitional periods for state sovereignty to be established. The brutal state massacre in the Alevi-Kurdish region of Dêrsim in 1937/38, in which up to 70,000 people are believed to have been killed after a rebellion led by Seyit Riza, seemed to have settled the 'Kurdish issue' in Turkey for the time being. Meanwhile, Kurdish political movements in Iraq and Iran recorded steps towards autonomy. In Iraq, rebellions led by Mullah Mistefa Barzanî from the 1940s onward confronted several Iraqi regimes. In 1946, Qazî Mihemed became the president of the Republic of Kurdistan, the only modern Kurdish state in history. The republic was crushed by Iran and the leader was publicly hanged. The historical emergence of the nation-state imposed new forms of individual and collective identity. In the first quarter of the twentieth century, while Kurdish men with land, status, arms, property, or any form of social or political capital were pursuing through diplomatic efforts an inclusion into the League of Nations model of a world community of nations, these new frameworks, identities, and relations remained either inaccessible or irrelevant for the majority of people in Kurdistan, who were not only bureau-cratically 'without a state' but also mentally and emotionally.

Over the past decades, much effort has been put into reconstructing a history of the Kurds.[5] This has proven challenging; whenever the existence of the Kurds has been acknowledged, it was usually defined by hegemonic powers or political interests. Tribalism, as well as regional, linguistic, and religious differences are often highlighted in Eurocentric perspectives that use rigid and homogenizing understandings of categories like 'nation', when claiming that the Kurds are too diverse to constitute a coherent identity and thus do not meet the criteria for independence. The Kurdish political spectrum is indeed diverse and full of internal contradictions. Different concepts of freedom inform ongoing political battles, ranging from civic action to armed guerrilla struggle. It makes little sense, however, to attribute, in essentialist fashion, intra-Kurdish disputes mainly to perceived national characteristics like tribalism or differences in dialect, when powerful regional and international dynamics regularly harness Kurdistan's geopolitical fragmentation for their own purposes. Framed as a transnational 'problem', Kurdistan is often employed as a 'destabilizing' factor by regional and global powers. It is however also possible to do an alternative reading of the diversity among Kurds and other peoples, namely, as expressing a level of autonomy from and resistance against central governance. In this sense, for example, the specific experience of the Kurds inspired the Kurdistan freedom movement to develop concepts and theories around autonomy and confederalism rooted in locally lived legacies.

The reshuffling of the global order in the 1990s after the collapse of the Soviet Union had radical implications for the Middle East region. For the Kurds, devel-opments in the early twenty-first century, specifically wars and crises in Iraq and Syria, opened spaces and opportunities to re-enter the geopolitical stage. In Iran and Turkey, different Kurdish political groups continue in diverse ways to resist against the oppressive regimes that deprive them of their collective rights through violence, imprisonment, censorship, and dispossession. Regime changes in the region have not eliminated violence and oppression against minorities. For instance, Kurdish people and political parties such as the Revolutionary Organization of the Toilers of Iranian Kurdistan (Komala) and Kurdistan Democratic Party-Iran (KDP-I) participated in the 1979 revolution against the former shah of Iran, Mohammad Reza Pahlavi, and in some regions established local self-governing councils, but faced targeted violence with the

Islamist takeover. Several Kurdish political leaders have been assassinated by the Islamic Republic in European cities, and more recently inside Iraqi borders.[6]

The Kurdistan Regional Government of Iraq (KRG) is a federal unit within the Iraqi state, with its own parliament, governmental structures and diplomacy. It is the only part of Kurdistan in which the right to language and culture are formally recognized. As a result of the 'Revolution of Rojava', declared in 2012, the Autonomous Administration of North and East Syria (AANES), which largely overlaps with the Kurdish regions of Syria, is currently exercizing self-government but without holding any international status. Genealogically, these build on two distinct transborder political legacies: while the former evolved since the time of the Republic of Kurdistan (with several key parties having branched out of the Kurdistan Democratic Party, KDP), with the prominent role of the Barzanî tribe, often lionized for its past military achievements, the latter builds on the socialist PKK movement, which emerged in the 1970s under the leadership of Abdullah Öcalan. These two Kurdish-led self-governance projects in many ways epitomize the two competing hegemonic freedom concepts in Kurdistan today: one is the quest for an independent nation-state integrated into the world-system, the other is a plurinational democratic confederal system under construction outside of the dominant order.

* * *

Much of the literature on the history of the Kurds is characterized by a focus on the male-dominated world of power. To show that Kurds, too, have history, people often emphasized their role in the history of kingdoms, religious battles, empires, and modern nation-states. Such tendencies to make sense of historical subjectivities in a manner that privileges relations vis-à-vis state power impacted histories of Kurdish women.

Kurdish women's relationship to history and knowledge production is intrinsically linked to their antagonistic relationship to the state. As Kurds and as women, both the absence of 'evidence' of their existence and their contribution to history have been enabled by and have further enabled systematic eradication, denial, and forced assimilation. Middle Eastern feminists have broken ground on the sexual politics of the state and its use of women's bodies as markers of tradition and modernity, especially in the aftermath of the collapse of the Ottoman Empire, but unfortunately, historically, many influential works either ignored the situation of Kurdish women or only marginally mentioned the specific impact of state policies on them.[7] This is even more striking considering that the relationship between authorities and women at the margins of state power is predominantly one of violence and dispossession, and therefore provides deep insights into the workings of the nation-state. For instance, even as the Turkish Republic brought about progressive reforms in society, such as education and work opportunities for women, permissible femininity required compliance with the nationalist framework of the state. The first female pilot in Turkey, Sabiha Gökçen, adopted daughter of the republic's founder, Mustafa Kemal, took part in the devastating bombardment of civilians in the Alevi-Kurdish region of Dêrsim (renamed by the state as 'Tunceli') in the late 1930s and continues to be praised as a symbol for the 'modern' values of the republic. Genocides and massacres against Armenians, Assyrians, Syriacs, and Chaldeans, as well as the Dêrsim massacre, were large-scale episodes of feminicide through rape, abduction, and forced marriage in the context of Turkey's early state-building.[8]

Strong female characters, stubborn and strong-willed, are not rare in the unwritten, oral archives of Kurdish art and culture, such as in the tradition of *dengbêjî*, a Kurdish art of musical story-telling.[9] When it comes to written sources on Kurdish women in history, however, we still rely mainly on works by Kurdish men or European travellers.[10] Many of the personalities listed in seminal works on Kurdish history are often members of important families or tribes. While some are remembered for administering entire regions upon their husbands' death, others were community elders, fighters, poets, singers, writers, translators, and artists. Among the most prominent Kurdish women in history is Fatê Reş (Black Fatma), who is believed to have commanded several hundred men in the Ottoman army and fought against the Russians in Cilicia.

As early as the late nineteenth century, the 'women's question' played a role in early Kurdish national aspirations that were framed along Eurocentric civilizational, modernist discourses. The earliest known Kurdish women's organization is the Ottoman era 'Society for the Advancement of Kurdish Women', founded by the Society for the Advancement of Kurdistan in 1919. With the first quarter of the twentieth century, individual Kurdish women began supporting the general national struggle for liberation through political activities, including armed struggle. Some profiles are documented in archives, others are remembered in narrative form. Zarife was among the Alevi-Kurdish women from the Dêrsim region, who participated in the armed rebellion during the Qoçgirî Uprising in 1920. Qedem Xeyr was a Feyli Kurd, who took part in the armed resistance in Loristan during Kurdish leader Simko Şikak's rebellion against the Iranian Shah in the 1930s. Born at the end of the nineteenth century, Hepse Xan-î Neqeb of Silêmanî was a teacher, political organizer, and leader, who formed the Kurdish Women's Association, possibly the second Kurdish women's organization in history. She is credited with establishing one of the first schools for women in Iraq, supported the armed Kurdish uprising against British colonial rule, and was outspoken about Qazî Mihemed's founding of the Republic of Kurdistan in 1946. The short-lived republic around Mahabad in Rojhelat/Iran itself enshrined equality between women and men in public affairs in its constitution.[11] It formulated the advancement of women and girls as an important element of national progress. Especially in the city, education, work, and political activities were offered to women to support the national course.

During the 1960s, a time of global revolutionary uprising and protest, women in the Middle East took part in anti-colonial and worker's movements, socialist and communist struggles, internationalist efforts against imperialism and militarism, and women's organizing. Kurdish women participated within these country-wide regional social struggles, not always with explicit reference to their Kurdish identity. For example, Kurdish women often joined the Iraqi Communist Party, including as armed fighters. The Revolutionary Organization of the Toilers of Iranian Kurdistan (Komala) included the progress of women as part of its programme for self-determination and was the first Kurdish movement to have women among the armed ranks on a larger scale. Women in the Komala party and Kurdistan Democratic Party-Iran (KDP-I) continue to take part in the struggle against Iran as pêşmerge fighters.*

With the 1970s, Kurdish women became more active in the resistance against oppressive regimes. Born to a poor family from Xaneqîn, Leyla Qasim, member of the Kurdistan Democratic Party (KDP) and the Kurdish student movement, was a political activist and organizer against the Iraqi government. In 1974, she was imprisoned, tortured and hanged for exposing the crimes of the Ba'athist regime. In Turkey, her contemporary Sakine Cansız was one of the only two women at the PKK's founding congress in 1978. In her early 20s, she was tasked by Abdullah Öcalan with building the Kurdish women's movement. Only a few years after Leyla Qasim's execution, Cansız organized a commemoration for Qasim in Diyarbakır prison, where she herself underwent unimaginable forms of torture by the Turkish state. In 2013, Cansız was assassinated by an agent with the Turkish intelligence, along with Fidan Doğan and Leyla Şaylemez in Paris. Had they not been killed, Leyla Qasim and Sakine Cansız would have been roughly the same age today. In her autobiography, Cansız (2019) described Qasim as a hero, who contributed to the liberation of all women through her participation in the struggle: 'There had to be many more Leylas'.

More names of Kurdish women could be listed here. However, this book aims to tell the stories not of individually powerful women, but a collective story of individuals, who came together to organize a powerful women's movement – the art of raising 'more Leylas'.

---

* The word 'pêşmerge' translates to 'those who face death' and is widely used by different Kurdish armed movements and groups, especially in Başûr and Rojhelat.

2

The Kurdistan Revolutionaries

In some ways, the Kurdistan Workers' Party arrived 'late' in history. As a national liberation struggle, it emerged after most of the anti-colonial movements in Africa and Asia. It obtained mass following for its revolutionary cause only after the collapse of the Soviet Union. Its socialist ideology spread in Kurdistan at a time in which capitalism institutionalized itself as a world-system. Post-colonial disputes were supposed to be settled; the borders of the world had come to stay.

The 1960s coup d'état had been followed by a relatively liberal Turkish constitution that enabled leftist groups to establish political organizations. Soon enough, the 1971 coup led to major crackdowns on the revolutionary left in Turkey. Leading revolutionaries such as Deniz Gezmiş, Yusuf Aslan, Hüseyin Inan, and Mahir Çayan were executed or killed by the state. Many youth-led groups on the radical left rejected Kemalism, the foundational ideology of the Turkish Republic, as a colonial and bourgeois nationalist idea that obstructed the country's liberation from imperialism. The early 1970s were marked by a rise of Kurdish national consciousness and ideological fragmentation in the left in Turkey. Increasingly, the phrase 'Kurdistan is a colony' was on people's lips.[1]

All of these developments influenced Abdullah Öcalan, nicknamed 'Apo', a poor, young Kurd from Amara (Ömerli) village in Halfeti, Riha (Urfa), who was briefly imprisoned for his involvement in student strikes against the state's killing of revolutionaries in the early 1970s. The small group of mainly young, lower-class students, including Turks, that formed in Ankara in 1973 around Apo, a political science student at the prestigious Ankara University, a hub of the revolutionary youth movement at the time, was soon known as the 'Kurdistan Revolutionaries' and later the 'National Liberation Army' (UKO). The group's means were limited compared to others. Lacking publications, venues, and even a name at the beginning, they turned up at revolutionary events to engage people in the taboo-ized Kurdistan question.[2] In her autobiography, Sakine Cansız, one of the only two women at the founding meeting of the PKK, recalls a visit from a member of the early group in her family home in Dêrsim in the early 1970s to speak to her and her brother. The two teenage children of genocide survivors found out for the first time that they were Kurds from a revolutionary, who told them about liberation struggles in places like Angola, Cuba, and Vietnam. He told them that the Turkish state, not the Turkish people, were the Kurds' enemy, but that for the wider revolution to succeed, a separate organization was needed to respond to the specific conditions of Kurdistan. The group's first and primary activities in the 1970s were such face-to-face meetings to recruit new members, as well as secretly held study groups and seminars in communal flats on socialist theory and the colonization of Kurdistan. The first all-women's gatherings began as early as then.

On 18 May 1977, Haki Karer, a Turkish member of the group, one of Öcalan's closest comrades, was killed by a rival leftist organization. His death is described as having sparked the decision to form a party. The secret foundational congress took place on 26–27 November 1978 in a mud-brick house in the village of Fis in Amed.[3] Öcalan called this his 'second birth'.

The PKK is sometimes described as a 'Kurdish nationalist split' from the revolutionary left in Turkey. However, this misconception ignores the group's critiques of the discourses on the Turkish left at the time.[4] As Cansız describes, leftists in the country, who downplayed the oppression and exploitation of the Kurdish people in the name of anti-imperialist internationalism, criticized the Kurdistan Revolutionaries as nationalist for their anti-colonial approach to the Turkish state. On this issue, guerrilla fighter Heja, a Turkish woman from the Black Sea region, who joined the PKK from the Turkish left in the 1990s, gave the following assessment when I spoke to her in the Qendîl mountains:

Great revolutionaries like Deniz Gezmiş, Mahir Çayan, or Ibrahim Kay-pakkaya had created strong revolutionary solidarity bonds, bridges of internationalism, as they faced execution. But others, with their nationalistic approaches, drew borders in their struggle and failed to build common grounds. After the death of these individuals, who refused to divorce the struggles from each other, the left in Turkey became increasingly more marginal, isolated and separated from Kurdistan. Later, too, leftists in Turkey developed a rightful reflex of solidarity with the Palestinian struggle, but ignored the many popular uprisings in Kurdistan, the village destructions, the state massacres right in front of them.

At the same time as it criticized the left in Turkey, the group rejected 'primitive Kurdish nationalism' as a reactionary perspective. In this sense, the formation of a party was seen by co-founders of the PKK as a conscious decision to take the political initiative to formulate an autonomous anti-colonial and socialist identity against the two dominant lines at the time: conservative Kurdish nationalism without revolutionary politics or leftist Turkish 'social chauvinism' without consideration of Kurdistan's colonization. In fact, the earliest documents of the party explicitly emphasized the desire to build a wider independent socialist federation for the Middle East. The right to national self-determination was therefore never interpreted in the form of a narrow nationalist project. Forming a democratic and socialist state was not the ultimate aim, but seen as a necessary step on the way towards the broader liberation of all peoples from imperialism by way of world proletarian revolution. The foundational manifesto 'The Way of the Kurdistan Revolution' outlined an analysis of classed society, colonialism, and the state, and put the conditions of the Kurdistan revolution in a world historical context, referring to liberation struggles in places like Vietnam, Mozambique, Angola, Eritrea, Palestine, Cuba, and various other places in Africa, Latin America, and Asia.

From the beginning, the PKK understood itself as a movement of and for the poor, disadvantaged, marginalized, and oppressed. As German ethnologist and feminist activist Anja Flach (2007), who has actively participated in the Kurdish women's struggle as an internationalist since the 1990s, explains in her German-language books on the Kurdish women's guerrilla, unlike movements drawing on the idea of *kurdayetî* (Kurdishness), from the beginning, the PKK's target support base was not a general Kurdish polity, but the disadvantaged sections of society. The PKK's founding document explicitly privileges the mobilization of the working class, peasantry, women, and youth, and expresses hostility towards the bourgeoisie and traditional land-owning elites.[5] Women barely featured in the manifesto, but they were listed as being among the sections of society that must be organized in particular, because 'women have been enslaved at the very beginning of classed society.' The text described women as the part of society that has been 'the least influenced by foreign hegemony' and therefore less assimilated into the dominant state's culture.

In the same year as the PKK's foundation, which was announced the spring after, a fascist mob of the ultra-nationalist Grey Wolves and religious extremists massacred more than 100 mainly Alevi-Kurdish people in the city of Maraş. The violent clashes between left-revolutionary groups and fascist cells in Turkey in those years was used as one pretext to stage the infamous military coup d'état of 12 September 1980, led by Kenan Evren. The junta suspended the parliament and constitution, banned political parties, and formed a brutal military regime. Police brutality, mass arrests, extra-judicial killings, detention torture, and executions had a decimating effect on what at the time was the powerful revolutionary left in Kurdistan and Turkey. The politicized university youth were specifically targeted by these measures. Like the rest of the oppositional groups, it became impossible for the PKK to engage in legal political activity inside Turkey. In the summer of 1979, in an atmosphere foreshadowing the military coup, Öcalan and a handful of members of the PKK, which was less than one year old at the time, crossed the border into Syria. Many leading cadres and supporters were arrested. Their resistance in prison launched the rise of the PKK, which presented itself as Kurdistan's '29th uprising'.

3

Berxwedan jiyan e! –
The Diyarbakır prison resistance

Prison is where the early PKK started its first uprising and where it consolidated its self-understanding as a party of cadres, who resist fascism to the death rather than surrender. Prison was also the first site of direct confrontation between the Turkish state and revolutionary Kurdish women. In the early 1980s, in the aftermath of the military coup, Diyarbakır prison (or 'Prison #5') became the symbol for both the Turkish military regime's cruelty and the revolutionary resistance against it. Placed under martial law, the prison was run by ultra-nationalist officials that made use of their extra-judicial powers with impunity. Prisoners, mainly Kurds and more generally, leftists and people who opposed the regime, were sentenced in show trials in military courts. Countless prisoners were killed or severely disabled in the prison. Although prisoners from many left groups were engaged in resistance actions against the torture and violence in Diyarbakır prison, the PKK soon became the main target of the state. Judges, prosecutors, police, medical staff, and the media made themselves complicit by covering up the atrocities behind the walls (among others, recording deaths under torture as accidents or suicides). The full scale of the systematic torture committed in Diyarbakır prison is still unknown, but the following graphic excerpt from work by sociologist Yeşim Yaprak Yıldız (2016) is illustrative of the horrors inside the prison walls at the time:

Diyarbakır prison was particularly notorious with humiliating and sexualised torture techniques including rape, forcing the prisoners to rape each other, inserting objects into the rectum, tying or lifting the prisoners by genitals, choking in prison sewers, forced eating of excretion, mucus, detergent, mice, and so on. The prisoner's entire day was filled with a cycle of torture, 'military training', and 'lectures'. Any interaction with fellow prisoners, talking, coughing or making any noise outside the control of the prison guards was banned. Speaking in Kurdish was strictly forbidden including during the prison visits of the families who only spoke Kurdish. The visitors and the lawyers of the prisoners were also subjected to judicial and physical harassment and violence. The bodies of the prisoners in Diyarbakır prison were turned into mnemonic devices reminding them and the wider Kurdish population that the power of life and death lay with the state.

As memoirs of former PKK prisoners like Sakine Cansız, Muzaffer Ayata, or Fuat Kav tell, for the state, the mere admission of guilt was not enough, the techniques employed in prison further served to make prisoners denounce the idea of revolution entirely. Through humiliation, degradation and violence, Kurdish prisoners had to be turned into obedient, Kemalist Turkish citizens. Forced confessions, as Yıldız notes, were not just a coercive method to obtain intelligence; making prisoners publicly repent helped pacify political organization and hope. The torture was meant to send a psychological, disciplining message to the wider Kurdish society. In some cases, the state succeeded in recruiting leading co-founders and members as agents who revealed vital information to the state, leading to further arrests. Despite major blows, the continuous physical and psychological torture tactics of the state were answered with anti-colonial ideological defences in court, cultural celebrations, educational work, physical violence, jailbreaks, death fasts, and self-immolations in the cells. Some of the members that had gone over to the state were 'pulled back from the abyss of treason' by the resistance. The families of the prisoners, often harassed and abused by the authorities during visits, increasingly turned to organized political action.

Prisoners usually engaged in resistance actions the moment they were arrested, but what is referred to as the 'Diyarbakır prison uprising' was sparked on Newroz day in 1982, when the 27-year-old PKK co-founder Mazlum Doğan lit his cell on fire with three matches and hanged himself to protest the conditions. While the state portrayed the death of Doğan, a high-level cadre, as a sign of despair and defeat, the organization interpreted his decision as a call for rebellion. As Doğan's comrade and fellow prisoner, Sakine Cansız later wrote in her prison memoir: 'Earlier [Mazlum Doğan] had written: "Surrender leads to betrayal, resistance to victory". Slowly we realized that he'd intended to send us a Newroz message: Resistance is Life!' Doğan's action came to be seen as a protest not merely against the physical conditions of prison, but also the destruction of personalities. In Cansız' words: 'Mazlum's action became a milestone event for PKK resistance. From now on, we would all measure ourselves against his commitment. On one side was the infamy of betrayal in a situation of terror; on the other side was the greatness of Mazlum's heroic act.'[1]

On 18 May of the same year, on the anniversary of Haki Karer's death, the party cadres and prisoners Ferhat Kurtay, Eşref Anyık, Necmi Önen, and Mahmut Zengin lit themselves on fire in protest. In the letter they left behind, they urged the people of Kurdistan to organize to resist imperialism and colonialism:

29

... All over the world the struggles of anti-imperialists, anti-fascists and anti-colonialists are progressing with pain, effort, life, blood and suffering ... If the wheel of history continues to turn today, we owe it to the Vietnamese, Cambodians, Cubans, Palestinians, the Kurdish people, the Russian, German, and Bulgarian proletariat, who paid for it with their blood and their lives.

The action of 'the Four' ignited further resistance within and beyond the prison walls. On 14 July 1982, PKK founding members Kemal Pir and Hayri Durmuş declared the beginning of a death fast to protest the prison conditions, in which they and two other central committee members, Akif Yılmaz and Ali Çiçek, later died. Kemal Pir, who was a Turk from the Black Sea region, lost his eyes before dying almost two months into his fast. His words 'We love life so much that we are willing to die for it' are seen as a guiding maxim in the PKK's notion of struggle, an insistence on life beyond the physical.

The majority of political prisoners were men, but women's role in the prison resistance in Diyarbakır not only surprised the state, it also impressed otherwise conservative male inmates. While the extent of the torture and abuse at Diyarbakır generally awaits full investigation, the violence against the female prisoners is even less accounted for. Sexual violence was used against all prisoners in Diyarbakır, but targeting women in particular was a way of demobilizing everyone by weaponizing concepts of 'honour' in society. In a Turkish-language book that she edited from prison, Gültan Kışanak (2018), former MP and later former co-mayor of Diyarbakır (Kurdish: Amed) municipality, who survived the torture in Diyarbakır prison herself, reflected on the fact that few women wrote down their experiences, noting:

But all women have the right to know this: despite the savagery in Diyarbakır prison, no informant came out of the women's ward. This is not because women were very heroic or because they experienced less torture; it has to do with the supportive affect of women's solidarity. All the women had clung onto each other so tightly that nobody could separate one from the rest. Sakine's role and labor in this solidarity was defining.

Due to her key role in the prison resistance, Sakine Cansız, at the time in her early 20s, became a legend during her lifetime. The merciless torturer and captain Esat Oktay Yıldıran, who terrorized the prisoners for years, was an ultra-nationalist committed to implementing the military junta's command to treat all prisoners like soldiers. Former prisoners recount that he enjoyed torturing people to unconsciousness. He was also a misogynist, who took particular excitement in abusing women. He deliberately mobilized notions of shame around women's bodies, especially their periods, as part of his humiliation methods. In her memoirs, Sakine Cansız described Oktay as an 'enemy of life and of beauty, his heart barren of love':

Esat loved hearing women's agonized screams – to him, they were like a beautiful melody, and he showed his love by inflicting the falanga on us for hours on end on the ice-cold concrete floor. The inmates in the next ward must have been wincing. Then he'd shriek, 'I'll have you sterilized! I'll wreck your fallopian tube so you can't have any more children, and your people will die out!' He wanted to extinguish the Kurdish people. At other times this sadist would show his love for women by snarling, 'Wish we didn't have any boards here!' and 'Soldiers gonna knock up those PKK girls.' And he'd beat us with a club between our legs till we bled, then threaten to 'shove up a club inside.'

The sexualized attacks backfired as women increasingly took collective action against the authorities. As remembered in Cansız' autobiography, women began theorizing the meaning of the violence they experienced and formulated common responses and action strategies against fascism's male-dominated nature. In a way, the first autonomous organization of women in the PKK came about with the decision of Diyarbakır prisoners to resist specifically as women against the Turkish state. Through solidarity and mutual aid, women collectively fought against the creeping atmosphere of mistrust brought about by agents and snitches especially in the men's ward. Moreover, many women, who were jailed for reasons unrelated to political causes, were politicized by the courage of the female political prisoners across different prisons, who offered support, education, and books to their cell mates. Women and men were held in separate wards but secretly coordinated joint actions. Some male prisoners felt hurt in their masculine pride in the face of sexualized attacks on the women, but many openly expressed their admiration for the women's resistance. In their writings, male former PKK prisoners at Diyarbakır often mention that the spirit in the women's ward strengthened their own determination and revived their will to live and continue the struggle. 'Nowadays, everybody can talk about Kurdistan and the Kurdish question. But back then, these were deadly terms. Those who did not bow down and stayed true to their history and reality paid with their lives to prepare for the present day', wrote PKK member and fellow Diyarbakır ex-prisoner Muzaffer Ayata (2011) in his memoirs after two decades in jail. In the foreword to his comrade's post-mortem memoirs, Ayata (2015) describes Cansız as a fearless militant, who protected prisoners through friendship and determination: 'In my eyes, Sakine represents the resistance spirit of the Diyarbakır dungeon.' Famously, Cansız spat in Esat Oktay Yıldıran's face during one of the many torture sessions. He was killed in 1988 by unknown assailants, who brought him 'greetings' from martyr Kemal Pir.

The PKK inmates' resistance in Diyarbakır prison, which had become synonymous with torture and death, gained them respect in the eyes of Kurdish people and other left organizations. It launched their rise from being one small revolutionary group among many to a popular movement. The violence experienced in prison sped up the group's plans to start guerrilla warfare, a decision that was formalized in the second congress in 1982, held in a Palestinian camp.

4

Vejîn! – The first bullet

In the summer of 1979, Öcalan and some leading PKK members crossed into Syria. In the last decade of the Cold War, the pro-Soviet Syrian regime under Hafez al-Assad, who hoped to establish himself as a regional leader, hosted various groups such as the Palestinian Liberation Organization (PLO) to counterbalance US (and NATO) influence in the region.[1] These were training in the Bekaa Valley of Lebanon, at the time occupied by Syria. As a small country, bordering the two most strategic regional allies of the US – Turkey and Israel – Syria tolerated, and in some cases, actively funded oppositional and leftist groups among Palestinians, Armenians, Turks, and Iraqis, as well as Kurds from the latter two, within the territories it controlled. Such factors made that region an attractive destination to the PKK, which needed a place to train for future guerrilla warfare. Upon arrival in Syria, they formed relationships with Kurdish communities, as well as revolutionary Palestinian and Armenian groups. The Assad regime itself, while denying rights to Kurds within its borders, saw the PKK as benign and a leverage against NATO member Turkey.[2] Syria was angered by Turkey's hosting of the Muslim Brotherhood as well as its intended Southeastern Anatolia Project (GAP), which would construct dams and irrigation systems on the Tigris and Euphrates at the expense of water supplies to Iraq and Syria. The 'Hatay question' was another point of tension; Syria continued its claims to the majority Arab region around Antakya that the French mandate rule in Syria had given to the Turkish Republic in the late 1930s in return for Turkey's neutrality in WWII. Despite this lenient attitude, these communications did not turn into strategic relations. PKK members and supporters recount regular waves of arrests and violence by the regime especially throughout the 1990s, and increasingly more under Bashar al-Assad.

The PKK co-founders' first destination in Syria was (later legendary) Kobanê, a small border town only an hour's drive away from Öcalan's hometown of Halfeti in Riha (Urfa). Upon arrival, cadres began educating local sympathizers about Kurdish history, colonization, and socialism. Relating to the local Kurdish community was not too difficult, since cultural and kinship relations had remained intact despite the border. The early political activities primarily served to mobilize for Bakur, where the Kurdistan revolution was supposed to be triggered, but the PKK's programme ultimately encompassed all of Kurdistan, at least in theory. While some cultural activities were public, educational and political meetings were held in secret, especially those involving women (since these would draw greater attention). With time, adults, who hid party material inside baby cradles, saw their children grow up among the '*heval*' ('friend' or 'comrade' in Kurdish) and join the guerrilla. Blood feuds and other disputes were often solved in the communities with the mediation of cadres. Generally, people from the lower classes, youth, and women began to see concrete changes in their lives.

Meanwhile, the PKK received military training from the Palestinian PLO in the Syrian-controlled mountainous Bekaa Valley of Lebanon. Years before launching the war on Turkey, 15 PKK members were imprisoned and eleven died fighting alongside the Palestinians against the Israeli invasion in 1982.

On 15 August 1984, Mahsum Korkmaz (*nom de guerre* Egîd) commanded the operation that fired the PKK's 'first bullet' against the Turkish state. Several soldiers and police officers were killed or injured in coordinated attacks on Turkish gendarmerie stations in Eruh in Sêrt (Siirt) and Şemzînan (Şemdinli) in Colemêrg (Hakkari). News quickly spread as banners, leaflets, and more attacks officially declared guerrilla war on the Turkish state. The operation, celebrated on its anniversary every year, is commonly referred to as *vejîn* – resurrection.

With the launch of the war against Turkey, the rural parts of Kurdistan became sites of illegal political activities, as guerrilla fighters established contacts with the locals to communicate their aims and seek support for the planned long war ahead. The targeting of exploitative landlords and tribal leaders increased the guerrillas' popularity among some sections of society. When the state partially lost control over some regions, many villagers began consulting not the state, but the PKK for the settlement of disputes. Among the emerging mass of sympathizers were young Kurds, who had been taught by their parents to deny their identity in school, university, and at work to avoid trouble. The PKK attracted both: those who were subjected to racism and forced assimilation in Turkey's metropoles, as well as those who experienced exploitation and state violence in Kurdistan. Though the emergence of the PKK was certainly not appreciated by all Kurds, especially due to its tendency to clash with tribes and rivals, it is widely acknowledged to have caused a rupture in the Kurdish psyche in Turkey at the time. Formerly scared villagers began risking their own lives to aid the guerrillas. People took notable risks to be able to recover dead guerrilla bodies to give them proper burials. Even the fiercest critics admit: after nearly half a century, the PKK broke the 'graveyard silence' in Bakur since the Dêrsim massacre in 1938.

Women were part of the guerrilla from the start. As early as the 1980s, women from diverse backgrounds, like Hanım Yaverkaya (Sunni Muslim from Riha), Rahime Kahraman (Alevi from Dêrsim), and Binevş Agal (Êzîdî from Êlih (Batman)) were among the first guerrillas and commanders of the PKK.

Women did not participate in the 15 August operation, which was conducted by a small unit, but they were commanders in the new guerrilla-held territories nearby. Before that date, the PKK had been clashing with state elements, various political groups and tribal leaders. Sultan Yavuz was one of the first PKK women to be involved in armed clashes with clans. Besê Anuş and Azime Demirtaş became the PKK's first female martyrs in 1981.

In Lebanon, Öcalan prioritized education for women, who organized in discussion groups among themselves, alongside military training. Shortly after the Kurdistan Liberation Forces (HRK) were formed, the first groups, including women, went back to Kurdistan to prepare for guerrilla war. At the third party congress in 1986, which formally founded the 'Mahsum Korkmaz Academy' in the Bekaa Valley, the HRK was restructured into the People's Liberation Army of Kurdistan (ARGK). The Union of Homeland-loving Women of Kurdistan (YJWK) was formed in Europe in 1987 as the first women's association affiliated to the movement; it was organized under the umbrella of the Kurdistan National Liberation Front (ERNK), which was also formed after the third congress.

In the early years, women guerrillas often wore loose headscarves to avoid being rejected by the communities they interacted with. At the same time, the presence of women encouraged many rural women to join the guerrilla. Women often secretly opened their homes to the guerrillas even when their male relatives refused. In the Qendîl mountains, I conducted a lengthy interview with Elif Ronahî, an Alevi woman from Maraş, and one of the first women in the PKK. She described the atmosphere of the early years:

> Women flooded to the PKK's ranks, leaving the realm of their families behind for the first time. This meant a radical break with our socializations as someone's daughter, sister, or wife and signified a rejection not only of the state but also of oppressive traditions and dominant conceptions of life.
>
> For the first time in the PKK, we met many other men and women outside of our families and found new ways of relating and living with each other. Women discovered themselves and each other and found that it is possible to live and organize without depending on men, without a husband, father, and society deciding and acting on our behalf. As the first women in the PKK, we may not have had a deep consciousness and analysis at the time. But we saw freedom calling in the PKK, a group that would talk to each human regardless of their background, point out to them their oppression and inform people that through resistance, they can overcome unfreedom. Women knew that we can create and find ourselves in this movement.

The 1990s marked the mass politicization of women in Bakur. Women increasingly joined protest actions in front of prisons, in city squares and in popular uprisings. Informal community interactions and family relations played an important role in mobilizing women of all ages, and educational and class backgrounds, as thousands of people were assaulted, arrested, and killed, with many joining the guerrilla ranks.

After the Turkish state failed to downplay the significance of the PKK in the Kurdish regions where authorities lost control, official discourse diminished the insurgent phenomenon with reference to poverty, illiteracy, and societal backwardness. Numerous Turkish-language books and academic theses dismiss the PKK's appeal to women as an insidious form of propaganda to recruit them as suicide bombers, when forced marriage and poverty are the only alternatives in conservative Kurdish society. Not rarely do such accounts use pseudo-scientific claims, as they cite emotionality, mental health issues, masculine traits, proneness to manipulation, self-confidence issues due to lacking attractiveness, and even 'father complexes' as reasons for women's participation in the guerrilla. As Shahrzad Mojab (2001) wrote: 'From a male chauvinist perspective, women could hardly qualify as brigands or terrorists; their sedition, revolt against the "indivisibility of the Turkish nation" and its "territorial integrity", had to be vilified in sexist terms.' The state, with the help of tribes and village guards, weaponized patriarchal notions of honour to spread rumours of Kurdish women's sexual exploitation in the mountains. Such claims are largely recognized as unfounded, but they continue to play a role in the right-wing discourse against the guerrilla to this day. Parallel to dismissing women's agency in the PKK, the state's army has historically targeted women guerrillas in sexualized ways, from so-called 'virginity tests' to displaying women's stripped and mutilated bodies. This decades-old culture of the Turkish state is now continued by Turkey's mercenary forces in its occupied areas in Syria.

5

Edî bes e! – The dirty war

In late 1996, a car crash in a town called Susurluk in Balıkesir province sent shock waves through Turkey. The so-called 'Susurluk scandal' confirmed what many human rights defenders and journalists had been claiming for years; namely, that the state was working through secret networks to systematically assassinate, torture, and terrorize dissenters and supporters of the Kurdish movement. The profiles of the victims, not all of whom died, revealed the money-driven, intimate relations between paid Kurdish clan leaders, far-right mafias, and the state.

In the years to come, numerous scandals, investigations, and reports began mapping out networks involved in the Turkish state's 'dirty war' on Kurdistan. This complex web of violence involves Kurdish clans and Islamists, ultra-nationalist Turkish fascist groups, as well as various elements of the police, justice, army, and intelligence, including what is referred to as the 'deep state'. The various groups, agencies, and departments may have different functions and methods, and their often-secret nature makes it hard to establish their links.[1] But to those victimized by their violence, they represent the highly organized character of Turkish nationalists' war on the Kurds.

The kontrgerilla (or Counter-Guerrilla) are considered to be the Turkish branch of Operation Gladio, a clandestine, anti-communist operations mechanism of NATO and affiliates. The US CIA-funded Turkey's later dismantled Special Warfare Department to pre-empt a possible Soviet occupation and to annihilate internal rebellions. For decades, the kontrgerilla employed and empowered paramilitary ultra-nationalist groups to use bombing, assassinations, and sabotage against the revolutionary left and later mainly against the PKK. These groups also played an important role in the violence that shaped the 1980 coup d'état period.

After the PKK's launch of guerrilla warfare, the Turkish state established the so-called village guard (köy korucu) system by arming and funding Kurdish villagers to collaborate with the state's military and counter-terrorism activities. The state recruited especially from conservative or tribal elements already hostile to the PKK. Many of these men abused their state-given powers and were involved in murder, drug trafficking, expropriation, bribery, and systematic sexual violence against women.[2] The korucu became one of the main targets of the PKK early on. The guerrillas made spectacles of punishing and executing many *korucu*, whom they saw as feudal collaborators.

In response to the guerrillas' increased relations to rural communities, in 1987, a 'state of emergency' rule was imposed on the Kurdish regions, allowing appointed governors and their officials to evacuate populations without notice, and control and disperse political activities with disproportionate use of force. Unaccountable for their actions, they systematically committed war crimes, and observers were increasingly banned from entering certain zones. The militarization of plateaus displaced many peasants and nomads and deprived them of their means of subsistence.

The formerly secret and unofficial intelligence and counter-terrorism agency of the gendarmerie, JITEM, is largely regarded as a core element of Turkey's 'deep state' effort to fight the guerrilla. Throughout the 1990s, it used death squads, including leading members of the Grey Wolves for forced disappearances, torture and extra-judicial killings against political figures, journalists, human rights defenders, lawyers, teachers, trade unionists, and businesspeople, who were seen as sympathetic to the PKK. The Kurdish Hizbullah (unrelated to the Hezbollah in Lebanon), a militant Islamist group based in Bakur, also actively engaged in violent actions against supporters of the PKK, which it saw as an 'infidel' rival. In those years, it was common to find bodies of well-known figures tortured to death in the middle of the street. The whereabouts of hundreds of people, who disappeared in the 1990s, are still unknown.

Political 'openings' to the Kurdish question in this period turned out to be insincere or were actively sabotaged by covert actors. The possibility of a political settlement of the conflict was first undermined in 1993, when Turkish president Turgut Özal, who had signalled openness to peace talks, died under suspicious circumstances, right after Öcalan declared the PKK's first unilateral ceasefire. Peace seemed far from reach, especially after the execution of nearly three dozen unarmed Turkish soldiers and civilians in an ambush commanded by former PKK commander Şemdin Sakık (nicknamed 'Fingerless Zeki'). Sakık, who defected, later testified during the highly politicized 'Ergenekon trials' in AKP-led Turkey that he believed that Turkish military officers had prior notice of his attack but sent unarmed soldiers to sabotage the peace efforts at the time. Testimonies of former high-level army officials during the trials revealed that numerous deaths blamed on the PKK had actually been false flag operations orchestrated by state elements. However, there were indeed PKK commanders, who committed atrocities, including civilian killings in this brutal period. Some, like Sakık, defected, others were executed by the party. These practices and phases were later analyzed and heavily criticized in movement congresses and publications. To this day, human rights organizations insist that truth and justice regarding the violence during the 1990s is a prerequisite for any prospect for peace.

*   *   *

As the first day of spring, 'Newroz' (21 March) is an ancient festival celebrated by many cultures and communities in western and central Asia. In the Kurdish context, Newroz is strongly associated with the legend of Kawa the Blacksmith (Kawayê Hesinkar), a mythical hero, who led a popular uprising against an oppressive tyrant. In his long poem 'Shahnameh', written around 1000 AD, the Persian poet Ferdowsi describes how the cruel king Dehak grew snakes from his shoulders that fed on the human brains of two youths a day. The cooks of the palace, however, mixed human brains with sheep brains, which led to the liberation of some individuals, who ran to the mountains – the Kurds. Kawa eventually became the one to overthrow and kill the oppressive king. He made a fire on a hill to tell everyone that the tyrant is dead. To spread and celebrate the good news, people lit fires all over the country. Modern Kurdish political movements creatively adapted variations of the story to construct it as an origin myth by turning Kawa into a prototype of the Kurds as a rebellious people.[3] The new year, marked by the beginning of spring as an end of the dark, cold, and deadly winter, is welcomed with fire as a symbol of life. The political meaning of Newroz as the festival of resistance and popular uprising developed behind a backdrop of the festival's criminalization by various states as 'modern day Dehaks' and Kawa-like Kurdish uprisings in response to repression. In the early 1990s, lighting the Newroz fire despite the Turkish state's policies of violence and forced assimilation became a matter of life or death in Bakur during the popular uprisings – the *serhildan*.

The *serhildan* in the first half of the 1990s were the first major revolts of Bakur since the 1930s. Some called them 'Kurdish intifadas', as they resembled the Palestinian popular uprisings against the Israeli occupation that had started a few years earlier. By the late 1980s, the PKK had already garnered support especially among communities in the Botan region, the south-eastern most corner of Turkey. Many young, unmarried women broke social taboos, as they joined the militants, who went from door to door to engage people in the struggle. The result of women's underground mobilization work revealed itself during the uprisings, with the widely circulated images of women, young and old, dressed in colourful traditional robes, chanting: 'Edî bes e!' (Enough!)

Binevş Agal (*nom de guerre* Bêrîvan) is often credited for having laid the foundations of women's politicization in Botan. She was born in a village near Êlih (Batman) province, but in the 1980s, her family migrated to Germany due to state violence. There, she joined the early PKK as one of the first Êzîdî

39

women. In the mid-1980s, she first travelled to Rojava for training and then crossed into Bakur. Her work inside the community in Cizîr (Cizre) put her on the state's radar and in January 1989, a raid on the house she stayed in erupted into a clash. It is believed that state forces tortured her to death after capture. Bêrîvan's death in combat in her early 20s left a big mark in Cizîr.

The first *serhildan* began with a funeral procession in the week before Newroz 1990 in Nisêbîn (Nusaybin), a border town in the Mêrdîn (Mardin) province. A week earlier, more than a dozen guerrilla fighters had died in clashes. The youth movement called on the people to turn the burial of guerrilla fighter Kamuran Dündar in Nisêbîn into a political protest. When thousands showed up, the security forces killed people, as they brutally dispersed the crowd. These events sparked riots in other Kurdish towns, where people built barricades to prevent the Turkish state's tanks from entering their neighbourhoods. Women and men, young and old, threw rocks at the army vehicles. Within days, several civilians across Botan were killed by state forces, while hundreds were wounded and more than 1,000 were detained.

With the *serhildan*, it was no longer possible for the state to portray the PKK as a small group of bandits. Turkish newspaper headlines at the time showed outrage at the tens of thousands of people in entire regions in the 'East' for collectively taking to the streets to openly resist the state on the side of 'separatists'. Meral Çiçek (2018), a leading Kurdish women's activist and journalist, writes on the Nisêbîn resistance: 'One of the fundamental messages that were declared at the *serhildan* was that the colonizing and occupying state had no legitimacy in Kurdistan ... The second fundamental message was that the repressive walls of fear had finally been destroyed.' She further writes that this was 'when the oppressor's fear of the dead manifested itself for the first time', as funeral ceremonies were obstructed and corpses were disappeared by officials.

At the time of the 1990 *serhildan* of Nisêbîn, Zekiye Alkan was a medical student at the Dicle University in Amed. On Newroz day, she self-immolated on the city walls surrounding the historic city centre. According to her family and friends, who spoke to her before her death shortly after in the hospital, she explained that she protested to draw attention to the oppression and injustice in Kurdistan. Similarly, in 1992, Rahşan Demirel, originally from Nisêbîn, lit herself on fire on top of the Kadifekale hilltop castle in Izmir, following a government announcement to ban Newroz activities. In the note she left behind, she said that she had to respond to the events in Botan by insisting on the celebration of Newroz, even if that meant 'becoming Newroz' herself.

The well-documented massacre in Cizîr in 1992 is widely narrated as the embodiment of the Newroz spirit. Dancing in their colourful traditional clothes and setting car wheels on fire, people started their festivities days ahead of Newroz. The celebrations were organized through committees in the neighbourhoods.

The big day was supposed to start with a march to the cemetery in Cizîr. Around 20,000 people had gathered with large colourful banners openly supporting the PKK and its struggle for Kurdistan. Soon, however, special forces teams with tanks tried to disperse the crowds. Heavily armed forces were positioned on the hills surrounding Cizîr, as helicopters cruised above the people. Existing footage shows special forces indiscriminately firing into crowds of terrified civilians; women in traditional clothes, elderly people, confused-looking children were rounded up and beaten. Protesters were assaulted and forced into army vehicles. Many of them later disappeared or died under torture. The wounded were unable to get to hospitals. Among the dead or wounded were also local and international journalists, who wanted to cover the events.

At the age of 17, Bêrîvan Cizîrî, who was part of the community's Newroz preparation committee, became the symbol of the *serhildan*. Bêrîvan had taken up her code name in honour of previously mentioned Binevş Agal. She had already witnessed the Turkish state's brutality from up close under torture in detention as a teenager. Footage from the Cizîr Newroz shows the young woman first leading the traditional dance during the celebrations, before leading the uprising itself. The confidence with which she directed the protest crowd under fire was an astonishing sight in the conservative Kurdish society at the time.

The *serhildan* spirit was echoed in the diaspora in Europe. In the 1990s, many Kurds sought asylum especially in Germany, where there was already a sizeable Kurdish population from Turkey that had migrated there as guest workers. In 1994, Ronahî (Bedriye Taş) and Bêrîvan (Nilgün Yıldırım) jointly self-immolated in Mannheim without warning, to draw attention to the Turkish state's destruction of villages in Kurdistan that were enabled by German tanks, assault rifles, and diplomatic relations.[4]

In response to the *serhildan*, the Turkish state collectively punished communities with torture, extra-judicial killings, enforced disappearances, and curfews. An estimated 4,000 villages in the area were destroyed within years. From the mid-1990s onward, the state began adopting a new language towards Newroz. After having committed massacres on several Newroz occasions over the years, the state suddenly claimed that 'Nevruz' (spelled without the separatist letter W) was in fact a Turkish holiday. Against this appropriation, the Kurdistan freedom movement continues to insist on the political meaning of the day.[5] Both the paradigm shift of the movement, as well as the 2015 peace process, were declared on Newroz. For many people in Kurdistan, Newroz remains an anti-fascist holiday.

Today, the name Bêrîvan is associated with the resistance of Botan. It is one of the most common names among women from the area and among Êzîdî women who join the movement.

6

Towards women's autonomy

We learned everything in action, we didn't even know how to walk properly at first! Shooting the first bullet, walking the first mile, planning the first operation; women gathered their first own life experiences in the guerrilla. In those years, what drove university women and village women alike to the mountain were two things, a commitment to liberating the Kurdish people and liberating ourselves as women. Women united these two causes not by opposing them but by struggling in an incredibly intertwined manner. – Elif Ronahî, Qendîl, 2015

In some ways, Kurdish women's journey towards autonomy began as a class struggle among women. In the 1990s, the PKK rapidly grew into a mass movement, as thousands of people from the destroyed villages joined the armed struggle. The first PKK members were mostly city-dwellers, often working-class students involved in revolutionary politics. The socio-economic make-up of this small socialist organization had already begun changing in the 1980s: in addition to Kurds from Syria, after 1984, people from the rural areas of Bakur started joining the guerrilla. Politically active youth in the diaspora in Europe, often university students, children of refugees, or migrant workers, relocated to Syria or to the mountains, among them not a small number of women. The third congress of the previously mentioned YJWK, held in Germany in 1991, was attended by approximately 1,500 women. The recent recruits were socially more conservative and often less formally educated than the early group. The socialist movement now had its own class contradictions, and this especially expressed itself among the women. Many among the first women, who joined the guerrilla during this time, had never communicated with men outside their families. The different socializations of women with urban, university-educated and/or seasoned left-revolutionary backgrounds and women from the villages, largely shaped by tribalism and religion, led to a formative social conflict in the ranks.

The 1980s and early 1990s were also marked by the corrupt practices of particular male commanders, who claimed disproportionate power over the individual units, which were at the time loosely organized and often disconnected from each other. In this period, some men openly expressed their disapproval of the presence of women in the guerrilla. Previously mentioned

42

Sakık claimed that women are soft and fragile 'like flowers'. He withdrew women from the fronts and went as far as kicking 300 out of the guerrilla in early 1993 (PJKK 2000). In some cases, some of these men, sometimes also known for making sexual advances towards women, turned out to be agents that had infiltrated the ranks. In any case, this phase was marked by high numbers of internal executions and civilian killings.

In the women's movement archives, the early period is also described as an intense gender struggle, with many women copying men's actions or behaviours and striving for recognition by entering alliances with men at the expense of other women. As described to me by women who lived through this chaotic period, some believed themselves to be already free and therefore not in need of self-development. Others were outright hostile to the men. Yet others sought shelter in the shadow of men, who played the women against each other. The generalized male-dominated climate at the time led to many women guerrillas rejecting aesthetics associated with femininity, wrapping their chests to hide their breasts, and adopting masculine ways of conduct and speech to display strength. In the absence of specific women's perspectives, masculinity became a measure by which courage, willpower, and ability were defined. Despite individual struggles and acts of courage, a shared understanding of womanhood as a collective struggle identity did not exist.

Figure 1   YJA Star guerrillas from Rojava and Bakur, building a new camp in the mountains. Xinerê. May 2015.

43

As documented in internal reports and conference transcripts, the years between 1987 and the mid-1990s constituted a difficult journey towards the formulation of shared principles around women's liberation. In this period, analyses made by Öcalan in his book *The Woman and Family Problem in Kurdistan*, and the martyrdoms of particular women were taken as occasions to take decisive steps towards women's autonomy.

The self-organization in the armed sphere (*artêşbûyîna jinê* – awkwardly translatable as women's 'army-fication'[1]), often narrated through the story of commander Berîtan, is seen as the first major milestone in the Kurdish women's movement's ideological and practical journey towards autonomy.

Born in Çewlik (Bingöl) to an Alevi-Kurdish family originally from Dêrsim region, Gülnaz Karataş (Berîtan) came in touch with the Kurdish Revolutionaries during her studies in Istanbul. At the age of 20, she joined the guerrilla following her short imprisonment for political activities. During the 'first South War', the name given by the movement to the escalations in 1992, in which the Kurdistan Democratic Party (KDP) and the Patriotic Union of Kurdistan (PUK) militarily allied with Turkey against the PKK's presence within Iraqi borders, Berîtan was commanding a unit of guerrillas in the Xakurkê region. She had fought to her last bullet, when she was surrounded by KDP pêşmerge fighters and driven to the edge of the mountain cliffs. It is said that Berîtan first broke her weapon to prevent its use by the enemy and then threw herself off the cliffs.[2] In the party's writings, her death, which came at a time in which certain groupings among male PKK commanders were trying to marginalize the women, is portrayed as a woman's stance against Kurdish men's tendency to collaborate with the occupier.

By the time of Berîtan's death in October 1992, there were already thousands of women in the PKK. The 'Freedom and Equality' committees were first steps towards separate women's units. Öcalan held a meeting with around 70 women to plan a national women's conference and to move towards autonomous structures. In December 1993, an order was sent to all guerrilla areas to begin women's independent military organization. The first separate women's teams formed in Amed, Dêrsim, Erzîrom, and Garzan in 1993. The work raised morale and self-confidence, but did not significantly contribute to developing a collective women's struggle identity. In the words of many women who took part in these developments, the meaning of the physical separation from men, the logic of autonomous organizing, was not fully grasped at the time. The women had begun organizing under the umbrella of TAJK (Kurdistan Women's Liberation Movement) and held a first conference in 1993, which they later nullified because of claims that it had taken place under the patriarchal influence of men. As thousands of women joined in the context of the serhildan, women's liberation became more prominent in the PKK's vocabulary and practice. In one early 1994 analysis,[3] for instance, Öcalan, who interrogated

Kurdish masculinities and femininities and addressed taboo-ized topics like 'honour', insisted that since power and male domination were deeply entangled, the women's revolution was the greatest of social revolutions and that the twenty-first century could be the era of the women's revolution. Men, in turn, could obtain their rights and freedom to the extent to which they participate in guaranteeing women's liberation.

At the fifth PKK congress in 1995, where Öcalan's analysis titled, 'Insistence on socialism is insistence on humanity' was read out, steps were taken towards transformation within the party in favour of decentralization, including removing the claim to independent statehood from the programme. The congress resolution (PKK 1995) referred to women's separate organization in the guerrilla as having the potential to 'destroy all ambitions of classed societies that uphold the status-quo' and called on women's 'army-fication' in all spheres of life through autonomous organization. After the congress, what is now called the first Kurdish Women's Liberation Congress was finally realized on 8–18 March 1995, with 350 delegates. It resulted in the creation of the autonomous women's army, the Kurdistan Women's Freedom Union (YAJK). The congress, which is sometimes referred to as the 'first national women's conference', allowed women in different areas to discuss their problems, criticize and self-criticize, lay out principles, organizational styles, and decision-making mechanisms. Previous women-specific formations were associates of the general structures. YAJK thus marked the first autonomous and separate organization of women. All the military, political, and social work of women, including activities in Europe, were tied to YAJK, which Öcalan referred to as: 'A means of revenge against all backwardness, fanaticism and especially all the dangerous characteristics of men.' For the first time in more depth, research was conducted to theorize concepts for women's liberation from patriarchy. The women's efforts benefited from Öcalan's perspective that 'killing the man is a primary principle of socialism'.

Early discussions in the movement already emphasized that the women's army must be qualitatively different from militarist and colonialist armies. Rather than merely integrating into a male-dominated realm, the women's army had to be a means to defend the oppressed. In their first publications, the women guerrillas analyzed their research on women's participation in socialist or national liberation struggles in Central and Latin America, China, Vietnam, Algeria, Palestine, Germany, Ireland, and the Basque Country. Many struggles, they noted, either lacked theoretical analyses of patriarchy and its links to other forms of oppression (colonialism, class, etc.), women's autonomous forms of organization and decision-making, and/or the ability to become mass movements. Neither reducing social contradictions to single-issue analyses nor removing themselves from society were concrete alternatives for women (PJKK

2000). Liberation struggles until this point, they wrote, traditionally had had 'male characteristics', and so, to meaningfully abolish systems of oppression in all spheres of life, one had to start with the oldest form of injustice: patriarchy.

Elif Ronahî, who witnessed these phases herself, said that despite all its problems, army-fication was not a gender segregation policy, but above all a necessary, temporary physical, and therefore mental and emotional break with patriarchy. Organized for the first time without men's mediation of thought and action, women started to build trust in themselves and each other by way of theorizing, living, building, and fighting together:

> When analyzing our own individual personalities, we saw that we all had different concepts of freedom. It was a great struggle to come to a basic common understanding, free from patriarchal concepts. In those years, we began analyzing and condemning slavery in women and power in men. We analyzed our gendered socializations. We understood the formation of a hegemonic, despotic masculinity as being related to other systems of power, which in turn are based on male-dominated mentalities.
>
> We physically separated from men for 3–4 years as a method to find our voice and confidence. We realized our own abilities when we created women-only spheres. In the mixed spaces, unless a woman had a strong consciousness, she could get under the influence of men's mentality and thought, admire his power and always see him as a saviour. We asked ourselves: 'What is a free woman? How did we live until now and how ought we to live in the future?' By becoming an army, we wanted to find answers to the question 'How to live?'

In this period in the 1990s, increasingly more internationalists, among them many women, joined the PKK.[4] Afitap Demirel (*nom de guerre* Ruken Çiya) is the first Turkish woman martyr of the PKK. After a period at the party school in Syria, she was given responsibilities in the Serhat region, but lost her life in an ambush in 1994. Nermin Akkuş (Hêlîn Çerkez) was a Circassian woman from Turkey, who joined the PKK from Austria. She went to the party school upon Öcalan's invitation, after she wrote him a letter on the situation of women in Circassian society. She believed that a federation of peoples in the region would also liberate the communities in the Caucasus. In 1998, she burnt to death under siege by enemy forces, who attacked with incendiary devices. In her early 30s, German anti-fascist socialist and former political prisoner Andrea Wolf (Ronahî) joined the PKK. In 1998, she died under torture by the Turkish army after being captured during clashes in Çatak in the province of Van (Wan). Her story drew many German revolutionaries to Kurdistan.[5] An international Jineolojî institute in Rojava is named after her.

Another Turkish woman, who joined in this period, is the previously mentioned Heja from the Black Sea region. Describing the roots of Turkish nationalism through genocides against Armenians, Syriacs, Assyrians, Chaldeans, Greeks, and Kurds, Heja claimed that while the PKK mobilized for social transformation within Kurdish society, it also constituted an occasion for Turkish people to radically reject their nationalistic upbringing:

> The state tried to design a sense of Turkishness based on diluting, oppressing, or annihilating other identities. In getting to know the Kurdish reality and Kurdistan I actually got to know the Turkish reality and the Turkish state. Getting to know Kurdistan, forced me to re-examine and re-formulate my own history in relation to the history of the Kurds, Armenians, Rum, Circassians, and others. Turkishness, the notion of the Turkish flag, Kemalism, nationalist sentiments – all of these are taught to us from an early age, starting in primary school. They tell us that each Turk is worth the whole world. In a context in which society and state had been so conflated, it is difficult to question the hegemonic culture of the state. But once people acknowledge that their 'superiority' had been designed by way of genocide and violence, they see how impoverished this identity is.

Heja believed that more Turkish women than Turkish men joined in the 1990s. She saw this as an indication of men's relationship to the state, but also of the value placed by the movement on change within society. She was inspired by the social struggles led by the working class in her city, but believed that due to gaps between theory and practice, many revolutionary movements at the time failed to attract ordinary people:

> Generally, in the daily life of the left in Turkey, there were very classical approaches between women and men. Freedom was understood in a very general manner. Relations in everyday life, our personalities were not questioned or touched by this broad notion of freedom. The question of freedom was left to a time after the revolution. This was not the case in the PKK.

On 30 June 1996, in her mid-20s, Zeynep Kınacı (*nom de guerre* Zîlan), a socialist university graduate from Malatya, detonated herself in a Turkish army checkpoint in Dêrsim, killing eight soldiers and wounding dozens.[6] The first Kurdish woman to conduct such an attack, Zîlan left behind a long letter that explained her motivation, decision, and action in detail. In her own words, she believed that in light of recent assassination attempts against Öcalan in Syria and the Turkish army's brutality in the villages, the guerrillas' response must be 'total resistance'. To justify her action, which she appears to have decided and planned by herself, she clarified that under certain conditions, 'voluntary death' could demonstrate determination against the colonizer, both to the enemy as well as to one's own people: 'By exploding a bomb against my body I want to protest against the policies of imperialism which enslave women and express the greatness of my rage and wrath and become a symbol of the resurrection of Kurdish women.' She warned that colonization not only occupied physical lands, but also people's way of thinking about themselves, others and history. The longest part of her letter addressed the oppression of women in Kurdistan in particular and in human society as a whole. Analyzing the subjugation of women in relation to the rise of classed society and colonization, she called for an organized women's struggle. She criticized socialist theory for not sufficiently addressing women's subjugation and stressed that Kurdish women, while they may have advanced since their participation in the national struggle, could not liberate themselves without specific focus on women's liberation. Upon receiving the news, Öcalan turned her letter and action into theory during his lectures, describing it as a 'manifesto of life' (YAJK 1999). He characterized her action as a criticism of the guerrilla war at the time, where neglectful commanders had caused avoidable losses. In his words, not Zîlan's calculated action against the army in a time of full-scale war, but guerrilla commanders' deadly lack of discipline and strategy was 'real suicide'.

As with Mazlum Doğan's action, Zîlan's attack was interpreted as a 'wake-up call', not least because it came at a time in which women were struggling against male corruption in the organization. Simultaneously, some men took openly hostile positions against women's self-organization, accusing it of a 'women's fascism' to split the movement at a time of war (PJKK 2000). In response to Zîlan's call to strengthen women's self-determination, concrete steps were taken at YAJK. Zîlan is thus described as the 'turning point' that paved the road towards the foundation of a women's party (today's Kurdistan Women's Freedom/Liberation Party – PAJK) and the 'Women's Liberation Ideology' (explained later), articulated from 1998 onwards.

Soon, women began developing several concepts and 'projects' in autonomous educations. The women's self-organization that had started in the guerrilla in 1993 was theorized with the 'break-off' theory. Beyond mere gender segregation it was conceptualized to mean a decolonization from patriarchy, a way of abolishing men's alienating influence over women's thought, emotions, and actions. The 'changing the man' project analyzed the 5,000-year-old male-dominated system and its effects on men's personalities. Women's efforts increased in Başûr, with the publication of the *Jiyanî Azad* newspaper, the formation of a women's association, and a YAJK headquarters all in one year (PJKK 2000). Increasingly, matricentric societies and the importance of ecology were stressed in party publications. In Damascus, women and Öcalan began to research women's history, and so male domination was increasingly analyzed as a system. The PKK was referred to by Öcalan as being 'a women's party or revolution'. On 8 March International Women's Day celebrations in 1998, he uttered the idea of a 'Women's Liberation Ideology' to theorize and strategize how to build the foundations for a free life without patriarchy. He argued that women must reclaim and develop the means of defining their own selves against sexist naming and meaning-giving practices. To that end, women needed spaces to debate their experiences and perspectives on every aspect of life, including taboo topics. He analyzed the nineteenth century as the century of bourgeois revolutions and the twentieth century as the century of workers' revolutions. In order to realize a true liberation of all of humanity, he argued that the twenty-first century must be the era of a women's revolution.

Weeks later, on the Newroz day of 1998, shortly after 8 March, political prisoner Sema Yüce self-immolated in her cell in Çanakkale prison. She had previously studied sociology at Ankara University. Two years after joining the PKK in 1990, she was imprisoned and sentenced to 22 years in jail for her political activities in her hometown Agirî (Ağrı). In the letter that she left behind, she defended her decision by drawing attention to the state's attempts to marginalize the movement by way of encouraging traditional gender roles and reactionary personalities. She drew a metaphor for the need to unify the autonomous women's liberation struggle with the revolutionary freedom struggle of Kurdistan by describing her desire to turn her body into a 'bridge of fire that stretches from 8 March (International Women's Day) to 21 March (Newroz)'. She wrote that just as it is impossible for two suns to illuminate the sky, women, who want to liberate themselves could not be torn between two ways of life or two sets of principles. She died after three months of hospital treatment. The women's movement's project of 'free life', on which the later formulated social contract was based, was dedicated to her memory.

Before leaving Syria on 9 October 1998, Öcalan gave separate perspectives to the women's movement and stressed that they needed to keep building their autonomy and protect themselves against the men, in increasingly more organized forms. He suggested a women's party formation to the sixth PKK congress in February 1999. That congress, however, coincided with his abduction.

7

International conspiracy and internal crisis

Abdullah Öcalan's kidnapping and imprisonment were the result of NATO cooperation.[1] The movement refers to his exodus from Syria as the beginning of the 'international conspiracy'. By the late 1990s, Turkey was threatening war on Syria in order to pressure Öcalan out. The ordeal that followed took him back and forth between Greece, Russia, and Italy. His aim was to seek asylum in Europe to work towards a political solution to the conflict, but states were put under pressure and closed their borders. He stayed temporarily in the Greek embassy in Kenya and planned to continue to Nelson Mandela's South Africa, where he would be granted asylum. However, a coordinated effort by (at least) the US, Israeli, and Turkish intelligence services with important roles played by the UK and Greece abducted him to Turkey on 15 February 1999. As images appeared of a blindfolded, bound, and evidently drugged Öcalan behind a Turkish flag, the kidnapping, referred to by Kurds as 'roja reş' (black day), sparked riots and protest around the world. More than 60 people self-immolated to condemn his capture.

Öcalan's imprisonment on İmralı Prison Island in the Marmara Sea, where he would be the sole prisoner for the first ten years of his sentence, caused a major internal crisis in the PKK. He was sentenced to death, a verdict that would be converted to life in prison in 2002, partly due to Turkey's EU membership endeavour. Öcalan apologized to the families of the Turkish people who were killed, and in his court defence, proposed a plan to resolve the Kurdish question and democratize Turkey to end further bloodshed. Many framed Öcalan's political defence in court as a sign of surrender, even betrayal of the Kurdish cause. The armed conflict was suspended after the summer of 1999, with a call by Öcalan to withdraw the guerrilla to outside of Turkey's borders. Several hundred guerrillas are believed to have been killed by the Turkish army to sabotage the process. The chaos and leadership vacuum led to the emergence of right-wing lines and deep power struggles within the party. This particularly affected the women's movement. In Öcalan's absence, some male cadres revealed more overtly that they had only tolerated the women's autonomy because of Öcalan.

Despite everything, the second YAJK women's congress took place with 140 delegates in March 1999, a month after Öcalan's abduction. It pledged to continue the fight for women's liberation, which Öcalan, writing from prison, referred to as his 'unfinished project'. The Kurdistan Women Worker's Party (PJKK) was formed with its own decision-making mechanisms and programmes. This constituted a major milestone similar to the army formation several years prior.

Excerpts from Öcalan's defence statements and meeting notes from his lawyers throughout the year of 1999 were prepared into a 'Political Report' titled 'Perspectives on the Transformation Period', which was presented to the extraordinary seventh congress, held in January 2000. Writing on death row and deeply influenced by his odyssey before the abduction, which, as he claimed, had revealed to him the Janus-faced nature of European democracy more intimately, Öcalan stressed the need to rearticulate the meaning of democracy and to form a joint democratic republic for the peoples of Turkey. He put the importance of such transformation within the context of a changing world: a democratization of socialism was required in the forthcoming century. 'National liberation' could only be realized through regional 'democratic liberation'. The Political Report (Öcalan 2000) focused on ongoing political developments, but the most emotional and ideological sections concerned women, whom he described as having more socialist personalities than men. He wrote that women must not leave their liberation to the mercy of men, including himself, and warned that men would not give up their power easily. Men who want to be comrades of women should not comment too much on women's struggles, he wrote, but rather show their solidarity in practice, above all by transforming themselves. Once again, as he had done before prison, he insisted that 'the twenty-first century will be the century of women's liberation'.

With the PKK's change in strategy in 2000 in favour of a solution to the conflict through 'democratic politics', the women's movement too restructured itself. The third women's congress, held in August 2000, dissolved the PJKK and founded PJA (Free Women's Party, dropping the word Kurdistan) to fully commit to developing the Women's Liberation Ideology as a radical global struggle paradigm. The congress resolved with the claim to enter the new millennium with a stronger commitment to women's internationalism by taking up intellectual tasks and exchanging with women from around the world. Dedicated to 'women's renaissance in the twenty-first century', PJA increasingly exchanged with global women's movements and organized joint actions with non-Kurdish women in the region. It drafted a new 'social contract' and presented it to women of the world to discuss women's participation in politics, economy, education, etc. and to formulate a blueprint to transform society. The guerrillas pledged to concern themselves more with women's issues in society, including labour, violence, poverty, and education. They engaged with Öcalan's prison writings that linked the idea of a 'democratic civilization' to the struggle against patriarchy.

In April 2002, following the eighth congress, the PKK was dissolved and instead the Kurdistan Freedom and Democracy Congress (KADEK) was formed as a people's parliament consisting of both party cadres and civilians. The new structuring was supposed to reflect the movement's transition from armed struggle towards a democratic and political project.[2] It declared a commitment to internally democratize by securing women's participation on all levels with the help of a 40 per cent quota. Furthermore, it encouraged Kurdish women 'to lead the struggle and to unite with all the democratic Arab, Turkish, and Persian women's movements in order to bring about a solution of the Kurdish Question by democratic means as well as by establishing peace, democracy, and improving the freedom of society in the world'. These and more decisive steps taken by the women's movement were obstructed by a feud between group formations within the organization. In a time of historic transformations in the region, marked by the US invasion of Iraq and the rise of the Justice and Development Party (AKP) in Turkey, the PKK went through its biggest crisis. The very principles and identity of the party were at stake. Several books anticipating the demise of the PKK were written around that period or immediately after.[3]

8

The battle for the PKK's soul

A new era began when, after a constitutional amendment following the land-slide victory of the Justice and Development Party (AKP) in 2002, Recep Tayyip Erdoğan became Prime Minister of Turkey days before the US invasion of Iraq in 2003. Documents published on WikiLeaks help construct a sense of the ways in which George W. Bush's 'freedom agenda', a neo-colonial imperial project to control the region in the name of reform parallel to military intervention, over time forced the new Turkish government to seek a renewed relationship with the Kurds, who were building a regional government inside post-Saddam Iraq. In this context, the AKP increased relations with conservative Kurdish parties inside and outside of Turkey's borders. At the same time as promising to solve the Kurdish issue politically, the government expanded military operations and cracked down on legal political parties.

The PKK calls the period between 2002 and 2004 'povajoyn tasfiyê', the liquidation period. The main protagonists of this process were two members of the PKK's presidential council, Öcalan's own brother Osman Öcalan ('Ferhat', hereafter Osman) and Nizamettin Taş ('Botan'), who rallied for a no longer socialist path. The rise of a conservative line within the PKK was influenced by US foreign policy in the region in the context of the 'war on terror'. In 1999, Abdullah Öcalan had warned that 'the US's demand to the PKK is a change of image' (Political Report). In the retrospective eyes of PKK members, with the promotion of 'reforms' the new US interventions in the region sought to co-opt the Kurds by pacifying the PKK, an enemy of NATO.

In this period, the women's movement had been critical of KADEK's inadequate implementation of the changes suggested in Öcalan's prison messages. In his defence for a court case in Athens, Öcalan proposed a structural change in the movement: a system of congresses. As a result, the short-lived KADEK was dissolved and Kongra-Gel (People's Congress) was formed in the second half of 2003. Öcalan also called for an end of the unilateral ceasefire in response to the state's lack of will to engage in talks. The PKK met to discuss the system change and the possibility of an end to the ceasefire, but members in executive positions such as Osman and Botan favoured giving up warfare for good. In his Turkish-language investigative book on the history of talks between the PKK and the Turkish state, Kurdish journalist Amed Dîcle (2017), who is affiliated to the movement, cites one central committee member, who later left the organization, as having said: 'Let us drop the word revolution from our literature.'[1]

The women's movement, which was the strongest proponent of Abdullah Öcalan's socialist line, was a target of Osman's group which openly advocated traditional, conservative gender roles. Using his authority within the party and the respect people paid him as the leader's brother, he nullified the decisions taken at a women's conference in 2003. In that period, once again, male members asserted that women's autonomous organization was splitting the party at a time of crisis. As noted in the women's movement's archives, Öcalan's new writings on democracy and decentralization were misrepresented by influential cadres as liberal individualism. Rotînda Engîn, at the time of our interview a KCK Executive Council member, witnessed this period first-hand. Her narrative of the struggle between 'two lines' – socialist/liberationist on one hand, economically liberal/socially conservative, i.e. collaborationist on the other – is representative of the women's movement's view of this period:

> In the spirit of liberalism, with the ideology of Britain and the US, Osman and Botan wanted to corrupt the PKK's line. Their first targets were relations between women and men. Their mentality failed to see that women's liberation was not a tactical matter to us. We had created the women's autonomous army, the women's party, the Women's Liberation Ideology to overcome patriarchy, to create a new life. But they wanted to manipulate the PKK's revolutionary way of life with bourgeois standards.
>
> As we developed criticism and self-criticism, they said that there is no need for change and transformation. We developed communality, did everything for the people, but they imposed individualism on us. We are a movement that grew with non-materialist values, but they put materialist values to the front. This is the ideology of capitalist modernity. Osman and Botan were individualism, liberalism, traditional gender relations, materialism. With the arguments of capitalist modernity, the void within our party opened a window for liberalism to enter the lives of the cadres. They would even insist that war and revolution are no longer needed. Everyone was after individualist life, people were looking to find someone to marry and settle.

The atmosphere resulted in a split of an estimated 1,500 people from the party and undermined the restructuring efforts. Many defected to the KDP or to the Turkish state. Osman left the party in 2004, married a fellow ex-cadre, whom he divorced later and married another woman nearly 30 years his junior. Osman, who lived under the auspices of powerful people in Başûr until his death in late 2021 due to Covid-19 complications, was regularly interviewed and quoted by media as a 'critic', who could provide insight into his old party's workings. For the Kurdish women's movement, however, he embodies the patriarchal mentality that tried to send them back into the home. The experiences in this phase shaped the women's movement's appreciation of the importance of women's autonomy and self-organization.

Öcalan's wrath at what the party had become is spelled out in his 2004 book *Bir halkı savunmak* (In Defence of a People; English title: *Beyond State, Power and Violence*). As activists tried to recover and rebuild trust, Öcalan proposed to refound the PKK as a purely ideological, revolutionary cadre party. In the midst of the chaos, the guerrillas announced an end to the long ceasefire period with a turn to 'active defence'. The 1 June 2004 manoeuvre, which reignited the guerrilla war, is narrated in party history as being as important as the firing of the first bullet 20 years earlier. Framed as a resurrection from the abyss, its significance as a 'wake-up call' is compared to the early prison resistance. After the reformation of the PKK and the revival of armed struggle, nearly 300 delegates met in the summer of 2004 for the fifth women's congress which dissolved PJA and formed today's PAJK, the ideological cadre party of the women's movement, the autonomous counterpart to the PKK. All these steps were crowned by Öcalan's announcement of Democratic Confederalism on Newroz day of 2005. A new, woman-centric paradigm had arrived. This was Apo's 'third birth'.

9

Enter Democratic Confederalism

The Kurdistan freedom movement's 'paradigm shift' away from the desire to create a Kurdish nation-state towards stateless democracy was not a sudden command from Imralı Prison that dramatically remade the organization – a story frequently repeated in casual accounts. In reality, the 'freedom paradigm' has its roots in the 1990s and the transition to the new framework was not at all an abrupt switch; it was a long and difficult, conflict-ridden process of discussion and contention and it is still ongoing. In any case, to many cadres and sympathizers, the idea of establishing a state was an abstract notion and not necessarily rooted in nationalistic sentiments; the state rather stood in as a shorthand for independence from colonization and imperialism. Long-term members of the movement always stress that the radical democratic, women's liberationist and ecological paradigm for freedom (in short, 'the new paradigm') was not merely a transformation of traditional movement practice; it above all redefined the scale of the Kurdistan revolution's freedom imagination.

Socialist revolutions in places like Russia and China, and the many anti-colonial national liberation movements of the twentieth century, had greatly shaped the movement's theory and practice, explained Elif Ronahî, as she recounted the chaotic collective processes of grasping the meaning and implications of Öcalan's new writings:

> Already after the collapse of actually existing socialism, our leadership and movement considered questions relating to state and power on our agenda, but the new paradigm was a radical challenge to the basic principles and ideas that had informed our struggle until then. 'Were we giving up Kurdistan?'
>
> In discussions about actually existing socialism and the ways in which it understood or practised democracy, socialism, and freedom, we started asking whether its statist approach managed to solve people's social issues and bring them closer to freedom. What about women's liberation? What were socialists' analyses of society and history? What sections of society do we exclude when focussing only on the proletariat as the revolutionary subject? What were actually existing socialism and national liberationism's effects on our own personalities and mentalities? As a result, we gave a deep self-criticism of our practice to date and asserted that we were not giving up freedom ideals. Instead, we changed our paradigm, philosophy, methods,

means, with new global conditions in mind. We renewed our promise to freedom with a more realistic and radical theory and practice. Our current paradigm encompasses the entire world, the previous one was limited to the Kurdish people. This is an ideological change and requires a new strategy, system, and understanding of alliance accordingly.

The previously mentioned developments in the region in the first years of the twenty-first century, in particular the US invasion of Iraq, the rise of the AKP, and the newly established KRG and its relationship to the US and Turkey, contributed to shifts in emphases in Öcalan's language; thoughts about the possibility of a shared democratic republic with a new identity and vision increasingly gave way to a radical democratic autonomy beyond borders.

In May 2005, the extraordinary congress of Kongra-Gel announced the new system it would begin building along Democratic Confederalism. Soon after, a women's congress formed the High Women's Council (KJB) to build an autonomous women's system in Kurdistan. With the new paradigm, women were no longer simply 'half of the nation' or 'a section' of the community, but rather, alongside the youth, the driving force of the liberation of society, the radical left-wing in the democratic confederal system. Initially, the Union of Free Women (YJA) was envisioned as an umbrella for the social and political organizational efforts, with YJA Star as women's legitimate self-defence force and PAJK as the ideological perspective-giving cadre party. In KJB's extraordinary congress in March 2014, KJB and YJA merged into today's Kurdistan Women's Communities (KJK), to organize a women's democratic confederal system, and YJA Star remains the women's guerrilla army, the HPG's counterpart. While PAJK continues to be the militant, ideological party based in the mountains, the KJK is charged with practical tasks of women's confederal self-organization and alliance-building. The KJK is the autonomous counterpart to the Kurdistan Communities Union (KCK), announced in 2007 as the Kurdistan freedom movement's umbrella administrative coordination for establishing Democratic Confederalism in Kurdistan. The woman co-presidents of all structures affiliated with the system are chosen by the autonomous women's movement. The structures can criticize each other and make recommendations, but only the women can intervene in the general structures by way of veto, and not the other way around. These two parallel, complementary systems (*xweser* and *gişti*, autonomous and general, respectively) have different missions and priorities, but are nonetheless part of one freedom struggle 'to liberate society from the state'. In addition to these umbrella structures, there are movements and self-defence units for the different parts of Kurdistan.[1]

In the new perspectives of the movement, an internationalism of the twenty-first century should be defined by relations between communities, liberationist movements, and struggles, not states. In fact, even the term internationalism is considered to be no longer sufficient to describe the urgent need to build alliances beyond borders and state-defined identities. As part of the effort of building democratic confederal systems, 'people's diplomacy' is supposed to draw on and foster millennia-old legacies of mutual, symbiotic neighbourly relations between peoples. In the same spirit, women's and youth diplomacy are organized autonomously and focus on building local and global alliances with social movements and civil society. World Democratic Women's Confederalism is envisioned as a world-system for and by women. In her article on this vision, which she describes as 'a way of building a political system of world-women', Meral Çiçek (2020) clarifies that beyond forming yet another international umbrella organization, the coordination of women's self-determination on a global scale constitutes

> a transnational grassroots democracy of women based on a perfect balance between local and global as well as partial and universal. This is different from a network, a federation or a union, for example. But it would also not be just a loose entity that comes together from time to time, discusses and diverges again. Rather, we need a mechanism by which the intellectual and practical potential of world women can take concrete shape at the global level and an effective counterforce to patriarchy can emerge.

As explained in later sections, self-defence, physical and political, cultural and economic are key to the protection of the women's system. The women's army YJA Star constitutes the self-defence force of the women's democratic confederal project for all parts of Kurdistan and beyond. They run parallel to the People's Defence Forces, HPG. Although the units are based in the mountains, in theory and practice, YJA Star knows no borders in its defence of women in Kurdistan and the Middle East. Derya, a guerrilla from Hewlêr (Erbil), contrasted this to regional practices of local, tribal, or government-linked militias: 'Our movement created an army of revolutionaries from four parts of Kurdistan willing to fight to death beyond their individual village, region or "part". Revolutionary homeland love means learning to defend Mexmûr, Sheikhan or Afrîn equally.'

YJA Star inspired the creation of autonomous Kurdish women's armies for different parts of Kurdistan.[2] All of these structures differ in size and are not all equally active; the intensity of war varies in the different regions. They also have different statuses in the eyes of states and international institutions. While the YJA Star is considered terrorist in the West, the YPJ has been part of the US-led coalition to defeat Daesh. Although they do not operate under the same command structures and have different targets and claims, what unites these armed units is a shared ideology and their function as the protective force of social and political structures of the respective women's structures they are part of. Collectively, they serve as the guarantee for the envisioned women's confederal system.

As I hope to show in later parts of this book, to its builders and defenders, Democratic Confederalism is not merely a material structure: it is also a moral and political attitude, a way of life, a philosophy, a revolutionary social contract, and it is already under construction in hearts and minds of people who imagine life without the state. In an environment in which politics, citizenship, and democracy are increasingly tied to the state and the capitalist world-system, with neoliberal non-governmental organizations playing a growing role, the Kurdistan freedom movement creates ungovernable organized communities outside of the gaze and control of the state.

PART II

Theory

Jineolojî, the women's academies, women's news agencies ... all of these create new concepts, perceptions, and claims about the world. They are part of a collective effort of women's truth-seeking. – Jînda, Women's Academy in Sur, 2015

Theory has historically played a major role in the fight against oppression. It can offer vocabularies and frameworks to articulate what is wrong and what must change, and why. It validates otherwise repressed and criminalized perspectives, ideas, and feelings. However, as bell hooks (1991) noted: 'Theory is not inherently healing, liberatory, or revolutionary. It fulfills this function only when we ask that it do so and direct our theorizing towards this end.' Having been systematically deprived of the power to name the world, the oppressed have a complicated relationship to theory. Questions around the use of theory for liberation remain relevant especially because of highly inaccessible and elitist language common in the world of critical theory. As a system, academia often acts as a cultural gatekeeper even of radical ideas. Politically engaged scholars and activists argue that academia can moreover have a depoliticizing and disciplining impact on people's ability to both fully grasp the stakes inherent to struggles for freedom and to appreciate knowledge produced within struggles for liberation. The apolitical, casual use of the term 'decolonization' in universities is one manifestation of this.

The chapters below provide a rough non-exhaustive sketch of the role of theory in the movement's view on history, society, and politics, as well as theory's relationship to the revolutionary practice. While the works of Öcalan are taken as a foundational basis for the movement's theory, knowledge is broadly produced and reproduced in the wider struggle ecology, and in conversation with other radical movements. The Kurdistan freedom movement's literature ranges from books, archives, pamphlets, newspapers, magazines, conference and congress transcripts, guerrilla diaries and prison letters, and converses especially with bodies of work on Middle East and women's history, radical democracy, feminism, ecology, socialism, world-system theory, anarchism, and critical theory. Largely invisible to the outside world, communicating intellectual ideas and debates to oppressed and dispossessed communities is one of the movement's most strategic and time-consuming efforts in its work of 'mental' decolonization.

One of the most important threads within the movement's philosophy is the critique of positivism in the study of social life. Positivism is an approach to knowledge that privileges scientific facts and principles (e.g. evidence based on observable facts, quantifiable measurement, testability, etc.). That positivist methods have been used by the powerful to legitimize their claims to truth and objectivity has long been criticized in scholarship and struggles around the globe. Ironically, although feminist or anti-colonial movements continue to produce rich criticisms of positivism, positivist methodology, deeply embedded in a secular worldview, often dominates the study of social movements, especially in European universities. In the context of the Kurdistan freedom movement, a common approach among researchers has been to triangulate superficial engagement with Öcalan's writings with snapshot-like ethnographic impressions or news articles about the movement's practice in order to 'assess' the relationship between theory and practice of a mass movement. Literature on the movement rarely recognizes the insights that this movement has collectively accumulated as sociological knowledge over the course of several decades of transnational mass mobilization of lower classes, refugees, genocide survivors, prisoners, and marginalized communities in political, military, social, cultural, and economic spheres. Another common tendency is to judge the movement's theories, especially its ideas about paradigmatic changes in social relations since the Neolithic revolution, on their scientific accuracy. Undoubtedly, there is value in doing so, especially in light of recent works that radically rethink the history of civilization against the state.[1] But it is perhaps more interesting to consider the subtextual and spiritual meaning, affect, and purpose, pedagogical and political, of such theses. For example, the term 'civaka xweser' (natural society) in Öcalan's work signifies the social world in the pre-state era. Activists often talk about how 'civaka xweser' manifests itself today within the cultures, life worlds, and practices in rural and otherwise marginalized communities, even if fragmented or residual. This is not far from (e.g.) decolonial and indigenous feminists' analyses of the violent ruptures in the fabric of life caused by colonization and the state.[2] One more interesting path of engagement is perhaps to understand the dynamic interaction between theory, society, and history: the PKK movement has spent years turning an anti-state hypothesis into a mantra, a ritual, a way of life, a political programme for millions of people who have been victimized by the colonial nation-state system. From a political perspective, insisting on an anti-state interpretation of early human history is less about contributing to anthropological theories than it is a pedagogical device to demystify and dethrone the state from one's relationship to history and society. Isn't a popular movement's sacrificial devotion to such ideas not in itself an ongoing episode of non-state history, theory, and practice?

10

'Struggling woman': Ideology and identity

In many ways, one can define the Kurdish women's movement's march towards autonomy as a journey from *hebûn* (existing) to *xwebûn* (being oneself). From a struggle to assert the mere existence of the Kurdish people, the women's movement, as the revolutionary force within the revolution, came to develop new social contracts, vocabularies, and practices to rearticulate the terms of Kurdish life. The role of theory was crucial in this process.

As mentioned in the previous section, the Kurdish women's movement began to deepen its theoretical perspectives in the 1990s, in conversation with Öcalan. Here, it is important to note that struggles over theory, concepts, and ideas evolved through contradiction, dialogue, disagreement, and discussion. The collective and transversal character of these debates makes it impossible to clearly attribute authorship to particular individuals. The insights gathered were published and used as educational material as well as to initiate conversations with other women's struggles. For example, in its 'Social Contract Declaration' published at the turn of the millennium in several languages, PJA, the predecessor of today's PAJK, offered its analyses on the reformulation of social relations in all spheres of life, from law to art, for discussion with women and movements around the world. The document is one of the early reflections of the Kurdish women's movement's articulation of its thesis that revolution is only possible with women's liberation as a universal freedom measure. Here, PJA outlined a rough framework for women to reverse dominant social contracts modelled after the patriarchal Sumerian state. In the multi-volume book, *Women's Army-fication*, published in 2004, the women's movement offers its perspectives on the historical relationship between women, violence, and self-defence (PJA 2004a). Its brief profiles of women's roles in revolutions and resistance movements in Vietnam, Algeria, Nicaragua, China, Chiapas, Palestine, Cuba, Ireland, the Soviet Union, and the Basque Country were also meant to enrich Kurdish women's knowledge of other women's experiences.

Over the years, the women began developing a theory of revolutionary women's militancy – the identity of the 'struggling woman'. This is not a uniform category, but rather any woman, who is on a quest to liberate herself from patriarchal definitions that confine her to an existence solely as another person's mother, daughter, sister, lover, or wife. Women's experiences, analyses, and martyrdoms became the basis for the 'Women's Liberation Ideology' in the 1990s. The idea is that in a world in which dominant media, culture, and politics are sexist, without ideology, women will be co-opted or instrumentalized by the system. For the struggle to succeed, commitment to ideology is seen as a guarantor to protect women from co-optation into conservative or liberalist ideas or systems. Elif Ronahî explained this to me with emphasis on the importance of trailblazing cadres:

> Without an ideology, you will be dragged into the system or be instrumentalized. For example, some feminist movements became detached from societal realities, because they created no alternative to the system, no militancy to struggle. They were active but not very radical or threatening. And that's what the system needs to be able to say: 'Look what I do for women, I give her rights, I include them'. For a radical struggle, there need to be women who dedicate themselves 24 hours. To not become collaborators in the capitalist modernist system, women need an alternative ideology.
>
> The Women's Liberation Ideology can be applied by women in all countries and adapted to their own contexts. We believed that to the extent to which women are liberated, revolution will be possible. This is the most radical work that we are currently doing. Otherwise, we too would have turned into a movement which defers women's liberation to a later point. We took our precautions accordingly to ensure that women will not merely serve revolutions which marginalize their freedom. On the contrary, we are the revolution's pioneers and creative force.

The five basic revolutionary principles of the Women's Liberation Ideology are valid in the women's movement to this day: love for the homeland, free thought and free will, organization, struggle, and ethics-aesthetics.

The Kurdish word *welatparêzî* translates to 'loving and protecting one's homeland'. Unlike the patriarchal connotation of the Latin-based word 'patriotism', it is gender neutral. In the movement's thought, *welatparêzî* is conceptualized as a commitment to liberate the lands from colonization, occupation, and militarism. Women's love for the homeland is read against male-dominated notions of borders, nations, and states, as universal love for humanity and the earth combined with an attachment to one's ancestral lands and ecology. Protecting cultures, identities, and geographies from genocide and forced assimilation is seen as indivisible from self-defence. Therefore, women's love for the homeland means a fight against state terror and other forms of exploitation and oppression, with an inherent commitment to internationalism. Drawing on this notion of *welatparêzî*, the movement often encourages internationalists, who have complicated relationships to their countries' problematic colonial and imperial histories, to dissociate their social history from that of the state and the ruling classes and seek traces of resistance legacies in their own cities and regions, to find references for democratic values and practices in their local contexts.

By way of the second principle of *fikra azad, vîna azad*, 'free thought and free will', women ought to break with both traditionalist as well as capitalist-modernist definitions of morality, politics, and society that frequently objectify women. Building on this, the third principle, *rêxistinî*, 'organizedness' or 'organization', is described as a guarantor for women's struggles to succeed. While women may individually have courage and willpower, they need to be organized in all spheres of life to translate their efforts into forms, whether that be a party or a commune. For this, women must develop their independent and autonomous struggle, concepts, and praxes to make sure that they do not reproduce male-dominated thinking. Organization and thought, however, must not resort to dogmatic or static ways of seeing society and life, but must be based on a commitment to permanent *têkoşîn* or 'struggle'. *Têkoşîn*, the fourth principle, is supposed to encourage adaptation, flexibility, and transformation. Although theory is important for liberation, a revolutionary must above all also be willing to fight and sacrifice to build practical alternatives. Creative struggle methods are also important to resist settling for less than freedom. The fifth principle, aesthetics (*estetîk*), advocates women's liberation from patriarchal, capitalist, and colonial standards. Beauty is reconceptualized as transcending the physical realm and relating to ethics and self-determination. Aesthetics ought to be informed by a commitment to justice, autonomy, truth, and liberation. Such free essence will manifest itself in free form: a struggling and organized woman's aura, posture, thought, speech, and consciousness have an aestheticizing effect on her environment to transform herself, other women, men, and society as a whole. In an article by Zozan Sima (2018) from the Jineolojî Academy, beauty is described as a value created in the process of liberating life:

> Women, who democratize politics, women, who risk their lives to protect communities and other women, women who educate themselves and those around them, women who live communally, women who save the ecological equilibrium, women who struggle to raise children in free countries, with their own identities, and many others are all women who become beautiful through struggle. In today's world full of ugliness, injustice and evil, not physical, augmented forms of aesthetics constitute beauty; only women who defend life through struggle can create beauty. In this sense, is there anything more beautiful than the young women, who fight against Daesh fascism?

The Women's Liberation Ideology is not a framework reserved for women. It is also taught to male cadres, whose militancy gets measured by their approach to women's liberation and by their engagement with 'men's freedom problem', i.e. patriarchy's imposition of violence and domination-based features on men's personalities. The movement's concept of '*hevjiyana azad*' (free co-life) as a proposal for egalitarian relationships between genders, societies, and species; its project to 'kill the dominant man'; and its notions of self-defence beyond the realm of the physicial are all aspects of the movement's philosophical, moral, and political struggle to braid new social relations. The broadness of these principles means that the Women's Liberation Ideology can be applied by women in all countries and adapted to their own contexts. For the Kurdish women's movement, they offer a framework through which it can organize its militancy and articulate radically different social relations for the guerrilla sphere, for Kurdish and Middle Eastern society, and for the world. Later chapters describe the engagement of these theories and concepts in practice.

11

Building 'democratic modernity'

'History' is commonly equated with the beginning of 'civilization', starting in the fourth millennium BC, and defined by the rise of the Sumerian city-state in ancient Mesopotamia. Anything before the first forms of writing, bureaucracy, formal laws, and standing armies, and technologies such as metallurgy – the hundreds of thousands of years since the first appearance of *Homo sapiens* and the social life that preceded the rise of the city-state – has conventionally been described as 'pre-history'.

Mesopotamia is 'the land between two rivers', the Tigris (Dîcle) and Euphrates (Firat), both of which have been a source of life for thousands of years. The region grew with women's contributions to the development of human societies in the Neolithic revolution, such as knowledge of nature that created agriculture. It worshiped powerful, complex female and male deities among the patrons of the first village and city communities. With the rise of the first city states, debt, institutionalized religion and military, bureaucracy, and surplus production gradually established a hierarchical, power-based social system. Feminist historians like Gerda Lerner (1986) have written on the evolution of deepening patriarchal turns in law, economy, and religion in ancient Mesopotamia. Today, the geography around this area is widely seen as one of the worst places to be a woman.

This 5,000-year trajectory plays a key role for Öcalan's thinking, but his notion of freedom references a scale that begins with the creation of the universe. His interest in quantum physics in the discussion about consciousness, truth, action, and existence leads him to ask whether uncertainty and spontaneity, as driving elements of the universe, signify that freedom is an essential part of the unfolding of life. The dual quality that is inherent to all phenomena in the universe, he writes in the methodology discussions of his manifesto, is the contradiction between being and non-being, generating internal, dynamic movement. If this flexibility creates freedom, then freedom creates diversity. It is within the 'quantum moment', the chaos interval, as a period of transition generative of qualitative change, that struggle is the decisive factor to determine outcomes, 'moments of creation', even within seconds (Öcalan 2015). As such, the option of freedom exists at all times, but struggle is the driving force, the principle of life. Duality – not binary – is another phenomenon that enables life, as expressed in the relationship between the feminine and the masculine, as well as fluid realities beyond.

Impacted by thinkers like Fernand Braudel or Murray Bookchin, Öcalan draws on a longue durée approach to history. He locates humanity's original freedom question in terms of the flow of two rivers: the 'democratic civilization' is the rendered-invisible stream in history, among others, made up of women as the true owners of the economy; workers, artistic groups, and marginalized communities in the cities; oppressed peoples insisting on survival and sovereignty, and organic communal units in the rural areas that resisted the city's exploitation, and the youth spirit. Despite all sorts of attacks by the parallel running 'statist' or 'mainstream civilization', the male-dominated world of kings, emperors, and ruling classes, this underground civilization survived through everyday practices or conscious resistance. Through violence, ideology, and economic organization, the colourful, animate world was suppressed by hierarchical divisions of life. Power and authority came to be represented by punishing, exploitative gods, whose demands are executed and protected by the main upholders of the state – an alliance of priests, elders, and warriors. The externalization of the sacred and good to abstract realms (heaven, afterlife, etc.) developed an increasingly classed and anti-ecological character. This major historic 'rupture' was a coup against women in this perspective. The domination of women became part and parcel of all oppressive systems since Sumerian times and normalized all other sorts of violence in the world. Hence, inspired by feminist scholarship, Öcalan refers to women as the first colony, class, and nation in human history, and to feminism as the 'rebellion of the oldest colony'.

Within this 5,000-year trajectory, Öcalan defines the era of capitalist modernity as a further institutionalization of power through sexism, colonialism, liberalism, imperialism, nation-state, positivism, industrialism, and ecological catastrophe. Industrialism not only physically destroyed nature, but also broke ties between people and lands, driving populations to migrate to increasingly unmanageable, anonymous cities, where politics and the economy would be delegated to the affairs of a central state. In his third volume, *Sociology of Freedom*, Öcalan (2020) relates oppression under capitalism to the hegemony of positivism. Pointing out that only in the last quarter of the twentieth century did the social sciences begin to pay increased attention to women as an object of study as an outcome of the feminist struggle, he dedicates several sections in his works to the sexist character of dominant notions of science. Similar to other system-critical thinkers, Öcalan views liberalism as a European ideology that claims universality within a state-centric epistemic framework that precludes people's hopes for freedom. As a pillar of capitalist modernity, it seemingly tolerates different views, while monopolizing the claim to truth and to the judgement over good/evil. Power and profit make up the morality that drives liberalism, 'the worst anti-social ideology and practice; individualism is a state of war against society as much as state and power are'. Liberalism also normalizes sexism in society. According to Öcalan, more than any other system before it, capitalism deprived women of political, economic, social, and cultural power, while disguising its deeply inherent sexism. Öcalan invokes the concept of 'Housewifization', a term developed by Marxist-feminists Maria Mies, Claudia von Werlhof, and others to describe the coercive process through which capitalist primitive accumulation subjugated women by appropriating, exploiting, and devaluing their labour.[1] Housewifization relies on a male-dominated configuration of public space and detaches women from the means of production, self-determined reproduction, and self-defence, all of which constitute basic needs for survival. He uses the concept also to describe 'submitted society', that is, a society rendered unfree, powerless and passive. In this sense, Öcalan suggests analyzing women's objectified status under capitalism as the 'summary of the entire system'.

The predicament of the great socialist thinkers, in Öcalan's view, has been their reliance on the progress of capitalist modernity and its tools. The bourgeois, urban character of social democrats at best leads to reformism without meaningful challenges to the system. He criticizes Marxists for what he perceives as an insufficient critique of modernity and the state, despite having undeniably genuine freedom utopias. National liberation struggles often develop profound analyses of colonialism and empire, but run the risk of copying the system of their oppressors. Anarchists, while providing radical theoretical and moral objections to power and authoritarianism, often fail to build wider societal alternatives, 'preferring the anarchist individual over democratic society'. Likewise, ecologists and feminists, while leading great justice struggles, sometimes turn into marginal elites out of touch with society, meanwhile not building concrete anti-capitalist, societal, political, and economic alternatives.

Against capitalist modernity, 'democratic modernity' is Öcalan's proposal to build, based on a multitude of liberationist legacies, a 'freedom utopia of equality within differences'. Built on the heritage of the democratic civilization, democratic modernity is perceived as already existing in the world of struggles for justice, rebellious artists, resisting women, and social movements for change. However, it also must be consciously and concretely built through struggle, autonomy, creativity, broad democratic alliances, and artistic courage, with women and the youth as its pioneering forces. Different autonomous structures are like self-directed cells that communicate and relate to each other in a confederal manner, as part of a larger eco-system. In this sense, autonomy does not merely relate to local self-organization structures vis-à-vis the state; it also expresses a symbiotic relation within the democratic confederal project. Ultimately, on the horizon of Democratic Confederalism is an alternative world confederation of communities, movements, and alliances, a 'commune of the communes' against the world-system based on nation-states. Öcalan's view of civil society as a counter-hegemonic force against the state's ability to name, define, and govern life encompasses building democratic, mutual relations within and between communities, tribes, faith groups, and movements. As the fundamental unit of democratic modernity, the moral-political society is what the nation-state is to statist civilization. The 'moral-political society' is expressed locally in communes, intentional communities, justice campaigns, movements, and self-organizing spaces. The moral-political society is a way of locally developing ecological and feminine characteristics against 'society-cide'.

In the fourth volume of his manifesto particularly, Öcalan (2010a) proposes what he calls an anti-Orientalist, but also anti-sexist, anti-modernist, non-statist, social history of the Middle East in order to develop a socialism from the region's perspective. He claims that the regional social fabric, especially people's attachment to the non-material, spiritual world, would not permit the forces of capitalist modernity to establish themselves in the region. To decolonize, however, Middle East culture needed a renaissance or 'truth revolution', a change in mentality and everyday political life to rescue the self from capitalist modernity's ideological hegemony and from reactionary forms of resistance against it (such as nationalism or religious extremism). These analyses lead to his proposal of the 'democratic nation solution', spelled out in the final volume of the manifesto (Öcalan 2013).

If Democratic Confederalism is the commune of the communes, the democratic nation is 'a community of communities'. Öcalan views nationalism as an ideology that developed with capitalism and the rise of the nation-state, representing a divisive and artificial form of organizing society deprived of moral meaning. It is responsible for all sorts of bloodshed in the name of flags, borders, identities, and symbols. Ethnic and religious problems in the region are seen as products of a particular conception of identity imposed by capitalist modernity, namely, a monopolistic, centralist, and homogenized one at odds with the region's social fabric. As such, Öcalan seeks to dissociate the term 'nation' from state-centric definitions of identity, in favour of a more plural-istic arrangement. The term nation is intentionally left open to allow a variety of flexible formations around language, religion, culture, and other forms of belonging, beyond narrow definitions that contain and standardize identities within the artificial borders of states. This approach to nationhood potentially opens interesting options for identity formation beyond essentialist ideas.

In its literature, the movement positions 'Kurdish-ness' not as a static identity, but rather as a phenomenon within a resistance/collaboration dialectic in an atmosphere of colonial and imperial violence. As regional and international forces treat the Kurds as 'destabilizing' factors, Öcalan believes that the Kurds' statelessness in a geography where the first states flourished can be turned into an opportunity for the democratization of the region. In a way, similar to the role that the revolutionary cadre plays for the development of Kurdish democratic society and politics, the Kurdistan revolution can play in the advancement of Middle Eastern democratic modernity. In this way, if it gets defined and redefined in the struggle for liberation, Kurdish-ness can come to signify a wider insistence on democratic life against the state. This, however, should not disregard people's perceptions and emotional attachments to their Kurdish identity as meaningless or irrelevant. In the context of oppression, the protection of Kurdish culture, language, and identity is seen as a duty to save a dynamic and diverse form of life from extinction. In the context of genocide, self-determined, 'free Kurdish-ness' becomes an ontological category, defined by an ability to become an organized force against assimilation, domination, and violence. In the same vein, as long as states and political groups instrumentalize Islam to justify violence against others, faith communities such as Êzîdîs and Alevis ought to protect their cultures from annihilation.

The representation of minoritized and othered identities is considered paramount under the given regional circumstances, but the ability to express identities is not viewed as an end in itself. Social and cultural identities are conceived of in dynamic terms and are above all tasked with self-democratization through self-education, criticism/self-criticism, and social and political activism.[2] In this notion of politics, the liberation of the self and the other are interconnected, with the more vulnerable component tasked with a revolutionary mission: an individual's self-realization, selfhood, and self-defence are a necessary condition for the liberation of society; women's autonomy is a condition for the possibility of liberating everyone from patriarchy; the self-determined existence of one community is a dynamic force that will democratize wider regions around it. Since centres of power and hierarchy cannot be expected to accept the will-power of entities they consider subordinate, autonomy is necessarily always an outcome of struggle and conflict even among allies. Young women, because they stand furthest away from power, are seen as embodying the non-dogmatic, generative energy that enables free life. Having been removed from the means of knowledge production, politics, economy, and self-defence by systems of power, they constitute the embodiment of a world-in-the-making, creating new aesthetics and ethics as they organize. Young women are also the ones with the greatest potential to pursue one of the most important tasks for liberation to succeed, namely, connecting with liberation quests around the world.

While democratic autonomy is practised through grassroots structures for people's daily affairs, engagement with 'statist politics' is framed as a relationship of 'negotiation and struggle'. Political parties engaging in electoral politics are supposed to represent the will of confederally organized autonomous structures. Their mission is to strengthen the hand of communities by forcing the state to democratize without surrendering politics to it. In the context of nationalist and authoritarian states, the political party also needs to make explicit its commitment to represent oppressed and excluded groups. In any case, even as it decentres state-centric laws and legal systems, in a world-system based on these frameworks, the movement does engage with them as one way of demanding the Kurds' right to freely exercise their own language and culture, and be equal participants in political life within imposed borders.

In ethnically, linguistically, and religiously diverse countries in the Middle East, like Turkey, Lebanon, or Syria, people often use the term 'mosaic' to acknowledge or celebrate a sense of cultural richness and co-existence. Mosaics are made up of differently coloured stones fixated in a controlled manner to reflect an aesthetically pleasing, representative image. Stones usually symbolize the opposite of change or transformation; mosaics thus evoke state-crafted, often artificial social relations, and obscure power dynamics. Carpet-weaving, in many cultures associated with women's craftiness, is perhaps a more suitable metaphor for the democratic nation vision: whether symbolizing individuals or collective identities, differently coloured, flexible threads relate to each other creatively, reversibly through re-/un-doable structures, patterns, and motifs – in this case, principles, values, and social contracts. Carpets, unlike mosaics, are about home-making also.

In some ways, the democratic nation solution is similar to what the Zapatistas refer to as 'a world in which many worlds fit'. In different sites of the struggle, this is already expressed on the ground. From the plurinational self-administration in Rojava to progressive alliances within Turkish borders, the term is used by the movement across contexts, to develop solidarity-based social relations among Middle Eastern communities. The Kurdish youth movement's anti-fascist coalitions built with internationalists in places like Europe also prefigure the formation of new cultures and identities along democratic values. As a Turkish woman, Heja (introduced elsewhere) described the generative nature of the democratic nation proposal:

> Dogmatic leftists struggle to understand us, because they don't overcome fixed ideas around nationhood, the state, and exploitation. We don't believe that certain conditions must ripen before people start organizing themselves. We create new terms for this process, such as the 'democratic nation line' against old ideas around self-determination that depend on states.
>
> Democratic confederal self-organization represents an alternative cultural mentality, in which oppressed identities get expressed, at the same time as

74

open-minded, creative forms of life are developed. It is a system of friendship, comradeship, a struggle-based democracy. Against the idea of one nation, one religion, one state, one language and one flag, ours is an identity quest based on the plurality of our communities. It is ultimately a quest for a sense of belonging based on freedom. As Nâzım Hikmet said:

> 'To live! Like a tree alone and free,
> To live! Like a forest in fraternity.'

12

Jineolojî: 'A science of woman and life'

Şahmaran, the 'ruler of the snakes' is a prominent mythical creature in Kurdish art. There are different versions of the anonymous folkloric story of the beautiful queen, whose lower body moulds into the shape of a serpent. In some oral accounts, a young man falls into a well and discovers Şahmaran's magnificent underground cave garden. As a guardian of knowledge and wisdom, Şahmaran, whose body has both toxic and healing qualities, agrees to teach him about herbs and medicine. One day, under torture, the man reveals her secret whereabouts to the terminally ill king, who wants to consume Şahmaran's miraculous flesh. In some versions, the king heals from her body, while one of his men dies from it. The young lover obtains her eternal knowledge upon consumption. In other versions, Şahmaran's ancient wisdom is lost forever upon her death at the hands of greedy men. Serpents have been associated with knowledge and immortality since the Epic of Gilgamesh, one of the oldest preserved epics in the world. Over the course of millennia, through Medusas and Eves, patriarchal ideas originated in this part of the world that likened women to snakes: untrustworthy, conspiratorial, and to be blamed for the failures of men. From past to present, in many schools of faith or thought, women have historically been excluded from knowledge and the means of knowledge production, and punished for knowing too much. The European witch-hunts, which Silvia Federici (2004) puts in the context of the rise of colonialism and capitalism, was a regional, systematic feminicide over centuries, orchestrated by state, nobility, and church, against tens of thousands of women and an attack on their knowledges, practices, and communal economies. Sexist ideas about women's relationship to knowledge condition everyday misogynistic language around the world. The witch-hunt-like murder of Şahmaran also represents the ways in which women's knowledge is harvested, persecuted, and betrayed. No wonder then that Şahmaran's omniscient gaze decorates many sites of Kurdish women's radical knowledge production – from guerrilla art to the mud-brick walls of Jinwar Women's Village in Rojava.

The word Jineolojî was first coined in 2008 in Öcalan's *Sociology of Freedom*, the third volume of his *Manifesto for a Democratic Civilization*, published in 2009. Following an extensive critique of the Eurocentric, male-dominated, and positivist nature of dominant strands in the fragmented social sciences, he suggested that the Kurdish women's movement develop a radical intervention in

Figure 2   Guerrillas admiring the decoration of the venue for the first Jineolojî
conference in the mountains. The image portrays Şahmaran, the 'ruler of the snakes'.
Xinerê, May 2015

the realm of knowledge. Not long after, the movement began internal discussions in Kurdistan and the diaspora to formulate a theoretical framework, methodology, and philosophy of knowledge against the oppressive ways in which women and life have been treated in interpretations of the world to date. With reference to a common root between the words *jin* (woman) and *jiyan* (life), Jineolojî (Kurdish: *jin* = woman; Greek: *logos* = science) is defined as the 'science of woman and life'. Jineolojî is presented as a women's science that encompasses also feminism and that seeks solutions to global social issues towards liberation. As noted in numerous publications, Jineolojî is not antagonistic or 'an alternative to feminism', rather, it builds on the legacy of all historical women's struggles and knowledges, including feminisms.[1]

Trying to pin down a singular definition of the evolving, collective world of Jineolojî would do injustice to the discussions among a growing number of women, who co-develop and deepen Jineolojî's content, scope, process, and meaning as they go.[2] For our purposes here, it is more useful to try and understand Jineolojî's intellectual and mobilizational role in the movement.

Jineolojî is often described as being many things at once, a worldview, a form of knowledge production, a set of methods for interpretation, a struggle for meaning- giving, and an organizational effort. The creation of a new science had to happen in an organized way, and so the Jineolojî committee in the mountains was formed in 2011 to begin an initial stage of research. To claim to develop a 'science' and not another critical theory implied the development of a theory of knowledge (epistemology), a philosophy of being (ontology), and ways of obtaining knowledge (methodology). The committee co-authored one of the first publications on Jineolojî, the book *Introduction to Jineolojî* ('Jineolojîye giriş') (2015), which begins by reading the layers of women's colonization from the viewpoint of the Middle East: from the early institutionalization of patriarchy in the early city-states through centralization, surplus accumulation, and male-dominated intrigues and alliances, to the rise of monotheistic religions, culminating in capitalism's objectification of every inch of women's bodies. Alongside studying women's worldwide critiques of the sciences, traces of matri-centric cultures and practices in Kurdistan and the region were 'dug up' in the early Jineolojî works. Archaeological terminology comes up often; as activists often claim, over millennia, starting with the Sumerian priests, 'layers' of patri-archal definitions of life are weighing down on the regional geography. All forms of interpreting the world, all schools of thought and their methods – including mythology, religion, philosophy, and science – must therefore be reassessed through the 'Jineolojî sift'. To solve social issues, Jineolojî promises to be a science that can render '*hevjiyana azad*' (free co-life) possible, as it develops research, perspective, and politics along nine dimensions: history, ethics and aesthetics, demography, health, education, self-defence, economy, politics, and ecology.

Jineolojî quickly transcended the mountain, as working groups formed in the civilian sphere in Kurdistan and the diaspora. Following the first Jineolojî conference in 2012 in Başûr, a first conference on Jineolojî was held in 2014 in Germany, with participants from countries like South Africa and the Philippines, to discuss radical readings of women's history, feminist methodologies and epis-temologies, and Jineolojî's potential contributions. In May 2015, surveilled by Turkish and Iranian drones, more than a hundred guerrillas gathered for the first Jineolojî conference in the mountains, after which the effort of taking Jineolojî everywhere reached new levels. The *Jineolojî Journal* is a quarterly theoretical publication produced in Bakur with contributions from activists and academics, including political prisoners. Jineolojî workshops are regularly organized in Kurdistan, Europe, and parts of Turkey and Syria on topics like ecology, resistance history, ethics-aesthetics, sexism, world politics, and methodology. In Rojava and Mexmûr, Jineolojî is part of high schools and higher education curricula. The Rojava-based Andrea Wolf International Jineolojî Institute is a centre of gravity for internationalists to advance the works on a global scale. There is a Jineolojî faculty at Rojava University. A Jineolojî Centre exists in Belgium, in addition to various Jineolojî committees in more than a dozen regions in Europe. Although not everyone is as actively or concretely involved in developing it, Jineolojî permeates all spheres of the women's movement's work. For example, in Rojava, the Jineolojî Academy and its various centres and institutions cooperate with the school system or structures like the *mal a jin* (women's houses, explained later) on strategic issues as well as on one-off projects.

Over the course of more than a decade, Jineolojî provided hundreds of autonomous discussion platforms, especially in the Middle East, Europe, and Latin America. As more women from different parts of the world entered these conversations, the contents, nature, and methods of the Jineolojî works became more diverse and global.

In the early years, much effort was put into justifying the existence of Jineolojî. 'Why Jineolojî? Is feminist theory not enough? What about gender and women's studies?' were among the questions that came up whenever Kurdish women introduced Jineolojî. These questions are far from being settled, but such dialogues in fact helped anchor Jineolojî in its politically and ideologically engaged effort to liberate knowledge production from the hands of the system.

In Jineolojî's perspectives, knowledge of the world is obtained not only by the principle of objectivity of the scientific principle, which is grounded in a highly secular worldview and conditioned by systems of power. Methodologically, Jineolojî values a diversity of approaches that can transcend the object/subject dichotomy rooted in much of Western intellectual thought, and holistically account for emotions, experiences, intuitions, notions of truth relating to *al-ma'nawi* (Arabic: the non-materialist, the spiritual, and impalpable) beyond the realm of the quantifiable, testable, or measurable. The definition of knowledge as a 'broad approach to meaning-giving' allows for the possibility of multiple interpretations of phenomena, for example 'woman'. Recognizing that phenomena around women's bodies, like pregnancy and menstruation, have historically been weaponized by male-dominated systems against women through sexist codes, womanhood is not reduced to being a matter of biology in Jineolojî's emerging body of literature. Nor is womanhood a social construction only. A material analysis of the colonization of women by way of historical critique is seen as important to make sense of the relationship between patriarchy and monotheistic religions, capitalism, and science. Approaching an answer to the question 'Who is woman?' is not an attempt to reach one essentialist definition, it is rather a path of critical inquiry to undo male-centric definitions and understand women as a fluid and dynamic social existence. Less interested in highlighting the heroism of individuals in its re-reading/re-writing of women's history, Jineolojî's main questions relate to understanding the material and ideological conditions through which women have been denied their contribution to life. For example, how was 'being' defined in any given era and what gendered implications did that have on social lives? How are sexualities generated or controlled by different economic systems? Research also focuses on ways in which systems of knowledge (mythology, philosophy, religion, and science) produce and are themselves reproduced.

Jineolojî is also a history-writing effort from below. It assembles and validates the experiences, thoughts, and feelings of those who have historically been excluded from history-writing and theory-making. Members of Jineolojî works often note that there are entire worlds of women who 'have simply never been asked for their opinion'. In their field trips to villages, Jineolojî researchers survey the fragments of women's knowledge rendered useless or invalid. Such personal interactions, and the solidarities, friendships, and possibly, organizational relations that evolve in the course are valued more than 'finished' texts, written as single-authored products to be presented for 'professional' scrutiny. Traditional knowledge, for example, rural women's understanding of herbs and natural cycles, is not only valued but also taken as an occasion to philosophically discuss the purpose and role of knowledge in human sociability. Such interactions are fed back as perspectives and bases for future works. The engagement with oral histories, local traditions, and regional myths is seen as a source to understand 'societal wisdom' and resistance against assimilation into capitalist modernity.

Jineolojî does not seek acceptance or recognition by the dominant academic systems, whose Eurocentrism, Orientalism, and positivism it criticizes; its engagement with academia is in fact concerned with helping it overcome its tendency to fragment life and to monopolize and patent knowledge and knowledge production.[3] Drawing on the movement's own sociological insights, which are based on nearly half a century of revolutionary mass organizing, Jineolojî critically examines the often highly inaccessible language of feminist and queer theory, noting that women's, queer, or gender studies, feminist theory or queer theory run the risk of being removed from their radical histories and independent critiques, as they are institutionalized through state, money, bureaucracy, and mechanisms of gatekeeping. Against the isolating, individual manner in which most social science research gets conducted today, Jineolojî encourages methods to commune knowledge and make it more democratically and freely accessible. Committees conduct research on topics that they believe will benefit communities. They also develop perspectives on the women's movement's social work and write analyses of political events. The findings of this collective accumulation are made accessible through TV programmes, publications, and popular discussion. With Jineolojî, the Kurdish women's movement collectively develops a 'big picture' analysis, something that is often seen as the business of states, professionalized classes, or grandiose individual thinkers. Thereby, the women's movement is shrinking the classed gap between the ability of illiterate home-makers and university degree-holders for developing system-critical analyses.

PART III

Practice

Autonomous organization is crucial for women to retake all that has been stolen from them, one by one, no matter how long it may take. It means creating spaces for women to express their language, colours, perspectives, independent from the patriarchal gaze. It means recognizing and valuing women's labor and struggle in all realms of society. Autonomy is an ideological principle, around which we assert, create, and transform ourselves. – Devrim, KJK Press, Qendîl, 2015

13

Stateless society

In 2013, a cell phone-filmed YouTube video from Istanbul's famous Taksim Square, home of the Gezi Park protests, went viral.

In broad daylight, in one of the busiest public spaces in Turkey, a band named Koma Sê Bira, consisting of three young men with two guitars, daringly performed songs that praised Öcalan, the political prisoners, and the guerrilla. The curious crowd, like the song compilation in the video, was a potpourri, crossing class and age divides. Gentle smiles of middle-aged men, their arms crossed behind their backs, radiated astonishment, content, and shock, as professional-looking adults, working-class boys, and young women with and without head scarves morphed into a jumpy Kurdish line dance.

When the lead singer animated the growing crowd with the words *Bê serok* (without the leader ...), some crowd members responded with *jiyan nabe!* (... there is no life). Levels of comfort appeared to rise as people looked around to see who else engaged in the criminal act of singing along with separatist songs. Clearly, a substantial number of strangers knew some of the lyrics, like *Em dimeşin bi mîlyona, em kurd in, em in Apocî!* (We march by the millions, we are Kurds, Apoists we are!) and *Bijî gerîlla li serê çiya!* (Long live the guerrilla on the mountains!). Many in the crowd knew exactly where to ululate, clap or 'whoo' during 'Oramar', one of the catchiest Kurdish guerrilla songs of all time. In the midst of this ecstasy, a little girl raised her victory-signalling fingers, as though it came naturally to her. It is almost as though the PKK, Turkey's archenemy, a 'terrorist organization', had sympathizers among the ordinary people in Istanbul's construction sites, universities, bazaars, and middle-class cafes. And it does.

People active in the Kurdistan freedom movement often claim that they would recognize each other anywhere in the world even if they never met before. This may sound like an exaggeration, but PKK members or supporters do in fact share a set of shared aesthetic values and behaviours that were developed over time in prison, streets, the war, and family homes.

Being *Apocî* (Apoist) has criteria; not only is it a political identity against the colonizer state, but a philosophy and culture for a different way of life. *Hevaltî* (friendship), more specifically *rêhevaltî* (companionship or 'friendship on the same path'), *welatparêzî* (homeland love), and *mîlîtantî* (militancy) are crucial terms that define social relations in the movement, which is mainly composed of people from the lower classes. The class character of the movement and the lack of value it places on material wealth and status are an important element in the movement's moral-political world. While having distinct, formalized social codes that structure interactions, the social world of the Apocî is above all seen as being marked by affectionate relations, relying on a deep sense of friendship and mutual aid. Relations between people are not mere political acquaintances; many people are also each other's relatives, partners, or fellow village or tribe members. Family-like bonds exist among people, who lost relatives in the same incidents or visit relatives in the same prison cells or graveyards.

Protests are an important method in its political toolkit, but it would be a mischaracterization to refer to the Kurdistan freedom movement as a 'protest movement'. Protests and festivals are usually highly coordinated and ritualized and therefore – now more than in the past – less about mobilization than about political socialization and regeneration. In addition to voicing objection to massacres, political repression, and other issues, people attend events to reconnect with long-term comrades, recharge morale and motivation, and honour shared histories and renew promises. To many, the struggle is above all a sensuous, visceral space for collective healing and meaning-making in a world that normalizes and even gratifies individuals' alienation and isolation from society.

There is no dedicated section in this book on this, but the movement's popular culture has a vibrant and rich music tradition, which historically played a notable role for political mobilization and for cultural revival against assimilation. Funerals and martyr commemorations are the only gatherings where line dances are absent.

Figure 3   Newroz celebration in Amed, attended by thousands of people, including international delegations. Amed. March 2015.

The emphasis on the emotionality of revolutionary politics is pronounced throughout the movement's literature and cultural outputs. For decades, cadres have been documenting their feelings in poems, memoirs, and diaries, often noting that they turned to militant struggle because they could no longer accept the violence of the state, especially against the poor. In the first volume of her memoirs, Sakine Cansız (2018) wrote that the PKK developed not merely from socialist theory, but from the ability to 'feel the people's pain'. She narrated her teenage fascination with the Kurdistan Revolutionaries – whom she later joined – a group of poor students, who spoke of revolution to people in her community while barely having anything to eat. Witnessing the wretched state of people in other cities beyond her Alevi-Kurdish hometown, meeting impoverished Roma women, exploited factory workers, imprisoned sex workers, and traumatized genocide survivors, she wrote that a solid approach to leadership could transform people into subjects of the revolution. Cansız criticized the shabby aesthetics and sometimes vulgar conduct of other revolutionary groups in late 1970s Turkey for alienating instead of attracting people: 'The point was to make clear that they rejected the existing system with its material possibilities. Instead of working towards a renewal and beautification of life, they created a culture of helplessness.' In her eyes, the revolutionary had to go through life as an example of strength in order to change the world. To decolonize Kurdistan, the cadres had to radiate revolutionary discipline and organization in their personalities when visiting the homes of the people: 'The first impression played a crucial role, because as yet no liberated life existed that one could point to. Everyone shared certain political theories and general truths, but not everyone had really internalized what it meant to be a revolutionary.'

The early PKK worked on a model of Marxist-Leninist vanguardism and Maoist militancy, heavily reliant on rural populations and clandestine urban networks. Over the years, its transformed view of society as the force of revolutionary social change (along with its view of 'the party' as an ideological, more than organizational institution) also foresaw a shift in the role of the party cadre. In the now confederally organized system, leadership works in a variety of ways through different spheres and relations. The highly criminalized movement continues to function through the 24-hour dedication of a network of revolutionary cadres, who are, in theory, tasked with organizing society's ability to lead itself. This paradox means that hierarchical, centralist approaches and patriarchal styles of leadership do manifest themselves within the movement. They are, however, tackled through reporting systems (and disciplinary action if needed), education, collective decision-making by the youth, and above all the feminization of leadership models. Transcripts of entire congresses, including criticisms and self-criticisms, are archived and often made available to the public.

The movement's perspective on society relies on a belief that individual and collective transformation and successful struggle are mutually dependent. In Öcalan's analysis, movements and organizations genuinely concerned about change must neither turn into elites, nor become mere reflections of society. Instead, what Öcalan describes as the dialectic between a revolutionary organization and the society it wants to transform must turn moral societal impulses into transformative energies for self-organization. In his eyes, the militant of freedom needs to carry the heritage of democratic civilization's accumulation of wisdom and struggle within herself, embodying and activating society's conscience (ethics) and organized action (politics). As a person, who has taken an oath to revolution, the cadre embodies the abolition of the distinction between the personal and political in her own life.

The vast majority of cadres come from the movement's support community, which is comprised of 'homeland-loving families' (*malbatên welatparêz*). Tavîn, a guerrilla in her early 20s, who joined the PKK from such a family in Europe and whom I met in Kerkûk, has a representative trajectory. As a young woman growing up in a western European state that oppressed and criminalized her based on her migrant and political identity, she was disillusioned by the European promise of liberal democracy. As a guerrilla, she developed an interest in philosophy and literature – things she did not value as much in her market-oriented education in Europe. She explained that many guerrillas experience a sense of self-realization upon joining, which in turn strengthens their belief in social change.

> This entire movement is built on people's ability to change. We are all from this society, are part of this people. When we analyze ourselves, transcend and overcome ourselves by achieving things we did not think possible, we gain the confidence that society too can radically change. We believe that no matter how alienated a person has become, they retain a quest inside of them. The system may corrupt and delineate this quest, but our task is to be a light in a dark room. As cadres, we must develop the ability to understand and feel with all of humanity, all its peoples. And these feelings of affection and rage, we must politicize. Our faith in humanity is not something we can find externally but must be sought in our individual selves. If we cannot create ourselves, we will not have faith in our neighbour. Hope is the human being herself.

Tavîn's words, moreover, describe the social role of the cadre as the organizer and embodiment of the wider revolutionary transformation that the movement seeks in society. The cadres' distinct, disciplined posture, speech, tone, look, walk, and conduct stand out to the 'Apocî' community. Cadres are not only measured by their ability to organize, but are also expected to lead a personal struggle to overcome internalized colonization, patriarchy, and liberalism to be able to move society forward. In other words, 'leaving the system' by taking the oath to formally join the movement does not suffice to be a revolutionary; one must actively work on personal development and become a living example of an alternative world, the slow realization of utopia. The individual revolution begins with the process of developing what is called a 'militant personality' and the development of one's own willpower (*vîn/irade*). From organizing one's individual day to being able to excite other people for social and political engagement, from surviving under adverse conditions in war to negotiating for peace, an Apoist militant is supposed to be the walking spirit of the revolution, wherever they are, whether in the mountain or in an office. Whether in casual conversations in private homes, political events, or cultural centres, PKK cadres have no problem spending great amounts of time and energy conversing with people from all walks of life, from children to the elderly. They are, as one older cadre once described Sakine Cansız, 'always ready to leave but work as if they were staying forever'. Militancy in this sense does not only encompass a physical fight against the army, but a lifelong and incessant commitment to revolution, which is reflected especially in the guerrilla's way of life but not limited to it.

At the Şehîd Dilan Academy, camping in the guerrilla held Xinerê region in the mountains, Narîn explained the importance of leadership and its relationship to revolutionary pedagogy and organizing. As a decades-old PKK member from Rojava, who has commanded major battles, Narîn unpacked the tension between revolutionary leadership and radical democracy.

> The sort of system we desire cannot be built without 'forerunning cadres' (*kadroyên pêşeng*). To be able to organize a people, you need a dedicated and educated ideological group. Although there are certain standards of militancy, the cadre must not stand outside or beyond society. The cadres' mission is not to strive for power and control or segregate themselves from society but rather to open its path through sacrifice.
>
> We should not think that we know everything better just because we are cadres. We are cadres only if we enable people to self-organize and develop willpower, otherwise we are redundant. I am a trailblazer, a PKK cadre to the extent to which I facilitate the people's self-organization. There is no self-praise in our movement. Everyone knows that every victory is a product of collective work. Without our organization, people, ideology, and comrades, nobody can succeed.

Narîn said that criticizing 'the illness of power' was an important element in the movement's view of leadership. To resonate with society, a revolutionary had to be modest and should never belittle the people she wants to organize. Neither should she romanticize abstract ideas around formless people power, but instead organize concrete institutions for grassroots self-determination to render social change lasting. This in turn required creativity:

A revolutionary should not simply theorize in the abstract. Our understanding of leadership and democracy is connected to our ability to develop people's consciousness and will-power, expressed in organized forms. It's a sign of defeatism for revolutionaries to not believe in the power of people. Liberal, pragmatist, centralist approaches often come up more frequently among men. Pragmatism or opportunism are normalized as men's ways of thinking. This is a point of discussion in our education, for instance. Likewise, a dogmatic revolutionary with fixed ideas on how to organize people will not go far. Institutions must be built not as ends in themselves, but as means of meeting concrete, ever-evolving needs. Creating a uniform system from the top down would amount to social engineering. That's state formation. It has little to do with revolution. A people's system must find answers to unemployment, poverty, violence. Each village needs a tailored self-administration. Those answers can only be found if you yourself are rooted in the community. We need to be flexible, if we want to change society from the depths of oppression. Our institutions must not be formed because of purist ideas. Organization above all requires a proper analysis of these needs, which is precisely why our system is based not on the state but on autonomy.

As later parts of the book demonstrate, the *welatparêz* (homeland lovers) – i.e. civilian organizers and sympathizers – are not a passive social 'base' but are seen as conscious political subjects that build self-organization through people's and women's assemblies. Active political participation, community responsibilities such as peace and reconciliation work, cultural initiatives, especially around the Kurdish language, and an effort to engage their own families in political work are seen as more valuable than displaying flags and symbols. The *welatparêz* are expected to develop themselves intellectually by reading books and participating in discussions on philosophy, history, and world politics. Caring for disabled, ill, and wounded comrades is seen as a collective revolutionary duty.

The cadres and the *welatparêz* families from Kurdistan to Europe, now increasingly joined by non-Kurds, over time formed a diverse intentional community of people, who collectively learn to organize their lives against and despite the state system. In this sense, *welatparêzî* culture formed new, revolutionary social relations beyond the family, village, tribe, region, or ethnically defined nation. The idea of the 'democratic nation', as a society based on principles, is partly an outcome of this concrete, moral-political world, which formed in the diaspora as much as it did in Kurdistan. The Kurdistan freedom movement has over decades strategically invested in fostering relations with anti-system movements in different parts of the world, from Brazil to the Philippines. The politicized Kurdish diaspora in Europe is a dynamic part of local, regional, and global struggles against police violence, discriminatory migration policies, prison, surveillance, arms trade, patriarchal violence, and racism. It proactively offers educations about its theory and practice to other political organizers and movements. Seeing internationalists with tattoos and piercings converse with members of religious associations during Newroz festivals in Europe is not unusual for people exposed to 'Apocî culture'.

14

Öcalan: Leader, prisoner, comrade

Bijî Serok Apo! (Long live leader Apo), a slogan that two generations of Kurdish children grew up with, is a way for millions of Kurds to passionately declare their opposition to fascism. The slogan animated watersheds in recent Kurdish history, such as the rescue operation of Şengal and the resistance of Kobanê.[1] The internet is full of videos of Kurdish communities celebrating their victories – from the HDP's election results to the defeat of Daesh – by line dancing to decades-old songs dedicated to the leader with the iconic moustache. Photos of Öcalan – banned in some parts of the world and on Facebook – are essential to the aesthetics of countless Kurdish community centres, family homes, refugee and guerrilla camps, youth and women's congresses, and cultural festivals. Non-Kurdish people drawn to the movement for its progressive politics are often uncomfortable with Öcalan's omnipresence, associating it with authoritarian leadership cults. People on the radical left are rightfully sceptical of strong leadership because its relationship to power and authority makes it incompatible with values like democracy, liberty, and creativity. Most people are perplexed whenever Kurdish women point to an 'unelected' man from a feudal-conservative region like Riha as their leader in their construction of an anti-patriarchal, radical democratic life. Drawing on liberal democratic ideas about politics and leadership – and likely influenced by Orientalist thinking – some even go as far as taking Öcalan's role as an occasion to deny the Kurdistan freedom movement any liberationist credentials. So, what does Öcalan signify to a people whose very existence has been historically denied and who continue to enjoy no formal status in a world of nation-states? Despite two decades of imprisonment, why do millions of people insist on '*Serok Apo*'?

Against the many attempts to stigmatize or marginalize him, over the past two decades, millions of Kurdish people engaged in thousands of large-scale protests, several hunger strikes, signature campaigns, and even self-immolations to demand Öcalan's freedom. In the aftermath of his illegal abduction, the International Initiative for the Freedom of Abdullah Öcalan – Peace in Kurdistan was formed as an alliance of human rights defenders, intellectuals, and civil organizations.[2] Between 2005 and 2006, in Turkey's environment of criminalization and arrest, 3.5 million Kurdish people openly signed a petition called 'Abdullah Öcalan represents my political will'. With the work of thousands of volunteers, from 2012 to 2015, 10.3 million people worldwide signed the campaign to demand his freedom. Havîn Güneşer (2015), a spokeswoman of the International Initiative and translator of several of his books, remarks on the meaning of such grassroots campaigns:

Kurdish people as a whole have no officially recognized right as a people to elections or referendum. Thus, such campaigns, despite the hardship and oppression they face, have a huge significance in declaring the demands and will of the Kurdish people. Indeed, the campaign that ran between 2005–2006 was also a response to the colonial insistence by Turkey and European states on the Kurds to 'Find yourselves another leader.'

Her words refer to the common tendency among (especially Western) academics and journalists to profile other political figures – 'not Öcalan' – as 'the Kurdish Mandela', even as the same figures embrace Öcalan's key role for the political solution process.[3] In fact, veteran South African anti-apartheid activists, including comrades of Nelson Mandela, are today at the forefront of demanding Öcalan's freedom.[4] In the past years, other Middle Eastern women, as well as internationalists, especially in Latin America and Europe, where the movement organizes, have joined the calls of Kurdish women to demand Öcalan's freedom as an urgent feminist cause.

Öcalan was the sole prisoner on Imralı Island, guarded by 1,000 soldiers for the first eleven years of his imprisonment since 1999. His ongoing isolation is a violation of Turkish, European, and international law. The United Nations Revised Standard Minimum Rules for the Treatment of Prisoners, known as the Nelson Mandela Rules, define this form of solitary confinement as torture. Since Turkey is a member of the Council of Europe, the latter's Committee for the Prevention of Torture (CPT) has the responsibility to monitor Öcalan's rights and well-being. In the past, the CPT paid visits to Imralı Prison Island only after several hunger strikes and political escalations by Kurdish activists, for instance in 2007, when Öcalan was suspected of being slowly poisoned. The political prisoners' mass hunger strike in 2012 was a major factor that moved the state towards the peace process with Abdullah Öcalan soon after.

The critical work of Black abolitionist feminists like Angela Y. Davis, Joy James, Gina Dent, and Ruth Wilson Gilmore theorize the 'prison-industrial complex' as a site of racial capitalism's ordering and bordering practices.[5] In reflections they offer on incarceration, segregation, and dispossession in places like Brazil, Palestine, and other parts of the world, these revolutionary thinkers emphasize the need to think transnationally and intersectionally about the meaning of abolishing systems of power and domination, in favour of building liberated life for all. To the Kurdistan freedom movement, peace and justice are entangled with the abolition of the Imralı Prison complex. Öcalan's imprison-

91

ment on the island is a key reference point for the movement's prioritization of resistance over international legalistic mechanisms in its quests for justice and liberation. Not only is his isolation one of the biggest obstacles to a political solution of a decades-old conflict, his case is also a 'human rights issue' that leading human rights organizations neglect for political reasons, in the eyes of Öcalan and the movement, due to their bonds with the nation-state system under capitalist modernity. This politicized treatment led his lawyers to theorize Imralı Prison as a kind of Guatanamo of Europe. To the movement, Imralı is not merely a prison island, but a lawless, colony-like complex that institutionalizes the state of exception through a regime of isolation and absolute control. As argued by Öcalan's lawyers, the system of annihilation normalized on Imralı has especially after the 2016 coup attempt been extrapolated to a state of emergency in the entire country.[6] By the movement, Imralı is also seen as a generative space for justice quests beyond law, Öcalan's defence-as-manifesto court submissions being a protest against international legal systems' reduction of historical injustice to individualized cases. Activists often describe Öcalan's work from prison, including the *Roadmap for Negotiations* and his five-volume *Manifesto for a Democratic Civilization* as Öcalan rendering himself 'ungovernable'. By implementing his thought into practice, the Kurdistan freedom movement aims to destroy the Imralı torture system and with that, the monopolization of justice in the hands of the world state system.

Towards the end of 2018, Leyla Güven, an activist of the Kurdish women's movement, former mayor, co-chair of the Democratic Society Congress (KCD/DTK), and Peoples' Democratic Party (HDP) MP, elected from prison, announced during a trial session that she would no longer defend herself in court, but enter a hunger strike to break the isolation regime at Imralı. Öcalan had not been allowed to meet any family members for three years, in addition to eight years without lawyer visits. There was suspicion that he could have been harmed when the prison island was attacked during the 2016 failed coup. An estimated 7,000 political prisoners, as well as Kurdish activists around the world, including elected officials, joined the historic hunger strike.

Among the many actions in support of the hunger strike was the International Women's Initiative for Leyla Güven, a call which was supported by thousands of feminist activists and women's movements around the globe. Güven was visited by Palestinian revolutionary Leila Khaled and Argentinian co-founder of the Plaza de Mayo Mothers Nora Morales de Cortiñas. Having gone on hunger strike in prison in 1970 herself, Angela Y. Davis (2019) wrote a *New York Times* op-ed in support of Leyla Güven and the political prisoners, which included the following words:

Those of us here in the United States who have protested the expansion of the prison-industrial complex have been emboldened over the years by the courageous actions of Kurdish political prisoners – especially by the women who have resisted American-type prisons in Turkey. We should now follow the example and leadership of Ms. Güven in protesting the isolation of Mr. Öcalan, who is recognized as the chief negotiator representing the Kurds in the peace talks with Turkey, and who has declared that the fight for women's equality is central to the revolutionary process.

Actions escalated as the hunger strikers' health was deteriorating. Several prisoners took their own lives in protest of the silence. Two groups of volunteers entered a death fast. Enduring police assaults in their protests, street sit-ins, and occupations of parliament venues, the Peace Mothers, blamed the slow death of their hunger-striking children on the state, which refused to return to the peace process by isolating Öcalan. Across Europe, Kurdish students and their friends disrupted seminars in universities. After six months of silence by the organization, Kurdish activists occupied the Amnesty International headquarters in London for its politically motivated behaviour. The UK trade union movement mobilized branches across the country for the demand to free Öcalan. South African women's activists and anti-apartheid veterans mobilized on 8 March International Women's Day action in front of the Turkish embassy in support of Leyla Güven. In the spring of 2019, this several months-long coordinated global resistance, led by political prisoners, eventually led to the first meeting between Öcalan and his lawyers after nearly a decade.

*   *   *

People who met Öcalan personally often describe him as a person who barely sleeps more than a few hours every night, lives plainly by a disciplined daily structure, and instantly notes changes in a room's atmosphere or a person's emotional state. Besê and Esma, at the time of our interview executive members of the KJK administration, directly worked with Öcalan in the 1990s. In our conversation in Qendîl, the two guerrillas explained the movement's approach to his leadership as constituting a unifying 'institution' beyond his individual personality. By way of anecdotes about the *rêber* ('guide', his preferred term over '*serok*', president), they narrated his active encouragement for women's liberation and autonomy throughout the struggle.

In his own writings and messages, Öcalan acknowledges the immense power that lies in his hands due to people's emotional attachments and encourages cadres to not overly rely on him. Besê similarly warned of glorifying him without understanding him. She claimed that although collective resistance to

93

centralization formed a key part of the Kurdish ethos, Öcalan's leadership style resonated with the masses because it activated drives for self-determination beyond the parameters offered by the hegemonic state system.

Abdullah Öcalan must be understood through the history and geography of this region. His hometown Riha (Urfa) is a centre of the Neolithic revolution and also known as the city of prophets. Building on the legacy of this region's cultures, faith schools, and revolutions, he managed to turn his life philosophy into a way of life in Kurdistan. Our movement's culture represents that alternative life today. Its magic lies in revealing a reality that fundamentally threatens systems of power: namely, that even a single individual can spark a revolution and shake the foundations of the order of things. These are personality traits that frighten the capitalist system because they open the path to a kind of individuality based on societal freedom struggle, not on liberal individualism.

Öcalan's entire struggle is based on a rejection of dominant conditions as fate. It's a quest for a different life. Whatever unjust condition, oppressive system or problematic social issue there may be, he will question and refuse to accept it. Moreover, he does not dogmatically make predictions about the future, but rather helps create the conditions to put things in practice in the here and now. This is a notion of liberation that understands the importance of organization and struggle above all.

In Besê's eyes, Öcalan's utopianism gave people the tools to practically and emotionally break with systems that oppress them. This particularly came out in his relationship to women:

His comradeship with women was not based on flattering or praising us. It was a critique, a refusal on his part to accept the woman created by the system, just like he refused to accept the dominant male. Analyzing above all his own marriage and relationship to Kesire Yıldırım, he explained the need to overcome the traditional masculinities and femininities imposed by the system, which lead to conflict-ridden, problematic relationships based on power, exploitation, possession, and unfreedom. This was a refusal to accept the hegemonic life system itself, a rejection of capitalist modernity's models of social relations. His concern was to create a lifestyle outside of capitalism.

As a people's leader and comrade of women, he presents a standard for a different masculinity by which we can measure our expectations. As we continue to organize our communities, we do not settle for anything less than the revolutionary standards he set for Kurdish men. The most essential aspect of his theory and practice is driven by a struggle for love and he understands that this is only possible with liberated, free women on his side. Our leader represents in his personage a quest for a life in which love is possible. In this sense, Kurdish women are lucky to have a friend, a comrade like Apo.

Öcalan could be extremely harsh in his criticisms, but was very soft in his interactions with children and elderly people. With anecdotes, Esma characterized him as a leader who would dedicate time to each individual and their progress over time. Always glad to receive visitors, he welcomed impoverished locals and influential tribal and religious leaders alike.

When I first met him, he personally greeted me at the door, with food on his moustache, smiled and gave me a big hug! This startled me immensely, I had imagined a very different kind of leader. Through laughter and jokes, he tried his best to establish a joyful atmosphere, while maintaining revolutionary discipline and seriousness. In a society in which women's existence is devalued and rendered invisible, he went out of his way to make us feel comfortable around him. He didn't take his militants for granted. He looked after us, he knew the meaning of women becoming revolutionaries. Rêber Apo created an atmosphere in which nobody would feel excluded, no matter how new or inexperienced they may be. He gave every cadre and civilian personal attention and made sure we develop our individual talents and potentials, sometimes despite ourselves.

In lectures, he especially wanted the men to reconnect with life, with animateness, with care, by giving them seemingly odd tasks. I once witnessed him hand a tiny bird to a male comrade, saying 'You must look after this bird now, feed it, protect it, until it can fly away'. To tell the Kurdish man, who has been socialized into seeing himself as the centre of the world, as the patriarchal head of society, to be responsible for a little bird!

He had gotten up very early one morning to bring each one of us a flower. 'It's 8 March', he said, 'International Women's Day'. At the time, we didn't even know what 8 March is. Our curiosity, knowledge of women's history developed with his active role. He normalized a culture of women's struggle in our movement and society with his thought and practice, including with subtle gestures. As a result, in a society in which men don't allow women to breathe freely, he confided in our power and helped us see that we can do absolutely everything in this world.

In a different location, Rotînda, another guerrilla, who trained with him, said that his leadership succeeded because it empowered both the individual, as well as societies. The ways in which she described Öcalan's significance echo how many 'Apoists' view their relationship to him, namely, as a symbol for a Kurdish insistence on revolutionary socialism.

Capitalist utopianism means having a house, a car, a career, a spouse, and maybe fame. In contrast, his utopia is about creating the power to realize one's ideals without relying on the system. This idea of utopia requires creativity and belief in victory. A leader sparks curiosity in people to understand the universe, nature, life, and death. Without actual care for the world around us, we cannot expect to be able to change it. He would ask us: 'How many times have you listened to the birds when walking through the mountains? Do you ever notice the flower petals open? Do you pay attention to eroded soil? Don't let anything become a routine in your life.'

One time, he said to me: 'Love! But love in such a way that the entire world fits in your heart'. At first, I didn't understand the meaning of these words. But guerrilla life teaches you that the impossible does not exist, especially when you see your own will-power as you live and survive under storm, rain, snow, and heat in the mountains. And so, I learned to love my own ability to struggle and the more I struggled, I learned to love my labour. Seeing my own power for the first time taught me to see the same potential in all of society. As guerrillas, it is our comradeship, our martyrs, our people's resistance and sacrifices that keep us alive, physically and emotionally. This collective labour increases the love and responsibility we feel towards our people. Fighting for a people's just cause in these beautiful mountains fosters personalities that cannot help but love humanity, nature, life. Öcalan's foresighted leadership created a new notion of politics for us; we no longer wait for someone to come and lead us forward, we learned how to be a self-organized people.

Despite his more than two decades-long imprisonment, Öcalan is not an abstract, mythical figure for generations of Kurds. For two decades, thousands of mainly poor people received educations from Öcalan in Syria or Lebanon in the 1980s and 1990s. Among them were home-makers, who, deprived of education and generally depending on their often-abusive husbands, were astonished by the leader's active encouragement for women's liberation. Women from this generation have photos of Öcalan visiting their family homes, and many of them are currently active in the revolution in Rojava at old age. 'Our women's revolution did not start in 2012. It started in 1979 when our leader arrived in Kobanê' is a common phrase among politically engaged elderly women across Rojava.

Dirsin from Kobanê, an elderly mother of nine, at the time of our interview spokesperson for the umbrella women's movement in Çil Axa (al-Jawadiya), a small town close to the border with Iraq and Turkey, participated in Öcalan's educations decades prior to the revolution. One of her daughters joined the PKK, two of her sons were part of Rojava's internal security forces (*asayîş*), one of whom lost both eyes in the war, and another son was in the YPG ranks in Afrîn at the time:

> Let me give you an example of a conversation I had with Serok Apo. He asked me what I do every day. I told him that we usually visit our neighbours. He asked whether they are Kurdish, and I said yes. He said: 'You are Kurds, so protect your identity. However, it does not matter to us whether someone is a Kurd or not. Whoever is oppressed, we will be on their side'. With this, he wanted us to understand that we shall never make a difference between ourselves and others. The fight is not between nations, but against oppression.

Nafiyah was an administrator at a *mal a jin* ('women's house') in Qamişlo when I met her. She was only 14 when she was married against her will and became a mother the year after. In her mid-20s, in 1980, she first met the PKK. Nafiyah took up political tasks early on, although she had small children to look after. In doing so, she clashed with society and her land-owning agha family. Nafiyah's many children, whom she claimed to have raised with 'the PKK's

Figure 4 Ilham (see Chapter 26), member of a *mal a jin* (women's house) in Qamişlo, with a photo of Abdullah Öcalan edited to go with the Kongreya Star logo. Qamişlo. July 2015.

97

ethics', were participating in the revolution as teachers, municipality workers, commune coordinators, journalists, and neighbourhood defence members. Similar to other women in her age group, she narrated a rupture in the lives of women in Rojava. The international appeal of the Rojava Revolution affirmed the universality of their cause in her eyes:

> There were politically active people in the past in Rojava, but no women. Apo directly went to the women to organize and educate them. With Apo, women became revolutionaries... In the 1980s, so many doors were shut to us, we struggled to organize our own people. Today, the world is coming to Rojava. Young people leave their comfortable homes in Europe behind and fall martyr here... Without this decades-old experience, we would have been massacred by Daesh. We too, would be sold in slave markets across Syria today. Wherever Apo's ideas exist, women will no longer die.

15

Revolutionizing love

Love, the strongest and deepest element in all life, the harbinger of hope, of joy, of ecstasy; love, the defier of all laws, of all conventions; love, the freest, the most powerful moulder of human destiny; how can such an all-compelling force be synonymous with that poor little State and Church-begotten weed, marriage? – Emma Goldman[1]

It is not true that men are unwilling to change. It is true that many men are afraid to change. It is true that masses of men have not even begun to look at the ways that patriarchy keeps them from knowing themselves, from being in touch with their feelings, from loving. To know love, men must be able to let go the will to dominate. They must be able to choose life over death. They must be willing to change. – bell hooks[2]

Kurdish music, poetry, and art are full of references to love, but every year thousands of women get murdered, mutilated, raped, harassed, beaten, or driven to suicide in Kurdistan in the name of love.

Liberating love from oppression, violence, and exploitation is at the heart of many resistance struggles that try to reclaim forms of expressing care, love, and relating to others outside of the exploitative logic of patriarchy and capitalism. For at least 100 years, feminists have pointed out that the institution of marriage is not merely a relationship between two people; it is also a sexual contract with the state, a form of organizing the deepest, and most untamable emotions of love, sensuality, and intimacy along heteropatriarchal societal expectations, economic calculations and official ideologies. Historically, colonialism and capitalism have (often together) fundamentally altered or eradicated numerous forms in which care and kinship have been differently organized around the world. Especially socialist feminists, from Marxists to anarchists, argue that the confinement of romantic love into the institution of marriage, usually in the form of a heterosexual relationship between one man and one woman, culturally advances a model of intimacy that is fundamentally private, enclosed, atomizing, and exclusionary in nature under capitalism. Along its economic and political interests, the state, often drawing on religious ideas, infiltrates people's bedrooms by elevating a particular type of relationship as the norm. Culturally, this criminalizes or pathologizes non-conforming arrangements for loving, living, caring, and reproducing. Of course, alternative relationship forms, no matter how courageous they may be in their circumstances, do not automatically constitute a liberation from domination and violence.

Thinking about the cultural role of love always implies considering the family, labour, reproduction, and care. One direct consequence of capitalism's division of life into private and public in a waged economy is devaluation of women's unwaged care work for social reproduction. Feminists like Silvia Federici, Tithi Bhattacharya, and Camille Barbagallo stress that social reproduction and care work is the work that makes all other work in society possible. Rethinking the modes of social reproduction would amount to a transformation of all the ways in which life is organized, from childcare to industrial production. Devaluing life-making work therefore means devaluing life. This in turn feeds back to the notion of love. Capitalism's politics of death, tragically illustrated in governments' handling of Covid-19, empties everyday life of meaning, spirituality, and purpose. In the absence of solidarity-based economies and community, individually experienced romantic love, no matter how toxic, becomes a refuge in a world of isolation, alienation, and uncertainty. The hypersexualization of love, the limitation of intimacy to the superficially physical – the pornographic, rather than the erotic, as Black lesbian feminist poet Audre Lorde (1984) suggests, atomizes individuals and in many ways culturally streamlines jealousy, possessiveness, and even violence as expressions of love.

> No matter what kind of life a woman chooses for herself, she must never ever allow herself to be totally tied to a man. Her life energy, work, inner world should not be surrendered to one man. Women must protect themselves from fake ideas of love that only serve to undermine their willpower, self-determination and ability to be themselves. Love based on ownership and domination is instant gratification, conflict, and deception. This doesn't do justice to the idea of love. – Besê, Qendîl, 2015

The literature of the Kurdish women's movement claims that in a context of colonization (of Kurdistan in particular and life in general, by state, capitalism, and patriarchy) not only freedom, but also love is rendered impossible. The Kurdish women's movement defends women's and all people's rights to bodily self-determination. However, when a person professionally joins the PKK, they do not only give up the prospect of a life in comfort, with money, a house, and career. They also give up sexual and romantic relations. For the feminist struggles that fought for sexual liberation for decades, this can appear as a conservative, even backward approach. In academic literature, some have attributed the phenomenon of guerrilla abstinence to a compromise with feudal Kurdish society, whose conservatism demands the safe-guarding of virginity, while

100

others describe it as a new form of bodily control over women's bodies. Both of these arguments, one overemphasizing tradition, the other the loss of individual liberties, tend to ignore decades of theorizing by revolutionary feminists and the Kurdish women's movement on gender, coercive or compulsory sexuality, and the conditions for love under the current system. They also rarely acknowledge that men, too, practice abstinence. As a social function, the abolition of sexual relations in the realm of the guerrillas/cadres in favour of new forms of revolutionary intimacy based on comradeship and sacrifice disrupts, mainly in favour of women, an important realm used to mobilize and establish power and hierarchy in traditional Kurdish society. Removing the ability of weaponizing sex and sexuality as sites of reproducing power relations creates new grounds for social interaction. This is not seen as something that needs to be maintained forever; abstinence can be read as an oath by cadres to commit to the building of a life in which interpersonal relations, including sex and love, can exist without revenge, shame, and control.

During my stay in Qendîl, I spoke to previously mentioned Esma and Besê, both decades-old guerrillas and coordinating members of the KJK, about love, its possibility and impossibility under patriarchy. They explained that modern love, as lived between two people and mostly confined to the nuclear family model is too narrow and enclosing as to capture individuals' need and desire for intimacy, care, and trust. In some ways, their views on the carceral character of Kurdish love, squeezed between conservative tradition and state terror, reminded me of arguments made by Black feminists, who believe that the abolition of oppressive systems such as the prison-industrial complex must go hand in hand with the creation of an alternative society, one that finds sustainable solutions to the problems that the state avoids solving peacefully when it resorts to mass incarceration (of mostly men): inequality, poverty, mental health, education, rape culture, etc. In Kurdistan, where women's bodies and sexuality are highly taboo-ized and socially policed, the imagination or prefiguration of 'free' relations often remains dangerous, abstract or limited to individual lifestyles. Love in Kurdistan and beyond, according to the ideological perspectives of the movement, needs to undergo revolution in order for relationships to be truly free. To enable a life with love, revolutionaries in particular ought to overcome regressive patterns of traditional love in the system and 'politicize their emotions' in their quests to abolish patriarchy. Esma explained:

Feminism should not be about equality between women and men. Men have to change, they must. To the extent to which I see change, I can feel attracted to him. Otherwise I can't love the man of this system. What I mean is that we are seeking new standards for love. Otherwise, ethical sociability is impossible. No matter how you call your utopia for liberation, it must be based on freedom-based social relations. Otherwise, power will continue to manifest itself in different ways, even deepen in fact. When we say 'love is a free life', we say that we can only imagine the possibility of love inside a free society, a society with a different masculinity than the one that dominates today's world.

Esma referred to the movement's concept of '*hevjiyana azad*' (free co-life) as 'a struggle against the system in every possible way'. In order to reconcile with the men, women had to 'declare a total war on the status quo masculinity'. This process of struggle against men in all spheres of life, parallel to women's autonomous quests for self-determination, in turn would enable new possibilities of interaction, thereby creating a new social contract.

We cannot say that we have reached *hevjiyana azad*, even in our movement. Instead, we are in constant struggle, and only with this struggle dynamic, we can keep on approaching a free life. We cannot say that love does or does not exist. But I can say that individually, I have new values, different expectations now. Through our struggle, women and men began setting new acceptable standards for relating to one another. We don't measure ourselves by conservative classical roles anymore. Of course, we also don't see ourselves as

Figure 5   YJA Star guerrilla with an Êzîdî child after the protest to commemorate the first anniversary of the genocide. Mount Şengal. August 2015.

separate from society in general. In loving one person, one must be able to love people in general, and in fact, love the universe. In a way we live love in a very special way here. Outsiders look at us and say that we 'forbid' love. That is not correct. We say: 'We consciously reject relationships in this system, and we struggle to make love meaningful'.

Similarly, Besê argued that in a fundamentally patriarchal world, it is hard to prefiguratively or concretely imagine, beyond individual lifestyles, what a liberated society with liberated gender identities and relations would look like, since new concepts and approaches develop during and through the difficult act of organization and struggle. Struggling towards alternative horizons in the here and now, however, already created new identities and possibilities for love, intimacy, and friendship.

Love is not a phenomenon that can be separated from social conditions. It can manifest itself more genuinely in a liberated society that abolishes unfree relations. Above all, you need to create a new type of human being, new terms of relating that can make love possible. The patriarchal family as it stands today is like a black hole that swallows women up, segregating them from society and life. How can we be our true, loving, social selves in a capitalist, liberalist system that glorifies individualism and domesticates women, isolating them in patriarchal homes and relationships? How can we be ourselves when this system destroys our culture and history daily?

Another form of relationship is possible, one that creates equal partners as well as social relations that have the power to embrace the entire world in their hearts through a struggle for justice. For that to happen, against the toxic patriarchal system, we must figure out what kind of man is loveable: we say the one that struggles for a different society, the one whose approach to us is not objectifying, exploitative and power-driven. If such men don't exist, we must develop and create them through struggle. We refuse to accept the dominant male in our lives. Likewise, without liberation, women can't be loveable either. True love must be based on principles. If you love me, then let us struggle for freedom together, for a world in which love can be set free.

'KILLING THE MAN'

Remember, we are talking about a masculinity that cannot be bothered to make a cup of tea for itself. A man who does not care to consult his partner before taking important decisions on their household. In our community work, we approach issues with examples from daily life. We ask: 'What is the role of the big brother, of the father in our families? How and why do mothers

uphold the rule of the men? Why does the state put so much value in the family? How does the patriarchal family model feed the state?'
– Jînda, Women's Academy in Sur, 2015

The Kurdistan freedom movement is an intergenerational struggle that managed to collectively politicize entire families and tribes. It's not uncommon for families to have lost several members in the struggle. There are stories of siblings who join the guerrilla at different times, and meet again years later in the mountains. That young people would leave the prospect of a life in marriage and property behind to fight for Kurdistan constituted a radical break with tradition and social taboos. Despite patriarchal backlash, over the decades the guerrilla had a transformative impact on traditional gender roles. Still, as fixed notions of Kurdish womanhood increasingly gave way to the emergence of diverse images such as protesting mothers at demos, fighting guerrillas in the mountains, speech-giving politicians in parliament, and later with the feminization of spheres like direct democracy, media, art, and culture, Kurdish masculinity often remained frozen in time.

According to Öcalan, 'revolution is possible with neither the enslaved woman, nor the dominant man'. Öcalan's critiques of the 'enslavement' of women in Kurdish society are thus complemented by his insistence on tackling another, equally crucial front: the importance of breaking the one-sided power of men as a condition for the liberation of life. As early as the 1980s, before diving more deeply into patriarchy's 5,000-year-old trajectory, Öcalan's writings drew parallels between colonization and male Kurdish privilege. In his early analysis, which has parallels to Martinican psychiatrist and anti-colonial revolutionary Frantz Fanon's assessment of colonialism's impact on the native's inner world, he claims that Kurdish men were acculturated into the state's nationalist culture through education, work, and military service and thus developed a relationship with the city and the state in a manner different to the less socially mobile women. Drawing on his own life story, he describes how men are assimilated into the hegemonic culture through enchantment with modernity. Men learn not only to work with the state, either by incentive or coercion, but also to admire and fear its power. In this continuum, so-called honour killings, which he describes as ridiculous symbolic acts, are men's pitiful attempt at re-establishing a meaningless notion of dignity based on patriarchal 'honour', domination, and violence. The analyses were greatly informed by his personal history, his strong, authoritarian mother and meek father, the taboo-ization of interactions with girls in his neighbourhood in his childhood, the forced marriage of his sister Havva, his troubled marriage to Kesire Yıldırım, and his direct engagement with the personal experiences of young women who had joined the movement, or illiterate home-makers attending his educations.

Joining the revolution with expectations and ideals, many women cadres experienced new forms of authoritarian masculinity, this time by political men they were not related to. According to previously mentioned Elif Ronahî, state violence had taught the already patriarchal Kurdish men new methods of obedience and control. Her analysis is representative of how women and men in the movement explain the intersections between patriarchy and the colonizer state in Kurdistan.

With the state's brutality against the uprisings, men were taught to see the state as all-powerful. The Kurdish man learned to equate the most insignificant state official, who would take care of a bureaucratic issue for him, with the state. He would timidly button up his shirt when seeing an official. He would enter government buildings, thinking: 'I must not clash with the state. They must not find out that I am Kurdish. I need to run my errands and leave quickly'. The Kurdish man, withered and with a broken will in front of the state, experiences this rage deep in his core. With this inferiority complex, he regrets not being as powerful as the state and resorts to his only sphere of influence and authority and which he can call his property: the family and the woman. He compensates for his defeat by becoming his own state in the household.

Walking through the day with constant humiliation by authorities, the first thing he does when arriving at home is to shout at his wife and daughter to assert his power, to make them shake in submission ... He renders the woman needy and dependent on him, creating an atmosphere of violence and domination in his house, where he gets to be the small emperor, the small replica of the state. A man, who commits all sorts of atrocities towards woman, but at the same time attributes to her body his sense of honour, ready to kill anyone who approaches her.

Since mimicking the state had become a way for colonized Kurdish men to assert their individuality, new masculinities needed to be enabled for the possibility of free life. In early phases, men were often purposely given kitchen duties while women had time and space for self-education. Between 2002 and 2004, the Free Women's Academy of the newly founded women's party offered several 'Killing the man' education programmes to male cadres. This phase coincided with the rise of previously mentioned right-wing, male-dominated lines promoted by Botan and Ferhat and as such, participants were sometimes mocked by others as emasculated. Still, the lectures and discussions on women's history, sexism, masculinity, patriarchal notions of love and honour, and perspectives on rearticulating gender relations had impact. The women guerrillas asked the men to write reports on the manifestation of patriarchy within their personalities and on how they intended to struggle to become better comrades to women. The participants were challenged to reflect on their upbringing and everyday behaviour. The discussions were transcribed and made available as further educational material. These classes for small groups of men were eventually discontinued in favour of including women's history and liberation ideology in the general education for all guerrillas.

Transforming the men is one of the most strategic works of the Kurdish women's movement, which does not believe that men will change by themselves, not because they are inherently unable but because state, capitalism, and patriarchy reproduce and enable male domination on a daily basis. Critically reflecting on past attitudes and methods that 'rejected men, rather than try to transform them', previously mentioned Narîn, whom I interviewed at the Şehîd Zîlan Academy of PAJK, the continuation of the Free Women's Academy, noted that society, including male revolutionaries, can only change if women, whose oppression renders them objectively more interested in social revolution, save them from the hegemonic ideology of power and violence: 'Every day, we struggle against our male comrades. Every day, in their personage, we fight the ruling system in our midst.'

Despite persistence of patriarchal behaviours among the men, the movement's organizational mechanisms are set up in a manner that defends women and ostracizes the resort to traditional oppressive roles. The prefiguratively horizontal gender relations in the guerrilla are presented as inspiration for all of society. The feminization of the movement's aesthetics is reflected in the conduct of male cadres, who are encouraged to radiate the emotions that patriarchy deprives them of: empathy, care, friendship not based on power, vulnerability, attention to detail and collectivity. In the movement's social culture, the de-sexualized male revolutionary is not seen as emasculated, but as embodying a more ethical, humane, and dynamic personhood, reconnecting with the enchantedness of life. The women's movement's perspectives on *hevjiyana azad* are thematized in all sites of the struggle. The movement's media frequently explores the topic by interviewing guerrillas as well as civilian families. Based on Öcalan's often-quoted 'Truth is love, love is a free life', local and regional love epics such as Mem and Zîn, Dewrêş and Edulê, or Şîrîn and Ferhad are reinterpreted through the movement's analyses of the obstacles to love under conditions of war and occupation as well as the urgency to struggle for *hevjiyana azad* as a revolutionary principle. With time, individual guerrillas such as long-time cadre Atakan Mahir, who lost his life in battle in 2018, and whose writings on masculinity and power are widely read in the movement, became modern reference points for the importance of leading gender struggle within the self and for society parallel to the fight against colonization.

Much of the movement's social work, which is largely invisible to the outside world, consists of 'democratizing the family'. This is highly sensitive, especially as most *welatparêz* families perceive issues such as domestic violence as private matters. In neighbourhoods that overwhelmingly support the movement, more context-specific engagements are possible. Jînda (not her real name), based at the Women's Academy in the Sur district of Amed, described their social work in the poor neighbourhood as a slow, but vitally important part of the revolution:

When it comes to the family, there are still prejudices towards our movement. Of course, we don't want to abolish the family. The social fabric of the Middle East would not permit this anyway. People will want to live together, have children, families. But to what extent are these forms of relationships dependent on the dominant system? What alternative family models can there be? How can people raise children and live together democratically, equally and freely?

We analyze the patriarchal family historically to point out that it is a specific model that the ruling system is imposing on our communities. The nuclear family institution as it exists today is the prototype of the state. The state is to the citizen what the family is to woman. Our aim could not be to remove or change the family in a manner akin to social engineering, but we do believe that it is possible to democratize the family. We can turn the family into a space without annihilation, a place in which socialist life is possible. A loving family without violence, a place that is open to society, not enclosing.

Jînda's words demonstrate an interesting struggle paradox: while on one hand, the movement aims to reconfigure social relations in the long term, it acknowledges the contemporary social realities in Middle Eastern cultures and communities. Rather than making an aggressive intervention into people's private lives, its 'slow' revolution claims to challenge the domination and hierarchy-based aspects of institutions like marriage and family, while building on their positive features (e.g. solidarity, care, trust, etc.). This is a shift from the movement's previous practices that were more dismissive towards these.

People doing social work in the movement say that transformation is slow-paced and often painful. As Jînda explained, as an institution built on Öcalan's thought, their academy usually enjoys respect from men close to the movement, at least more than state-linked NGOs operating in the city. According to Jînda, men that sympathize with the movement and read Öcalan tend to confidently describe and define patriarchy, and even speak of killing masculinity, however, not all do so by 'looking in the mirror'. A common habit is to criticize the shortcomings of the women's movement, for example low protest attendance, while keeping one's own partner from joining public activities. Jînda mentioned that when taking classes with the academy, men were often surprised to learn about their partners' mental and physical labour in planning the household and sustaining the family. Often, men started crying in educations. Some admitted to have beaten their wives up until the time of the classes.

> In our classes, we ask: 'Do you ever tell jokes to your wife? Do you drink tea in the balcony together? Do you ever discuss the peace process? If not, then why are you married? What is the meaning of your togetherness? What is that woman's position in your life?'
>
> One man had given his kidney to his father, and so everyone was feeling sorry for him. He beat his wife, when she asked him whether he wanted to drink water or whether he had a headache. He said he beat her because he didn't want to be felt sorry for. He cried a lot. Others fall into silence, unable to speak.
>
> In general, we lead a united freedom movement against an outside enemy, but our internal gender struggle is ongoing. We cannot reject men, if we want to share society with them. But we cannot continue living this way without transformation and change. Our struggles for democratic nation, autonomy, ecology, communal economy – they can only be led together with the men.

The Mesopotamia Academy for Social Sciences was created in Qamişlo (Rojava) in 2014 as a critical higher education centre. In its first year, I had the chance to sit in on some of the classes, run by teachers that were often also students. At the Academy, where young people live together and organize their daily life communally, I spoke to male students, who were taking Jineolojî classes for the first time. One of the student-teachers of the academy at the time was 24-year-old Malik, who previously studied literature at a Syrian university. He said that the academy's approach to social science and history encouraged him to analyze patriarchy in his own person:

> Male domination provides endless comfort and power to young Kurdish men like me. Back in high school, I couldn't even accept when a girl performed better in class than me. I didn't care about other boys getting better grades, but girls couldn't be smarter than me. This mindset dominated our family homes, schools, everywhere. When a woman had something to say, we said: 'She is a woman, what does she know?'
>
> As we research the male-dominated system, we realize that we ourselves are that dominant man! I personally feel a sense of shame, whenever we learn about the many instances in which men used violence to subjugate women,

as well as all the cases of women's resistance against male domination. We understand how much we as individuals benefit from this system of male supremacy.

It's important to historically understand how different events and developments, above all capitalism, lead to the domination of women. Women created the values of democratic life at the beginning of human history. They were at the heart of building up human society. With male domination, women's power and leading qualities were systematically destroyed. Studying Mesopotamian mythology, especially Babylonian and Sumerian, has been enlightening to understand how imaginaries and thought-systems turned patriarchy into a fact of life.

Malik's words describe the consciousness-raising impact of teaching patriarchy as a long-term, created system, departing from apolitical tendencies that advocate equality in a manner divorced from historical analysis. Organized women's resistance, too (as opposed to celebrations of individually successful women) seems to be a powerful teacher. Malik admitted that he had been taken by surprise when 'the girls I didn't take seriously in my neighbourhood took up arms against Daesh, organized their assemblies, and developed their own agendas. They became respected leaders, politicians, educators, journalists, community organizers. Their labor for the revolution is beyond measure.' Like other men in Rojava told me, Malik's perspective began to shift as a direct outcome of the emergence of the organized women's struggle in Rojava, especially their resistance against Daesh, a group epitomizing male domination.

That these developments surprised men shows how much we were raised to think that women are naturally incapable, weak, unable. The revolution taught us to see women as our partners in the struggle for free life. We learn to no longer see women our age merely as potential girlfriends, wives, and mothers of our children. Now, we develop a culture of interaction based on respect and freedom, with which we can finally form meaningful friendships not based on possession. We walk, laugh, discuss, share things with our female friends, less and less afraid of what they may think and do, even if what they think and do challenges our position as men in society.

It would be arrogant and dangerous to think that we have overcome our patriarchal attitudes. However, I can say that today, as a result of our education, I'm more sensitive to sexism in daily life. I feel outraged whenever I see women being treated unfairly. I feel responsible to challenge the problems I see and intervene whenever I can.

The struggle against violence and for egalitarian relationships has a long path ahead. In the civilian sphere, the movement's political culture actively seeks to de-normalize gender-based domination, from TV programmes on the women's struggle to community accountability against domestic violence. In Kurdistan and the diaspora, married couples who support each other's engagement in political work are often praised for their embodiment of the movement's vision of democratizing the family. In places like Rojava where many neighbourhoods organize as communes, the movement encourages solidarity-based communal forms of organizing childcare, production, and so on, as opposed to the state-reliant private nuclear family model. For couples of the younger generation, who grew up exposed to the movement's ideals, it is becoming more common to share family responsibilities such as childcare and household chores in a way that allows more equal engagement in social, economic, and political activities. In Kurdish community centres, seminars are given on how to raise children in a way that does not reinforce sexist gender roles. TV programmes or written publications of the women's movement have increasingly focused on non-sexist education in the recent past. These perspectives are enriched with the research efforts of Jineolojî committees. There is no ready-made formula, but guerrilla relationship advice such as the above comments permeate the daily lives of Kurdish women in the civilian sphere around the movement.

It is difficult to make claims about whether or to what extent Kurdish masculinity has transformed as a result of the movement. When men joke to the women's movement about taking things 'a bit too far sometimes', this is often an expression of both admiration and anxiety. In the movement's social circles, as a result of the women's autonomous structures and Öcalan's writings, Kurdish men are at least expected to acknowledge the value of equality. While this creates a critical minimum moral standard in the community, safeguarded by mechanisms like autonomous assemblies or co-presidency, men's approaches can also turn into mere lip service. As experienced especially by young women, even as they voice their respect to the women's struggle, men in the movement can tend to drive moralistic wedges between Kurdish women by categorizing them, one of the oldest practices of patriarchy: 'revolutionary/liberated' versus 'classical/traditional', the guerrilla versus the marriable woman, the activist versus the home-maker. The women's movement tries to defend women and their gains against such new and divisive forms of patriarchal control over women's conduct, bodies and thought with a dual approach: creating autonomous organizational mechanisms that represent women's collective will in the struggle on one hand, and engaging in the 'mission' to transform the men on the other. In autonomous educations, from the guerrilla sphere to community centres in the diaspora, women critique patriarchal categorizations of women and redefine what it means to be a 'traditional' or a 'struggling woman', beyond the male-imposed divisions relating to individuals' personal or political status. In any case, men are not issued certificates for having 'killed' their dominant sides. Killing the man is a continuous and dynamic individual and social process of reflection and transformation. It is part of a constantly evolving revolution to 'liberate life', a collective struggle that only succeeds if everyone also personally feels responsible for it.

16

Mothers

My son was only thirteen when he was arrested and received a heavy sentence. Our children are exposed to all sorts of harassment, violence, and torture by authorities from a young age. Of course, they don't accept this treatment and go to the mountains. More than anything else, we want them to be here with us. We long for their voices, their smells. Because of the draft, many families have children both in the guerrilla and in the army. The state is the one that makes brothers fight. The state is responsible for this bloodshed. The violence that we experienced by the state is unspeakable, and yet Erdoğan claims that the Kurdish issue does not exist.*

The ignorant 'Eastern' woman dressed in folkloric clothes, with too many children, who is complicit in the oppression of her own gender through her refusal to modernize, is a stereotypical character in Turkey's popular culture. Standing in contrast to the (also problematic) representation of the successful, conventionally attractive, Westernized Istanbulite corporate woman on TV, the stubborn, yet powerless village woman pops up in soap operas as the only state-approved representation of Kurdish womanhood. Even as they mobilize traditional 'motherly' values to incite nationalistic sentiments to support domestic and foreign wars and impose conservative gender roles on all women in the country, Turkish nationalist discourses regularly demonize politically active Kurdish mothers. Handan Çağlayan (2007; 2013) was among the first to argue that the political Kurdish mother is portrayed as a traitor and terror sympathizer, whose grief does not matter as much as those of mothers of Turkish soldiers in flag-draped coffins. Indeed, when it comes to Kurdish women in traditional clothes, who chant 'death to fascism' in broken Turkish, differences vanish between the otherwise divisive gender politics among Kemalists and Erdoğan supporters. The politically active Kurdish mother is not part of the Turkish state's unresolved modernity dispute either way.

Feminists are critical of tendencies that bestow patriarchal ideas around motherhood upon women's bodies. Equating 'mother' with 'homeland' often

---

* Since some Peace Mothers are currently in Turkish jails on terrorism charges, I do not identify the names of individuals in this chapter to avoid further criminalization. While this erases the women's individuality, it does convey a sense of the collective voice that the Peace Mothers often use themselves.

serves to glorify the political project of the nation-state, which many see as a macro-version of the patriarchal family. Busy with childrearing and housework, the mother is almost universally portrayed as having no public agenda in her own right. In war and peace, the essentialist image of the infantilized and sanctified mother and her child ('womenandchildren' to use Cynthia Enloe's term) represents innocence and suffering. Ironically, the characterization of motherhood as a morally charged identity makes the ostensibly apolitical 'mother's voice' a useful tool for political propaganda. The romantic image of the selflessly caring mother, who is fulfilled by the chance to sacrifice her own happiness for her family, is often evoked across ideologies – from fascism to anti-colonialism – to kindle emotional responses in times of crisis and mobilization.

In the age of social media, the spectacle of human misery acquired near pornographic qualities. The quietly sobbing mother holding her child is a universal branding trope in the humanitarian sector. Meanwhile, parties to conflicts increasingly understand that by occasionally giving 'womenandchildren' controlled access to public platforms, they can subtly yet dramatically streamline their agendas or distract from their violence. A convincing crying scene can be staged to stir up patriarchal feelings of revenge and honour. A mother's tears can even cover up atrocities committed by her next of kin. Ironically perhaps, truly respecting mothers' complex personhood and agency may mean liberating them from the patronizing burden of innocence – in other words, acknowledging that mothers too can lie and deceive, especially in times of war and violence.

At the same time, it must be said that the seemingly apolitical concept of mother is a product of patriarchal systems that have over long periods of time promoted male-dominated divisions of life into 'private' and 'public' spheres. Despite all sorts of devaluation and exploitation, throughout history, in different parts of the world, motherhood was and still is often a positive source of legitimacy and authority.

The work of feminist historians, indigenous scholars, and women from different parts of the South shows that the depoliticization of women, including mothers, is often a direct product of capitalist relations and colonial regimes. The notion that motherhood has to be oppressive and burdensome is maintained by ideology. As Silvia Federici (2020) put it in reference to dominant forms of glorifying the nuclear family model and the role it assigns to mothers, 'This [capitalist] ideology that opposes the family (or the community) to the factory, the personal to the social, the private to the public, productive to unproductive work, is functional to our enslavement to the home, which, in the absence of a wage, has always appeared as an act of love.' Liberating motherhood and childrearing from patriarchal frameworks and capitalist interests by creating material conditions that enable bodily and economic autonomy and choice against cycles of dependency and coercion continues to be a feminist priority around the world.

The common oppressive codes around motherhood apply also in Kurdish culture. Similar to other contexts, it is common for Kurdish men to sanctify their mothers. Kurdish mothers in turn are expected to prefer their sons over their daughters and help police the movements of female relatives, including their 'brides', often through surveillance and abuse. Such powers often increase with age. One different, gendered, socially accepted assertion of agency relates to peacemaking. It is said that when Kurdish women throw their headscarves on the floor, feuding parties should end their fighting in the village. In the Kurdistan freedom movement, one particular group has over time turned this otherwise symbolic peacemaking practice into a political statement: the Peace Mothers. In the movement's cultural discourse around peace and justice, the Peace Mothers with their recognizable thin, white headscarves, often with embroidered edges, clearly standing apart from the style of veiling associated with the Turkish government, signify the infusion of traditional Kurdish culture with revolutionary politics. They symbolize an insistence on political agency and 'dignified' peace based in justice. The gendered role given to mothers in the struggle offers an interesting perspective on non-pacifist peace politics from below.

* * *

The Peace Mothers were formed in 1996 with the first association branches in places like Amed, Wan, and Istanbul. At the height of the war, these mothers, whose children have either been killed in the war or are currently in the guerrilla ranks, began organizing themselves. While sympathetic and supportive of each other's cause, the Peace Mothers are distinct from the slightly older organization of the Saturday Mothers, who for many years have been protesting weekly in Istanbul's Galatasaray Square for truth and justice for the forced disappearance and extra-judicial killing of their children, similar to the Argentinian Plaza de Mayo Mothers.

The Peace Mothers are organized in an umbrella fashion, with local assemblies in several dozen cities. They are mainly based in Bakur/Turkey, but Peace Mother groups exist in Rojava, Başûr, and Europe as well. Even though they primarily focus on putting an end to the war and demanding freedom for political prisoners, they also organize against violence against women. Some elderly and ill mothers, who do not have the ability to physically participate in activities, are honoured with symbolic membership. In addition to their assembly meetings and protests, they mobilize around 8 March, 25 November, or Newroz, among other events. They send delegates to the movement's congresses and other structures and their opinion is consulted by the guerrillas, legal political parties, and human rights organizations. Some Peace Mothers are currently in prison on terrorism charges.

Peace Mothers have a special place in this movement. We are a direct bridge of communication between the people and the PKK, as well as the state and the PKK. We are able to reach places that others cannot. That is our mission, to function as a force of peace and dialogue. Peace Mothers are not bound by anybody, we act as we find appropriate. Of course, we coordinate with other parts of the movement, but in general, we stay away from formalities. We stand for peace, our only commitment. Peace is also what we represent in the women's movement, of which we are a part. When the peace process began, we knew we had to play our role as those who push the process forward with all means available to us.

In their public interventions, from rallies to occupations, which often help rapidly escalate wider Kurdish political action against the state, the Peace Mothers capitalize on the state's refusal to take them seriously as interlocutors. In some (even if limited) ways, this informal, yet distinct, emotionally charged identity helps evade legibility, giving Peace Mothers more fluid room for manoeuvre compared to more institutionalized political actors. Parallel to its mobilizational function, the clarity of the Peace Mothers' basic demand – peace, not war – has a moralistic effect: 'Everyone knows that we work from our heart and soul. There is no money, no profit, and no ulterior motive in what we do. Everybody knows that our concern is to stop our children from dying.' The mothers' claims are simultaneously selfless and therefore universal on one hand, and motivated by personal interest (family) and therefore highly subjective on the other. Due to their intimate blood ties to the mountain-dwellers, Peace Mothers are perhaps the civilian constituency least apologetic for their support for the guerrillas. They are also among the furthest away from state power in terms of class. Their critique of the state may not be as theoretical, but it is rooted in concrete experience. As one Peace Mother said: 'What has the state given me up to this point other than oppression? I don't expect anything.'

The individuality of their stories matters greatly, but the accumulation and narration of their often similar stories of state violence, politicization, and resistance constitute an oral archive for the collective memory of war. Peace Mothers often narrate other people's stories as though these were their own:

My son has been in jail for 21 years now, twelve years in solitary confinement. Even though he is ill, he can't get proper treatment. He is far away, I don't have

115

the means to visit him more than once a year. Every 15 days, we speak on the phone for ten minutes.

That mother over there? Her son joined the mountains and then disappeared one day. To this day, we don't know if he is alive or dead. In this situation, what else can we do as mothers other than organize? Reuniting with our loved ones is our only wish and this is only possible through peace.

The Peace Mothers often use the words *bi rihê seferberiyê* ('with the spirit of mobilization') to describe their energy. Their non-bureaucratic form of organization, which in their words is fuelled by their emotions, means that unlike formal institutions, their schedules are not confined to office hours, but rather determined by the urgency of conditions created by life. This 24-hour dedication and their uniform-like scarves in a way resemble the guerrilla's non-capitalist organization of time and space. Unlike the political parties or human rights associations they support, beyond daily developments, the mothers' way of 'seeing' combines various aspects of violence into a decolonizing narrative of justice-seeking that comes from a place of wisdom rooted in feelings of love. However, they do not want to preserve any life unconditionally – they demand dignified life.

Our eyes are open. We understand the meaning of the tanks, military presence, pressure water – violence is a normal part of our relationship to the state. We are criminal by virtue of being Kurds, but without our resistance, we would be extinct today. After the imposition of the village guard system, our villages were destroyed and our homes were looted. Many of us here came to Amed city because of state violence. Some of our people had to migrate to places like Ankara, Istanbul or Antalya and became poor workers. The people of this country have nothing, they barely make their day's bread and live in rented homes, while the tyrant sits in his palace on the back of the poor. We protect our values against this state that has no conscience, mercy or justice. We resist against this undignified life. We resist for our homes, our land, soil, water, language, and identity. But he? He is just a tyrant, a tyrant! May God give Erdoğan reason so he leaves the path of Saddam!

Another Peace Mother added:

On their TV programmes, they always ask: 'What do the Kurds want?' For decades, we have very clearly voiced our demands: our right to live freely, without oppression, with our language, culture, and political means on our homeland. It is peace that we want, peace, peace, peace! We also empathize with the mothers of the soldiers and police. We don't want anyone to die, but for that to happen, we need to struggle against this oppressive tyranny.

In the Kurdish women's movement's discourse, the ancient Mother-Goddess embodies the heart and soul of moral political leadership in social organization. Nazan Üstündağ (2019) reads Kurdish political motherhood in the context of the Kurdish movement's analysis of the family in the longue durée of patriarchal domination, in which the Mother-Goddess has lost her societal status to the conspiracies of men. In the movement's understanding then, the Kurdish father is prone to be a collaborator whereas the mother is a force of restorative justice: 'Therefore, while the man has to be symbolically killed, the mother can be redeemed.' Üstündağ argues that the mother's identity allows her an exceptional sort of power and right to life that is beyond law and political discourse of the nation-state.[1]

Indeed, the movement encourages religious communities, tribes, and social roles such as motherhood to mobilize those of their qualities that serve societal ethics in a way that advances communities towards democratic values. Care, love, and suffering should shed their oppressive and reactionary elements and be turned into occasions for struggle, which amounts to what the movement often refers to as the 'politicization of emotions'. In this setting, political motherhood can erupt as a manifesto of self-determination, a conscious renaming of the world and redefinition of societal relations on new terms. As argued by Nisa Göksel (2018), instead of pacifying or paralyzing them, the mothers' really experienced traumatic pain of losing one's loved one becomes a platform to voice objection, disobedience, and non-compliance with the colonizer's definitions of life and death. The act of loving and caring thus acquires new meaning and quality when channelled into political and moral sovereignty.

The political Kurdish mother also symbolically clears the battleground for the revolutionary children of future generations, who want to part from tradition and do things differently. Their children may have been the reason for their politicization in the Kurdish movement, but lifelong engagement in the struggle turns many mothers and fathers into respected activists in their own right. Sultan Uğraş, a beloved, originally Arab member of the Kurdistan freedom movement's community in Europe, was in her late 60s when she was stabbed in the throat by AKP supporters at the Turkish consulate in Belgium during the 2017 referendum on the presidential system. 'Mother Sultan', who lost several children in the guerrilla, spoke the following words in an interview with Firat News Agency (ANF): 'Those fascists should be ashamed of themselves. They can never intimidate me. We remain standing and we will continue our struggle. As a mother and woman, I am not afraid of them.'

A mother of four, Remziye Tosun survived the military lockdown in Amed's Sur district after more than three months in 2015/16. She was then jailed for 15 months along with her infant Berîtan on charges of supporting terrorism for staying in place during the fighting. In 2018, she was elected as an MP for Amed. During her campaign, she declared that she would wear the symbolic white scarf in office, in honour of women such as Taybet Inan, a 57-year old, who was shot by the Turkish armed forces in the streets of Silopî and whose body was left to rot for seven days during the siege, or Emine Çağırga, who had to put her teenage daughter Cemile's dead body in a freezer during the army siege of Cizîr around the same time. Like a warning or a cry of conscience, the Peace Mother's white scarf entered the parliament of a state that is accused of knowing no law or morality.

*   *   *

The emotive image of the 'mother-as-homeland' is often used as a romanticized symbol in a way that erases complex personhoods and reinforces patriarchal nationalist ideologies. This applies in some ways to the role of mothers in the Kurdish struggle as well. However, the glorification of motherhood also comes from innocent feelings of love, care, and longing for serenity. As a child, I used to believe that the sequins from women's traditional dresses had magical qualities. At the very least, I thought, they might bring imaginative dreams if put under the pillow at night. (Once in a festival, I even tried to sell the idea to other children!) As a teenager, my friends and I were always fed delicious homemade food made by women from different regions on our regular hours-long community bus trips to protests and festivals organized by the movement in different parts of Europe. I no longer searched the floors during political/cultural events, but I always wondered how the bodies of the ululating, joyfully dancing Kurdish mothers in their 60s making victory signs, dressed with accessories they often hand-crafted themselves never seem to tire during hour-long rallies or festivals. The Kurdish women in my community often have chronic health issues such as pain as a result of housework, childbearing, and/or untreated mental and physical conditions. But something about political participation seems to have a healing effect on our mothers.

In my travels in Kurdistan, there were some elderly mothers I repeatedly encountered in surprising places. Mother Qadifa, an elderly Êzîdî woman, whom I had interviewed at the women's house in Tirbêspiyê (al-Qahtaniyah) in Rojava, laughed at my surprised face when I saw her again a few days later on the other side of the Syrian-Iraqi border, in the Şengal mountains, where she protested on the first anniversary of the Daesh genocide. In Amed, in a rather official building, I ran into two elderly mothers I had briefly met during

118

their visit to the guerrilla on the other side of the Turkish-Iraqi border, in the Qendîl mountains several months prior. Their demand to 'shhh!' turned into conspiratorial giggles at my astonishment.

The white headscarf, as a single-use, last-resort type of artefact may well have at some point been Kurdish women's only means of disrupting male-caused conflict in their intimate communities. Today, its power derives from its ability to express one colour out of many in an organized, intergenerational mass women's movement that seeks to be a collective quest for peace and justice against patriarchy and the state.

17

Self-defence

The roses of resistance are born in the asphalt. We receive roses, but we will be with our fists clenched speaking of our existence against the push and pull that affects our lives. – Marielle Franco

Guerillahood is giving the most precious thing a person has – their life – to speak one's language freely, in Kurdistan, where a language and culture were forbidden under the shadow of genocide. It's to weather the most difficult storm, including life in the mountains, with belief and willpower, to ensure that a people can embrace their language and culture, which are their most natural rights, and their freedom, the most vital thing. No other guerrilla movement has braided itself ideologically, politically, socially, culturally, morally, and ethically on the basis of women's social freedom – in other words, on women's autonomous army-fication – for as long as we have. We tried to fit every stage of the liberation struggle into guerrillahood, becoming, at times, poets with our pens, at times directors and master theatre actresses on the freedom stage. To the mountain peaks, we play the songs and sounds that are so existential to our people; we become authors of novels. Each woman guerrilla has a different story, but together, they are a militant collective that longs to realize their freedom ideals. – Sakine Cansız, Europe, 2012

The mountain-dwelling warrior phenomenon resonates with many regional traditions and stories, from those of nomadic spirituals to those of what anthropologist James C. Scott (2009) refers to as rebellious 'state-evading' communities. The mountainous geography of Kurdistan is sprinkled with footprints of different groups that have taken up armed struggle against occupation over the period of a century. Under extreme conditions, people from all parts of Kurdistan and from all walks of life created intentional communities for common causes in the mountains. Starting with the first pêşmerge – which translates as 'those who face death', people who are not blood relatives lived communally with each other, frequently transcending tribes, dialects, and regions of Kurdistan and beyond. Whether they were called pêşmerge or guerrilla, generations of Kurds grew up with the images, stories, and songs of the sacrificial freedom fighter, who is not subordinated to any state system. As such, many Kurdish practices of self-defence historically formed beyond the moral-political realm of the state.

In modern history, the mountains served as headquarters for Kurdish groups in their fight against European colonialists, Iraqi monarchies and republics, the Iranian armies both under the Shah and under the Islamic Republic, the second-largest NATO army of Turkey, as well as Daesh.

The mountain is one of the only commons left in the enclosing grasp of neoliberalism in the Middle East. In the context of the Kurdistan freedom movement, the mountain is also seen as a sphere 'outside of the system'. The entire logistical structure, routine, and social mentality of guerrilla life embodies a sociability outside of capitalist relations. Equipped with an AK47, wearing a tailored militant uniform with enough pockets for small useful items, a guerrilla never owns more than she can carry. Apart from the weapon, her most valuable possessions are diaries, scarves, pens, perhaps a USB-stick with music and photos, and hand-made gifts from comrades. The guerrillas' moneyless way of life and willingness to sacrifice themselves without personal reward is seen as signifying a Kurdish will to freedom beyond materiality. In many ways, the PKK's ideals of communal economy, women's autonomy, and permanent self-organization and self-reliance that it envisions for the community were prefigured in the mountain before turning into perspectives for all of society.

To be in the guerrilla is not only seen as a physical stance, but also as a relationship to life. Ideas and ideals associated with guerrilla life include selflessness, generosity, sacrifice, wisdom, care, communality, and willpower, all of which developed in different sites of the struggle throughout the movement's history. During my stay in guerrilla camps, I met former factory workers, peasants, children of wealthy land-owning rural aghas, dentists, engineers, journalists, musicians, social scientists, formally uneducated people, and graduates of elite universities. Among the guerrillas were Kurds from all parts of Kurdistan and the diaspora, as well as Arabs, Turks, Latin Americans, and Europeans. For many young Kurdish women and men, the idea of 'going up the mountain' presents an anchor in their self-conceptions: the knowledge that a different life is nothing more than one decision away. It is a concrete option for direct action that, just like the mountain itself, is always there. This knowledge materially shapes women's identities and decisions. It impacts personal and communal histories, regardless of how many actually make use of that option.

The first phase of the guerrilla war was largely shaped by an attitude to prove that the Kurds exist and that their existence needs protection from massacre and assimilation by the state. The guerrilla practice of the 1980s and 1990s drew on the Maoist strategy of protracted 'revolutionary people's war'. The later paradigm shift impacted not only the movement's ideological perspective, but also its relationship to violence. Women's autonomous organization actively shaped the articulation of new concepts of self-defence.

Kurdish women in the various armed units I visited often mentioned that for 5,000 years, only men were allowed to protect themselves and society. In their view, considering that all beings in nature have self-defence mechanisms, it was women's natural right to create their own means. Anti-patriarchal self-defence had to create radical concepts for the protection of the diversity of life. Today, the movement conceptualizes 'legitimate self-defence' (*xweparastina rewa*) as one of the nine fundamental dimensions of Democratic Confederalism. In fact, the women's movement theorizes this question more thoroughly than the general movement.

Guerrillas emphasize that their armed struggle is not only qualitatively different from the cruel methods of specific states, but also different from that of the state system in general, which relies on the monopolization of force for the purpose of control, domination, and exploitation. It was not to kill, but to protect and enable life, they often said. YJA Star guerrilla Arjîn was guarding the area around the Mexmûr Refugee Camp from Daesh attacks at the time of our conversation in late 2015. In early human societies, she said, clans often functioned based on the principle of 'one for all, all for one'. This solidarity logic was turned upside down by the state, and especially the nation-state. Through law and other means, the state imposes its power on society. The state not only takes freedoms away; in the name of national interest, it also profits from making people sacrifice themselves for causes that have nothing to do with them. She criticized the totalitarian turn made by socialist states, partly due to their militarization, bureaucratic state apparatuses, and a modernist fascination with technology.

> The Red Army was built to be the defence of the working class, but it turned into a militaristic vehicle for power. It failed to be society's self-defence, it became an agent of state interest, resembling the armies of the systems it claimed to dismantle. The guerrilla's notion of self-defence is independent. It relies on an understanding of struggle, not power. To create its own protection is society's most natural right, but how can we liberate self-defence from the state's monopoly? How can we build self-governing communities? How to free the idea of protection from the violence of power?

The movement's war propaganda involves many catchy songs about the armed struggle, but, in theory, the guerrillas are not supposed to glorify the act of violence itself, something perceived as an unwelcome expression of hyper-masculinity. The notion of revenge (*tolhildan*) is often evoked when speaking about taking a stance against the state and its agents. While especially in the early years of the movement, this often quite literally amounted to spectacular executions of individuals, such as tribal heads, police chiefs, rival groups, and 'traitors', revenge is today seen as an act that needs to be mainly directed at systems of oppression, although spies, occupiers, and collaborators still don't get spared. As an act of rectifying an injustice, targeted revenge must be a one-off warning, radical in its purpose and practice, but not brutal or senseless. Cruel practices are punishable by disciplinary measures.

The movement's non-statist self-defence concept became particularly relevant during the Daesh war, in which entire communities were massacred as regional and global states abandoned them. The regional wars themselves, guerrillas never fail to point out, are an outcome of the nationalist and sectarian policies created by the nation-state system, imperialism, and the military-industrial complex. Accordingly, since states are at war against their own societies, all societies, not just those 'without states' needed independent and autonomous self-defence measures. As Arjîn put it:

> We resort to armed struggle because we are culturally, economically, and socially under genocidal siege. A society's defence is not up for rent or negotiation. Just as women cannot rely on the mercy of men to achieve their freedom, we believe that communities' futures cannot be left to power-driven states and their security paradigms. Communities whose names the world no longer knows have been wiped out. Acting in this awareness, we encourage Syriacs, Assyrians, Arabs, all peoples of the region – to consider the meaning and importance of creating mechanisms of self-defence.

In the political perspectives proposed by the movement, self-defence is not just the duty that professional cadres take up in war. In the movement's literature, reproduction, nourishment, and protection are described as the fundamental reflexes of any living being, including human beings and their societies. The 'theory of the rose', Öcalan's elaboration on the concept of self-defence, distinguishes the notion of self-defence from hierarchical power systems and asserts that since every atom, every cell exists to the extent to which it can preserve itself, society can only flourish if it secures its existential base. Similar to the bee's sting or the rose's thorns, human beings must create their individual and collective means of self-defence as a moral duty to life. Beyond mere physical survival, self-defence must encompass political, economic, social, and cultural institutions to defend individuals' and communities' ability to live on their own, self-determined terms. Narîn, who we heard from in previous chapters, put it in this way: 'Education, consciousness, and self-defence go hand in hand. We are not just an army. Our organized-ness is our real defence system: against man, state, and tradition. An unorganized woman is a woman who lost her self-defence. Without it, she can be finished by her brother, husband or father.'

The aim is not only to defend communities and lands from state violence, colonization, and fascist groups. In theory, if communities successfully build their autonomous, self-reliant systems, even formal structures like the currently exisiting guerrilla armies would ultimately be abolished in the future.

These perspectives may sound utopian for the time being, but on the ground, the movement has already begun laying the foundations for these ideals. Inside the self-organizing communities created by the movement in different geographies, including in Europe, procedures are in place to directly intervene in incidents of violence and resolve conflict. These are seen as more reliable and solid than the neglectful and misogynistic attitudes among police and courts that perpetuate rape and feminicide culture. For example, men engaged in domestic violence or any form of misogynistic behaviour or harassment get suspended from their roles and community spaces. They are held accountable by the women's assemblies and are, unless they change, ostracized. Justice committees or women's assemblies intervene especially when requested by someone affected. Over time, sensitivity towards violence against women increased in the circles around the movement, and people talk about existing cases informally, so that even rumours are enough to trigger check-ins by the women's movement. Often, anxiety about the possibility that the organized structures may find out about an incident is enough deterrent for men, who feel committed to the movement, to abandon abusive behaviours. In acute moments, the movement's structures help women remove themselves from dangerous situations and support them with sustainable next steps. The general movement must respect the women's movement's decisions on these issues, i.e. it cannot veto any matters that involve patriarchal violence.

Self-defence, therefore, is seen as not just a matter in contexts of war and large-scale violence, but as a legitimate question wherever capitalism, state, and patriarchy destabilize, disrupt, and attack life. Today, around the world, states advance their technologies for surveillance and police brutality and criminalize protest. Questions around collective ideological, social, political, cultural, and economic self-defence are therefore relevant, especially for feminists, who do not view the carceral means of the state as a protection or solution. In the words of Hêlîn Dirik (2021):

> How do solidarity and community work when the prevailing system is based on isolation, individualism and property? How can we support friends experiencing repression? How do we deal with violence, how do we support those affected, and what happens to perpetrators? How can a community take charge of conflict? This means not leaving friends and siblings to fend for themselves when they are being bullied, harassed, threatened, insulted, face violence, get arrested, controlled, deported or imprisoned. This includes

strikes, blockades, occupations and demonstrations, but also the ability to create alternatives, safe places and self-defence mechanisms. Because only in collective revolutionary action can we truly fill words like feminism, anti racism and class struggle with content, and only then may our ideas of a world free of police violence, racism, isolation and exploitation find fertile ground.

18

Martyrs

Şehîd namirin – 'martyrs are immortal' is one of the most chanted slogans of the Kurdish movement. Nearly every person close to the movement has at least one martyr in their inner circle. To this day, more than 40 years after party formation, no PKK member has died of old age, a testimony of its emergence as a youth movement. Except in cases of illness, all of the deaths up until this point have been a result of combat, assassination, or self-sacrifice actions, including hunger strike, self-immolation, or self-detonation. Although the origins of the word 'şehîd', commonly used to glorify deceased heroes of various causes, is religious, it is also used by secular movements without reference to religion. This does not make the martyr less mythical. Martyr-related rituals are an important aspect of the Kurdistan freedom movement's spiritual meaning-making. Since the beginning, particular martyrs such as earlier mentioned Mazlum Doğan or Zeynep Kınacı have been theorized as 'turning points' and 'values' for the movement's ideology and practice.

Assembly meetings, educations, congresses, and festivals always begin with a minute of silence for the tens of thousands of martyrs of Kurdistan's freedom struggle or the women's liberation struggle (which also include women like Rosa Luxemburg or the Sisters Mirabal), often followed by the words: 'May their light illuminate our path.' Regular commemorations bring people together, who renew their promise to the martyrs to continue their struggle. New fighters often take up the names of martyrs and sometimes fighters change their *nom de guerre* into the names of their fallen comrades. Parents often name their children after martyred members of their families. Cultural or social buildings, festivals, music bands, refugee camps, education periods, communes, academies, self-defence units, cooperatives, and assemblies are frequently named after individual martyrs. In Rojava, neighbourhoods, streets, hospitals, and self-organized structures are often remembered with the names of martyrs, who died defending these. In addition to countless songs, several documentaries, feature films, and books have been produced about individual martyrs and deadly battles. Guerrillas often act in films about their fallen comrades.[1] As part of the movement's archival work, guerrillas are often interviewed about their life in the mountains, their reason for joining the revolution or their thoughts on political developments.

'Self-sacrifice' actions, both as attacks on the enemy or as self-directed protests, have a long history in the movement but occurred more frequently in the 1990s. The movement generally does not normalize such attacks as a method of action. Öcalan and the movement more generally usually pay tribute and give meaning to specific actions of this kind, while discouraging them. Whenever they happen, such actions are interpreted as 'wake-up calls' for the movement at moments of ideological and political crisis. In other words, militants engage in 'self-sacrifice', knowing that these actions will be read as a criticism of the organization for failing to achieve a goal by other means.

Community support in times of death is very much rooted in Southern culture. In places with organized movement structures, the community gets together to collectively assist the grieving family with their needs. Careful attention is paid to respect the family's religious beliefs and customs. Martyrs' families often organize in the form of associations or are represented in 'martyrs' families committees' within Kurdish people's assemblies.

Guerrillas are aware that their own death may not be far away, which is why they often write diaries and letters. They braid bracelets or make necklaces, decorate their scarves with beads, dry flowers, and herbs to paste into notebooks, and give these tokens away. As they do not carry many things with them, the little that they leave behind after death is treated with utmost care. Their clothes, notebooks, letters, watches, and handicrafts are usually handed to their families, but sometimes they can be displayed in cemeteries or community centres. Since it is not always possible to bury the martyrs in their hometowns, there are several guerrilla cemeteries in the mountains of Kurdistan. The importance of the martyrs is well understood by the Turkish state, which routinely bombs guerrilla graveyards. Some have referred to this seemingly absurd practice as 'killing the dead beyond their death'. Mutilating, stripping or otherwise dese- crating especially women's dead bodies, and circulating images of these war crimes has been a practice of the Turkish state since the 1990s and has been adopted by its proxy forces in Turkish-occupied regions of northern Syria since 2018. As the final parts of this book show, recent years have seen the often-targeted killing of politically active Kurdish women, leading the women's movement to expand the definition of martyr to wider civilian constituencies.

Similar to the image of Jesus Christ on the cross, the macabre presence of martyr images in everyday settings has a haunting-humbling effect. Honouring martyrs is not merely an act of political identity-making; in many ways – as seen in the movement's literature references to historical figures like Mansour al-Hallaj or Giordano Bruno – giving meaning to the death of individuals who sacrifice themselves for their ideals also serves as a mechanism for collective spiritual detachment from the individualistic and assimilationist organization of time and space under capitalist modernity. Ritualizing remembrance of the martyrs and their sacrifices is also a way of summoning, in a secular-yet-mythical fashion, the ghosts of one's ancestors; not bloodties, but rather the experience of having shed blood for the same cause of freedom formulates the basis for such political kinship. In the context of anti-colonial struggle, martyr remembrance also presents an alternative history to that of the oppressor, in this case, the nation-state system. By animating the dead, the movement brings into being the unwritten and erased history of a people, whose existence has been denied by the state (and statist civilization more broadly), through its social history of resistance. Every territory in which a martyrdom occurred becomes a spot on the map of decolonization. Even if that same spot is eventually occupied, the martyr's spectre looms over it, haunting and thus symbolically overwriting the dominant history of the colonizer.

Figure 6 Martyr's memorial centre of the Mexmûr Refugee Camp. Children looking at photos of people who died over the course of the history of their refugee camp. Mexmûr Refugee Camp. May 2015.

19

Prisoners

Those who fight against oppression are thrown into dungeons, rather than those who perpetuate it. The prolonged torture of solitary confinement is being used, not only as a weapon against political dissent, but as a weapon against anyone who protests any of the injustices of the system. How can you fight against injustice, without demanding the liberation of political prisoners? – Assata Shakur

According to a 2021 report by Penal Reform International, more women are in prison than ever before. Between 2010 and 2020, the ten years after the adoption of the UN Rules for the Treatment of Women Prisoners and Non-custodial Measures for Women Offenders (commonly known as Bangkok Rules), the global female prison population is estimated to have risen by 17 per cent. Regardless of their gender, people who are poor and racialized are overrepresented in prison demographics. Like others, many women are charged for crimes relating to poverty, such as theft or substance use. Women are disproportionately jailed under laws criminalizing abortion, witchcraft, and sex work. Women also serve sentences for self-defence against patriarchal violence. Around the world, there are thousands of women locked up for their political beliefs.

It is symptomatic of the state's monopolistic influence on the public imagination that prison is the first thing that comes to mind when we think about justice. But incarceration rarely solves social problems that lead to crime; violence flourishes behind bars. As the work of Black abolitionist feminists has long demonstrated, race and class serve as organizing principles of the punitive and vengeful ideology that underpins the 'prison-industrial complex'. Prisons serve to remove 'problems' from view and signify a lack of hope in individuals' and society's ability to change. The resistance against prison systems is therefore about society reclaiming justice, rehabilitation, and reparations from the state and tackling the structures that generate the issues that lead to the incarceration of (disproportionately poor and racialized) people. The state's claim of a monopoly on justice and its equation of justice with punishment makes the question of prisons fundamentally a feminist issue. To cite Angela Y. Davis (2003):

In other words, we would not be looking for prisonlike substitutes for the prison, such as house arrest safeguarded by electronic surveillance bracelets.

Rather, positing decarceration as our overarching strategy, we would try to envision a continuum of alternatives to imprisonment demilitarization of schools, revitalization of education at all levels, a health system that provides free physical and mental care to all, and a justice system based on reparation and reconciliation rather than retribution and vengeance.

Both mass arrest and mass prisoner resistance have a long history in Kurdistan. With the 1980 military coup d'état, Turkey's jails were increasingly modelled after the US prison system and over time introduced isolation mechanisms to suppress the collective forms of resistance. At the moment, there are tens of thousands of political prisoners in Turkey, among them thousands of Kurdish women.[1] Turkey has one of the highest total populations of women prisoners and is believed to be among the countries with the greatest number of women political prisoners. Iran, a country that regularly tortures and executes dissenters in captivity, is another mass jailer of Kurdish (among other) political activists, journalists, teachers, and rights defenders. The UN Special Rapporteur on the situation of human rights in the Islamic Republic of Iran, published in the summer of 2019, claimed that 'Kurdish political prisoners charged with national security offences represent almost half of the total number of political prisoners in the Islamic Republic of Iran and constitute a disproportionately high number of those who received the death penalty and are executed.' In one of her final letters written from Iran's infamous Evin Prison, Şîrîn Alamhouli, a member of the Kurdistan freedom movement, described her horrifying experience of torture. She was hanged in May 2010 along with four other Kurdish political prisoners for being an 'enemy of God'.[2] Due to the difficulty of organizing communities within Iranian borders, among the priority works of KJAR, the Kurdish women's movement's organization in Rojhelat, are prisoner solidarity campaigns. One of the best-known cases is that of Zeynab Jalalian, who has gradually been losing her eyesight in her imprisonment since 2007.

From 2009 onward, and more so after 2011, the Turkish state arrested an estimated 10,000 civilians on terrorism charges for their involvement in the democratic autonomy efforts in Bakur.[3] Another wave of mass arrest came with the collapse of the peace process in 2015 after the state ended the dialogue with Öcalan in April. Especially after the 2016 coup attempt in Turkey, thousands of political activists, among them elected MPs and mayors, were put behind bars. Community members, rights defenders, lawyers, trade unionists, politicians, journalists, researchers, and artists, especially those organized in the Kurdish freedom movement's structures, were targeted. According to Reporters without Borders, Turkey has been the biggest jailer of journalists for several consecutive years.

130

At the time of writing, a significant number of people are held in prison without trial or court sentence. Hundreds of small children spend their most formative years in prison with their mothers. Prisoners also include elderly people with severe health issues and inadequate or no treatment. LGBTQI+ prisoners, many of whom are active in political struggles, are subjected to all sorts of violence and abuse. Prisoners with disabilities are often not appropriately accommodated. Many ill people die as a result of deliberate neglect.[4] The state released thousands of people from prison during the Covid-19 pandemic without ensuring the safety of the women that abusive men returned to, which led to several feminicides. At the same time, it excluded from the amnesty political prisoners, among them countless women's rights defenders and health-compromised individuals. The atmosphere of state violence, suppression, and censorship in Turkey prevents investigations into prison conditions. But as human rights defenders have made clear, cases such as that of 28-year-old Kurdish political prisoner Garibe Gezer, who in December 2021 died under suspicious circumstances in her prison cell after months of resisting sexual and physical torture, should not be treated as exceptional.

* * *

Prison is the material manifestation of the state holding society hostage. Ideologically, the prison's mission is to render people meaningless, corrupt, and absurd. We view the prison as a space of enclosure by the state, a controlled and surveilled environment, deprived of creativity and spontaneity. – Besime Konca, Amed, 2015

In Amed, only a few months after her release in 2014, I interviewed Besime Konca, who was imprisoned on terror charges twice. Her political engagement was strongly influenced by the massacre committed in her Alevi-Kurdish hometown Maraş (sometimes 'Gurgum' in Kurdish) in 1978 by Islamists and fascists. First arrested in her youth in the early 1990s when involved in preparing banned Newroz festivities, she was re-arrested during the so-called 'KCK trials' in 2009. In total, she spent 16 years in prison. Her experience resonates with that of many Kurdish political prisoners since the 1990s. Months after our interview, she was elected to parliament.

Prison is a sphere of isolation, loneliness, quarantine, condemnation, where the state imposes its own definition of you. Its message to the prisoner is: 'You are no longer a normal human being. You are abnormal, separated from society. You are now under my rule and you will passively bow down to your punishment.' You must insist on the justness of your struggle most radically

131

in prison. To the extent to which you grasp the meaning of prison, you can organize yourself against its system of destruction.

Taking women out of their homes and imprisoning them, the state imposes household life on women in jail. Once inside, the state reminds you of your femininity at every level and stage. The personnel are usually men, who use insult, harassment, and torture to break your will. Even if some guards are women, they follow the orders of men. The entire system is designed by a male mentality.

Initially, women and men were usually in separate wards in the same prisons. In Besime's account, authorities frequently weaponized conservative gender roles during attacks to cause confusion and escalation. She described that when authorities attacked the women's ward, male prisoners wondered why they had not been targeted. Likewise, when men were attacked, women would riot in solidarity. The state's later approach was to keep all women in one place. A women's prison was opened in Sivas in the mid-1990s shortly after Islamists had torched the Madimak Hotel, killing 37 intellectuals and artists participating in an Alevi cultural festival. Political women were brought to Sivas, after they had participated in the prison resistance. Besime, who stayed there for nine years, said that Sivas' newspapers at the time were deliberately publishing reports that the locals do not want 'immoral women' in their city.

Due to the mass arrests in the 1990s, we were often 20 or 30 people in one hall. During searches, officials would tear our clothes, break our few items, and disturb any sense of privacy. Every morning, we were made to stand up for the prisoner count. We rejected this policy, a remnant of the coup regime. We refused to follow the system and schedule imposed by the prison. Instead, we created meaningful, collective time. Together, we prepared breakfast, worked out, and organized regular educations and activities.

We shared books, equipment, everything, to overcome different family circumstances. Prison life tends to be egalitarian and disciplined. Since we had a lot of time on our hands, we organized it productively to get a sense of structure. We turned prison into a space of knowledge production. People would volunteer to read up on topics and later present their research to other prisoners. Poetry, art, theatre, and other cultural activities made our daily life. We had to organize actions just to have the right to activities. We went on hunger strike when our books and newspapers were taken away as a form of punishment. We demanded access to certain channels on the shared TVs. Random, unnecessary restrictions were issued solely to ridicule and frustrate prisoners. In turn, we fought for every single one of our rights, such as visits, newspapers, leisure time, etc. Our resistance forced change in the prisons.

To undermine the prison solidarity works, the state frequently transferred prisoners to jails far away from the Kurdish cities. This also exposed the prisoners and their families to more harassment and attacks. Soon, seeing political prisoners' ability to mass mobilize, the state introduced the F-type high-security prisons in the 2000s. Hundreds of prisoners from numerous revolutionary groups protested the anticipated measures with death fasts. In part to break this resistance, authorities deployed thousands of soldiers for the infamous 'Return to Life' operations in late 2000 across approximately 20 prisons to transfer political prisoners into F-type prisons, where up to three people would be confined to small cells. Dozens of prisoners and soldiers died in this violent process.

Besime continued:

Any kind of relaxation or passivity in prison will result in further attacks or a total loss of your control over your life, a surrender to the state. Since the state tries to destroy your personality and will through isolation, you must become a free person to defeat the prison system. Beyond insistence on access to specific rights, resistance becomes a rationale to assert your subjective agency. This isn't an abstract, theoretical issue. Quite practically, your ability to resist is connected to your ability to remain your own person. This is tied to your belief that you are right and your ability to stay alert. Especially as a woman, resistance makes you more conscious of your own power, your confidence in your existence increases. The prison shows the importance and possibility of individual resistance against assimilation.

Imprisoned activists continue their work from prison, regularly sending messages to those struggling outside. As previously mentioned, from prison, jailed Kurdish women politicians published a book on Kurdish women's political participation (Kışanak 2018). Journalist and artist Zehra Doğan, who, while trapped in the military lockdown, painted the Turkish army's destruction of Nisêbîn, based on a photo shared by the armed forces, spent nearly three years in jail for her art. In prison, she joined the other jailed journalists' efforts to create prison newspapers, while continuing to produce art through means available to her, such as hair, tomato paste, turmeric, period blood, and bird crap. Imprisoned women regularly write for publications including the *Jineolojî Journal*. They are consulted on their opinions by the movement outside. Although political prisoners are subjected to a regime of isolation, they have repeatedly demonstrated their collective ability to put pressure on the Turkish state. Often using their bodies as the only weapons available to them, political prisoners continue to symbolize conscience, disobedience, and permanent resistance against the state. A democratic solution to the Kurdish question is inherently tied to their freedom.

133

20

Education

Political education is a strategic area of work for revolutionary movements that value the role of individual and collective transformation. Rich, radical pedagogical traditions evolved within homes, prisons, camps, in the works of early feminists, in numerous anti-colonial struggles across the Third World, in anarchist cultures, in organizations like the Black Panther Party for Self-Defense, or the indigenous-led Zapatista uprising, to name a few. As articulated in the critical work of revolutionary Brazilian educator and philosopher Paulo Freire (1970), liberation-oriented approaches to learning must refuse capitalist educational models that treat human beings as vessels to be filled, and instead view education as a humanizing process, especially for the oppressed, racialized, poor, and marginalized. Just as education can be a tool for discipline, control, and obedience, it can be a journey towards liberation and hope. Political education can offer concrete tools to act upon the world with the aim of changing it.

Nationalist education has been one of the primary tools of states to assimilate, criminalize, and eradicate Kurdish identity. In all four states which overlap the territory of Kurdistan, to varying degrees, Kurds were taught to be embarrassed about their identity, which was stigmatized as ferocious, backward, and uncivilized. Some of the first concrete roads in rural Bakur were built to lead students to Turkish state schools, although people would have needed other basic infrastructure as well. Decades of aggressive policies of assimilation and denial, parallel to genocidal violence, have meant that many parents stopped speaking Kurdish with their children. To this day, as social media videos show, abusive teachers continue to physically and psychologically humiliate and punish Kurdish children for their inadequate Turkish-language skills. Historically, advocacy for the Kurdish language has often been framed as a security threat and taken as an occasion for criminalization. As seen in the recent prison sentence of Iranian authorities against young Kurdish teacher and cultural activist Zara Mohammadi in Sine (Sanandaj), this state practice continues to this day. To many Kurdish people, the protection of their language symbolizes their ability to express their voice and is therefore central to their fight for freedom.

Early on, the PKK positioned education (*perwerde*) at the heart of its concept of revolution. The first cadres began their work by self-educating and in many ways relearning Kurdish history, politics, and society within a socialist and anti-colonial framework.[1] In the 1980s and 1990s, Öcalan's speeches, recorded and transcribed were circulated through the party's media outlets and publications, reaching Kurdish communities in the diaspora. Öcalan's methods included using daily incidents to illustrate how capitalist and colonial systems concretely manifest in the lives of individuals. For instance, he told stories from his childhood and shared insights from his relationship with Kesîre Yıldırım to critique patriarchy and tradition. One of his methods involved asking lecture attendants to share their story and to criticize their own personalities in front of all. This approach was formulated at the party's third congress in 1986 as follows: 'Today, we analyze not the current moment, but history, not individual person, but class and society.'

Even though education, both ideological and military, was from the beginning seen as an important and permanent part of the formation of militant personalities, the 'dirty war' of the 1990s, in which the PKK suffered many losses, led to a neglect of the educational activities in the mountain sphere. According to the party literature, this contributed to authoritarian, brutal, and gang-like behaviour in some guerrilla units. Yet, as described in this book's first part, the same decade also marked a rising emphasis on ideological-educational work, especially among the women. Today, women's liberation and history are core aspects of all educational activities of the movement.

With the paradigm shift, the movement's education system was radically restructured, with people's and autonomous women's academies becoming essential to the wider efforts of building radical democracy. There are permanent as well as 'travelling' academies of the Kurdistan freedom movement, whose education workers frequently insist that it is possible to create an academy even 'in the shadow of a tree'. Outside of the academies, regular commune and assembly meetings also constitute sites of learning through discussion and planning. The movement's media outlets are platforms of political education for hundreds of thousands of people, many of whom are without formal education. On any day, one can check movement-affiliated TV or publications and learn, in Kurdish and in other Middle Eastern and European languages, about global social movements, including women's resistance struggles. The media is also used to disseminate information on ongoing social campaigns led by the movement, such as campaigns against child labour, child marriage, feminicide and other forms of patriarchal violence.

On one hand, education reinstates a sense of identity against internalized inferiority resulting from colonization, nationalistic curricula, and anti-Kurdish racism. On the other hand, on a more profound level, it serves to decolonize society from patriarchy, and human history from statist civilizational narratives. This sort of education is not designed to prepare individuals for professional life under capitalism. Rather, it is defined as an ideological formation to foster

135

internationalist, anti-capitalist and anti-colonial personalities among historically marginalized and dispossessed people.

*   *   *

Teachers and students in the educational works I attended in Rojava, Bakur,
Başûr, Europe, and the mountains often referred to education as a form of
self-defence. At the Abdullah Öcalan Academy for Social Sciences, which
nomadically travels through the mountains, I spoke to Zelal, who had been with
the movement since 1993. 'Etymologically, the Kurdish word for education,
perwerde, implies a relationship of loving and protecting. A living being, a
human, is meaningful only to the extent to which it is allowed to creatively
unfold its existence in the entirety of its being', Zelal said, giving an overview
of the movement's perspectives and practices on the issue of education as a
method of mental liberation from the state.

> Violence is part of the state's education. Anywhere in the world, criticizing
> the state can take you to jail. Look at all the young people around the world,
> who protest against injustice and are beaten with police clubs in response.
> The state tries to break their dignity and honour when beating, dragging, or
> otherwise humiliating them for daring to object.
>
> The state knows the importance of education. At all the formative stages,
> children and youth are shaped in accordance with state ideals. The capitalist
> education system feeds children with ideas that promote selfishness and
> competition, instead of solidarity. Its monopolist pedagogical logic tries
> to shape, form, and mass produce obedient personalities to sustain state
> interest. Passive, unquestioning, unorganized individuals serve as satellites
> of the state, a type of human being that easily surrenders to power. This kind
> of anti-social, authoritarian education normalizes the idea that anyone, who
> questions the system and refuses to submit to it, can be marginalized, crimi-
> nalized, and assaulted.

After sharing her memories of experience with Turkish teachers' racism
towards Kurdish children, Zelal said that education was an occasion to either
learn or unlearn any kind of internalized hierarchy, including misogyny:

> The state system's schools are sexist. In their content and method, they
> attribute traditional gender roles that especially discriminate against girls.
> The education system deepens the gendered socialization of the population
> to consolidate patriarchal mentality and culture. Strict limits are set early on
> as to what women and men respectively can or cannot do. I remember the

'home economics' classes in school, where we were taught to stitch and cook, while the boys learned woodwork. They taught us to know our place ...

Since the beginning of our struggle, education affected how we walked and talked. From her tone of voice to her hair and nails, women's bodies had been objectified according to patriarchal terms and needs. Her feelings were dismissed, her thought always defined as lacking, insignificant, stupid. Psychologically, mentally, women had been deprived of self-confidence and the ability of independent thought.

Outsiders often perceive the PKK's party education, usually involving hours and days of reading and discussing Öcalan's writings, as a form of indoctrination. State-affiliated outlets even call it 'brain-washing'. Based on her fieldwork among PKK guerrillas, critical education scientist Kariane Westrheim (2008) argues instead that the organization's pedagogy in mountains, prisons, and streets creates 'organic intellectuals' in the sense described by Antonio Gramsci. She writes: 'The PKK emphasizes that political education also entails a language of identity, belonging, possibility, and hope. Seen against this background, the PKK movement proclaims the pedagogy of hope in a Freirian sense.' This sense of humanization through party education was a common sentiment among the guerrillas I interviewed and it resonated with Zelal, who placed more importance on the emotional impact of the collective learning and thinking process than on the absorption of exact facts:

Rather than making people memorize events, we aim to strengthen people's ability to express themselves, to systematize their thinking, and to have faith in the validity of their thought. Analytical thought by itself, without emotionality, leads to mechanization, as we can see in the depressed state of Europe. This matters especially when we consider that consumerist culture promotes physical, material pleasures at the expense of people's emotional and mental depth. This consumerism is imposed on the Middle Eastern communities today, where there is still a lot of value put into non-materiality. Sharing life is an important part of meaning-giving. Despite the wars and massacres here, people continue to latch onto finding meaning and purpose in life. You can see the unbuyability of happiness in the friendships, neighborhood and family relations in the Middle East.

Zelal said that unlike the capitalist state, the movement did not put any limits on what education entails. Likening the discussion-based and social format of learning in the movement to the Socratic method of inquiry, she thought about learning as a lifelong and intergenerational experience.

In the state system, there is no value in educating someone past the age of 50. Why bother? Elderly people are either seen as incapable of further learning or their education is seen as useless, because they are seen as past their most productive, thus profitable age. In our struggle, all individuals, regardless of their age, are agents of political, social, and intellectual life. Our notion of knowledge does not limit itself to strict definitions. Of course, an elderly mother can still shape her community's future with her contributions. Her life experience is a source of knowledge and wisdom. Youth are full of dynamism, energy, potential, drive – they hold the future in their hands. These generations have a lot to give to each other. Our revolutionary struggle itself is an intergenerational school.

Education serves the movement as a constant reminder of the class realities in Kurdistan. At the Şehîd Zîlan Women's Academy in the mountains, previously mentioned guerrilla Narîn also described education as an essential part of the revolutionary quest to 'rescue' people from nihilism.

Our educational system tries to save people from egotism, individualism, a struggle against capitalist modernity's toxic influences on the individual. To save ourselves from being divorced from history and the realm of non-materiality, the language and level of discussion must be accessible to everyone, otherwise we cannot reproduce ourselves as a revolutionary movement. Everyone is tasked with developing each other. This is also a class struggle: people with university degrees and people without formal education, villager and city-dweller – we struggle against hegemony, elitist arrogance, and immodesty. This creates revolutionary synergy.

In the autonomous women's academies, women struggle with and against themselves as women in an atmosphere in which they discuss and criticize and self-criticize comfortably in the absence of men. As Narîn told me in a break session during the ongoing PAJK education period she was attending at Şehîd Zîlan Academy:

Our autonomous educations present occasions to struggle against and with each other as women. There, we criticize each other very openly, without reservation. We must be able to self-criticize and criticize, in a genuine and constructive way. We don't criticize other women in the same way in the mixed spaces, because there, men will use those points against us. The divisive and harmful gaze of men is absent in the autonomous sphere. There, we grow together. A traditional woman cannot change herself, another person, or society. In our individual transformation, we develop women more generally. This women's consciousness in turn influences the men. Because of our education system, you can recognize a PKK woman from the way she walks through life. Our education desires to create a struggling woman. A free woman is conscious, organizing, struggling, aware of herself. A woman who questions, who lives philosophically.

Throughout the movement, beyond the guerrilla, numerous seminars and lessons are offered to civilians. Formats vary, but they generally cover different elements of the movement's history, ideology, and practice. Most of the time, attendees sleep and eat in the same venue. Sessions conclude with criticisms and self-criticisms, in more advanced stages with 'platforms'. These are group analyses of individuals and are meant to create a space for reflection, improvement, and comradely honesty. The purpose is to solve personal or collective problems and conflicts in a radically transparent and constructive way. Songs, dance, music, theatre, and martyr memories mark the end of educational periods.

Apart from temporary academies, physical academies enable people to research, develop their own concepts, theories, knowledges, and perspectives outside the statist gaze. While academies in the guerrilla sphere move through the mountains, in places like Mexmûr or Rojava people have been able to establish permanent spaces for educational activities, ranging from school systems for children to popular education academies for youth and adults. These institutions are inspired by Öcalan's ideas about the role of the academy for the revolution, but they are not necessarily organizationally linked to the PKK.

Most of the academies in Bakur were forcibly closed by the Turkish state, their members facing terrorism-related charges. When war started after the peace process in 2015, Sur, one of the poorest districts of Amed city, was nearly fully destroyed and much of its population displaced. Ever since, the Turkish state has been engaged in aggressively gentrifying the area to attract tourists.

Before the war, during my stay in Amed, I attended a few Jineolojî workshops at the Women's Academy in Sur. The institution was located in a typical historic Amed house, with a large courtyard and many chambers to accommodate multiple families. There, previously mentioned Jînda, a coordinator, explained to me the work of the academy. Although their door was open to all, the people participating usually came from the already organized autonomous structures in Amed. The different assemblies, unions or cooperatives were able to request specific classes or trainings from the Women's Academy to educate their members on topics like ecology or sexism.

These people are from the grassroots base of the Kurdistan freedom movement, which has grown over a period of 40 years. They are experi-

Figure 7 A guerrilla bookshelf with translations of international works on history, sociology, and political science, as well as the movement's own literature. Qendîl. April 2015.

enced, politicized people, who know the struggle, gave sacrifices, and feel affinity to Öcalan and the movement. In this sense, people in this community share political memories, values, and practices. Therefore, they appreciate what the academy represents, they know that we approach them to discuss Öcalan's perspectives. It would be a different story if a civil society organization from Ankara came here to teach people.

Jînda argued that women's autonomous education was crucial because it was not possible to expect women to play a leadership role in the struggle without considering that women's identities, personalities, lives, and work had been historically colonized.

140

Sometimes women get up in mixed spaces and say: 'But there are bad women, too! Our mothers are oppressive as well!' Such discourses don't see male domination as a system; they are used by men against our women's struggle. This way, men are empowered to say: 'Look even women agree with me', reinforcing the lie that women are each other's rivals and enemies. To avoid this, we encourage women to join autonomous educations before participating in mixed ones.

We approach different sections in society differently. There are very radical young women, willing to resist the state, but lacking gender consciousness. Obviously, capitalism's use of images and language specifically targets young women and their vulnerabilities. We explain to them what objectification is, we try to enter their world with referencing things that are relevant to them. On the other hand, the mothers in the neighbourhood don't have access to theoretical language and concepts. We use practical examples from their daily lives to encourage questioning. One education alone can sometimes initiate visible change in a woman's stance. Freedom consciousness develops as people set their standards for acceptance and rejection around different aspects of life.

Apart from the revolutionary function it plays for the internal transformation of Kurdish communities, education is also seen as crucial for peace and justice between the peoples of the region. Separating democratic histories of societies from states' tales of power and domination is seen as a strategic intellectual task by cadres working in the movement's education, media, and social spheres. As Zelal put it, insisting on the 'democratic nation solution' meant insisting on developing free individuals that can express themselves and their communities in all their colours:

We live with Armenians, Arabs, Syriacs, Laz, and Turks and so on. How can we look for solutions if we don't even know our common or each other's history? Similarly, the Kurdish people have diverse dialects. Everyone should be able to speak in their own way and know the culture and history of the place that gave birth to them. At the same time, they need to actively learn about the wider region with all its cultures. Neither chauvinism, nor assimilation. If we had it our way, we would enable everyone to learn and speak their own languages. We envision such projects, but we haven't reached such stage of implementation. This education system develops in the harshest conditions. We are leading a life-or-death struggle, alongside a fight to freely express our thought and belong to ourselves. Amid massacres, we create a new life.

21

Media

Headlines like 'Angry husband stabbed his cheating wife to death' endorse the idea that a woman experiencing violence deserved what happened to her. This normalizes feminicide. If a woman gets murdered, we must create platforms to ask: What to do to stop feminicide? What are the economic conditions, the social and political systems and structures, family concepts that led up to this? Press work is a medium for consciousness and liberation. – Devrim, KJK Press, Qendîl, 2015

Media, like education, plays a key role in the ways in which we make sense of the world around us. What stories matter and why? Whose existence is represented how and by whom? The stakes of such questions are high in a world in which dominant narratives are produced by powerful corporations and states. Feminists have often claimed that when they are represented at all, women and other oppressed sections of society are usually portrayed in ways that stereotype, stigmatize, target, or otherwise 'other' them, usually through the gaze and for the entertainment of the able-bodied, well-off, white man, who has been rendered as the universal human being. No surprise then that media has been a major front in efforts to reclaim repressed stories in all their complexity and diversity.

The increase of mainstream representation of minoritized identities over time is not due to a change of heart among those who control news and entertainment media; it is the result of many individual and collective struggles. At the same time, corporations have appropriated feminist aesthetics and language in ways that almost mirror the harmful gender tropes that people long fought against. Incentives to enact a politics of victimhood invite self-essentializing and individualistic performances, pacifying collective political agency while depriving people of ways to express more complex personhood. In the name of 'giving voice' to women and the oppressed, dominant discourses often caricaturize and freeze people in time. Moreover, the fetishization of cherry-picked 'first-woman-tos' as resilient change-makers overshadows information about the achievements of radical mass women's movements in different parts of the world.

Anti-capitalist feminist approaches to media and art can capture the difference between the photogenic and the beautiful. In this spirit, the Kurdish women's movement sees women's autonomous media as an important site of self-defence against the erasure and co-optation of women's struggles. Besides reporting news, documenting one's struggle is also a way of preserving gains and creating radical collective horizons.

In 1995, the PKK-affiliated movement launched the first Kurdish satellite television channel in history: MedTV. At the time, the ability to watch and hear Kurdish on the TV screen felt 'like a dream come true' to many people. Generally, newspapers, magazines, pamphlets, radios, and TV channels historically played a crucial role in Kurdish political resistance. Despite repression by different regimes, media reported on state violence, but also provided space to express criminalized Kurdish language, politics, culture, and art. Media has also been one of the main areas of Kurdish women's political involvement. Kurdish women worked as editors and authors of Ottoman women's publications, as well as in the first Kurdish papers.[1] Today, there are hundreds of Kurdish women's magazines, newspapers, programmes, and journals, many of which are run by women only.

The 'free media' (*ragihandina azad*) is what people call the broad network of newspapers, agencies, and TV channels, general and autonomous, affiliated to and often built by the thousands of media workers of the Kurdistan freedom movement, operating in nearly a dozen countries. If 'free' is measured by liberal media criteria, the strongly ideological and partisan *ragihandina azad* may not make the cut. From the revolutionary media workers' perspective, however, they are 'free' as 'truth-seekers' outside of the norms of the nation-state-based capitalist system. With all its shortcomings and problems, the movement's media system is almost entirely run by people with no conventional professional training and sustained by the movement's own means, without any funding from governments or foundations.

The 1990s saw a rise in Kurdish women's magazines, brochures, and newspapers.[2] The mobilizational publications of the Kurdish freedom movement, compiled by guerrillas and political activists, drew attention to the relationship between patriarchy, colonialism, and the state. Sometimes women followed these publications secretly, hiding them from their families. In 1993, the women's magazine *Jina Serbilind* started circulation in the diaspora in Europe. From the mid-1990s onward, the weekly *Jiyanî Azad*, based in Başûr, was the movement's first women's newspaper. After the paradigm shift, the movement's media content featured women's liberationist perspectives more prominently. Especially in the 2010s, a number of all-women Kurdish media outlets were launched to develop alternative concepts, styles, formats. To give a (non-exhaustive) sense: *Newaya Jin* is a women's monthly Kurdish- and Turkish-language newspaper published in Europe since 2005. Run by women only, it publishes articles on global women's struggles, revolutionary women's biographies, and various topics relating to political developments, ecology, health, history, and art/culture. Formed on 8 March International Women's Day in Bakur in 2012, *JinHa* became the first all-women's news agency in the Middle East. It was shut down by the Turkish authorities in the aftermath of the failed coup attempt in the summer of 2016. Its short-lived successor *Sujîn* was banned soon after. At the moment, *JinNews* is building on their legacy, with women reporting from different parts of Kurdistan and beyond. On 9 January 2018, the fifth anniversary of the Paris murders, *JinTV*, an all-women television station in Kurdish, Arabic, Turkish, and English, was announced. Following its launch, it began broadcasting programmes – from documentary dossiers to discussion fora – on politics, economy, culture, society, and Jineolojî.[3] Kurdish women's armed self-defence units such as the YPJ or YJA Star have their own press offices and websites.

Thanks to the movement's media institutions, tens of thousands of Kurdish home-makers, from London to Kobanê, access information in their own language about women's resistance around the world – from the anti-rapist self-defence collective 'Gulabi Gang' in India to the 'Ni Una Menos' protests in Latin America.

Numerous guerrilla fighters worked as journalists before going to the mountains. Others took up media work upon joining. Over time, guerrilla art, including poetry, literature, music, drama, photography, painting/drawing, and film became an important genre of the culture associated with the movement. Gurbetelli Ersöz (*nom de guerre* Zeynep Agir) from Palu/Elazığ was the first female editor-in-chief in Turkey. Upon her release from prison for her political activities, she worked at the left-wing Özgür Gündem newspaper, which had

Figure 8 Kurdish women performing traditional songs with drums (known as *daf* or *erbanê*) as part of the activities to host the World Women's March. Mêrdîn (Mardin). March 2015.

been refounded to continue reporting on the Turkish state's war crimes and human rights abuses. Ersöz continued journalism upon joining the guerrilla, where she participated in the first steps taken towards women's autonomous organization. She was killed in 1997, when the Turkish army and the KDP collaborated in the war against the PKK. Her diaries, rich in both critical reflection and humour, are seen as a precious source to gain insight into the harsh conditions of guerrilla life in the 1990s.

At the time of our interview in Qendîl, Devrim was part of the KJK's press work. Amid technical equipment in a guerrilla tent by a mountain spring, Devrim told me that her interest in journalism started when she witnessed underreported state violence as a teenager in the 1990s. A few years after joining the PKK, she began working in the guerrilla's press. At the press academy in the mountains, the mainly young members studied a variety of topics around world-system analysis, sociology, psychology, and history, in addition to technical training.

The mission we attribute to media differs from the mission given to media by states and hegemonic systems, which normalize war, destruction, and exploitation. The media is often weaponized to incite conflict between communities, to justify war in the eyes of people. States use media as a special war method against people, who want to build alternatives. Dominant media narratives can facilitate the annihilation of entire worlds and communities. In this sense, media is important for peace, for the development of a more ethical society.

Devrim stressed that media should amplify the voices of the oppressed and innocent. To do that, reporting needed to avoid sensationalism and instead provide sociological and historical context when describing issues like violence or social inequalities. Although a women's lens was not radical or alternative in itself, as she pointed out, it presented an occasion to challenge dominant languages and framings. According to Devrim, male comrades tended to think in a linear manner, less focused on nuance and connections, less vested in 'truly feeling with the population', and therefore prone to objectifying society. This in turn affected their understanding of the relationship between the different issues they reported on.

In 2013, the women's autonomous umbrella media association RAJIN (*Ragihandina Jinê*) was formed in the mountains following the movement's second Women's Press Conference. Like in most other spheres of the struggle, it was a difficult journey to get men in the movement to accept the need for autonomous structures in the realm of media. Even women did not see the need initially. Devrim noted that although gender relations were more progressive

145

in the guerrilla compared to the rest of society, male comrades still tended to centre themselves in work or claim ownership of women's labour. The presence of women in both media spheres, general (*gişti*) and autonomous (*xweser*), caused confusion about the purpose of the latter. In Devrim's view, women's media had to report not just on women, but on all of life, but, when doing so, be qualitatively different and push for transformation in all media structures.

> The point was not to separate people along their genders for the sake of it. The autonomous sphere truly is more advanced and radical, with a different kind of mentality and atmosphere. It's a constantly evolving space that accumulates and appreciates women's labour and renders it visible and lasting. Moreover, it is a space of organizing, creating a common mindset among women, enabling them to express themselves more sincerely, both collectively and individually. Away from the stifling patriarchal gaze and atmosphere, women are able to express themselves more openly, honestly, critically, and flexibly.

The women's movement views media as an important part of its social work. For instance, it has a role to play for the de-normalization of violence against women. In addition, people who did not previously know about the movement are drawn to its ideas through its media or through conversations with activists, who distribute print publications.

The fall of Saddam Hussein led to a rise in media outlets across Iraq, including the Kurdistan Region. While critical, independent, and progressive voices are now able to voice their concerns and perspectives more openly, the liberalization of the media landscape has largely been shaped by corporate structures, owned by wealthy political parties or powerful individuals. This was criticized by Viyan (not her real name), a young woman in her early 20s and main spokeswoman of *Truske* at the time of our interview in late 2015. Launched in 2004 first as a fortnightly newspaper, the Başûr-based monthly magazine *Truske* means 'spark' in the Soranî dialect of Kurdish, in which it was published. The magazine featured individual women's resistance stories especially from Başûr, social analyses, philosophy, culture, economy, politics, and research.

> During Saddam's rule, people were aware of the regime's full control over the media. Things are less clear, more complicated now. Increasingly, the word belongs to the few, a new upper class that also has most of the power in the economy and in politics. Naturally, they have better means to communicate their message to the people and to the outside world. Their ideology, their thought becomes hegemonic. The press should, however, be a voice of societal critique, a means to hold elites accountable. That is our philosophy, our project at *Truske*.

Viyan explained that while some platforms critically discussed the root causes of social problems, such as the mass migration abroad, sometimes under censorship pressure, society was not seen as an interlocutor by the main media outlets. This impacted women in particular: while women's issues and voices were largely absent, women were at the same time highly sexualized on television.

> The women on TV are usually quite separated from ordinary women in society. The ones who get to voice their thoughts on TV don't speak to the worlds of the working women, the poor, the illiterate. Women who host programmes often simply implement media agendas set by male bosses. They reproduce the language of men. Male editors-in-chief decide how to report on violence against women. Women become more visible but without having a say in the content and format. Issues remain at the level of information; statistics about divorce rates, violence, and killings are important, but what is our alternative?

Her words broadly apply to the media landscape in the Middle East more generally. TV channels with links to ultra-conservative governments or religious movements that otherwise harshly police women's bodies in public often employ liberally dressed women, deemed as attractive, as news anchors to attract views. Viyan complained that while knowledge of Kurdish women's struggles in other parts of Kurdistan remained superficial as a result of marginalization, problematic Turkish soap operas regularly made it into family homes in Başûr, promoting misogynistic ideas about women. Coupled with the glorification of hegemonic Western cultures, in Viyan's view, this led to the youth feeling alienated from their culture and thus constantly looking westward in their life choices. Yet, despite its limited reach, *Truske* wanted to 'spark' curiosity for alternatives, especially among rural communities:

> Many media outlets use websites and social media, but the vast majority of ordinary women, especially in rural parts don't have access to these platforms. That's why we go from house to house to physically hand our magazine to women. This also gives us the chance to interact with readers directly. It surprises many women to see that someone makes the effort to give them something to read.

At the time of our interview, Sarya (not her real name) was a reporter for *JinHa* news agency in Başûr.[4] Reporting mainly on violence against women, she believed that things like social conservatism, withdrawal to the household, the desire to maintain control over life were partly also products of the genocidal violence that people experienced, regardless of their gender. The anecdotes that Sarya shared about being pushed around and harassed by male reporters during her work resonate with stories from many female journalists across contexts. Reporting on life, especially when dressed in colourful clothes, presented in her eyes a way of disrupting power:

> In these male-dominated streets, we go from city to city to interview people and we are often the only female reporters. With our street reporting, we also quite practically break taboos around women's presence in the public sphere. By interviewing women workers, poets, artists, farmers, even children, we show them that we care about their thoughts and feelings. We try to practically support the work of struggling women by documenting and archiving their resistance. That is why we don't simply report on violence, we also follow up on incidents to actively support quests for justice ...
>
> In a war-torn place like the Middle East, there is no neutral media, all media takes sides. When uncritically normalizing social inequalities and other problems, the media can uphold the idea that only the powerful's version of truth is accurate. Women's media is important to have hope, against the idea that there can be no alternative to those in power. Often, women only appear on programmes to discuss culture-related matters, but with our reporting on all spheres of life, we refuse to surrender politics to men. People think that professionalism equals European standards, but we don't need to be like corporate media to hold ourselves to high standards. We want to show our community that we can create our own ways of journalism.

Alternative media is an important ideological defence mechanism in a time in which mainstream media, including social media, actively generate disinformation on radical movements and render alternative world-making projects invisible or unfeasable. As a site of collective horizon-making, women's autonomous media is a conscious effort to resist state-held, corporate, and male-dominated forms of storytelling. It represents a form of radical memory.

22

Ecology

While we have capitalism, this planet will not be saved. Capitalism is contrary to life, to the environment, to human beings, to women – to all forms of life.
– Berta Cáceres

The cover of this book shows my several hours-long hike with guerrilla Dorşîn. During what must have been the most scenic intellectual conversation of my life, we discussed the evolution of the role of ecology in the movement. I was particularly interested in her take on the influences of different thinkers on the movement's perspectives around ecology. Acknowledging several names, Dorşîn, a member of the Jineolojî works, affirmed: 'Look around you. Look at these mountains, these trees, this sky. Do you think we as guerrillas needed much theory to appreciate and respect nature?'

Ecological catastrophe is one of the most urgent issues faced by our planet today. It is no longer possible even for the main culprits of climate change to deny this. Similar to gender struggles, climate justice is not a single-issue cause. Rather, it is about radically reorganizing the social and economic systems and structures according to a mentality that values life over exploitation, domination, and profit. Against the 'green-washing' trends advanced by states and corporate actors like weapons and fossil fuels industries, social movements around the world emphasize the interconnectedness between exploitative mentalities and deadly economies. Women from different indigenous communities stress that it is not possible to measure the violence of environmental destruction through numbers and statistics alone. To many of them, the interplay between colonial state policies and extractive capitalist industries normalizes patriarchal violence, past and present. In other words, feminicide, genocide, and ecocide are inseparable. Refusing to let care for the environment be depoliticized by emphases on individual lifestyles and consumption choices, anti-capitalist and anti-colonial perspectives call for demilitarization, decolonization, and degrowth on a global scale. On their agendas are strategies for reparations to colonized regions, economic and political sovereignty, alternative energy and production systems, and the redistribution of resources.

Critiquing the logic that normalizes and establishes hierarchy and domination in the world has long been a major front of struggles to protect nature from destruction. The drive for expansion and profit tore apart, sometimes irreversibly, social fabrics, eco-systems, and relations between and within species. Social ecology, a philosophy and praxis first developed by Murray Bookchin, defends the perspective that power and domination within human societies is based on the domination of humans over nature. Ecological problems and social problems must therefore be solved together. For decades, critical scholars have connected the industrial-scale killing of nature to key paradigm shifts in Western intellectual thought over time, entangled with the history of empire. Over the course of centuries, capitalist and colonial patriarchy normalized violence against all that is deemed unproductive (in narrowly economic terms) and not (yet) exploitable: the feminine, the 'wild', the creative, common, queer, untamable, 'irrational', magical, spiritual. In *The Death of Nature: Women, Ecology, and the Scientific Revolution*, Carolyn Merchant (1980) argued that with capitalism, an 'organic worldview', which regarded the universe as an animate, ecologically connected, complex interdependent system with each part constituting a vital, autonomous element of the whole, was replaced by the rationalistic metaphor of a mechanical order. These opposing attitudes normatively impacted value systems and cultural, social, and economic practices. Analyzing formative philosophical, religious, and political texts, perspectives, schools, and systems of Western culture, Merchant traced the shift in the view of nature from a respectable, feminine, nurturing, and sacred instance to a commodifiable, inferior object of use at the disposal of men.

Marxist-feminists and eco-feminists have long pointed out that the colonization and commodification of nature goes hand in hand with the colonization and commodification of women. Drawing on Rosa Luxemburg's work on imperialism, many linked the parasitic nature of capitalism to the exploitation of women, nature, and colonies as free commodities to generate surplus and accumulate profit. Maria Mies (1986) argued that the process of this ongoing primitive accumulation of bodies, labour, and resources through the witch-hunts, settler colonialist mass murder and ecocidal industrialism was necessarily based on violence and presented the foundation for Enlightenment and modernity in Europe. As Silvia Federici (2004) noted, early European capitalism's rise not only encompassed the enclosures of the commons (forests, waters, fens, fields, etc.) and the exploitation of colonies, but also the appropriation of women's bodies and systems of knowledge to institutionalize a new social and economic order. Against the capitalist logic of neo-colonial development agendas that emerged in the second half of the twentieth century, Maria Mies and Vandana Shiva (1993) proposed what they called the 'subsistence perspective', a cooperation-based, sustainable ethical alternative framework for living, with nature, with balance and peace.

In many parts of the world, the idea of a mutual interdependence and symbiotic interplay between human societies and the environments they inhabit is not a conclusion reached from science but rooted in ancestral knowledge and embodied ways of life. In the lives of lower-class women and women in colonized contexts, the struggle for autonomy and sovereignty over the body and over territories are therefore entangled. To quote Lorena Cabnal (2015):

> To undertake resistance in the defense of the territory land without forgetting about our bodies is a political act of hope so that other generations of women and peoples may contribute to the construction of a new world, moving us from oppressions to emancipations. It is disturbing for the system, that in the midst of its threatening neoliberal patriarchal model, we have the energy to release our demands with joy and with our sense of indignation.

Similar to the above-mentioned perspectives, the Kurdistan freedom movement draws on traditional communal practices of living with nature and combines them with new scientific and political/ideological insights. References to local cosmologies and spiritualities, especially those that locate sacredness not in the world of the beyond but as embodied in the sensuousness of immediate life, aim to encourage solutions through love and respect for nature, not through enchantment with technological progress. In the movement's literature, holistic decolonization is linked to dissociation from statist, high modernist mindsets that promote limitless growth and view nature as a 'resource' rather than as a vital aspect of life. While local cosmologies, traditional ways of life, and everyday practices of rural communities still alive in Kurdistan and the Middle East present a big part of the movement's perspective on socialism, Murray Bookchin's work on social ecology[1] actively influenced Öcalan's conscious treatment of ecology as both a principle and condition for freedom. The movement also draws on and connects with feminists especially in the South and indigenous communities who link capitalism-induced destruction or commodification of land, water, and other commons to the subjugation of women. Beyond practical implementation and beyond viewing it as an attitude towards nature, the movement's understanding of ecology expresses a spiritual mentality, a form of creating relationships among beings based on autonomy and symbiosis. This makes ecology ideologically entangled with the women's liberation struggle. In the words of Azize Aslan (2021): 'Anti-patriarchal autonomy, therefore, is a fundamental organizational perspective for the Kurdish struggle; a perspective that constitutes the heart of the ecological aspect of democratic confederalism.' Aryen at the Şehîd Jiyan Women's Academy at Mexmûr Refugee Camp, described in the next section, believes that an insistence on ecology is important for development of the tools to survive and struggle:

151

When you attribute meaning to the notion of animateness, if you view yourself as part of a nature that is alive, you can feel your existence beyond materiality. Capitalism created itself by destroying ecologies and distorting the world's balance. Capitalist modernity annihilates non-materiality. Its mentality is the opposite of love, patience, and labor. This is the mind of male domination. Nature is exploited and put in the service of capitalists to generate further profit. This colonial relationship is mirrored in how society abuses women. What kind of life philosophy can we expect from a system that is so oblivious to beings that realize themselves? ...

Under capitalist modernity, people are less and less inclined to feel the need for human social interaction. Modern technologies and communication methods create a mechanization of social relations. Capitalism is the mental structure and understanding of life that is responsible for so many psychological issues, for sexism, for violence and despair. It is the main enemy of humanity and nature ...

Even without the means, we try to create ecological mindsets at the camp. Despite water shortages, people here still insist on watering the trees they planted in front of their homes. We believe that we come from nature. And to live as part of nature, we need to create the foundations for us to live within it in a balanced manner. That is impossible in the current cancerous forms of urbanization in Kurdistan. How to find meaning amid concrete walls that were built on exploited labor? Nature, gazing at the sky, that is what opens our horizon.

Environmental degradation often comes disguised as 'development'. The environmental destruction inflicted in Kurdistan and the Middle East more generally is a result of war and occupation, forced migration, governmental neglect, and profit-oriented economies, all of which are interrelated. The industrial state-building efforts in the Middle East region in the twentieth century often disrupted local subsistence economies in favour of central economic policies. Profit-driven planning, including large infrastructure projects often amounted to the – sometimes irreversible – breakdown of eco-systems and a decline in biodiversity. The centralization of national economies drove the atomization of households in rural communities, which previously had traditions of commoning, as well as sharing production and surplus. As national economies merged with the increasingly globalizing economy, pre-existing local subsistence and solidarity economies further diminished. According to Ercan Ayboğa (2021), a Kurdish environmental engineer, academic, and co-founding activist of the Mesopotamia Ecology Movement, the 1970s marked an era of unprecedented environmental destruction in various parts of Kurdistan in the context of regional neoliberalization.

Over decades, military operations by states have often been accompanied by large-scale attacks on nature. In recent years, as part of its war and occupation, the Turkish state has been preventing populations in northern Syria from accessing water. In 2021, Turkey increased its systematic deforestation of areas in the Kurdistan Regional Government as part of its war on the PKK. The deliberate targeting by states of Kurdistan's geography often sustains nationalist attempts to eradicate local histories. The attacks on nature target community knowledges and spiritual worlds.[2] In different parts of Kurdistan, existing state efforts for the preservation of nature and cultural heritage serve the purpose of attracting tourism and generating profit.[3] 'What some have called 'state-led gentrification' is a method of the Turkish state to promote national and inter-national tourism in places like the historic city centre in Sur district in Amed, where the population has been forcibly displaced by war.[4]

Constructions of dams and roads often serve population control and coun-terinsurgency purposes. The Ilisu Dam is part of the larger Southeast Anatolia Project within the neoliberal development framework in Turkey. In 2019, the Turkish state flooded the 12,000-year-old human settlement area of Hasankeyf for this medium-term project. The dam displaced tens of thousands of local majority Kurdish people, whose livelihoods were connected to the eco-system now submerged. The Turkish state moved what it deemed as the archaeologically 'valuable' parts of the site. The colonial aesthetics were unmissable in circulated videos at the time. elderly Kurdish locals cried and lamented the pieces of history that were draped in Turkish flags as they were driven away. Heart-wrenching photos showed the elderly wave goodbye to their flooding valley.

Compared to the other two pillars (radical democracy and women's liberation), the question of ecology is much less developed in the movement's practice. Yet, with the turn of the millennium, municipalities in Bakur became the first sites to implement the movement's ecological perspectives. Starting in the 2000s, diverse initiatives for conservation, river cleaning, organic seeds, and agricultural coop-eratives were accompanied by public discussions around the environmental implications of large-scale infrastructural and economic development projects. Building on the ideas offered by social ecology and Democratic Confederalism, the Mesopotamia Ecology Movement was formed out of the Mesopotamia Ecology Council in 2011.[5] In addition to proposing sustainable perspectives for self-determination in Kurdistan, the ecology movement, which organizes con-federally through local committees or assemblies, develops strategic relations with ecologists and environmental organizations and initiatives around the world such as the Middle Eastern 'Save the Tigris' initiative. The Mesopotamia Ecology Movement is critical of NGO-ized forms of environmental activism and encourages ecology movements to be proactively anti-capitalist and feminist in their approach. The movement opposes megaprojects, encourages

153

renewable energy and advocates for society's active participation in decisions concerning energy. It furthermore foresees a decolonization of village/city relations wherein rural communities get governed and exploited by the speedily growing urban centres.

The question of ecology is closely tied to questions around land and labour: the economy, one of the most important sites in the struggle for self-determination. Entire sections of societies, writes Öcalan, above all women – whom he refers to as the original economy-runners – are rendered 'economy-less' under capitalism. Against capitalism's 'anti-economy' regime (a reference to historian Fernand Braudel), Öcalan writes that a truly economic, anti-monopolist, and ecological society should organize every sphere of life along solidarity values and in balance with nature. To this end, the movement aspires to create possibilities of shared, communal life, as opposed to individualist, consumerist social relations. It is argued that democratic-ecological societies are best embodied in sovereign eco-communities that can produce and decide for themselves (Öcalan 2020), though there is no exact blueprint on how to go about this.

The movement began building autonomous women's cooperatives in the early 2000s. Over the years, these collective efforts, supported by municipalities and the women's movement, were able to open several shops to sell women's products, from honey to traditional clothing.[6] Azize Aslan (2016), a young Kurdish scholar of social movements and political economy, writes that women's self-determination, ecological consciousness, and anti-capitalist economic independence are mutually constitutive. As her fieldwork on communal economy practices (especially autonomous women's cooperatives) in Rojava and Bakur shows, the movement's approach is not fundamentally concerned with reforming labour conditions under capitalism as it is with developing direct opportunities for communities to sustain themselves through sovereignty and active political decision-making in all spheres of life. The moral-political nature of cooperative and organic production is seen as de-alienating people from their labour, which gets exploited in the capitalist wage relation.

Much of the future of any territory-based emancipatory project relies on its ability to offer economic self-determination for populations. Working together with the administration's commission for municipalities and ecology, the Internationalist Commune of Rojava launched the 'Make Rojava Green Again' campaign to play an organized role in the works to protect and rewild eco-systems in the area. Efforts and projects vary in scale and include research and practical works (including public education) on water management, renewable energies, tree-planting, waste disposal, and sustainable farming.[7] Commenting that the ongoing efforts are far from being sufficient in addressing the urgent issues, the Commune writes (2018): 'Rojava exemplifies how ecological problems are interwoven with social and economic issues, how centralisation, capitalist economics, and the exploitation of humans and nature are interconnected.'

The Jinwar Women's Village near Dirbêsiyê was built by a collective of women with material and logistical help of the local administration. The women made mudbricks and used materials available in the surrounding areas to create an accessible and green space with recreational facilities. As a practical project of the Jineolojî committee in Rojava, the village aspires to build a sovereign and self-sustaining women's commune, which organizes around communal democratic and ecological principles through assemblies and cooperatives.

Developing a belief that alternatives to capitalism are possible remains difficult in a context of poverty, authoritarianism, and political violence. For example, due to Turkey's Operation Peace Spring, Jinwar had to evacuate. The urgency of having to struggle against male or state violence often makes ecological considerations be perceived as luxury items on the radical agenda. In light of this, in times of war and climate catastrophe, insistence on ecology will prove to be a litmus test for the Kurdistan freedom movement and other struggles around the world. For such efforts in the South to flourish, resisting the military-industrial complex, one of the most corrupt and ecocidal industries in the world, should be an urgent matter for environmental justice movements worldwide.

Figure 9   Guerrillas taking a break during the first Jineolojî conference in 2015. Xinerê. May 2015.

23

Mexmûr: From displacement
to self-determination

Mexmûr camp embodies our larger vision for a system in which all peoples, with all the colours of their cultures can live together by participating in all affairs of life. In Mexmûr, we want to create the prototype of the democratic confederal system that we envision. – Aryen, Şehîd Jiyan Women's Academy Mexmûr Refugee Camp, 2015

In her book *Border and Rule*, Harsha Walia (2021) writes that 'Borders are not fixed or static lines; they are productive regimes concurrently generated by and producing social relations of dominance. In addition to migration being a consequence of empire, capitalism, climate catastrophe, and oppressive hierarchies, contemporary migration is *itself* a mode of global governance, capital accumulation, and gendered racial class formation.' Consequently, thinking through and against borders means radically interrogating the ways in which the nation-states-based world-system envelops people, controls their movement, and measures the value of life. Borders, especially colonially drawn borders, not only artificially cut through lands, they also sever life worlds, histories, and social relations. In many ways, they symbolize the worldview of a system that organizes life not through solidarity and cooperation, but through violence, nationalism, and profit.

Borders marked the beginning of the modern 'Kurdish issue' and in many ways, they continue to reproduce it. Over the course of the past century, in several episodes of large-scale state violence, tens of millions of Kurdish people were forced to cross, often multiple times, the borders between Turkey, Iraq, Iran, and Syria. Millions left the region to live in Europe, North America, and Australia. In recent years, countless dead Kurdish bodies were recovered in the seas and territories in different parts of the world, as tragic scenes and stories emerged of people losing their lives on the way to seeking safety, work, or peace. In 2015, the dead body of the drowned toddler Alan Kurdi from Rojava, washed up on a beach in Turkey, came to symbolize the so-called 'refugee crisis'. To draw attention to the inhumane conditions of migrants and refugees under Australia's dangerous border externalization policies, Behrouz Boochani (2018), a Kurdish journalist and political activist from Rojhelat, wrote a book on his phone during his six years in detention on Manus Island. To mention only one out of many instances, in late 2021, 27 mostly Kurdish people from Başûr drowned in the English Channel on their way to the UK. Increasingly, regular mass deaths at sea get normalized as governments use right-wing discourses to avoid states' responsibilities under international law. These and other stories show that Kurdish forced displacement is an international issue and entangled with the fate of millions around the world, who, for various reasons, leave their home behind and tragically lose their lives to the violence of state and border regimes.

Recent years have seen a rise of technology-oriented 'solutions' to the global migration 'crisis'. Whether it is integrating refugees into the capitalist market or establishing colony-like refugee statelets, it is evident that the worldview underlying such Eurocentric, high-modernist, efficiency-driven visions is part of the problem. Approaches that try to turn 'crisis' into economic opportunity are often celebrated by institutions like the IMF or World Bank. They often focus on improving the refugee experience instead of exposing the root causes of forced migration, such as (neo-)colonialism, militarism, political violence, economic injustice, and climate change. How can the same states, institutions, and businesses that directly contribute to and profit from warfare and injustice in different parts of the world find solutions to forced migration? How can we speak about forced migration without centring capitalism in our analysis? As well known examples such as the forced displacement of Palestinians show, humanitarian systems are deeply intertwined with Western state interests and often function as pillars to preserve the status quo.

In the context of the so-called 'refugee crisis' of 2015, the Turkish state succeeded in blackmailing the European Union when striking a deal to curb refugee influx into Europe. By praising Turkey's 'generosity' and, in Orientalist fashion, representing Turkey's handling of Syrian refugees as an expression of a regional hospitality culture, countless academics and policy-makers made themselves complicit in covering up for the fact that the deal was essentially a geopolitically motivated, cynical trade on human lives. Turkey materially benefited from this trade, which further legitimized its militaristic ventures. The hundreds of kilometres of walls that Turkey erected at its borders over the past decade are claimed to serve to stop 'irregular' migration especially of Syrians and Afghans (crossing through Iran), believed to be the two largest refugee communities in Turkey. However, these walls also function as a way to symbolically and physically separate Kurdish-inhabited areas from each other, not least to create obstacles for guerrillas.

Parallel to such border policies, which sparked the liberal #RefugeesWelcome discourses, radicals in Europe understood that – whether organizing shelter, conducting sea rescue, or resisting arms companies – acting for refugees is an internationalist, revolutionary task. In southern European countries such as

Greece and Italy, for example, the radical left was at the forefront of developing solutions when states busied themselves with restricting immigration, building walls, and arranging deportations. No surprise then that solidarity activism is increasingly being criminalized parallel to migration.

Meanwhile, as states outsource their obligations, the humanitarian sector is increasingly spotlighting (and sponsoring) so-called 'refugee-led organizations'. But who benefits from neoliberal language around 'self-reliance', and whose self-determination is deemed 'too political'? Depoliticizing refugeehood is, after all, a way in which European states assimilate and control otherwise activated communities (in fact, states gather intelligence about states and political movements in resettlement processes). The democratic autonomy structures of the Kurdistan freedom movement in Europe (including social centres, people's and women's assemblies, the youth movement, etc.) were largely set up by former refugees and are routinely targeted by surveillance and criminalization.

Democratic Confederalism as a political project aims to challenge existing borders by building transnational politics from below. In doing so, it ultimately aspires to render existing regimes meaningless in the lives of self-organized people. For now, the Kurdistan freedom movement's efforts have hardly dismantled borders in any physical sense; people continue to drown or get shot at border-crossings. They do, however, encourage people to imagine a borderless Kurdistan as a stateless democratic society and to meanwhile rehabilitate communal relations within and between peoples and their neighbours. Symbolically, it was a refugee camp that became the first site to locally implement democratic autonomy.

* * *

The 'Martyr Rustem Cudî Camp' or Mexmûr (Makhmour) Refugee Camp is inhabited by approximately 12,000 Kurds from Bakur, who left their villages during the 1990s war after refusing to cooperate with the Turkish state against the guerrillas. It is precariously located on disputed territory, depending on the geopolitical mood of the day, sometimes within and sometimes beyond the central Iraqi state and the Kurdistan Regional Government's respective spheres of influence. The camp population understands itself as an organic and active part of the Kurdistan freedom movement and organizes itself through assemblies, communes, and academies.

In oral history accounts, Mexmûr's residents often stress that their displacement is a result of their conscious decision to not become 'collaborators'. The following words by one resident are a common way of narrating Mexmûr's story:

When we first arrived, we found ourselves in the middle of a desert without water or shelter. Children died from mines, scorpions, and snakes. But every family picked up a tool and helped build up this place that first consisted of tents, then became a village and is now a small town in which we implement an alternative democratic system.

The different stages of the camp's history – villagers' refusal to collaborate with the Turkish state, their experience of several episodes of displacement and violence, and their building up of an autonomous self-governance system from zero – represent the trajectory of the movement's journey from insisting on bare Kurdish existence to developing a transborder system for autonomy. Over the years, the camp established its own civil society structures, education and health care system, and economy. Local and regional governments, as well as the United Nations High Commissioner for Refugees (UNHCR) often caused more harm than good for this community. From the beginning, Turkey, Iraq, the regionally dominant KDP, and the UNHCR viewed this political population as a liability or in actively hostile terms. Evidence of the calculations between these institutions over the lives of the thousands of displaced and endangered people emerged on WikiLeaks. Based on their negative experience, Mexmûr's residents often believe that governments and state-centric aid institutions pose obstacles to the self-determination of forcibly displaced communities. In many ways,

Figure 10   Seventh conference of the People's Assembly of Mexmûr Camp. Mexmûr Refugee Camp. May 2015.

Mexmûris present their camp as an autonomous alternative to the nation-state system, which they view as the main driver of forced displacement. Their model for radical sovereignty, at odds with the global managerial regimes that handle seemingly never-ending 'crisis' in a manner confined within borders, raises important questions about the predicaments of international law and humanitarianism, embedded in the nation-statist order of the world.

REFUGEE AUTONOMY VS NATION-STATIST HUMANITARIANISM

Mexmûr camp consists of a community of people from different villages mainly around Şirnex province. Upon consulting with each other in one of the most violent periods of the war in Bakur, a group of villagers decided against fleeing to Europe or the Turkish metropoles. Soon, in the spring of 1994 approximately 15,000 people crossed the Turkish-Iraqi border. At the time, a US-led 'No-Fly Zone' in Iraq had been in place since 1991 from the 36th parallel northwards with the aim of protecting the civilian Kurdish population in the aftermath of Saddam Hussein's genocide campaign. The Kurdish refugees thus fled Turkey to another part of Kurdistan that had only recently been the site of mass exodus, embargo, and violence. Kevser's family was one of the first to leave the village of Mijin village in Şirnex. In autumn 2015 at the camp, she told me:

Our village is empty now, because it refused to become part of the village guard system. Why should we collaborate with the state against the guerrillas? They are the children of the people of these villages. Our brothers and sisters had gone to the mountains to fight for us, and the state wanted us to help kill them. We were not going to let ourselves be used as a pawn in the state's game. We became refugees due to the Turkish state's oppression and violence and because we refused to become collaborators.

In the oral history of the camp, the residents were displaced eight times within the first four years of seeking refuge within Iraqi borders before finally settling in Mexmûr in 1998. Upon crossing the border, people were exposed to freezing temperatures, and lacked supplies, including clean drinking water. In the summer, they suffered from the scorching heat. Early on, the community published its political perspective on the Kurdish question and a list of humanitarian demands. In the early days, the UNHCR offered limited aid, but did not recognize the community as refugees, due to the entanglement with the PKK. The establishment of formal camps and the recognition of the displaced as refugees came about through a series of protest marches, hunger strikes, rallies, and direct actions. Eventually, the UNHCR began to provide limited assistance, but disciplined the camp for decades by way of incentives and aid withdrawal, to comply with its apolitical model and with geopolitical demands. For example, the question of finding a location for the displaced community turned into a source of tension. Originally, the residents' plan was to stay near the border, in proximity to their homes on the other side. According to people who experienced this first phase as adults, Turkey, the KDP, and UNHCR officials coordinated in various constellations to ensure that the refugee population was as far away from the PKK points as possible. Turkish helicopters bombarded areas and engaged in a variety of military tactics to harass and intimidate the community. When the UNHCR stopped assistance due to the camp's political affiliations, the residents moved to another camp, which they had set up themselves in response to the Turkish army's actions. Several other camps were created and dismantled by 1995 when the Turkish army and the KDP launched their second major joint operation against the PKK, and targeted and killed members of the displaced population, which they viewed as an extension of the guerrilla. In a 1996 article for UNHCR, current OHCHR spokesperson Rupert Colville offered these striking words: '[The refugees] resisted UNHCR's initial attempts to move them down to a camp well away from the border, until a couple of cross-border bombing raids helped change their minds'.

Threatened by the Turkish army, the refugees were put under pressure to move to Atroush, hundreds of kilometres away from the border. Mechanisms were put in place by the UNHCR to separate the population and monitor movement in and out of the camps. The refugees were further surrounded by intelligence and security forces. Efforts by the residents to demonstrate the civilian nature of the population failed as the UNHCR decided in the mid-1990s to close several camps due to militant presence. Residents told me about several instances in which the UNHCR seems to have deliberately looked away when the Turkish army's attacks wounded and even killed civilians in Atroush. In this period, people also died from preventable diseases. The adherence of the UNHCR to Turkish pressure to remove the displaced as far away from the border as possible forced the population to move closer to areas held by the Saddam Hussein regime. In late spring of 1998, following negotiations between the UNHCR and the Iraqi state, the community was transported from Nineveh to Mexmûr, their final destination. In Mexmûr, the UNHCR provided a small number of tents. In the hostile environment, people had to take long, often risky marches to wells to carry water to their homes.

The trail of the residents' displacement is marked by burials. Today, a large building, maintained by the martyrs' families committee of the camp, is filled with hundreds of photos of all the people that lost their life in the history of the community. Some were civilians targeted by the Turkish state, Saddam's regime or the KDP, while others were former Mexmûr residents, who joined the guerrilla and died in combat. Yet others died defending the camp against Daesh since 2014. Mexmûr's residents still condemn the UNHCR's acceptance of claims made by Turkey and the KDP that refer to the camp as a military recruitment camp, arguments that seem to have supported decisions to limit or withdraw aid. For many residents, the humanitarian organization's condition to depoliticize the camp makes no sense. As one member of the women's assembly at the camp put it:

> The PKK is a party of the poor, of our very own people. They don't protect our people for money. They don't take a single day off in their defence of our communities. They are the children, who grew up in the freedom struggle and are now defending us. How could we split from something that is part of us?

BUILDING A SOCIETY IN DISPLACEMENT

Social relations in the community that constitutes Mexmûr today were upset in the context of displacement early on, as members of different tribes and villages turned into one society, primarily united by their refusal to become village guards. Although the small, self-contained nature of the camp presents a set of logistical, economic, and political difficulties for the implementation of the movement's ideals in practice, socially, it is a relatively homogeneous community of political Kurdish families from the same region, which makes the acceptance of certain principles and organizational modes easier. These conditions mean that, on one hand, ethnic and religious differences do not need to be considered for the camp's organization. On the other hand, the residents' ability to be economically self-sufficient or to become a politically relevant site are heavily limited due to their settlement's identity as a refugee camp in the middle of nowhere in the wider context of Iraq.

The camp is divided into around half a dozen districts, with neighbourhoods organizing themselves in the form of communes with various committees. The communes in the districts meet once a week and are represented in the district councils, which send delegates to form the camp-wide People's Assembly (*meclîsa gel*). Roughly, the People's Assembly constitutes the umbrella in which all assemblies, associations, and institutions are represented. For example, martyrs' families, health, education are organized in the form of councils with their own administrative structures, including co-presidents. They send delegates to the People's Assembly, as do the women's and youth assemblies, worker's associations, and media and culture workers. The practical works of the People's Assembly are primarily organized through committees in charge of implementing the decisions taken in the assembly. The Ishtar Women's Assembly and the

Revolutionary Youth Assembly have their own decision-making procedures and planning. People from different assemblies (women, youth, martyrs' families, etc.) can be on different committees of the People's Assembly (e.g. economy, health, etc.), as long as they do not take up other commitments. Information flows across the assemblies, its committees, and other structures through the activists' involvement in the different works. The relationship between the different institutions is not strictly formal but shaped also by intimate social relations. Organizers have a sense of people's expectations not only from the deliberative meetings and discussions, but also because their own families and friends talk about plans and projects in their living rooms.

The People's Assembly and the camp's municipal administration are two separate, but complementary institutions. The latter, also with two co-chairs, primarily concerns itself with public services, including electricity, waste collection, water, registration, construction work, food and health supplies, and security. It formally represents the camp to external institutions, for instance to arrange project funding, but it cannot claim to politically speak on behalf of the camp – that is the role of the Assembly, which represents the organized form of the popular will. The municipal council has representatives in the People's Assembly and like all the other structures of the camp, it is accountable and answerable to it. Every few months, the municipal council presents a report to the People's Assembly and the individual districts. A committee accounts for the camp's finances, which are presented regularly to the Assembly and communes. Any projects that the municipality applies for must be approved by the Assembly. Excepting a few facilities for health and education, the majority of purpose buildings were created by residents following collective decisions. Only in recent years, contract-based and often fluctuating salaries of some teachers and municipal workers have been paid by the KRG or the UNHCR. Residents are proud of the fact that some of the doctors of the camp were raised there. A committee of the health assembly is trying to file knowledge of traditional medicine and revive natural healing practices. The shortage or lack of specialist surgeons, ambulances, medication, and other specific facilities means that camp residents are largely reliant on trips to the city.

As a self-governing, green village-like settlement between desert and rapid urbanization, Mexmûr is viewed by the movement as a lived non-capitalist alternative in an increasingly neoliberalizing region spiralling into market dependency. The camp's self-reliance grew stronger upon Saddam Hussein's fall, as the newly gained freedom of movement opened opportunities to earn incomes from outside. Students and workers that regularly leave the camp and interact with the outside system are part of associations to protect the residents from exploitation and injustice. However, the camp's actual ability to live ecologically and independently of the economies around it is limited to some cooperatives

163

and small-scale food production. Since the economy of the camp barely covers the needs of the large families, many people are forced to find low-waged work in the city, mainly in the construction and agricultural industries.

Alongside negotiating with humanitarian institutions and the local and central government, the diplomacy committee also raises political questions on different platforms. The women's assembly and other structures, such as the education and health works, send delegates to the diplomacy committee and also have their own diplomacy committees, which inform and coordinate with the central camp diplomacy efforts. The People's Assembly and the women's assembly regularly issue statements about developments in Kurdish politics. They organize protests and panels at the camp in solidarity with other sites of the Kurdish struggle.

In the past, children had to sit on the floor in makeshift school tents or on rocks, sharing notebooks and pencils, sometimes erasing their writing to recycle the material. The majority of Mexmûr's first teachers had not finished high school themselves, but could at least teach others to read and write.[1] Today, each district has a nursery and a primary school, while there are several middle and high schools. The residents created their own teaching material themselves, largely drawing on the movement's philosophy. When the self-organized school system at Mexmûr became recognized by the UNHCR and KRG in the mid-2000s, this enabled hundreds of youth to pursue higher education outside the camp. Some of the university graduates return to the camp as teachers. Mexmûr's school system laid the foundations for Kurmancî language education in Rojava and Bakur.

Teachers explain that the natural sciences were similar to what is taught in the rest of the world, but not prioritized over other subjects. In the words of a woman whom I will call Hêvîdar, who helped set up the camp's education system: 'We refuse to devalue literature, art, sociology, philosophy, history. The depreciation of these subjects is state logic – for efficiency, they say, these subjects are not necessary. But they play an important role for our camp's life philosophy.'

Hêvîdar further elaborated that 'knowledge production must be anti-sexist'. Unlike the surrounding state systems, Mexmûr's schools were not teaching students gendered ideas on how to be proper women or men.

Critiquing traditional ideas that confine people enables more meaningful friendships against a system and culture in which men were raised to view women only as potential lovers or sexual objects. In Jineolojî classes, we discuss women's history, sexism and how to overcome it. Democratic nation is a topic of study from middle school onward. Ecology is taught within sociology classes. In the future, ecology can become its own class, especially

164

considering the rise of climate issues. We must urgently raise ecological humans, humans with ecological consciousness.

Mexmûr's education system benefited from and continues to study alternative education models from around the world. This affects discussions about the shape, format, and purpose of classrooms. The schools employ the movement's practices of *tekmîl* and criticism and self-criticism as ways of undoing hierarchies between teacher and student and of enabling students to give constructive feedback on their learning experience. The points raised are taken up by the teacher's assembly for further reflection for the future. Violence against students is strictly forbidden.

We have two co-chairing class presidents, one girl, one boy. Students rotate responsibilities. Through communal activities, such as looking after the classroom together, we teach children in practice that autonomy and responsibility are interlinked. Here, there is no state or state representative that will come and clean after you. If you want to live beautifully, you must take social responsibility.

In addition to the regular school system, adults benefit from literacy classes as well as the many political educations and training opportunities (health,

Figure 11   Centre of the Revolutionary Youth Movement. Mexmûr Refugee Camp. October 2015.

language, IT, media, tailoring, etc.). At the Ferhat Kurtay Academy,[2] which was opened in 2012, the movement's theory and practice are taught, with topics including Democratic Confederalism and women's history. Music bands, dance groups, theatre ensembles, and choirs regularly perform at annual celebrations. The youth organizes tournaments for the several football teams at the camp. Sports and culture festivals take place regularly.

WOMEN'S AUTONOMY IN MEXMÛR

The settlement in Mexmûr in 1998 coincided with the rise in the movement's focus on women's autonomy. As such, projects like the women's centre were among the first institutions of the camp. The Ishtar Women's Assembly, formed in 2003, is the umbrella structure that encompasses all the autonomous women's institutions of the camp. It also represents the women that have responsibilities in the mixed structures. As in the case in other sites of the movement, women in Mexmûr organize the nine dimensions of the democratic nation – society, culture and art, economy, self-defence, law/justice, democratic relations and alliances (diplomacy), health and education, ecology, and politics – by way of committees. The Young Women's Assembly is organized under the umbrella of Ishtar Women's Assembly, but it takes its own decisions and comes up with its own perspectives and plans. It is also a core part of the Youth Assembly, where it has its autonomous decision-making mechanisms. The Peace Mothers of Mexmûr are involved in a variety of other activities of the women's assembly or in the martyrs' families' council.

The Ishtar Women's Assembly meets regularly, bringing together the administration, committees, and delegates from institutions and structures. Like the different committees, the administration rotates and meets on a weekly basis to assess the progress of the planned works. Regularly, larger gatherings with women from all districts and institutions discuss issues and plan activities. The women's committees in the districts carry the assembly's decisions and plans to the local communities by way of home visits. During these tours, organizers get a sense of women's overall situation in the camp. Visits allow women to share their problems and concerns with the women's movement, while receiving updates on planned activities.

The People's Assembly and the Women's Assembly each hold large biennial conferences to evaluate all efforts, elect new representatives and committee members, and set out plans for the next period. The Women's Assembly gets to propose women to the leadership of the People's Assembly, but the latter does not hold the mandate to make recommendations to the autonomous assembly. Similarly, the Women's Assembly shares its decisions and planned activities with the People's Assembly without seeking the latter's approval.

Formed in 2009, Şehîd Jiyan Women's Academy is named after Zeynep Erdem, *nom de guerre* Jiyan, who was killed by KDP forces in a camp protest in 1995. Women from the communes often stay in the academy collectively for a specified period to get away from housework and enjoy the stimulating atmosphere. In the past, men were invited to the academy to reflect on sexism and male domination. Women were given the chance to criticize their partners' patriarchal behaviour. Such works are now spread out to spheres of the camp beyond the institution. The academy prepares perspectives for the teachers at the schools and academies. It is also a space in which traditionally taboo topics like sexual health and contraception are discussed.

At the academy, I interviewed Aryen, who was part of its administration at the time and told me that women often complained about their husbands belittling or abusing them. Some women also show little interest in overcoming internalized sexism. Nevertheless, Aryen said, 'despite the undeniable prevalence of oppressive conservative mindsets, there is a system in place that aims to create a change in social relations, a shift in consciousness, based on an understanding that struggling for liberation is an important condition for a self-determined life here'. The academy offers classes on women's history, including the evolution of the Kurdish women's struggle, self-defence, Democratic Confederalism, health, ecology, and other topics.

> Our education system also includes discussions on how to organize and solve our issues ourselves, instead of appealing to higher instances. Through institutions for accountability, a notion of social ethics develops, which takes up an important role in the process of problem-solving. Creating a society in which people learn to trust each other enables meaningful possibilities for justice.

Social harmony and justice are vital for life at Mexmûr camp indeed. As a self-contained space that tries to render itself independent of external authorities, the ability to maintain social peace is an important test for the autonomous system. People are free to move away from the camp and nobody is required to actively participate in the self-organization structures, but everyone benefits from them. However, as long as they do live there, people have to respect the camp's social contract. Rather than law – unchangeable and imposed – the camp's social contract is seen as a framework that emerged out of a process of consultation and discussion. The different assemblies and structures have their own guidelines. The women's assembly's social contract lays out principles and regulations against violence and discrimination against women, including domestic abuse, bride price, forced and child marriage, and polygamy. The women's social contract is binding for the People's Assembly, which also has principles and regulations of gender equality and women's liberation. In this complementary way, it is not only the women's movement's, but the entire camp's organized structures' duty to implement practices for women's justice. In theory, the idea is to foster an understanding among people that violations of the social contract, drafted and adapted in a long process of participatory consultation and discussion, damage the community's values and way of life. Unlike the state system's individual rights and punishment approach to social ills, any problem in the community – violence, theft, disputes, etc. – is seen as relating to social relations. Instead of relying on law and authority, the camp's system and philosophy of justice and peace are safeguarded from below by a variety of dynamically interacting mechanisms at the camp, from criticism and self-criticism to the People's Assembly social contract.

Due to the camp's close-knit social relations, things such as murder or theft are rare, but conflicts in society, including domestic violence, economic issues, and family disputes, remain. There are no prisons at the camp, but security forces, accountable to the assembly, ensure peace and safety in case of escalations and can detain people for up to a few days. Any problem gets addressed first by the most immediate institution in charge, in the commune or other local institutions before referral to the larger assembly. Individuals are held accountable by their respective communes, committees, or assemblies. If someone who has violated an aspect of social life currently occupies a position in self-organization structures, they get temporarily suspended until a decision has been taken regarding their conduct. Usually, a critical self-evaluation and apology is in order. If the relevant institution believes that the person is genuine in their self-criticism and will not repeat the mistake, they can resume their work. Since people know each other, being summoned for investigation is already a source of embarrassment.

Issues concerning women are directly brought to the women's autonomous structures. Camp security forces can isolate an abusive partner from the family for a specified period, in which the person in question is given the opportunity to reflect, self-criticize, and apologize. In the meantime, measures are undertaken to consult the affected woman about her ideas on how to move forward. If an issue does not get resolved, the 'people's platform', consisting of delegations of structures and individuals, gets activated. The abusive man is made to listen to criticism, which he can address, after which proposals are being made regarding the next steps. It is up to the concerned woman and the women's assembly to issue a final decision. Generally, disciplinary measures involve writing a self-critical report, reading up on topics, or taking up specific duties in the organized structures. The worst scenario is the exclusion from the camp. This rare move is a last resort; ultimately, the movement's philosophy of justice is a hopeful one that believes in individual and collective transformation and rehabilitation.

*   *   *

In interviews, statements, and publications, the residents of Mexmûr repeatedly stress that return to their villages in Bakur is conditional on justice and a dignified, democratic solution of the Kurdish question. Only if the Turkish state shows an openness to transforming itself from being a nationalist state that dènies the existence and rights of the Kurds will it be possible to speak of the existence of conditions that make return meaningful. The camp residents refuse to normalize their displacement by continuously insisting on return and by actively participating in the political struggle. But as long as they continue their existence in refugeehood, they build their democratic autonomous institutions in the here and now, and along the way gather experience of self-organization for the future social, economic, and political structures that they want to build in their native villages.

24

Bakur: Women against politicide

> The women, who had come from the women's struggle in the streets and squares, used the parliamentary seat for women's liberation. – Sebahat Tuncel, Diyarbakır E-Type Prison[1]

In 1990, the People's Labour Party (HEP)[2] became the first legal political party in Turkey to enter politics with an explicitly Kurdish agenda. In the following year, Leyla Zana became the first Kurdish woman in the Turkish parliament, one of only eight women in a parliament with (at the time) 450 seats.[3] From a traditional background and without formal education, she was politicized by the imprisonment of her husband Mehdi Zana, a well-known Kurdish politician. Zana wore the traditional Kurdish colours (green, red, and yellow) in her hairband when she took her parliamentary oath, which she finished with a sentence in Kurdish: 'I take this oath for the fraternity of the Kurdish and the Turkish people.' For this act of 'separatism', she served ten years in jail.

Three decades after Zana's election, Kurdish women are no longer an exception in Turkey's political landscape. In fact, the organized Kurdish women's struggle is a vibrant political opposition against the patriarchal and authoritarian, nationalist state. The Kurdish women elected as MPs or (co-)mayors in the past decades in Turkey are a mixture of women with many years of political experience and those with no prior political engagement. While some are university-educated, others did not graduate from high school. Many are former or current political prisoners.[4] Most have become political after experience with state violence, and many were hospitalized due to state violence during protests while in office. Their creative protest actions, both in parliament and in the streets, made female Kurdish politicians targets of the government, its security forces and supporters in explicitly gendered ways, from sexist media portrayals to harassment and physical assault.

This chapter focuses on Kurdish women's struggle-ridden engagement in 'statist' or mainstream legal politics in the context of Turkey to offer a sense of the possibilities and limitations of radical democratic politics in the context of authoritarianism. However, it must be stressed that much of the women's movement's work takes place outside of this realm and includes grassroots politics in the streets, urban neighbourhoods and rural villages through political education in popular academies, radical democratic assemblies and consciousness-raising initiatives. These include large-scale grassroots campaigns against rape culture, patriarchal notions of honour, child marriage, and domestic violence and have historically had a defining impact on the legal political struggle. Streets, barricades, universities, workplaces, and villages are all sites in which organized Kurdish communities, together with democratic-leftist and minoritized groups, mobilize against state violence and repression and offer alternative political horizons. This is at once a struggle for autonomy as it is one for peace, democratization, and the solidarity of peoples.

Just as in all other spheres of the movement, Kurdish women in the realm of conventional legal politics are seen as 'natural members of the women's movement', accountable to women's structures they are affiliated with. Their engagement in politics has a dual mission: to help build up the autonomous women's system in society and to transform the male-dominated character of traditional politics. Elected women are usually pre-selected by large umbrella structures of the women's movement in the respective constituency to represent women's collective interests. Women's politics is therefore not about the mere inclusion of individual women into spheres of power, but an organizational and ideological front to dismantle the monopoly of statist, patriarchal, and bureaucratic notions of politics.

The book *The Purple Colour of Kurdish Politics*, published in 2018 in the Turkish language from prison, features essays written by incarcerated women politicians. Through their life stories, the women connect their individual struggles against tradition and sexism to collective women's struggles against patriarchy in the family and the party and the wider struggle against state power. Gültan Kışanak, a former MP and later co-mayor of Amed metropolitan municipality, who edited the book in jail, writes that an autonomous women's approach to politics cannot divide sites and methods of struggle from each other; questions of representation, mobilization, policy, leadership, and organization are dynamically interlinked. In her words: 'Women's willpower can be expressed through women's organization; representation is the reflection of this willpower' (Kışanak 2018).

TRANSFORMING THE PARTY, RETHINKING POLITICS

Today's Peoples' Democratic Party (HDP), which secured more than 90 per cent of votes in numerous cities and towns in different elections since its first emergence, is a continuation of a decades-old trajectory of the Kurdish people's legal political struggle vis-à-vis the Turkish state. The HDP frequently presents itself as a 'third way' in a polarized country dominated by two powerful political state projects – the elitist militarist and chauvinist nationalism of the Kemalists around the Republican People's Party (CHP) and the conservative, populist, and neoliberal Islamism represented by the Justice and Development Party (AKP), both of which frequently ally themselves with the proto-fascist Nationalist Movement Party (MHP). The emergence of new parties in recent years, most notably the İYİ Parti (Good Party), led by Meral Akşener, is seen as just another incarnation or shade in the familiar spectrum of Turkish nationalism.

In the period after the infamous 12 September 1980 coup d'état, the first successful Kurdish entrance into the legal political realm in the 1990s came several years into the guerrilla war and was over time accompanied by a wider civil society effort; trade unions, human rights associations, press, and student activities to demand justice and accountability for village destructions, war crimes, corruption, and enforced disappearances. In the 1990s, the first forms of women's collective action often led to mass arrest. Early debates around undoing men as a reference point and developing autonomous women's concepts, ethics, and aesthetics in politics often mirrored the developments in the guerrilla sphere.

In-depth research by Handan Çağlayan (2007, 2013) shows that a commitment to specific women's issues in the realm of electoral politics only occurred from the mid-1990s onward with the formation of the People's Democracy Party (HADEP). The creation of women's commissions in districts and towns, which held community gatherings and engaged in door-to-door mobilization efforts, meant that much of the women's work was more powerful on the local level than at the party centre. In 1997, a central women's commission was formed by women in the party assembly. A women's quota (>25 per cent) for elections and administrative positions was first formalized in the HADEP congress in 2000, shortly after a new law allowed political parties to found youth and women's branches. Under the Democratic People's Party (DEHAP), established in 2003 after HADEP's ban, the quota rose to 35 per cent. In the mid-2000s, it reached 40 per cent with the later formed Democratic Society Party (DTP), which also introduced the co-presidency principle. Over time, in addition to the establishment of women's separate and autonomous organizing in the party programmes, allocated women's budgets and women's electoral commissions were created. Furthermore, women set criteria to the party, such as zero tolerance for gender-based violence and abuse. Today, parties in this tradition operate on the principle of 'equal participation, equal representation', aiming to achieve parity at all levels of the party. The co-chair system is implemented at all levels at the party and in municipalities.

Party programmes increasingly adopted equality formally over time, but women carried the burden of the fight. For example, the initial lack of a separate budget for women's efforts often put women in a position in which they had to justify funding their activities to the men. In an essay written from prison, former co-mayor of Dêrsim, Nurhayat Altun, wrote that running men in 'winnable' places and women in 'unwinnable' places used to be an 'unwritten rule' in the party (Altun in Kişanak 2018). This made women visible during election campaigns, but they were likely to lose. Women were also held to higher standards and subject to harsher criticism than their male counterparts. As electoral losses were blamed on female candidates, women often avoided running for risky seats. Moreover, the 10 per cent general elections threshold, one of the highest worldwide, posed a structural barrier that undermined the effort to get women elected. Although Altun received 76 per cent of the votes in Batman province in the 2002 general elections, the party's failure to pass the nationwide threshold meant that men from conservative parties won seats from Batman province with far fewer votes. DEHAP's electoral failure that year became an occasion to rethink conventional methods of political participation.

The new paradigm expanded the movement's notion of the political, turning the women's movement into a vibrant political actor. The first half of the 2000s saw a growth of Kurdish women's research centres, associations, and educational institutions. The Democratic Free Women's Movement (DÖKH) formed in 2003 as an umbrella of the women's struggle in Bakur. Its horizontal organization and decentralized leadership, as well as its self-definition as a 'movement' rather than organization, gave it a flexible and spontaneous mode of action, which mattered especially on the local level. DÖKH – organizationally as well as through its individual activists – was always in direct relationship with the respective political party at any given time. Soon, the Democratic Peoples' Movement (DTH) was created as a joint effort of political parties and groups, social movements, civil society organizations, and intellectuals to reflect the new, pluralistic understanding of politics and democracy. Out of this progressive coalition, the Democratic Society Party (DTP) was formed. Born out of the new paradigm, the DTP embarked on the first exercises in implementing Öcalan's new proposals. Women convened ahead of the DTP's foundation and decided on the implementation of co-presidency, the 40 per cent gender quota and the restructuring of the women's wings into a women's assembly. According to activists involved in that period, although quota and autonomous organization were generally accepted in the party, co-presidency became a subject of debate. Nonetheless, together with the 40 per cent quota, it was included in the party constitution, and the ban on polygamy was formulated as a principle for party members. In the end, eight out of the party's 22 elected representatives in the 2007 general elections were women (out of 50 in the whole country). Sebahat Tuncel for example was elected as an MP for the third district of Istanbul, following an election campaign led from prison and with the joint efforts of the Kurdish women's movement and feminist struggles in western Turkey.[5] By the second half of the 2000s, the women's assembly was deciding on the female co-presidents and candidates for all elections. The Democratic Society Congress

(Turkish: DTK/Kurdish: KCD) was formed in 2007 on Öcalan's suggestion to counter the state's hegemony in the public realm. It assembles political parties, the women's and youth movements, civil society organizations, trade unions, and faith communities under one umbrella. The women's movement is an active unit of the DTK/KCD and works with the women's departments that were set up in some of the Kurdish municipalities. This meant that the women's movement's sanctions policies towards violent men in the struggle were usually backed by the assembly, party, and municipality.

This vibrant period, which saw a rise of the radical municipal agendas of self-organized institutions, was disrupted by the mass wave of arrests in 2009. The grassroots institutions that had been built all over the Kurdish regions were criminalized as being affiliated with the KCK and its 'separatist' agenda. An estimated 10,000 activists, including elected officials, were imprisoned. Despite the repression, hundreds of delegates gathered in Amed when DTP co-president Aysel Tuğluk announced the 'Call for Democratic Autonomy' in 2011, weeks after general elections. After DTP's forced closure, the Peace and Democracy Party (BDP) was formed in the intensified war period and worked to unify with progressive forces in the rest of Turkey. It spearheaded a broad left alliance, the Labour, Democracy, and Freedom Block, and secured 30 seats (11 women) in the 2011 general elections. The Peoples' Democratic Congress (HDK) was founded in the same year as a 'common struggle' umbrella for progressive, anti-capitalist, democratic, and minority sections of society in the form of confederated assembly structures.[6] The move away from 'people' to 'peoples' reflected the movement's shift in conceptualizing constituencies. While part of the Turkey-wide HDK, the Democratic Society Congress DTK/KCD, is primarily focused on Bakur. Following a consultation process, the Peoples' Democratic Party (HDP) held its first extraordinary general assembly to kickstart as a coalition of leftist, progressive movements, parties, and struggles. The BDP later restructured itself into the Democratic Regions Party (DBP) to focus on implementing democratic autonomy in Bakur. It delegates its stakes in Turkey-wide politics to the HDP as its sibling party. In 2015, the HDP entered parliament as the first party from the Kurdish tradition to have passed the 10 per cent threshold without running with independent candidates, causing the AKP to lose its majority for the first time. Out of 80 elected MPs, 32 were women (40 per cent).[7]

The HDP claims to represent the 'democratic nation' line against the 'one flag, one nation, one language' policies of the Turkish state. In its programme, it refers to the multicultural make-up of the country and claims to defend the historically oppressed and otherwise excluded. Strategically acting on behalf of the 'othered' in society, such as women, workers, oppressed peoples, religious minorities, migrants, refugees and IDPs, youth, and the LGBTQI+ community, at the same time as presenting a bridge between the militant PKK and civilian society, the HDP established functioning connections across different realms of politics. The centrality of organized struggle inside as well as outside of parliament and municipalities on behalf of all identities in Turkey is regarded as the differentiating factor that makes the HDP not only a party, but also a social movement. The HDP's desire to be as inclusive of different groups as possible meant accommodating different political cultures. There were concerns among Kurds when it came to trusting the new individuals and groups joining from western Turkey. In addition, whether progressive or conservative, most groups did not have a history of autonomous women's politics. As such, the party had to find a balance between including new societal sections and insisting on women's autonomy and equal representation and participation.

WOMEN'S LEADERSHIP IS ABOUT SOLIDARITY

To Edibe Şahin, the question 'How can all women – not just a select few – participate in political life?' became a central question in her life. An Alevi-Kurdish woman from Dêrsim, Edibe is one of the women who led the early grassroots women's work in the late 1990s, mainly among forcibly displaced Kurds in Istanbul. In 2009, she succeeded DTP's Songül Erol Abdil as the mayor of Dêrsim. Abdil had been the only woman to be the mayor of a province in Turkey. Building on her predecessor's work, Edibe helped develop the city in cooperation with the women's movement, the Mesopotamia Ecology Movement, and trade unions. Under her leadership, the statue of Seyit Riza, the executed leader of the 1937/8 Uprising, was erected in Dêrsim. She actively encouraged speaking to the endangered Kirmanckî (Zazakî) in the municipality.[8]

In our interview in early 2015, Edibe told me that her experiences as a socialist Alevi-Kurdish woman developed her understanding that life does not have to be as it is, but also that change cannot be expected to come about only 'after the revolution', as was strongly asserted by many left groups at the time. During the 1980 coup, Edibe was subjected to torture for weeks in detention. Narrating her journey from a young political activist during the military regime, to one of the first Kurdish women to be elected as mayors, while being a mother, she constantly drew parallels between her personal history, political developments and the increasing consciousness among Kurdish women about different forms of oppression.

How do we want to live? What kind of organization of life do we envision? Kurdish self-governance will not automatically lead to social change. As history shows, it is very well possible to reproduce the same oppressive system even while claiming to act in the name of the proletariat, the oppressed masses. We must rethink the very methods we use in our self-governance.

175

The women's struggle requires courage because it cannot succeed without resistance. Of course, in a patriarchal society, this means a major break with tradition and convention. It means burning bridges. Working for change is a struggle against dogmatism at the same time – a struggle against the dogma that everything will always remain as it is. Through struggle, even notions of time and space can radically change. We reject dogmatism, but we are protective of our principles. After all, often, our principles, our stance is the only way we can defend ourselves. Such is the Kurdish people's struggle, which started with the assertion 'we exist', before it took on more concrete expressions in all spheres of life.

In her prison essay, former HDP co-president Figen Yüksekdağ argues that when elected women inherit offices that other women had previously collectively struggled for, leadership is conceived of as following a path of resistance, rather than an opportunity to occupy a position of power.[9] Seen in this light, for women, leadership becomes a site of struggle against male domination and simultaneously an occasion to develop new forms of administration by building on earlier collective labour and effort.

The reproductive nature of a form of leadership based on women's solidarity is illustrated in the case of the poor Bağlar district of Amed. Under Yurdusev Özsökmenler, who became the first female mayor of Bağlar in 2004, Gültan Kışanak and Çağlar Demirel, both of whom later became both MPs and mayors at later times, were actively engaged in administering the new autonomous women's policies in the district. While Kışanak coordinated Bağlar's women's projects, including women's shelters, cultural projects, and educational work, Demirel was in charge of the Kardelen Women's House. Demirel became mayor of Dêrîk district of Mêrdîn in 2009, and initiated similar projects based on the experiences in Bağlar. Zeynep Sipçik, a young sociologist, was coordinating the activities of Peljîn Women's House in Dêrîk, before becoming co-mayor of Kerboran (Dargeçit) district of Mêrdîn. Kışanak first served as an MP before taking up the role of co-mayor of the Metropolitan Municipality of Amed. During her time as the co-mayor of Amed, the women's movement, of which she has been a part for many decades, was able to implement a variety of projects for women's employment, cultural activities, ecological initiatives, and anti-violence works.

Recognizing such trajectories is also a matter for the historical record. For example, international media outlets reported about Fatih Mehmet Maçoğlu of the Turkey Communist Party as 'Turkey's first communist mayor' first of Dêrsim's Ovacik district and then of Dêrsim province. Some attribute his victory to the HDP's shortcomings in the province, but singling him out as a revolutionary mayor erases the labour of Songül Erol Abdil, Edibe Şahin, and

Nurhayat Altun, three socialist Alevi-Kurdish women, who preceded him, built on each other's legacy amid state violence and criminalization, and were each sentenced to years in prison afterwards.

WOMEN'S UNITY AGAINST ERDOĞAN'S ONE-MAN RULE

The question is: who will win, Erdoğan's 'bear three children' policy or our women's liberation project? – Çağlar Demirel, Amed, 2015

The Justice and Development Party (AKP), led by Recep Tayyip Erdoğan, rose to power in a landslide victory in 2002, at a time in which anti-US sentiments were roaring in the Middle East region and beyond, in the context of the wars in Iraq and Afghanistan. Much to the dismay of the traditional Kemalist elites, the AKP agenda seemed to appeal to both the West (especially through EU accession efforts) as well as the East, the Islamicate world in particular. The AKP came to rise with the support of the secretive, but remarkably well-organized and internationally influential movement around the religious preacher and cleric Fethullah Gülen, who has been living in exile in the US since 1999.

Under Erdoğan's conservative and neoliberal rule (first as prime minister and afterwards as president), with the support of Gülenists, who had infiltrated the organs of the republic, Turkey saw an unprecedented series of socio-economic reforms and a major restructuring of the state and military apparatus. His focus on strengthening Turkey's economy through strategic investment in development uplifted large sections of society and created jobs and infrastructure in less developed parts of the country. His early statements signalled equality for all citizens of the country and promised to solve the Kurdish question democratically. Such pronouncements, along with his establishment of a Kurdish-language service of the state broadcast TRT, previously unheard of, gained him vital Kurdish votes. The later failed 'Oslo process' in 2009 was a first, secret attempt to initiate negotiations between the Turkish state and the PKK.

The rise of the AKP came at the same time as the Kurdistan freedom movement began articulating its new vision for the Middle East. Around that time, the Obama-led US was desperate to undo the damage caused to its image during the Bush era, while continuing its strategic military and economic interests in the region. In this time, NATO member Turkey began to be portrayed as a model example for a 'moderate Islamic' democracy: open-market oriented and (apart from occasional, symbolic condemnations) not hostile to Israel. While much of the first decade was marked by adherence to standards to join the EU, the AKP took a populist, ultra-nationalist and more explicitly Islamist turn in its third electoral period in the early 2010s. Soon, Turkey's 'Zero Problems with Neighbours' policy faded into oblivion.[10] The government's behaviour in the context of the emergence of the Arab Spring and the related Rojava Revolution, the beginning of the negotiation talks with the PKK, and the Gezi Park protests, all revealed different aspects of the AKP's increasingly militaristic, authoritarian and Islamist domestic and regional policies. As the war re-escalated in the early 2010s, Draconian anti-terror laws were broadly applied to protesters and activists. The Kurdish movement often likened the Turkish state's 'annihilation concept' to the 'Tamil solution' – a large-scale military plan leading to thousands of preventable deaths. As such, in the eyes of many oppositions, the AKP did not really 'shift' in the 2010s; rather, its mask fell off.

＊　＊　＊

Despite its secularist founding myth, the Turkish state never treated all religions equally. Turkish nationalism always upheld Sunni Islam, but regulated religious practice in public. The AKP's conservative, religious project, however, unveiled, deepened, and institutionalized this relationship. In marrying religion and nationalism, it reconfigured everyday life in the republic in many gendered ways. The lifting of the long-standing ban on the headscarf in the public sector caused polarizing debates about the principles of the republic, but allowed a great number of religious women to assume roles and jobs they had previously been excluded from. At the same time, the government propagated conservative gender roles and idealized the patriarchal family model. In an attempt to move away from Kemalist state feminism, Erdoğan frequently voiced that women and men have fundamentally different roles to play in society because of inherently different qualities. He repeatedly encouraged women to give birth to 'at least three children' and incentivized early marriage as a form of patriotic duty. Over the years, in addition to vilifying feminist and queer struggles (and banning and attacking protests), high-ranking members of the party, including ministers, repeatedly caused outrage with sexist statements that suggested 'proper' women should primarily concern themselves with being good mothers to many children, discouraging women from pursuing careers and joining the workforce. Pro-government academics, journalists, religious scholars, and state-affiliated NGOs regularly produce often pseudo-scientific content to promote conservative gender roles. Among the many scandals of the AKP's rule are several attempts at introducing versions of a bill that would give suspended sentences to inmates convicted of child sex offences if they marry the victim. The bill sparked outrage among women's rights groups that pointed out that it normalized rape, child abuse, and forced marriages. Reports show that violence against women, including feminicides, massively increased during the AKP's rule. The AKP's rhetoric is also explicitly homophobic and transphobic in a society in which discrimination and violence against queer people is already commonplace. LGBTQI+ individuals and groups in Turkey are framed as 'sick' people who want to impose Western lifestyles and as a conspiratorial attack on morality and the traditional family. The first organized LGBTQI+ organizations emerged in the 1990s in Turkey and historically took proactive political positions on issues like the oppression of the Kurds.[11] The HDP is often attacked for its stated commitment to struggle against violence and discrimination experienced by the LGBTQI+ community.[12]

The AKP's ultra-patriarchal regime became an occasion for women's and queer movements in the country to unite forces. Historically, the relationship between such struggles in the country had been shaped by tension and conflict. Existing cooperation revolved around state violence, human rights abuses, war crimes, forced displacement, and labour rights. A qualitative change in this relationship at the turn of the millennium reflects developments within the Kurdish women's movement. Rallying around the cause of women's liberation moved the movement's demands beyond things directly related to Kurdistan. The emergence of the HDP and the movement's local politics empowered independent struggles across the country to meet on joint platforms, initiate common campaigns, and rally behind causes in a time of hope and alliance-building in the context of the peace process initiated in 2013.[13]

The HDP's elected women politicians are connected to the women's struggle through its Women's Assembly, the umbrella women's movement in Bakur (Free Women's Movement TJA, formerly Free Women's Congress KJA), as well as other grassroots women's organizations and feminist institutions and platforms across Turkey. The Women's Assembly is a network of local women's assemblies, actively engaged in building relations with women's organizations in other parts of Kurdistan and around the world. The assembly references the radical democratic, ecological, and women's liberationist paradigm and views all historic women's struggles, including the women's revolution of Rojava, as part of its heritage. To 'share the parliamentary seat' with the women's struggle, in the words of activist, former MP, and current political prisoner Selma Irmak,[14] the women's group established by HDP members of parliament invited women's struggles and organizations, including trade unions, human rights activists, lawyers, writers, as well as delegates of young women, Peace Mothers, and different feminist initiatives. Consulting these groups was important to root the party's policies in actual women's movements.

Çağlar Demirel (reintroduced again in the next section), a long-time activist of the women's movement in Bakur, served as mayor of the Dêrîk district of Mêrdîn before being imprisoned. She was later elected as an MP before being imprisoned again. In our interview in 2015, which took place shortly after DÖKH was dismantled by the women's movement to found the Free Women's Congress (KJA), she explained:

Previously, DÖKH, as an umbrella organization, encompassed the academy, peace activists and political parties. With DÖKH and the women's wings in the political party, we laid the foundations towards a system of autonomous women's struggle. Holding the first Middle East Women's Conference, bringing women from all four parts of Kurdistan together, finding common struggle ground with women's organizations in Turkey – all of these were important milestones on our way. With the formation of KJA, we grew into a congress that can unite women's struggles in northern Kurdistan and Turkey and actively struggle alongside women's movements around the world.

Women were present in the negotiation process between the Turkish state and Abdullah Öcalan from the beginning. During the meetings with the HDP delegation at Imralı Prison, Öcalan proposed that it is not enough for individual women to participate in the delegation; rather, the women's movement should have an organized representation in the process. Following the formation of KJA in January 2015 in Amed, Ceylan Bağrıyanık became the representative of the organized collective political will of the women's movement in the Imralı delegation. As a result of these peace efforts, the Dolmabahçe Agreement,

Figure 12   KJA-led 8 March International Women's Day celebration in Amed. The banner says: 'The life that gains meaning with the struggle of Sakine (Cansız), Arîn (Mîrkan), and Kader (Ortakaya) will be liberated with women's organizedness'. Amed. March 2015.

published as a memorandum of understanding between the conflict parties, included guarantees for women's participation in life as a condition for meaningful peace and justice.

From 2013 onward, initiatives such as the Women's Platform for Peace or the Women's Freedom Assembly monitored the negotiation process from feminist perspectives. Some of these efforts preceded 2013, but gained traction with women's participation in the peace process. Drawing on the experiences of women in peace processes around the world, committees were formed to ensure that truth-seeking and reconciliation consider the gendered violence experienced by women over the course of decades of war.[15] Nazan Üstündağ (2020), who took part in these efforts, writes that the boundaries between the legal and illegal were blurred in this liminal time: 'Taboo and fetishized words and means, such as PKK, Öcalan, communalism, radical democracy, democratic autonomy, confederalism, people's tribunal and justice, communal self-defence, and international solidarity, entered our lived world.' The municipalities in Kurdistan benefited from broad feminist insights and in turn strengthened the hand of grassroots women's campaigns. These joint actions and projects became strategic platforms of struggle and organization beyond the peace process.

FEMINIZING THE MUNICIPALITY

I knew what it would mean for a woman like me to enter public life. I was scared I would get rejected, I know Kocaköy very well. But due to the Kurdish movement's support, I wasn't. In fact, people take me very seriously when I speak about violence. They know that I mean what I say. My words come from experience and that is why many women relate to them. When I was first elected, the media presented it as though I were the first woman to have experienced violence. I did not fall from the sky, there are thousands of women like me, but we are too ashamed to speak publicly about violence in our community. When I speak about my experience with violence, I don't talk about myself only. Mine is the story of thousands of women.

Bêrîvan Elif Kılıç, owner of the above words, had been elected as the co-mayor of Amed's Kocaköy district one year before I met her in 2015. A mother of two and in her mid-30s at the time, Bêrîvan's story had been covered by national and international newspapers, often with sensationalist headlines: 'from child bride to mayor'. Bêrîvan, who had been married as a teenager against her will, was outspoken about her abusive marriage. After an arduous process of getting divorced, she worked as a cleaner and hair stylist, and eventually managed to open her own small business, against everyone's expectations. Bêrîvan had never considered entering political life, but was moved by the Kurdish women's movement, which she followed from her TV screen. She said that she was 'not even allowed to look out the window for 14 years'. Upon joining the BDP, she was encouraged to take up political responsibilities. In addition to her municipal duties, she was dealing with her son's chronic health problems while remotely studying for a high school diploma.

At the time of my interview with Bêrîvan, the feminicide of 19-year-old student Özgecan Aslan in Mersin had just caused another wave of outcry across Turkey and was very much on the agenda of women in Amed. On her way home, Özgecan was brutally murdered by a minibus driver, who attempted to rape her and who cut off her hands and set her dead body on fire with the help of his father and a friend. Throughout our interview, Bêrîvan, who mourned the young woman, drew parallels between the Turkish state and her ex-husband. Despite her divorce, he was able to continue harassing her even after she was elected, in Bêrîvan's view, because he knew that the government and its justice system protect abusive men.

> In the past, if anything had happened to me, nobody would have heard, but now, because of the Kurdish women's movement, I have thousands of women behind me. No matter what happens to one of us, we will all rally to protect each other. I always say that I used to struggle alone but now I have thousands of women on my side. Before taking up office, I saw myself as Bêrîvan, who experienced violence. But then I became Bêrîvan, a representative for thousands of women who experience violence.
>
> I am Bêrîvan, not someone's wife. And that is exactly what most of society cannot handle: that I am *Bêrîvan*, that Bêrîvan *can*, by *herself*, and *not* as someone's lover, sister, or mother. This is our struggle: to help women develop their *own* identity, independent from male systems.

Bêrîvan, a practising Muslim, was particularly moved by the amount of men who would consult her opinion and send her messages of support and respect. Sharing powerful stories of interactions with women, who started to get politically engaged, Bêrîvan repeatedly stressed that she wants women, who can relate to her, to view her appointment as an encouragement to get organized. She wanted them to think 'If Bêrîvan can do it, so can I'.

> I only want to stay in politics for one period. In my time, I will open some parks, implement some projects, start some initiatives, but my main aim is to create more Bêrîvans as I go. When I leave office, the next woman can see what I missed and come up with new ideas. In my short time, I have seen the rise in our numbers at gatherings. Change is happening. A person, who sits in Ankara cannot understand our situation here. Likewise, an elite woman on

a high government salary cannot enter the life of women like me in Kocaköy. We understand ourselves the best, so we should be the ones to take charge of our lives.

Fifteen years before Bêrîvan's election, Kurdish women were first elected as mayors in 1999, when HADEP managed to win more than three dozen municipalities in local elections. Cihan Sincar (Qoser, Mêrdîn; Turkish: Kızıltepe, Mardin), Mukaddes Kubilay (Bazîd, Agirî; Turkish: Doğubeyazıt, Ağrı), and Ayşe Karadağ (Dêrîk, Mêrdîn; Turkish: Derik, Mardin) were among 20 women (out of more than 3,000 people in total) in all of Turkey to be elected as mayors. In 2004, HADEP's successor party DEHAP, which had formed a coalition with other socialist parties, elected nine women for 56 municipalities. Women of DEHAP made up half of all elected female mayors that year, partly also due to a rise in discussions on autonomous women's approaches to politics. The municipalities won by women constituted 16 per cent of the party's overall achievement; compared to a national average of 0.56 per cent. The 2009 local elections raised the number of Kurdish women mayors to 14. Following a women's conference, the co-chairing principle was for the first time applied in about one hundred municipalities in Kurdistan in 2014, with exceptions in a few places. While the change in the political parties' law had enabled a formal application of co-leadership, this did not apply to the municipalities. The de facto application meant that only one of the co-mayors was officially entitled to the office and its salary. In discussions on the implementation of the system, it was decided that the co-mayors must split all responsibilities and privileges of their office, including their salary. The majority of candidates put on the polls were men, but thanks to the co-chairing principle, the number of women rose to more than a hundred that year. According to KA.DER, an association for the support of women's candidates, only 7.89 per cent of all mayoral candidates in the local elections of 2019 were women. Twenty-four out of the 'officially elected' 45 women were from the HDP.[16] Three of the five women in the country who won provincial municipalities were from the HDP. These official numbers exclude the 'unofficial' co-mayors of the HDP. Having won 54 municipalities meant 54 women co-mayors in the Kurdish regions, which is higher than the number of officially elected women across the country. The municipal agenda presented by the women's assembly ahead of the 2019 local elections stressed its will to 'overcome the extortive, monopolistic, sectarian, and male dominated style of politics and to democratize politics' via anti-violence and anti-sexism campaigns, economic opportunities through cooperatives and local production to counter seasonal work dependency, investment in arts, culture and sporting activities for women, ecological initiatives, and accessibility of services for women with disabilities.

One striking theme in the writings of Kurdish women who served as both mayors and MPs in Turkey is the idea that men seem to have been more likely to accept women in parliament, while being reluctant to 'hand over' municipal administration to them. Parliament seems to have been perceived as more suitable to women, compared to jobs that are traditionally seen as men's work: administration, city planning, finance, construction, etc. The representative character of parliamentary politics offers a site of expressing one's stance vis-à-vis the state. Local politics, however, demand implementation of one's politics in action. Before 2014, most of the municipalities had never seen women in leadership positions and, in fact, some of them did not have female employees. For some of the municipalities, it was also the first time that a political party from the Kurdish movement's tradition was taking charge.

Testimonies of Kurdish women who served in local politics describe how men often confidently speak on behalf of 'the people', when arguing that 'society' is 'not ready' for some of the policies proposed by the women's movement. Yet, because of their grassroots work, activism-driven research and coordination with social struggles and movements, women often had a much less abstract idea of 'the people'. Through consultations in the neighbourhoods, they were able to demonstrate that many women favour an end to gender-based discrimination, child marriage, bride exchange, polygamy, and bride price. Women also demanded work, political participation, and justice for violence. First activities of women mayors included forming women's directorates or departments to develop women's liberationist perspectives on local governance, conducting surveys on gender-specific issues and needs, hiring women, and allocating budgets for social projects.

In an essay written from prison, Mukaddes Kubilay, who became one of the first Kurdish women mayors in 1999, claims that women's meetings often turned into mass gatherings in which women voiced their problems and demands for the first time openly.[17] At the time, women in her constituency in Dogubeyazit (Bazîd in Kurdish) did not have spaces to socialize outside of each other's homes, so a social centre was opened to meet this need. The demand to actively use the Kurdish language in public was another specific request of women, who, due to language barriers, often faced more obstacles than men when trying to access services. Although male colleagues seem to have been doubtful of her ability to win and succeed in office, she won a second time in 2004 after running against eight other male competitors in her party during the race for candidacy.

The lack of affiliated MPs as a result of the failure to pass the 10 per cent threshold in the 2002 general elections meant that at the time local politics had to represent the party's general politics as well. In the municipalities held by the party, equality commissions were formed early on. In addition to training municipal personnel on issues around sexism and violence against women,

Leyla Güven, who became mayor of Kücükdikilli district of Adana in 2004, introduced a set of sanctions on municipal council workers engaging in practices such as polygamy and domestic violence.[18] Together with civil society actors, including trade unions and women's organizations, she developed a social contract for the municipality. Güven's policies helped pave the way to some of the radical policies that would characterize the women's approach to municipalism in later years in a more institutional manner.

In an essay written during her imprisonment in 2018, Güven describes how other women mayors from Turkey were invited to Kurdistan to share with them their projects and perspectives. The cooperation between women-held municipalities in Kurdistan and women's civil society organizations from across Turkey further helped overcome some of the past obstacles for a common women's struggle. Güven credits the women-led character of her campaign for her victory (47.1 per cent) in Wêranşar, Riha (Viranşehir, Urfa) during the 2009 local elections against her AKP rival, who appears to have incited misogynistic sentiments among the tribes and village guards against her.[19]

Over time, the autonomous women's policies that were institutionalized and implemented in the political party and then in the municipalities spread to other spheres of public life. Similarly, approaches to radical democracy and ecology sparked new collaborations in civil society. Municipalities in Kurdistan commissioned research projects by sociologists, health workers, and environmental engineers. Academics, trade unions, and civil society organizations were actively engaged in developing perspectives and projects to help solve the socio-economic and infrastructural issues at the local level.[20]

One striking, but short-lived example of the popular local governance approach was exemplified by Diba Keskin, former co-mayor of the impoverished Erdîş (Erciş) district of Wan (Van). She held consultations in Kurdish and Turkish with local women regarding projects to further education, cultural activities, and infrastructural works in the neglected area. In an essay written from prison, she described arguing with examples of female leadership from the Holy Qur'an when developing women's projects.[21] Self-identifying as a conservative, practising Muslim, with experience in the movement's Democratic Islam Congress and the HDP's faith commission, Keskin's appointment constituted a grounded counterforce to the AKP's weaponization of Islam.

> People have been forced to get used to only one mode of politics: power-driven, masculine, nationalist, and centralist. Decisions taken in the municipalities can be overridden by orders from Ankara. To do politics differently, we must break with this sexist style and develop a political approach based on sharing, mutuality, and autonomy. Rather than viewing our municipal politics and its mechanisms and principles in a technical, bureaucratic sense, we approach

them politically and philosophically. Their purpose is social change and transformation, starting from the local and extrapolating from there. – Çağlar Demirel, Amed, 2015

Before her election as mayor of Dêrîk district of Mêrdîn in 2009, Çağlar Demirel was actively engaged in a variety of women's initiatives including anti-violence campaigns and autonomous cooperatives. As a trained nurse, she was offering education for municipalities on sexual health, gender-based violence, and women's bodily self-determination, while joining campaigns against feminicide and rape culture led by the women's platform in Amed. She co-founded the women's centre Kardelen in the poverty-stricken Bağlar district of Amed, which alongside counselling, offered consciousness-raising sessions, university preparation support, vocational training, music lessons, and seminars on sexism and gender-based violence. The centre and its workers frequently became targets of threats and violence by men.

Less than three years into her work in Dêrîk, she was jailed in 2011, in the mass arrest wave that had started against Kurdish political activists in 2009. The main charges pressed against her related to her engagement in the women's struggle. She was released in the summer of 2014, only a few months before our meeting. At the time of our interview in Sur district, where she grew up, she was working in the Union of Democratic Local Administrations, monitoring the implementation of the autonomous women's policies.

The interconnectedness of concepts such as democratic modernity, democratic autonomy, and democratic nation is perhaps expressed more concretely in municipal politics than in other spheres of the struggle. The obstacles created by male-domination in our own community to women's self-organization resemble the approaches of the state towards the Kurds. In this sense, our struggle is not only against the state's nationalist and authoritarian policies, but also an effort to change and transform the men right next to us.

Despite their egalitarian aspirations, HDP-held municipalities have experienced issues around inefficiency, corruption, and favouritism, not all of which can be blamed on the state. In Çağlar's eyes, a municipal approach that is untouched by women's hands and minds is prone to reproduce the administrative style and power structures of the state. She gave the example of local efforts to change the names of places to their original Kurdish names. Communities saw the arbitrary nature of the state's refusal to agree even to small changes (for instance, by arguing that certain letters do not exist in the Turkish alphabet) on one hand, and the municipality's insistence to struggle for these changes on behalf of its constituents on the other hand. The experience of local governance revealed that the idea that 'society would not accept change' was a self-fulfilling prophecy.

Ideologies will resonate in society, if they affect life itself. Anything we do happens through consultation, coordination, and cooperation with society. We don't just impose centrally taken decisions like the state.

Society accepted co-mayors faster than the state. Take co-chairing as an example: the state does not recognize co-chairing, because it does not recognize women to begin with. Instead, it tells women not only to give birth to children but also how many. It restricts access to abortion and normalizes harassment and rape by blaming these on women. It's this sort of understanding that we struggle against, in an environment in which five or six women are murdered every day, in a country where thousands of women are raped every day.

In the past, people were suspicious of women's ability to lead, but in practice they eventually felt affection for the female mayors. Egotism, self-interest, these things are much less pronounced among women. Once people saw that women can and that they actually can better, they did not want to give up on women anymore. Trust was gained through a beautiful style of women's politics that impact people's lives concretely. Now, in places where fifteen years ago, people insisted that women could never enter public life due to tribal power structures, women co-mayors are greatly respected and celebrated. It's a matter of belief that change is possible through organization.

CO-CHAIRING MEANS DISRUPTING POWER

Co-presidency presents a platform through which women, in an otherwise patriarchal system, say: 'I, too, am here. I, too, am a part of life and therefore have the right to take decisions.' – Çağlar Demirel, Amed, 2015

The co-chair system is one out of multiple practices of the Kurdistan freedom movement to secure women's equal representation and participation in political life. In the co-chair or co-presidency system (*hevserokatî*), one woman and one man are elected to co-lead any given structure jointly and equally. While everyone gets to elect the male co-chair, only women can vote for the woman. Co-chairing was first applied in the mid-2000s, for the first time in Bakur, in the DTP co-leadership of Aysel Tuğluk and Ahmet Türk. Today, it exists in almost all sites of the Kurdistan freedom movement, from urban community centres in Europe to small village communes in Rojava to the leadership of the KCK.[22]

While symbolically representing equality, co-chairing is framed as an anti-authoritarian pedagogical method for internal democratization, a way for women and men 'to learn how to lead together'. Potential conflict is implied in the form: two chairs mean two perspectives. This structurally pushes leadership towards consensus-oriented decision-making. Activists often describe co-chairing as a concrete site of individually learning democracy in action, a practice that promotes a leadership style based on criticism/self-criticism, collectivism, transparency, accountability, and equal responsibility and burden-sharing. In an essay written from prison, former HDP co-president Figen Yüksekdağ said: 'Co-chairing is not intended to mirror already existing equality but rather represents an aspiration to bring equality into existence in all forms.'[23]

Co-chairing also offers a way to represent the women's struggle in an organized form. The female co-chairs are chosen by autonomous women's structures and are accountable to them. This is to ensure that they will represent the collective will, interest, and concerns of women rather than that of an individual person, who happens to be a woman. As such, the female co-chair, having been selected by a particular constituency for a particular mission, constitutes the more radical and strategic one of the two office-holders. Not only does representing a collective political identity hold her accountable to the women's movement, it also strengthens her hand in the struggle against the classical style of politics represented by her male counterpart. This is a form of disrupting the 'one-sided power of men'. In this sense, in the movement's discourse, co-chairing is understood as a philosophical concept of leadership and moral style of administration that aims to build freedom in the here and now. In ethnically or religiously diverse contexts, such as in Rojava's political systems, the movement usually takes care to have the co-chairs' identities reflect the demography.

Despite its apparent rigidity in conceiving of gender, co-chairing is often narrated as being oriented towards transformation. The principle draws on two binary social categories – woman and man – with the aim of turning a shared platform into a site of dismantling power relations and formations. In this sense, co-presidency helps unlearn the traditional gender roles generated under a patriarchal system; to undo the 'enslaved woman' and 'dominant man' to enable 'free individuals'. The mechanism embodies the movement's broader project of 'free co-life' (*hevjiyana azad*), in which gender roles will no longer serve as tools or occasions for exploitation and domination. Rather than signifying a status, title or role, the co-presidency institution becomes a social relation marked by a permanent struggle between two partners in arms.

Patriarchal dynamics certainly prevail among co-chairs, but the purpose and value of this power-sharing system has become more widely accepted in organized Kurdish society over time. When the movement first implemented co-chairing in its own structures, there was confusion among party members and supporters alike. Currently imprisoned Aysel Tuğluk, who had the privilege and burden of being the first co-president of a Kurdish political party, alongside Ahmet Türk, has an anecdote with a restaurant worker, who called her *'yenge president'* – *yenge* being the Turkish word for one's sister-in-law or uncle's wife.[24] Many of the women co-chairs and co-mayors of parties, cantons, or municipalities that I interviewed in Bakur and Rojava told me about their individual battles to get recognized by their counterparts, their constituents, and the media. When Turkish authorities first rejected the request to formalize the co-chair policy, some men in the party were ready to give up on something that seemed not only impractical and unrealistic, but also legally impossible. Women, however, argued that implementation did not need state approval. As such, struggling to get it recognized turned into a political statement. The media often referred to the 'unofficial' co-president as 'assistant' or 'deputy'. In response, men in the movement often insisted on clarifying who should be the 'formally' elected position-holder. Only after women's collective actions and their insistence on applying co-chairs in a de facto manner was co-chairing formalized through a change in the political parties' law. This did not apply to the co-mayor system, which nevertheless continued to be practised in the HDP-held municipalities. In the words of Bêrîvan Elif Kılıç, co-mayor of Amed's Kocaköy district at the time of our interview, the unrecognized status of the co-mayorship was an occasion to raise questions about legitimacy:

Look, I may not be formally recognized by the state but I walk around my streets and people call me their mayor. They come to me with their problems, they see me as their interlocutor, they ask me for help. What does this say about whose word is recognized by our people? Is it the state's – or mine?

Çağlar Demirel expressed it similarly:

It does not matter if co-presidency is recognized by the state system or not. We don't sit and wait for the state to acknowledge it. The state authorities struggle to understand why it's so crucial for us to sign our documents with two names. We struggled to implement co-presidency and we will struggle for its formal recognition, but regardless of the outcome, we will implement it.

* * *

When I met Bêrîvan again during the 8 March celebrations in 2015 in Amed, she was surrounded by crowds of women who wanted to take photos with her.

189

Affection and solidarity radiated from this sight of women, nearly all of whom had little children playing between their colourful traditional dresses.

That year, the World Women's March had kicked off in Kurdistan in response to Kurdish women's resistance against Daesh. In the week of 8 March International Women's Day, thousands of women joined the international feminist caravan that launched in Nisêbîn, at the border to Rojava. When participating in the activities from Nisêbîn to Mêrdîn to Amed, I saw Nisêbîn's co-mayor Sara Kaya tirelessly run around and organize with a heart-warming smile, indistinguishable from all the other activists involved in the powerful march. On the other side of the border, in Qamişlo, the women's movement in Rojava also held a massive rally, mirroring the activities in Nisêbîn. Under Kaya's leadership, a women-only market named *Jiyana bê sinor* ('Borderless life') was planned at the border to Syria by the municipality's women's assembly.[25] Its aim was to enable women experiencing economic problems and domestic violence to socialize and make a living by selling products from the new women's communal and cooperative economy projects. Under the motto 'Not mines, but roses – not death, but life', a women-led effort was supposed to create a park with white

Figure 13 The launch of the World Women's March of 2015, with feminist delegates from around the world. The march was launched in Nusaybin (Nisêbîn) and included a celebration at the nearby Turkish-Syrian border, which was greeted by a parallel celebration on the other side of the border, organized by the women's movement in Rojava. This was one of the first activities led by the Free Women's Congress KJA, newly founded at the time. Months later, the peace process collapsed and KJA was eventually banned. Some of the participants of this gathering later joined the armed struggle. Others, such as Sêvê Demir, one of the organizers of this event, were civilians who were murdered by the Turkish state, which razed entire Kurdish towns to the ground in the months to come. The co-mayor of the town, Sara Kaya, who actively organized these activities has been in prison since 2016. Nisêbîn. March 2015.

190

roses – a former trademark of the town – in the militarized border region. During the 8 March activities, tens of thousands of women were saluting each other across the border between the twin cities of Nisêbîn and Qamişlo, which was guarded by mines and Turkish soldiers in armoured vehicles. The chants of women from around the world temporarily rendered the male-drawn and male-guarded borders dividing Nisêbîn and Qamişlo meaningless. Later, in different times, the army destroyed Nisêbîn and bombed Qamişlo. Most of the women mentioned in this chapter are now imprisoned.

25

Başûr: 'Freedom is more than the absence of dictatorship'

> The liberation of Kurdistan cannot be expected to take place in separate stages, with freedom for one part at a time. Oppression and liberation in the parts of Kurdistan are always interlinked. One cannot be liberated at the expense of another. – Rojgar, PAJK administration, Xinerê, 2015

The world's first author and first poet known by name is Enheduanna, a Mesopotamian high priestess, who lived in the late third millennium BCE in modern day Iraq. More than 4,000 years later, colonialism, dictatorship, war, religious extremism, and occupation turned Enheduanna's country into one of the worst places to be a woman.

In the past, Iraq was considered one of the progressive Middle Eastern countries with regards to women's rights. In his short rule before his assassination by the 1963 Ba'ath Party coup, General Abd al-Karim Qassim appointed the first woman minister of Iraq, prohibited polygamy, issued equality in inheritance and raised the minimum marriage age. With its modernist outlook, the Ba'athist Iraqi regime was less conservative on women's rights than neighbouring countries at the time or the subsequent governments after the regime fell. However, the regime amended personal status regulations and reverted earlier progressive policies in its last two decades in power. In any case, gestures of modernization meant little for women subjected to genocide, political persecution, sexualized torture dungeons, and executions by the state. The decades-old brutal rule of Saddam Hussein targeted entire populations and ways of life with the purpose of annihilation. Priding itself on a pan-Arabist ideology, the Ba'ath Party used a forceful divide-and-rule policy to consolidate its power: while on one hand mobilizing nationalism and, to a lesser extent, sectarianism, the state on the other hand tried to co-opt all ethnic and religious groups into its system of governance by punishment and reward.

In 1987, a governmental decree signed by Saddam Hussein's cousin, Ali Hassan al-Majid 'Chemical Ali', who was made governor of the Kurdish areas to annihilate the rebellions, declared that 'the armed forces must kill any human being or animal present within these areas'. The so-called al-Anfal ('spoils of war') genocide campaign of the Ba'ath Party amounted to the killing of an estimated (up to) 180,000 Kurdish people through massacre, executions, village destructions, forced relocations, and abandonment in hostile conditions. The unspeakable chemical attack on Halabja in 1988 murdered at least 5,000 civilians, mostly women and children, within a few hours. The consequences of the campaign are multiple, including widespread health issues, and continue to affect livelihoods to this day. In her ethnography of mass atrocity under the Ba'athist regime, feminist Kurdish poet and academic Choman Hardi (2011) writes that 'the majority of the women who survived al-Anfal were farmers who worked in their own farms, orchards, and vineyards and tended to sheep, goats, cows, and poultry. Al-Anfal deprived them of their homes and their means of production.'

The situation of women in Başûr cannot be separated from the past episodes of large-scale political violence and mass displacement during the Saddam era on one hand, and the present situation of Iraq since 2003 between instability, ethnic and sectarian conflict, geopolitical upheaval, neoliberalization, and corruption on the other. Minoo Alinia (2013), another feminist scholar of gender-based violence in Kurdistan, describes how decades of nearly permanent war shaped a type of Kurdish masculinity that is inseparable from the violence around it: 'Even in times of conflict and war, the state, tribes, and the Kurdish leadership were in tacit agreement about the organization and maintenance of women's subordination.' State violence continued after the al-Anfal campaign had devastated entire livelihoods in Kurdistan, such as when in 1991, encouraged by the US government under George Bush Sr., the popular Kurdish uprising – the *Raparîn* – was brutally answered with another wave of attacks by the regime, forcing 2 million people, among them al-Anfal survivors, to run towards Iran and Turkey. In response to international pressure, a US-led effort installed a 'No-Fly Zone' over Kurdistan, laying the foundation for autonomy. The end of the Saddam Hussein era was not just significant for Kurds from Başûr after decades of genocidal violence; the promise of freedom also opened a physical zone of relatively free movement for political groups from the other parts of Kurdistan. For exiled activists and politicians, Başûrê Kurdistan became a home.

Women in Başûr have a long history and memory of resistance. Over several decades, women took part in the liberation struggle as pêşmerge or faced brutal torture in prison for their political activities. Others resisted by refusing to leave their lands and by building and rebuilding their homes after multiple episodes of large-scale state violence. In my conversations in Başûr, experienced, urban women's rights activists often made a distinction between the time before and after the 1991 uprising, recounting a new sense of individual rights, parallel to their collective struggle for Kurdistan. Opportunities for contentious politics indeed emerged after 1991 and more so after 2003, when a rise in civil society organizations and grassroots campaigns led to law amendments and policy changes. Compared to other parts of Kurdistan, in an environment in which Kurdish identity is at least formally recognized, women's civil society organizations are able to flourish by focusing on a variety of social and economic issues. Most of the political parties have affiliated women's associations. Access to transnational networks and exposure to international standards helped local activists advocate for women's rights. At the same time, this presented an opportunity for the KRG's self-representation to the outside world as a liberal democratic, de facto state that is able and willing to live up to international standards of 'good governance', and therefore, deserving of statehood, or at least investment.

Over the past nearly two decades, as a result of the work of local women's rights defenders, governmental initiatives and bodies were established and important steps taken against gender-based violence in the KRG's constitution, which is in some ways more progressive on women's rights than its central Iraqi counterpart. Nevertheless, efforts to combat violence against women, including domestic abuse, so-called honour killings, suspicious self-immolations, and female genital mutilation, are often undermined by the rule of the two patriarchal families, the Barzanî (KDP) and the Talabanî (PUK) that control the region. Of the two, the PUK enjoys a more progressive image when it comes to social issues, but this is measured against a low standard. Both parties have been routinely accused by women's rights defenders of perpetuating violence and harassment against political dissenters, including targeted sexualized attacks on women. Widespread nepotism means that well-connected perpetrators of sexual violence, including rapists and child abusers, frequently evade justice and accountability. Western support for the two parties furthermore undermines the protests and labour of the younger generations that are disillusioned with the idea of a Kurdistan that benefits few elites and leaves workers, including civil servants, unpaid or unemployed. Over the years, Islamist parties and movements began to take hold in the region, leading to an increase in influence of conservative politics. Many of the refugees that have recently died on the way to Europe are young Kurds, who flee the repression and inequality caused by the corruption and authoritarian rule of the two parties.

While abuses by political parties are certainly part of the reproduction of social issues, including gendered violence and rights abuses, it is important to consider the precarity of Başûr's political and civic life in the wider context of Iraq and the region. The KRG's economic policies depend on the central Iraqi state budget and foreign investors. Alongside their interference in Iraqi politics in general, Turkey and Iran influence the Kurdistan Region's economic and political life in particular. Moreover, the post-2003 era was accompanied by the economic liberalization of Başûr. From the mid-2000s onward, the KRG passed bills to facilitate foreign investment and the privatization of the economic, health, and education sectors. With the erosion of subsistence economies, alternatives are difficult to realize in this environment, especially when the threat of war still permanently looms over life in Iraq. Shaping social progress along capitalism causes conflict and contradiction within people's expectations of justice and freedom. The work of young political economist Schluwa Sama (2015) puts class, capitalism, and freedom aspirations in the Kurdistan Region into historical context. Drawing attention to the impact of the extreme sanctions in the 1990s and decades of nearly permanent war on contemporary lives, she demonstrates the interrelatedness of socio-economic and geopolitical issues by studying new class and power formations in Kurdistan from critical materialist perspectives.

In the aftermath of the US invasion, as part of Bush's 'freedom agenda', foreign-funded NGOs working on violence against women mushroomed especially in the Kurdistan Region in a rapid way, training and employing vast numbers of especially young women.[1] A new constituency of Kurdish women working in the civil society sector emerged as part of the bridge between the KRG and the global. While many women working in this sphere (including activists that I interviewed in Başûr) are undoubtedly driven by a passion to put an end to gender inequality in their communities, the rise of organizations working on gender-related issues is directly connected to the KRG's investment-oriented economic policies. These relied on public discourses and diplomatic efforts which spent large sums on the stylization of the Kurdistan Region as a tolerant, pro-Western, yet authentic sphere in an otherwise unstable region. To polish its image, the KRG has been lobbying through neo-conservative institutions since 2004, even receiving consultancy services of advisors of the Bush administration.[2]

The project-based, funding-dependent sphere of women's empowerment work often also heavily relies on cooperation with political parties and the government, a matter that greatly compromises their independence and ability to challenge the system. In a co-authored piece, Aven Aziz, Houzan Mahmoud, Rega Rauf, and Shara Taher (2020) voiced their criticism of the NGO-ization of the causes of Kurdish women in Iraq, arguing that Western governments and institutions deliberately amplify and develop elite profiles and their voices since this 'version of feminism is compatible with neoliberalism, creating yet another layer of division and hierarchy recalling colonialist attitudes in a region ravaged by nepotism, war and genocide'. Even as they tarnish the work done by women's organizations and activists on the ground, who are frequently subject to harassment and violence by conservative circles, the two ruling parties often reap global praise even for minor and delayed steps towards equality. Journalists, academics, and activists I interviewed narrated how the two ruling parties use sexualized forms of intimidation through harassment, assault, and systematic bad-mouthing. During my several months-long stay in

Başûr in 2015, mainly between Hewlêr (Erbil) and Silêmanî (Sulaimaniyah), a group of women's rights activists had joined forces to start a campaign against harassment of women in the digital sphere, following the circulation of fake pornographic footage of women politicians by supporters of political parties. Many women (independent activists, as well as political party representatives[3]) told me that the ruling parties routinely deferred urgent social issues to the time after statehood, blaming all shortcomings on their dependency on the Iraqi state. Nevertheless, many activists across the legal political spectrum agreed that independence was necessary to assert meaningful changes in a smaller-scaled, Kurdish state. They claimed that their efforts to create a more equal society and system would be more successful in a country of one's own than in the legal, economic, and political context of the failed project of post-war Iraq. Others, however, are more inclined towards building anti-sectarian Iraq-wide alliances with progressive groups, youth, and women, while insisting on the Kurdish people's right to self-determination within a democratic framework. Younger people in particular are dynamically involved in issues around equality, transparency, education, culture and art, economy, and environmental issues. Many feel alienated by the family-based and partisan patronage system of the two ruling parties. To those who follow Kurdish politics in other parts, the experience of Başûr is also a critical lesson for the others to learn from.

THE PKK IN BAŞÛR: A TROUBLED RELATIONSHIP

In the summer of 2014, PKK guerrillas arrived in Kerkûk in large convoys from the Qendîl mountains to reinforce the pêşmerge's battle against Daesh. Videos of their arrival in pickup trucks with their flags and symbols showed scenes of celebration. For the first time in Kurdish history, the pêşmerge and the guerrillas were fighting and dying side by side against a common enemy. For a short period in those years, the PKK was able to interact relatively freely with the people of Başûr in an urban environment. Its flags and symbols, as well as Öcalan stencils, could be found in public squares at the time. Shopping malls even sold pens, magnets, and other kitsch items with Apo's face. An unprecedented number of young people joined the guerrillas from Başûr. At the height of the war, then president Mesûd Barzanî even paid a visit to PKK guerrilla units in Mexmûr to thank them for their role in the defence of the Kurdistan Region against Daesh. These sights were exceptional, considering the complicated history between the PKK and political parties in Başûr.

Founding members of the PKK first arrived in Başûr in the 1980s to establish contacts with Kurdish parties and organizations in the region. During Saddam Hussein's period, their activities, including educations, were held in the mountains. Later, limited organizing work was possible in certain

Kurdish cities. Soon, however, violent conflicts between the PKK, PUK, and KDP throughout the 1990s, particularly in the context of Turkey's military operations, tarnished the PKK's image among the population of Başûr. In the framework of the US-backed Washington Peace Agreement between the KDP and PUK, following their several years of infighting over resources (*birakujî* – fratricide), the two parties pledged to deny the PKK bases within Iraqi borders. Over the years, the leaders of both parties have routinely referred to the PKK as a terrorist organization that undermines the KRG's economic and diplomatic development, which relies on Turkish and Western investment.

Despite clashes, especially with the pro-Turkish KDP, the PKK's social and political work in the area grew in scale in the 1990s with the formation of various sometimes legally operating associations, including representations of the newly emerging women's structures. YAJK's first women's conference in Başûr was held in 1997, at a difficult time marked by intra-Kurdish wars. In this period, young women began supporting or joining the guerrilla.

To PKK members or sympathizers, the two parties, in particular the KDP, represent a consensus between regional and global powers on what kind of Kurdistan is non-threatening to the status quo in the Middle East. Öcalan as well as spokespeople within the Kurdistan freedom movement frequently speak of the two parties as having been 'given a role' by hegemonic powers to serve as their Kurdish proxies. They view the West's endorsement of the KRG as the only legitimate concept for Kurdistan, and the unanimous support for the Barzanî-led government as a way of keeping other Kurdish political movements in check, at the expense of dissenting voices within society. In Western political and media discourses, the two main ruling parties are presented as the representatives of the 'good Kurds', the ones interested in stability and investment, not chaos and revolution like the PKK. With the PKK's rise of global popularity in the mid-2010s, the KDP in particular openly backed the AKP over the HDP in Turkey during the peace process, rejected KCK-led calls for Kurdistan-wide national unity, and sabotaged political developments in Rojava by digging border trenches and restricting cross-border movement between Rojava and Başûr. Its political formations inside Rojava did not propose any oppositonal democratic frameworks, but rather act according to the interests of Turkey.

Women often reference Başûr's popular rebellious legacies on one hand, and the genocides experienced on the other hand, when arguing that the KRG's current system, a power share agreement between two parties, in many ways constituted a 'settling for less' than freedom. In my interviews, women from Başûr who joined the movement were unwilling to normalize the problems in the KRG as an outcome of the difficulty of state-building in the Middle East, an excuse often put forward by the billionaire leaders of the two families. Many of them viewed the corruption by two overwhelmingly male-dominated parties that criminalize protest, civil society work, and even journalism as being built into the system with international support. This corruption is not too different from the situation of many post-colonial governments, who remained economically colonized even after achieving independence.

Derya, a young woman from around Hewlêr, joined the PKK to the outrage of her KDP-affiliated family, which has members in high-ranking military or political positions. Social issues, especially widespread violence against women, economic injustice, and political impasse led her to familiarize herself with the PKK. In her view, male-dominated concepts of Kurdish freedom struggles normalized the marginalization of women.

> Episodes of violence, the Iran-Iraq war, the Turkish army's attacks, the Saddam regime, fratricidal wars between the Kurds, all of this normalized war, killing, and dying in the minds of people. The idea that 'we are dying anyway' influences how women think about their right to live. The sexist ruling parties eliminated leading women in their ranks quite early on. Today, women pêşmerge are excluded from combat, which makes them redundant, second-class soldiers with no power. The parties cover up cases of violence against women. They want to create and protect a system by and for men. What liberated Kurdistan do we speak of when we can see women being assaulted, trafficked, raped and murdered on a daily basis without much outrage?

In conversations, pro-movement, young women at Mexmûr, in the guerrilla or in the movement's social works across Başûr told me that local universities were sites of assimilation into the hegemony of Western knowledge production, not spheres for critique or radical politics. The contradictions faced by a Kurdistan between particular ideas around tradition and modernity were articulated by young cadre Kanî[4] in the following way:

> The universities follow neoliberal models. They assimilate our youth into capitalism, instead of constituting sites of uprising, rebellion and revolutionary youth spirit. Critical thinking is not actively supported in society and generally criticism of the system is met with violence. While the security forces shoot young protesters, TV shows, consumerism serve to distract people. On one hand, highly sexual themes are presented on TV, on the other hand, journalists get murdered here for writing articles saying, 'I fell in love with Mesûd Barzanî's daughter'.[5]

Similar to Derya, out of dissatisfaction with the system, Kanî joined the PKK at a young age from an area close to the border to Rojhelat. A poetic young woman, she speaks several regional languages and different Kurdish dialects fluently. When we met, she was part of the movement's efforts to build relations with women's organizations and movements in the Middle East. She told me that she refused to get used to a Middle East in which the killing of poor smugglers and the early deaths of children were normalized and warned of the risk of 'illusions of freedom', in which the advancement of selected groups is equated to a breakthrough in freedom for all of society.

This year, in Duhok, in the heartland of the KDP, a man married off his 12-year-old daughter to an old man. The girl could not bear it and ran back home. Her father tied her from the rooftop, brought two dogs and let them attack her. When she was all wounded, he murdered her. Where are the authorities? Freedom is not a personal experience; it is a societal phenomenon. Even though we are in the mountains, with weapons on our shoulders and heads held high, I cannot get my mind off the women experiencing violence in our society, in which a woman leaving her home by herself is treated like a criminal. Thousands of women living in the shadow of men – thousands of women being raped by their husbands every night – thousands of women taking their own lives to escape violence. How can we speak of freedom in these conditions?

Kanî believed that the promise of statehood by the ruling parties was a way of deflecting from their corruption and other, new causes for oppression and exploitation in Kurdistan.

People look at the violence they experience and say: 'This would not happen if we had our own state'. The constant promise of a state, regardless of likelihood, serves to pacify people. Otherwise, they cannot be governed. The parties have no ideological, philosophical view on the systems and forces that govern the world, no adequate understanding of history that would have prepared them for the establishment of a state. A Kurdish state – what an easy thing to sell without preparation or willingness to be democratic. Insisting on the establishment of a Kurdish state in this way – corrupt and dependent on the oppressors of Kurds – is a backward idea in a time in which more and more people seek democracy. It is very well possible to create a Kurdish state and perpetuate the ideas behind the Treaty of Lausanne that divided Kurdistan. The illusion of independence, created by nationalist slogans that blur the realities on the ground, is very attractive for a people subjected to so many genocides.

A generation older than Kanî, guerrilla fighter Rojgar was a member of the administration of PAJK at the time of our interview. From Silêmanî originally, she went to the mountain in the late 1990s, during her university years. Like many others of her age, she remembers the many times that her family home was destroyed and rebuilt in several waves of large-scale state violence. In her view, after so many episodes of violence, the people of Başûr deserved better than the system under construction in the KRG, which, in her eyes, was often instrumentalized to undermine other Kurdish freedom projects.

When the ruling parties of Başûr engage in policies that harm Kurds outside of the borders of Iraq, this is called 'diplomacy'. Yet, Kurdish-ness, Kurdish nationalism, independence are evoked whenever a new crisis emerges. An increasingly rich class exploits terms like 'freedom' and 'independence' to keep alive a dream that they them selves help undermine. This is what happens when neoliberalism suddenly hits a region with a long history of resistance and genocide, facilitated by a ruling class that profits on the back of its population, which has been traumatized by massacre, civil war, displacement, and poverty. Capitalism's imposition of individualism and liberalism fills spiritual emptiness, but at the same time, it degrades the immaterial values that drive resistance for freedom.

What kind of Kurdistan will do justice to these people's historic suffering and courage under decades of genocidal dictatorship? Because Kurdish

Figure 14   Protest to condemn the Turkish state's violence in the aftermath of the collapsed peace process. Rallies are frequently organized in various cities and towns across Başûr against the Turkish state's attacks on Kurdish people in different parts of Kurdistan. Silêmanî. September 2015.

freedom has always only been imagined in the form of a nation-state, people often believe that the PKK's paradigm shift means that we have given up on 'freedom'. Our vision of freedom is more radical than the model of a Kurdistan that can be commodified, exploited, and used against others.

Founded in 2002 under the name TJAK (Movement of Liberationist Women of Kurdistan), RJAK (Free Women's Organization of Kurdistan) is one of the oldest social institutions of the Kurdistan freedom movement within Iraqi borders. In the summer of 2015, I had the chance to join an ongoing education at RJAK's academy. The walls of the room in a building with a large garden were decorated with photos of women martyrs from all four parts of Kurdistan. The topic was economy. The woman holding the lecture was explaining the Greek roots of the word and went on to describe the process through which women were divorced from the means of production, despite their crucial role in sustaining economies.

Perwîn, a woman from Rwanduz and coordinator at RJAK at the time, contrasted the work of the academy to the well-funded international NGO work in the region. In her eyes, the prevalence of foreign-funded NGOs delegated important decisions, analyses, and plans to small numbers of people with resources or connections, amounting to a new 'elite class formation through an individualist notion of freedom':

NGOs and more generally, people, who come from abroad with their concepts, ideas and projects have the capital to implement their visions, regardless of their meaning or outcome. Plenty of men are involved as CEOs in women's projects that they don't believe in. A lot of money flows this way. A lot of intelligence is gathered through NGO work and their research projects.

Women, young people get taught to say things in certain ways with the aim of receiving money and support for further projects. The Eurocentric aesthetics and their bourgeois character express themselves in people's clothes, conduct, and attitude. This is seen as elitist by many people in society. An attitude that looks down at its own people cannot be activist or have a claim to lead society towards change. It's a performance and prevents people from developing autonomous analyses to help their communities.

Where does violence come from? Surely, it must be understood through wider systems and their expressions, including capitalism. But this is lacking in much of the work on women being done here. Increasing opportunities for small groups of individuals or reaching minor legal reforms are not the same as changing the system. What alternative concepts of freedom can sustain society's transformation? Beyond a womanhood that is stuck in a false binary between individualism and 'fate-ism' – what would a liberationist stance look like?

Around the same period, I had the chance to attend a workshop led by two UN agencies in Silêmanî's Ramada Hotel in which an Irish man, who admitted to never have been to Kurdistan before, gave a PowerPoint presentation to a room of invited 'women leaders' on a plan to make the city safer for women. It already worked in India and Tanzania, he unconvincingly insisted. Years later, I found out that millions had been spent on the project, whose concrete impact is impossible to determine.

*   *   *

Despite many aspirations, the movement's efforts to find political foothold in Başûr are arduous. Institutions, offices, and individuals representing the ideas of the freedom movement are routinely attacked by the security forces of the two parties. The PKK is often perceived as a radical communist and atheist group, whose leader no longer believes in Kurdistan. This is also related to the fact that many of the PKK defectors who abandoned socialism in favour of conservative, nationalist concepts of Kurdish freedom reside in Başûr, often under the auspices of powerful circles. Regularly cited in media, these men help shape perceptions on the PKK in Başûr. Yet, despite repression by the two parties, the Kurdistan freedom movement is actively supported by sizeable sections of society, and especially younger generations.

Affiliated with the freedom movement, the Democratic Solution Party of Kurdistan (PÇDK) was formed in Başûr in 2002. Early on, it implemented the movement's 40 per cent gender quota and enshrined principles in its bylaws (for example, men who want to marry more than one woman to be excluded). In 2014, the party dissolved itself to form Tevgerî Azadî Komelgey Kurdistan (Kurdistan Free Society Movement) as a broader effort to building democratic autonomous structures. In principle, Tevgerî Azadî aspires to organize its committees and assemblies everywhere, from Zaxo to Xaneqîn, but its access to regions is restricted by its own capacity as well as various political dynamics. Tevgerî Azadî has a self-proclaimed role to play for the unification of Kurdish politics based on mutual cooperation for wider issues around peace, democratization, and justice in the region. Şilan Şakir, a woman from Silêmanî, at the time co-president of Tevgerî Azadî, argued that an uncritical subscription to the idea of Kurdish nationalism, without political analyses around class, gender, and power, could easily amount to a betrayal of people's decades-old hopes for freedom. Radical democratic forms of politics were needed:

The mere shell of the idea of democracy does not automatically create democracy. Even if one hundred Kurdish parliaments and states were formed, this would not necessarily amount to a free Kurdish society. Freedom is not something that can be squeezed into institutions and serve the interest of a certain class. The current presidency crisis is a case in point.[6] It epitomizes the mentality of power. A rich, tribal man, who insists that he is forced to stay on his seat because there is nobody else to replace him at a moment of crisis.

Two ruling parties reap the fruits of the many uprisings and revolutions that have been led here. Two families control the distribution of wealth. It's not enough to say 'as long as we have some sort of Kurdish system', if this system is designed to create different classes of people within Kurdistan, with the rich selling the wealth of Kurdistan to other powers, instead of developing the country for the local population. This sort of 'Kurdish nationalism' is not patriotic, it is a structure that serves the interests of very few people and forces the rest of society to comply with a system based on money and power. As the elite owns politics, the lower classes are deprived of the ability to express themselves politically. Solving problems becomes difficult, when any challenge is dismissed as working against Kurdistan's interests and when those in power monopolize the idea of 'Kurdish interest'.

Şilan pointed out that land was bought by corporations, with revenues flowing into the hands of a few, while subsistence economies broke down. She explicitly linked this to the emergence of new values, styles, and conducts among people, who wanted to survive and advance in the environment of imposed capitalism:

What does it mean for historically self-reliant communities to lose their livelihoods for neoliberal progress? Development for whom? At what cost? The sanctions in the past and many new forms of economic dependency created an idea of progress along Western standards. The idea emerges that presenting oneself in a certain way, through one's clothes, speech, and behaviour, is a show of progress. In reality, this just creates moulded categories of women. In a patriarchal Kurdish system, women are forced to play by the rules of a game that was never their own creation.

In a similar vein, Tara Husen Mihamad, a woman from the Germiyan region in her 30s at the time and the deputy co-president, advocated a 'break with the masculine character of politics', arguing that true change could only come about if the liberation of women is a driver of Kurdistan's liberation. At the age of 16, Tara, who later became the co-president of the party, was married to her cousin and described a life with much economic hardship. Several years before our interview, she first became a regular member of the previous PÇDK before taking up greater responsibility.

> Pêşmerge-hood has a rooted meaning in people's lives. It is a symbol of courage and freedom, but what happens if an ideal gets converted into a regular paid job and tied to oppressive partisan politics? The commodification of the decades-old legacy of resistance here kills people's love for their homeland. The current political set-up exploits people's genuine feelings.
>
> Kurdish politics without self-criticism is dangerous. Those, who try to challenge the system face aggressive intimidation tactics. Women in particular are targeted. Their families get used against them; their reputation gets tarnished in the name of 'honour' until they go silent. This is why the women's struggle must never stop. Freedom for women in Kurdistan must not be reduced to the ability to dress and walk as we wish. Freedom is more magnificent than individual choice. It is not the mere absence of dictatorship. We can, through organization and consciousness, build a system of freedom, in which we live as meaningful, politically conscious individuals in a just and equal society. This is what we mean by democratic nation.

Around the time of my fieldwork, the PKK was actively organizing within communities in Başûr, from Şengal to Silêmanî, offering educations and building links with different political groups. In the context of the chaos caused by Daesh, the PKK guerrillas could roam around in their uniforms in certain areas. They began overtly organizing activities and opened academies. For the first time, the movement was directly interacting with the civilians of Başûr on a larger scale. Many guerrilla fighters from other parts I spoke to self-critically admitted that they perceive that part of Kurdistan through the lens of their past and present hostilities with the KDP and PUK.

In the 1970s, the Iraqi Ba'ath regime began settling Arabs in Kerkûk, forcing out local Kurdish, Turkmen, and Assyrian populations. Although Article 140 of the Iraqi constitution states that Kerkûk's status would be determined via a referendum, the city remained disputed territory, mainly due to its oil wealth, but also as a result of competing nationalist projects. In the aftermath of the large-scale Daesh raids in Iraq, the area around Kerkûk and Daquq, home of many different ethnic and religious communities, hosted the overt and covert presence of several, often competing armed groups for a number of years: Daesh, Iranian-backed Shi'ite militias (al-Hashd ash-Sha'bi), the decimated Iraqi army, the Turkish intelligence service (MIT), Kurdish pêşmerge forces (mainly PUK), and the PKK. From 2014 until 2017, Kerkûk was Kurdish-controlled. Hundreds of pêşmerge fighters died in the defence of Kerkûk.

In September 2015, I spent a few days between Daquq and Kerkûk with HPG and YJA Star units. They often complained that the local Kurdish media was not adequately broadcasting their participation in the defence of Başûr. In Kerkûk, I spoke to a YJA Star guerrilla named Gulan about the ongoing tensions between the PKK and the regional powers, in light of the differences between Kurdish political projects and ideologies.

People think of this as the liberated part of Kurdistan because there is a Kurdish system in place and that 'the PKK is a party for Turkey'. We always wanted to play an active role here in Başûr, but that space was never given to us. When we arrived, more people saw that the PKK does not fight only for one group of Kurds. Our fight against Daesh here created trust and hope but disturbed those in power.

The media did not convey our participation in the war properly, even as pêşmerge themselves appreciated us. There is a class difference between the pêşmerge, who courageously fight and die, and those who command them. There are groups of people, who materially profit from the sacrifices of the pêşmerge.

During the hottest phase of the war, political parties applauded the PKK, but once things settled down, they started saying 'We don't need you. Your organization does not belong here anyway. Go back to your own part of Kurdistan'. We were always pushed aside as a 'neighbor', a friendly but temporary presence out of fear that our military presence can transform into a political one. That is why we hear phrases by the regional government like 'The PKK is a guest here, they must leave eventually'. Official records did not document our sacrifices but the local people saw what they saw.

The movement's semi-openly operating political organizing efforts did not all last, as the guerrillas eventually had to end their public presence due to pressure by Turkey on the KRG, which led to the closing of several institutions. The 2017 Kurdistan independence referendum announced by Mesûd Barzanî, at the time president of the KRG, was followed by the first clash between Kurdish and Iraqi forces in years. The Iraqi army and the Iranian-backed Shi'ite Popular Mobilization Forces (al-Hashd ash-Sha'bi), supervised by Qasem Soleimani, brutally recaptured the city by force, after it had been held and protected against Daesh by Kurdish forces for several years.

In the years that followed, Turkey increased its military and intelligence presence in Başûr, especially with the cooperation of the KDP and by recruiting agents on the ground to gather information on PKK activity. In public statements, Turkish officials often frame their presence inside Iraqi borders with reference to Ottoman era claims to places like Mosul and Kerkûk. The AKP's activation

Figure 15   Kurdistan and PKK flag alongside each other on top of a PKK institution in Kerkûk, a short drive from territories that were Daesh-held at the time. Kerkûk. September 2015.

of Turkmen groups in these regions moreover reflects the use of pan-Turkist visions employed in its expansionist strategy. Meanwhile, Iran uses sectarianism and military and economic power to pursue its own geostrategic interests. Several times in recent years, Iran attacked targets inside Başûr with missiles. Iranian authorities often claim that these strikes inside Iraqi borders aim to retaliate against Israel and the US.

Such hostile conditions present obstacles for women when uniting their struggles. As a result, unity has been a main rallying point in the Kurdish women's movement's efforts to reach out to women's organizations across all the four parts. In the 2010s, Kurdish women's national unity conferences were jointly organized by the movement and other Kurdish women's organizations in Hewlêr, Amed, and Silêmanî to discuss ongoing conflicts and political and social issues affecting women in Kurdistan and regions beyond.

*   *   *

During my second trip to Rojava, I was alone at the makeshift Semalka/Faysh Khabour crossing between Rojava and Başûr. The KDP's border authorities were not letting me pass. My being a young Kurdish woman from 'Turkey' with a foreign passport travelling alone rang the usual alarm bells. The young woman my age, who was in charge of dealing with me, refused to listen to my request, with unnecessary hostility. Eventually, my hours-long protest, coupled with some help from individuals engaged in the movement's diplomacy efforts, worked. The strict tone of the young woman softened after her boss allowed me

206

passage. She was even kind enough to offer to help me carry my backpack to the crossing point. I declined, but she accompanied me anyway.

'Is it true what they say about what is happening over there?', she suddenly asked me with a lowered voice and an air of mystery. 'What do you mean?', I wondered. Her curious eyes glanced over to the strip of land on the other side of the Khabour river that I was about to cross on a ferryboat. 'Do you think women are free on that side?' She was genuine and I immediately forgave her earlier behaviour. For a few moments, the river no longer seemed like a border dividing two Kurdish projects. It was just water, somewhere in Mesopotamia and we were two girls wondering about the same question: *azadî*.

26

Rojava: A women's revolution

Revolutions stretch our imaginations and manifest our desires. Political struggle is a purpose and a practice. In between utopic romanticism and demobilizing fatalism – both of which foreclose the future as a process we generate – is our collective commitment to revolutionary struggles blossoming around us and ushering in a different world. – Harsha Walia

There were always women, who found inner strength, empowered by our leader and encouraged by the women *hevals*. But 2012 changed everyone's lives. Imagine you remove a heavy stone only to discover all the green, the life, underneath it. – Sara, Kongreya Star, Kobanê, 2018

On 19 July 2012, more than a year into the conflict in Syria, footage circulated of young women and men with AK47s, watching over Syrian governmental facilities, now decorated with yellow, green, and red banners. Kurdish communities occupied the streets, loudly chanting revolutionary Kurdish music, and announced that they had taken control first in Kobanê, then in Afrîn and cities across Cizîre (Jazeera) as regime officials and security forces withdrew. These scenes launched the declaration of the 'Revolution of Rojava'.

As such, over the course of a decade, 'Rojava' entered the vocabulary of radicals around the world. It created hope, courage, and solidarity. It generated discussions about the meaning of revolution in these times. Ten years after the declaration of the revolution, 'defining' Rojava is more difficult than ever. There is no knowledge production on Rojava that is not politicized and ideological. Rojava is at once an ideological promise, an ongoing revolutionary society-building effort, a disruptive historical political event, and a complex lived reality of millions of people. Its history is entangled with that of the revolutionary Kurdistan freedom movement, with that of the wider regional context, and with a longue durée history of freedom, including millennia of women's resistance against patriarchy. The scale of political activities in Rojava ranges from neighbourhoods to the world stage, and these unfold on a key frontline between NATO and its enemies. The revolution in Rojava has its autonomous dynamics, but it is also part of a wider context of war and displacement in Syria. It also offers lessons for revolutions to come.

To long-term supporters of the Kurdistan freedom movement, the liberation of territories and the subsequent building of democratic autonomous structures in Rojava represented the fruit of decades of intergenerational and transnational political labour and sacrifice. For many people in this constituency, securing a place like Rojava is not in itself the end goal of revolution. Rather, Rojava is viewed as the largest site of 'practical implementation' of the democratic, ecological, and women's liberationist paradigm proposed by Öcalan. In this sense, Rojava is a space to breathe and begin the concrete work of the long social revolution ahead.

Outside of this political community, to believers in the idea that 'another world is possible', Rojava's revolution appeared as one of the most radical and emancipatory political events in recent history. Both due to the organized popular resistance against fascism, as well as the self-organization towards an egalitarian political system and culture against patriarchy, capitalism, and the nation-state, Rojava has been likened to the Paris Commune of 1871, anti-fascist resistance in Catalunya during WWII, and the indigenous-led Zapatista uprising of 1994. Years before the international community of states took action against Daesh, Rojava had already become a destination for many internationalists organized in anti-capitalist struggles in different contexts. Rojava especially attracted women, who were interested in the explicitly articulated and institutionalized role of women in the revolutionary process. The global discourse took a turn when in 2014, at the height of Daesh's military victories, the organized armed forces in Rojava, the People's Protection Units (YPG) and Women's Protection Units (YPJ) first entered a tactical and temporary military alliance with the US and its allies. This relationship never translated into cooperation on a strategic and political level, however. Rojava's status is not internationally recognized, with the notable exception of the Catalan parliament's recognition in 2021.

Naturally, the events in Rojava were frequently compared and contrasted to the evolution of the protest and opposition movement that emerged across Syria against the Ba'athist regime of Bashar al-Assad in 2011. Crucially, these two parallel and connected trajectories had different relationships to the word 'revolution'. As Syrian activists have often written, unlike the anti-regime activities in the rest of the country, developments in Rojava did not emerge as a seemingly spontaneous and horizontal uprising, but through a coordinated effort by a cadre party with an ideological and organizational programme. In the eyes of actors in Rojava, early on wary of the interests of countries like the US and other Western states, Turkey, Qatar, and Saudi Arabia, what happened in the other parts of Syria was rebellion rather than revolution. Since the regime and the leadership in Rojava in many ways did share similar tactical interests early on in the war (e.g. common enemies), some opposition accounts compared the Democratic Union Party (PYD) to the Ba'ath Party, and called the former the latter's *shabbiha* (a term used for regime-affiliated armed thugs) working to undermine the Syrian revolution. Other Syrian accounts, especially those opposed to Western interventionism, criticize the alliance between the Kurdish-led military structures and the imperialist US after 2014 as an arrangement that undermines Syrian state sovereignty and divides the country. Yet other veteran revolutionaries from different parts of Syria view Rojava as the final bastion of hope for a free Syria.

While knowledge production on Rojava was initially limited to radical left circles (not least due to the Kurdistan freedom movement's old networks, diaspora, and media infrastructure), in later years, mainstream accounts of Rojava proliferated in markedly non-revolutionary ways after the US entered a tactical military alliance with Kurdish-led forces to fight Daesh after at least three years of covert training for rebels to fight the regime. Think tanks, as the ideological sphere of the world of states, military alliances, and intelligence, unsurprisingly represent the developments in Rojava through geostrategic lenses. Such securitizing frames are part of special warfare; they colonize history-writing and have a depoliticizing and alienating effect on constituencies that sympathize with any revolutionary promise.

Several other factors determine knowledge production on Rojava. References for democracy in Rojava have their roots in revolutionary philosophy and are not fundamentally based on legal frameworks such as human rights and international law. The political, social, and economic system that today constitutes the Autonomous Administration of North and East Syria (AANES) as an outcome of the Rojava Revolution was built with no external assistance and with no international monitoring. On the contrary, it was an indigenous process guided by a revolutionary party's principles and experiences. This means that questions like legitimacy, accountability, efficiency, and sustainability are not measured by the standards set by the bureaucracies of the international state system. Such dynamics raise critical philosophical questions about the meaning of politics and democracy, but are largely absent in knowledge production on Rojava, especially in works that, in positivist fashion, take liberal democratic ideologies or development indices as metrices to 'assess' what is essentially a vision for large-scale social transformation, spritiual liberation, and decolonization.

It is also crucial to note that while the Kurdistan freedom movement's media system generally operates on restricted terrain, in Rojava it is the hegemonic one. This means that the aims, works, and successes of the revolution are widely reported and mostly in positive light. Media workers do not operate in ideal conditions, often having to consult with authorities in order to keep their licences. Ongoing concerns about security and intelligence may be justified, but they also become opportunities to control information cycles and interfere with press freedom. Many reporters and outlets outside of the movement's political circles present themselves as 'independent', but are often funded by European or regional NGOs or affiliated with hostile Kurdish political parties. Their lack of professionalism fails to contribute to the creation of a meaningfully diverse and critical media landscape.

In light of these issues, it is impossible to do justice to the entirety of issues that are relevant to understanding all the structures that have been built by tens of thousands of people in this war-affected region. Political life in Rojava is as colourful as it is confusing to explain (and by the time people read this book, the system is likely to have changed already). Considering this, the following pages will mainly point to the continuity between the Kurdistan freedom movement's historical presence in the region and the ways in which Rojava's women's revolution presents itself as a contemporary political alternative in a region marked by foreign intervention, authoritarian and nationalist states, sectarianism and religious extremism. This chapter cannot claim to do justice to the complex and diverse experiences of millions of Syrians in other parts of the war-torn country.

THE KURDS UNDER BA'ATHIST RULE

By the 1930s, the northern parts of Syria had become a refuge for Armenian, Syriac, Assyrian, Chaldean, and Kurdish survivors of massacres committed under the Ottomans Empire and later the early Turkish Republic. Following the collapse of the Ottoman Empire, Syria was placed under a French mandate for several decades until independence in the mid-1940s.[1] Pan-Arab nationalisms, while presenting themselves in terms of unifying frameworks for anti-colonial resistance and progress, were in many ways chauvinistic state-building exercises that dispossessed and marginalized peoples outside of the dominant nationalist identity. In 1962, at a time of Kurdish rebellions in Iraq, a sloppy population census was ordered in the north-eastern Cizîre (Jazeera) in the Hesekê (al-Hasakah) province in Syria by presidential decree. Kurds, who could not prove their residency prior to 1945, had their citizenship revoked, which made at least 120,000 of them stateless, a number which later doubled as children inherited their parents' status. Following multiple regime changes, the pan-Arabist Ba'ath Party seized power in 1963 by way of a coup d'état. In the same year, Muhammad Talab Hilal, head of the political department of the secret service in al-Hasakah governorate presented a report, *A Study of the al-Jazeera Province from National, Social and Political Aspects,* for a solution to the state's concerns about the Kurds, particularly in the north-east corner of the country, bordering Iraq and Turkey. The racist document, full of pseudo-scientific claims, includes the idea that due to different 'forms, colours and heads', the Kurds have no history, no civilization, no language and not even a race. At most, they have the attributes of violence, ferocity and rigor. These are the features of the mountain inhabitants ... Consequently, there is no Kurdish nation, because it does not possess factors of a nation and thus, there is no national homeland for the Kurds.*

His portrayal of the Kurds as the agents of imperialism, as a 'cancer' to divide the Arab world – an image that prevails among Arab nationalists today – shaped the blueprint for the so-called 'Arab belt' policy of the Ba'ath Party: the settlement of Arabs in majority-Kurdish areas, the Arabization of names of majority-Kurdish villages, expropriation, displacement, impoverishment, unemployment, surveillance, citizenship deprivation, and with that the denial of political, civil, and economic rights. Parents were banned from giving their children Kurdish names. The Syrian curriculum does not feature the Kurds, who make up an estimated 10 per cent of the population. Generally, especially with the rise to power of Hafez al-Assad, the increasingly more powerful pervasive intelligence and security apparatus of the authoritarian regime suffocated all Syrians' political activity. Schools, media, and public events largely function in disciplinary ways to reproduce the dominance of the Ba'ath Party. All over the country, dissenters organized themselves clandestinely, at risk of imprisonment, torture, and death.

THE APOISTS ARRIVE

The first Syrian-Kurdish political parties were formed towards the end of the 1950s and largely comprised urban nationalists or rural elites, with varying degrees of conflict and cooperation with the state.[2] This landscape changed when Öcalan and his comrades arrived in Syria in 1979. Hanife, at the time of our interview a member of the Executive Council of the Movement for a Democratic Society (Tev-Dem), described her community's encounter with the PKK as the beginning of a new political phase for the Kurdish community in Syria. It brought in a new notion of socialism to impoverished Kurds in a country in which socialism had been tied to the Ba'ath Party's abusive authoritarian and racist policies:

The Apoist movement's arrival in Rojava opened a new horizon, a different style of doing politics, another life, a new mode of struggle. New concepts entered Rojava's political life, with the PKK as a Marxist-Leninist movement without primitive nationalist, religious or sexist connotations, one that struggles for socialism. They were not nationalist, they were against injustice.

---

* My translation from German (see Hilal 2013 [1963]).

It was a revolutionary movement of the poor. The cadres were intellectual, but modest, had nothing for themselves. They were young university students, who left everything behind and arrived here for revolution and to unite all parts of Kurdistan. Previous Kurdish struggles were led by tribal leaders or elites, there was no effort to fight on behalf of the proletarian class, the poor, the oppressed. Rojava's society is poor after all. In the minds of ordinary people of Rojava, these ideas slowly created freedom utopias. The way of life of the Apoist militants, the way they sat down and stood up influenced society. They were directly in touch with the people, lived, slept, and ate in people's homes.

Most importantly, with the arrival of the PKK, Kurdish women in Syria became politically active for the first time. Politically, women across Syria could not meaningfully organize outside of the Ba'ath Party's parameters. Likewise, traditional Kurdish political parties had (and continue to have) no women's agendas. Many women therefore see the arrival of Öcalan and the PKK women as a game changer in their lives. Hundreds of women joined the PKK especially from Afrîn, Kobanê, and Aleppo in the 1990s. Women's active participation in the struggle to liberate Kurdistan left a deep impression in the homes of thousands of *welatparêz* families. As home-makers hid party material and helped with logistics, younger women broke taboos by engaging in art and cultural work such as music and theatre. In the Qendîl mountains, Zaxo, a PKK member from Rojava, spoke of the atmosphere that shaped her youth years:

That women would go to the mountains to fight, be politically active, hold meetings, begin to talk in public, all of this was a strike against the dominant sexist and conservative mentality. People joined the PKK on their wedding nights, others donated their marriage gold to the movement. Many of those who did not join the guerrilla still dedicated themselves with voluntary activities. Seeing women become self-confident and active broke taboos and sexist conceptions that only men can be political. Many women cadres, who organized Rojava's society for years, later fell in the war. People saw that they lived the way they spoke and spoke the way they lived. People heard about Sakine Cansız' prison resistance, of Bêrîvan Cizîrî at the forefront of the *serhildan*. Dîcle from Kobanê joined the PKK on the night of her wedding and later fell martyr. These women proved in action that courage and heroism don't belong to men. Women became subjects with the PKK. Over time, this impacted the family. Violence became less acceptable in *welatparêz* circles, and it decreased. Men with extreme patriarchal behaviours were collectively frowned upon. They watched their actions at first out of fear of ostracism, but with time, they came to question themselves more genuinely. Traditional

213

masculinity was far from being overcome, but through Apo's freedom ethics, women's strong stance, and the many martyrdoms, it received a serious blow. Society's male emphasis started crumbling. A mental transformation cannot develop over night, but at least to some extent, patriarchy was shaking in Kurdistan.

Öcalan's sudden absence after 1998, after two decades, was difficult for the local movement to cope with, especially after the regime of Bashar al-Assad began improving its relationship with Turkey, after 2002 led by the AKP. Clandestine community work was weakened when sympathizers and cadres were arrested or killed. The 2003 founding of the Democratic Union Party (PYD) took place around the earlier outlined period of internal defection and crisis within the PKK. People I interviewed refer to the period after Öcalan's exodus as the beginning of a 'special war' strategy of the state to corrupt and pacify the organized sections of Kurdish society.

Following the establishment of Kurdish autonomy in Iraq in the context of the US invasion, anti-Kurdish sentiments were incited by Arab nationalists in Syria in a regional environment that collectively stigmatized the Kurds as agents of imperialism. In March 2004, violence broke out during a community football match in Qamişlo, when some fans began chanting racist, pro-Saddam slogans against the competing Kurdish team. In the riots that followed, security forces used live ammunition as Kurdish protesters targeted buildings and statues associated with the Ba'ath regime. Several dozens were believed to have been killed and hundreds were imprisoned or disappeared. Kurdish people often claim that the escalations were provoked and desired by the Syrian state to crack down on oppositions. From the perspective of the Syrian regime, an enemy of NATO states and their ally Israel, the United States' use of local uprisings in neighbouring Iraq for the aim of regime change gave reason to anticipate and prevent a similar scenario.

The Movement for a Democratic Society (Tev-Dem) was formed in this eventful time in 2005 in response to Öcalan's call to build Democratic Confederalism. It began the work of forming underground organizations and decision-making mechanisms based on councils. State repression, however, meant sometimes within a year, an entire council could be arrested, as described by one of the co-founders: 'until 2011, we secretly formed councils, they were destroyed, we formed new ones'. In January 2005, after decades of organizing in Rojava, the women's movement secretly formed Yekîtiya Star (the Union of Ishtar) as an umbrella organization. Similar to Tev-Dem, its activities had to remain underground. Politically active Kurdish women were threatened or imprisoned by the regime. According to activists, rumours were consciously spread to provoke families into preventing women's political engagement.

Yekîtiya Star (later transformed into a congress, Kongreya Star) and Tev-Dem became the primary entities to set up the communes, assemblies, cooperatives, and academies from 2011 onward.

WAR AND REVOLUTION(S)

The war in Syria is one of the greatest tragedies of the twenty-first century. According to various estimates, it has left more than half a million people dead and millions of people displaced from their homes. More than a decade into the conflict, no political solution appears in sight.

In the spring of 2011, the 'Syrian revolution' emerged as a protest movement demanding the end of the oppressive regime of Bashar al-Assad. Soon, popular protests reached different corners of the country. It appears that the Syrian state made sense of the events through its decades-old concerns about NATO warfare and Muslim Brotherhood-led insurgency inside Syria. Early on, the regime, closely observing the dramatic changes in other countries impacted by the regional 'Arab Spring', signalled openness for national dialogue, while dismissing some of the dynamics leading the protests as agitations coordinated from outside. Shootings at protests were justified with claims about the existence of armed militants. Meanwhile, promises for reform were dismissed by those who had suffered torture and death in the hands of the regime for decades. Many expected the Assad regime to be the next domino to fall.

Knowledge on the violent turn in the war remains elusive. The opposition in Syria has historically been ideologically diverse, the end of the Ba'ath Party's authoritarian, security and intelligence-based anti-democratic rule being one overarching demand. There is a diverse spectrum of opinions among Syrian political actors, from religious and political figures to activists and intellectuals, on the impact that the resort to armed violence had on their causes.[3] The turn to violence particularly alienated and marginalized the voices of women and minorities in the opposition.

With the explicit militarization of the conflict following the open formation of armed groups that operated under the loose umbrella of the 'Free Syrian Army', the situation spiralled into a web of proxy wars with a number of local and international actors with competing interests. As different rebel factions competed for legitimacy and external funding, infighting left civilians in the crossfire of power struggles. As many commentators noted, the term 'FSA' was a branding label. The incoherence is perhaps most strikingly illustrated in the fact that while some FSA battalions fought alongside or even joined with the YPG/YPJ (and later SDF), others merged with radical Islamist groups. That funding from countries like Saudi Arabia, Qatar, and Turkey enabled the rapid rise of the radical Islamist colours of anti-regime resistance is now widely recognized. In retrospect, it is clear that Western and regional countries' aid for regime change (as in Libya) was strenghtening groups like al-Qaeda.[4]

These developments fed into the regime's narrative that there was no real opposition in Syria. As the war dragged on, the regime resorted to indiscriminate killings and collective punishment, and continued its control over the population through securitization, torture, and detentions. Horrifying images revealed reports about the deadly fate of people in regime custody, most famously in the Saydnaya Prison.[5]

One episode in early June 2011 in Jisr al-Shughour in the northern province of Idlib, near the Turkish border, is often narrated as a turning point in the war.[6] Lieutenant Colonel Hussein Harmoush defected and announced the formation of the Free Officers Movement, which would later merge into the Free Syrian Army (FSA). In his account, members of the forces had refused to shoot at protesters, which led to mutiny and infighting in the ranks. He went to Turkey, where the state had in the meantime set up tents in its Hatay province to host thousands of refugees. That the refugees, who routinely protested in the camps against the regime, were grateful to Turkey was amplified by Western media and also echoed by US celebrity Angelina Jolie, who quickly travelled to Hatay to visit the displaced. Several journalists sympathetic towards the opposition retrospectively realized that they – and large mainstream agencies like AFP and AP – had been fed false information about what happened in Jisr al-Shughour when people later admitted to them that they had lied in order to blame the massacre on the regime.[7] As it turned out, in coordinated fashion, Islamist militants had killed at least 120 members of the Syrian regime's security forces in Jisr al-Shughour. Many of the bodies were beheaded, mutilated, and dropped into mass graves. The site was visited by diplomats, including then US ambassador Robert Ford. The 'origin story' of the escalation into violence in Syria, including Harmoush's 'heroic' defection story, has not been revised due to fears that it would de-legitimize the struggle against the dictatorship of Assad. Meanwhile, inhabitants of border areas had been seeing militants receive special treatment in Turkish hospitals, noting sectarian ideologies first-hand.[8]

The events of Jisr al-Shughour of course do not represent legitimate demands raised by democratic oppositions (who were unaware of such violent episodes at the time) and they do not erase the atrocities and war crimes committed by the Assad regime, which was later on aided by indiscriminate Russian military power. However, truth on the factors that reproduced cycles of violence and displacement, especially the role of external actors, will matter for any possibility of peace and justice. Uncritically lumping perpetrators of atrocities together with grassroots democratic opposition activists all under vague umbrella terms has been a useful blurring of lines for both the brutal regime and those who wanted regime change at all costs. But rendering the role of coordinated international action and well-organized reactionary groups (and their links to regional and global actors) as marginal to the story is a massive injustice to the millions of ordinary Syrians, who demanded change and have lost lives and futures to this war. This background is also important to help make sense of the ways in which actors in Rojava related to events in the country. Turkey's relationship to rebel groups and their cross-border coordination were major reasons for why the Kurdish movement, with eyes on both sides of the border, took an unapologetic attitude towards armed self-defence from the first moment of the Rojava Revolution.

Within weeks after protests started in March 2011, Bashar al-Assad issued various decrees, including one to give previously disenfranchised Kurds Syrian citizenship and ID cards. Many interpreted this as a way of discouraging the Kurds from collectively joining the country-wide protests. When the state forces withdrew from the north in 2012, suspicion increased that there was a secret agreement between the PYD and the regime. The regime's presence had already begun thinning as it started to concentrate its army and security forces in regions where armed groups had been capturing territories. In any case, Assad effectively cut the rebels' logistical lifeline to Turkey by enabling the Turkish state's greatest vendetta, the Kurds. Activists in the Syrian opposition often portrayed the PYD and its affiliates as being prejudicially against the movement based on Kurdish nationalist interests. Such accusations, however, ignored the regime's history of repression against the PYD and uncritically echoed the discourse of the Turkish state. Several articles of the Syrian Penal Code provisions permit actions that can be seen as inciting racial or sectarian strife, with one article specifically banning acts towards cutting off chunks of Syria with the aim of joining it to other countries. The prospect of mobilization in Kurdish areas is rooted in a decades-old anxiety of the Ba'ath regime; however, it is specifically the PKK movement that has the largest popular base and greatest organizing capacity in these regions. PYD spokespeople often stressed that their party and affiliated organizations had been among the main targets of the Ba'ath Party in the 2000s under Bashar al-Assad, especially after the latter's 1999 security deal with Turkey ('Adana agreement'). As noted in a Human Rights Watch report from 2009, protests and events organized by the movement (Newroz, 8 March, solidarity with Kurds in other parts) were frequently targeted with live ammunition; activists routinely disappeared in detention. Moreover, the heavily criminalized PYD has a long history of cooperation with left and secular elements of the opposition. In fact, it was embedded with the increasingly marginalized National Coordination Committee for Democratic Change (often referred to as 'internal opposition'), an alliance of political parties, who opposed foreign intervention and favoured de-escalation and dialogue with the regime.

Although the internationally supported exiled opposition around the Turkey-based, Muslim Brotherhood-dominated Syrian National Council (SNC) presented itself in anti-Ba'athist terms (with members having experienced violence and persecution under Ba'ath rule), its positions towards Kurdish rights, minor symbolic gestures aside, did not fundamentally differ from that of the Syrian regime. Leading spokespeople of the SNC repeatedly shut down Kurdish demands for decentralization or the recognition of the Kurds as a nation as 'secessionism'. If the Kurds' historical experience of regime reprisal (with little to no solidarity from opposition actors) discouraged some from joining the protests, these dynamics inside the opposition further alienated them.[9] Early on, the PYD's vision clashed with that of a camp of Kurdish parties with ties to the Barzanî rule on the other side of the border. A collective of these groups make up the Kurdish National Council in Syria (Kurdish acronym: ENKS) bloc, which initially joined the Turkey-based internationally supported SNC.[10] Kurds were tokenized along ideological lines within the SNC in the international sphere; the accepted representatives belonged to the ENKS, i.e. they shared strategic interests with Turkey. Leaders within the Rojava Revolution, who had been intimately familiar with Turkey's role within NATO for decades, did not view foreign-sponsored regime change as the preferred option. As such, political efforts in Rojava did not pursue a line of toppling the authoritarian regime at all costs. In meetings with delegates to Imralı Prison, Öcalan repeatedly stressed that the Kurds should be open to talk to anyone in Syria who is open to give them their democratic rights. He emphasized that resistance to Assad's authoritarian rule could not happen through reliance on external imperial powers or Islamists but by way of progressive alliances among Syrians.[11] In statements, political representatives and organizations stressed that while they had a long history of resisting the regime and that the status quo under Assad's dictatorship had to end, they did not want to get dragged into what they considered as sinister foreign agendas. In the absence of a strong independent opposition, willing to seriously accommodate Kurdish rights, and in light of increasing attacks by numerous foreign-armed and funded factions, they pushed their 'third way' – an autonomous Rojava within a secular, democratic, federal Syria. These political perspectives and efforts to reach out for democratic alliances are documented in press statements and official documents but they were largely ignored on the national and international level, especially due to Turkish pressure. During my first trip to Rojava in late 2014, Amina Osê, member of the PYD and at the time deputy spokesperson for the Board of Foreign Relations of the Jazeera canton, explained:

When we saw the developments in Tunisia, Egypt, and elsewhere, we knew Syria would be impacted soon. At our extraordinary congress in June 2011, we decided to forge alliances with progressive, democratic Arab groups. At the same time, we prepared the ground for our societal self-organization through councils, youth, and women's work. The regime remained silent on us, and it anyway had more urgent problems elsewhere. They knew our mobilization capacities. Compared to others, we knew the regime well. We knew that simply demanding a dictator to be removed is not sufficient. The entire system needed to change.

In the summer of 2011, the People's Self-Defence Units (YXG), as well as the first overt people's councils were formed by communities in Rojava who had long supported the PKK. The People's Council of Rojava Kurdistan (MGRK) launched in 2011. When the revolution was declared in 2012, Tev-Dem began offering educations and organizing popular participation in the grassroots democratic structures. In a country in which aspects of Kurdish culture were either marginalized or banned, suddenly Kurdish TV channels, radios, newspapers, books, films, and music groups were shooting up everywhere. At the same time, Rojava became a main target of radical Islamist groups such as Jabhat al-Nusra. Especially in 2013, al-Qaeda-linked groups launched attacks on Kurdish towns even from inside Turkey.

When Tev-Dem's calls for inclusion in international talks at Geneva, as well as cooperation with the more privileged Kurdish parties failed, in January 2014, the three cantons of Rojava, Kobanê, Afrîn, and Jazeera declared democratic autonomy in response. The Social Contract of Rojava was presented at the time in lieu of a constitution and outlined the movement's intention to build a secular, pluralistic, and gender egalitarian society from the bottom up. A commitment to justice and peace for all ethnic and religious communities accompanied a clearly spelled out desire to treat the abolition of discrimination and violence against women as a duty and burden on all of society. With the autonomy declaration began the ambitious work to build a large-scale self-governance system for millions of people in the middle of war.

Hediye Yusuf, at the time of our interview in 2015, co-president of Jazeera canton, elaborated on what she perceived as the difference between Rojava's model and other protest movements in the wider region, namely, a pre-existing (left) revolutionary network, a concretely emancipatory project to be implemented in a coordinated manner with the guidance of experienced cadres and organized political communities, and a reluctance to trust global or regional state agendas that claimed to demand freedom for Syrians in an abstract sense. In other words, coordination, not spontaneity, made Rojava's revolution:

There was an already organized community here, a pre-existing political culture. Experienced people provided farsighted perspectives and analyses

219

to lead the process of self-organization. Unlike other regions of the Arab Spring countries, we did not have a sudden outburst of events in Rojava. As the Syrian opposition was co-opted, as the Free Syrian Army splintered into dozens of groups, and as al-Nusra, Daesh, and similar groups took over, the narrative of the war in Syria turned from being a demand for freedom against dictatorship to a war on terrorism. The armed groups jumped from front to front with their weapons, whereas we liberated our own communities, secured their safety and immediately established people's councils.

Our fight was ideological. From the start, our priority was to express the will of the people in all communities, not the interests of one nation or one section of society. Our victories are not measured by lands conquered but by the ability to turn uneducated mothers into leaders in society. This perspective of ours empowered our ability to physically fight. For us, radical social change was at stake. From the start, our opponents claimed this: 'The Kurds want a state in Syria'. This is because their authoritarian mentality does not allow their horizon to go beyond the state as the liberator. In their logic, the co-existence of people is impossible, a farce. For us, it is the very cause we fight and die for.

Figure 16 Photos of Sakine Cansız (Sara), Fidan Doğan (Rojbîn), and Leyla Şaylemez (Ronahî), and Clara Zetkin and Rosa Luxemburg, above a statue of Mother Mary, at the Ishtar Women's Academy in Rojava. Rimelan. July 2015.

220

BUILDING THE SELF-ADMINISTRATION

For the first time, democratic autonomy was going to be put into practice on a larger scale, in a place colonized by an authoritarian regime. Nevertheless, we knew that a system created by women's hands would be qualitatively different from the nation-state mentality. We wanted to build a communal, democratic society, pioneered by women, without hierarchy and domination. From the start, we said absolutely no institution should be without women and we set minimum criteria. We said: if there is going to be revolution in Rojava, it must be led, formed, created, and thought by women. Beyond quotas, we needed women's representation to mean something radical. Women are decision-makers in all spheres of life in Rojava now. You cannot find a woman-less institution, assembly, or committee in the revolutionary institutions today. It's impossible because women are foundational to the philosophy of the system. – Nûda, Rojava, 2015

Democratic Confederalism had been declared in 2005, only seven years before the beginning of the revolution in Rojava. As such, the Kurdistan freedom movement had already been articulating a broad vision for a revolutionary self-governance system. In fact, it had even accumulated some experience with local self-governance, municipalism, and cooperative economies in Bakur and Mexmûr Refugee Camp. However, nothing could have prepared people for the enormous task of organizing the lives of millions in the midst of war. At a time in which terms like democratic autonomy, commune, cooperative, etc. still seemed abstract or esoteric even to long-term supporters of the movement, a whole field opened up to test these ideas in practice. This field was not a sterile lab, however, it was a war-torn country, and while Rojava is home to the oldest PKK sympathizers, there were also millions of unorganized people who had no reason to put faith in adventurous journeys. In this sense, much of the practical implementation of the movement's ideas in Rojava emerged from within the concrete needs, preferences, and priorities of diverse communities, besieged by conflict.

Naturally, the establishment of a new political system was not welcomed by everyone. There is a large number of people that has not involved itself and views the system through critical or neutral eyes. Some groups actively opposed the work. From the beginning, the KDP-affiliated ENKS (which largely aligned with the Turkey-backed opposition), voiced criticisms over the PYD's undertakings, accusing it of authoritarianism and collaboration with the Assad regime. Non-Kurdish communities, including tribes and religious minorities, often refrained from engagement, and some groups opposed the self-governance project due to political or ideological disagreements. Others are dissatisfied

221

with the revolutionary system's ability to deliver its promise. Several Syrian intellectuals and activists have written, mostly in Arabic, critical commentaries on the promises and limits of these proposals around federalism, decentralization, and citizenship.[12]

Revolutionary ideals were up against reality at every stage. Early on, the need was identified to create a representative system alongside the creation of communes and councils. As explained to me by various people involved in different aspects of the early process, it was unrealistic to expect people to suddenly accept new ways of doing things without explanation or proof of benefit and efficiency. Activists often describe this dual process of building revolutionary politics alongside more traditional forms of governance as part of the struggle to 'help people overcome the state mentality'.

The current political system is a hybrid and constantly evolving model that is made up of confederations of regions, assemblies, and communes. Following several restructuring efforts, such as the Democratic Federation of Rojava – northern Syria, whose establishment in 2016 was opposed by the US and Turkey, as well as the Syrian state and the SNC opposition, in 2018, the Autonomous Administration of North and East Syria (hereafter AANES) was declared. As of the time of writing, the AANES consists of seven regions: Jazeera (Cizîrê), Euphrates (Firat), Afrîn, Manbij, Tabqa, Raqqa, and Deir ez-Zor, making up an estimated population of 4–5 million. The area around Qamişlo and Hesekê is now part of the Jazeera canton, while Kobanê and Girê Spî are cantons of the Euphrates region. At the time of writing, a new social contract is being discussed and negotiated through various committees and public and specific consultations with plans to establish a board to develop and implement regulations for elections.

An election system has been in the making for several years, with disruptions caused by the Turkish invasions, but at large, the notion of democracy is not limited to elections in Rojava. The emphasis on the social means that democracy is also expressed in people's participation in the running of daily life. The most direct and concrete way in which people intervene in political action in Rojava happens within the communes and councils. Horizontally, committees are tied to the commune and councils, while vertically, they are tied to the respective region-wide committees, so that the highest level embodies the prototype of the lowest. The women, who are among the co-presidents, administration, and committees in any given general commune, are also members of the parallel women's commune, but they do not take up tasks within it and vice versa. The spokeswoman of the women's commune participates in meetings of the general commune administration. Likewise, the female co-president of the general commune joins the meetings of the women's commune administration. They coordinate with each other, but follow their own decisions and plans. The councils can only claim to be representatives of the communes, if people actively engage in the latter. The fact that many people do not participate presents a challenge and raises questions of legitimacy. As such, among the first major efforts of 'building' the Rojava Revolution was the establishment of people's academies for the public to learn and discuss the system, as well as autonomous youth and women's academies parallel to the general educational system for children and youth. The relationship between the direct democratic grassroots institutions and the representative self-administration is often described as 'negotiation and struggle'. As argued by Nazan Üstündağ (2016), the communes and councils are an effort to undo state-like tendencies of the self-administration. They do not necessarily seek representation but demand protection and services, while engaging in the act of self-organization in the neighbourhoods. Tev-Dem, which initially helped form the communes, councils, cooperatives, and academies now primarily focuses on developing the civil society sphere through cultural institutions, unions, and social justice campaigns. The Rojava Information Center (RIC 2019) describes Tev-Dem as a 'counter-power' to the Autonomous Administration, 'preventing it from reproducing itself as a state and protecting the values of democratic confederalism'. A young activist named Nûda, who had participated in the revolutionary process since the beginning, claimed that the system of Rojava derives its legitimacy from the bottom up: 'Notice how the last thing that was declared was the self-government. We did not create communes only afterwards. We started with the communes and extrapolated from there.'

The protagonists of this early revolutionary phase were a relatively defined group. Over time, new revolutionary subjectivities were produced and reproduced, as organizational efforts expanded to new constituencies previously untapped. Decades under an authoritarian regime had normalized power abuse and impunity. How could a revolutionary party-based movement fill a vacuum and create not only a whole system, democratic in its claims, but also mechanisms for checks and balances, rules and regulations, and spaces and conditions for oppositions and contentious politics? The self-administration evolved as a process of constant restructuring and renewal. It set up new parties, organizations, coalitions, etc. to form new publics that could organize daily affairs at the same time as debating complex issues like citizenship, decentralization, dialogue, and reconstruction. In this way, it acts as a front for a wider, less conservative agenda for revolutionary liberation.

While the administration is a site for the structural democratization of the wider region and therefore more conventional in its language and methods, the communes, assemblies, and all other direct democratic institutions privilege social and cultural transformation and thus employ more explicitly the aesthetics and approaches of the revolutionary struggle. One stream tries to bring together ideologically and politically divergent constituencies and interest groups in formal settings. It interacts with the other, which draws on the old, strong, and familiar bonds that connect the Apocî community. Tensions happen for example, when the autonomously organized revolutionary youth movement, whose stance is openly militant, bypasses the formal administration structures to target offices of individuals or organizations that it identifies as acting to undermine the revolution. Within the self-administration structures there are people who condemn as well as people who appreciate the youth's direct actions.

From day one, women played a central role in the building of the system, from taking part in the physical defence of the region to the drafting of the social contract. They did not do so only on an individual basis, but organizationally, as delegates of the revolutionary women's movement. From the start, the co-presidency system was introduced in the revolution's institutions. The creation of women's and youth associations, communes, and assemblies were among the first steps taken in 2012. In many places, the women's movement reappropriated the buildings of the regime and turned their contents upside down. For instance, the Ishtar Women's Academy in Rimelan, previously a Ba'ath Party guest house, is part of a gated complex that women repurposed and turned purple. Bombshells became flower-pots, and the walls are decorated with women like Rosa Luxemburg, Clara Zetkin, and Sakine Cansız. The Women's Board of the Jazeera canton is a good example of the symbiotic relationship between the self-administration and the radical democratic efforts in Rojava. It actively works with and stands in solidarity with the women's movement, supporting initiatives and projects of civil society organizations such as the anti-violence organization Sara or the Free Women's Foundation of Rojava (WJAR). When I visited, Emîne Omar, then head of the Board, explained that unlike the daily grassroots self-organization in the commune and council system, the Board was working on larger-scaled projects for the canton. Among their early projects were shelters, sports and health facilities, literacy classes, and economic initiatives. The Board compiled a canton-wide survey on women's literacy rates, education levels, employment, health, and economic situation and proposed projects based on the findings. Nurseries and orphanages were opened. The Board played a significant role in the drafting, issuing, and campaigning of the women's laws passed in 2014 and helped organize public seminars and educations to prepare society for them. They regularly met with representatives of the women's movement to get their perspective and share with them the problems of women in the administration.

The liberation of territories from Daesh beyond the majority Kurdish regions presented a vast set of new challenges to the self-administration system under construction since 2012. In line with the stated aim to represent all ethnic and religious components in the region in the spirit of the 'democratic nation', the Syrian Democratic Council (SDC) was formed. It comprises councils and offices made up of representatives from different political and cultural groups and seeks internal Syrian-Syrian dialogue for a political solution to the conflict. It is mainly in touch with progressive and secular opposition groups, and constitutes the body through which the AANES contacts the regime. It advocates a decentralized, federal, and secular Syria in which the rights and representation of all sections of society will be secured.

Despite systematic efforts to struggle against nationalism and chauvinism, sentiments of hostility and vengefulness, sometimes stemming from concrete life experiences, have not disappeared. It is not uncommon for Kurds to express their mistrust towards Arab members of the Syrian Democratic Forces (SDF) or civilian structures. Christians, who survived massacres committed by Kurdish-Arab alliances in the past, struggle to find incentives to involve themselves. Arabs I spoke to were not shy to admit their scepticism towards what many see as a Kurdish political project. While reservations and conflicts remain, with time, many new constituencies were 'won over' for a common governance system still under construction. In recent years, various Rojava-wide conferences and public consultations were held to improve the services and governance system in line with local demands and needs.

The SDC's Women's Office established the Syrian Women's Council as an umbrella to unite women's organizations, political party representatives, and individual activists from Syria, beyond Rojava. Through representatives, it organizes forums to discuss women's perspectives on the Syrian conflict, public events, trainings, and rallies on various issues. In 2021, the Zenobia Women's Rally was formed for the majority Arab regions of Tabqa, Raqqa, Deir ez-Zor, and Manbij to match the work of Kongreya Star at the local level.

Rojava's previous economic relationship to the Syrian state is often described by activists as colonial. After expropriating much of the land, the state banned the local growth of certain products.[13] This monoculture policy not only corrupted the soil, it also exploited the local populations, who neither reaped the fruits of their labour, nor were able to grow diversely for their own consumption. In the absence of much heavy industry and infrastructure, there were no major yawning gaps between classes in the area. Land, the main source of property, was either owned by the state or rural elites. In the past, Kurdish women were working their fields, but the economic strategy of the state robbed women off their subsistence economies. In the already conservative, increasingly impoverished community, girls were discouraged from going to school and more likely to marry young. Some engaged in precarious work as cheap labourers under subcontracts, picking cotton, lentils, and chickpeas, but their wages were often seized by fathers or husbands.

Economic works, including building vital infrastructure, started at the beginning of the revolution. Land previously owned by the state was allocated to communities to work on cooperatively. As a result, the area was largely spared from starvation and even managed to look after hundreds of thousands of IDPs from Syria and refugees from Iraq without foreign aid for the most part especially in the early years. Although each region runs its economy independently, committees oversee the inter-regional exchange economy and manage their coordination. In the context of war and specific embargoes on Rojava, the administration's stated aim was to create a social economy, relying mostly on the development of economic cooperatives to struggle against trade monopolies. The actual conditions of war, however, greatly limit capacities and mean a constant juggle between keeping the war economy going and assuring the basic needs of millions of people. Siham Karyo, a Syriac activist and politician, who was heading the Jazeera Canton's Board of Economy during my 2015 visit, told me that much of Syria's agriculture, animal husbandry, and petrol used to come from Gozarto, the Aramaic name for Jazeera. The Ba'athist administrators were mostly not from the local population and organized the economy according to state interest. In her view, the regime tried to control populations through dependency. This was achieved by dispossession and migration:

> We prioritize cooperatives to assure that the economy is in the hands of those who work. We are committed to democratize the economy, which means we

Figure 17 Members of the Young Women's Movement in Rojava in one of their centres. Qamişlo. December 2014.

cannot sign anything off without the approval of the communes. Once the embargo is lifted, individuals or entire systems will want to exploit the region or corrupt the communal economy we try to establish by turning it into a capitalist one. We oppose attempts from abroad to invest and profit off our backs. People can help our economy, but in a manner that helps us create our own institutions and efforts.

Ramziya Mihemed, who was heading the Board of Finance of Cizîrê canton at the time of our interview, argued that the KDP's border policies and embargoes were trying to turn the precarious and economically vulnerable populations against the new system under construction. She explained that the board, which at the time especially oversaw incomes from the semi-official, unrecognized Semalka-Faysh Khabour border, tried to protect the embargoed economy from exploitation and poor-quality products.

Since the beginning of the revolution, the women's movement created cooperatives for women to work in agriculture, food production, textile works among others. Aboriya Jin is the 'women's economy' commission that oversees the strategy for sustainable work opportunities for women. To enable economic independence, the women's movement allocates agricultural land, creates work opportunities, offers trainings and childcare options. Women still overwhelmingly rely on men economically, however, a shift in gendered notions of work is on the horizon of the women's movement, which coordinates with autonomous women's economy bodies within the administration.

Despite such perspectives and projects, the anti-capitalist promise of Rojava's economy remains compromised on several levels. The US extracts Syrian oil in SDF-held areas while imposing heavy sanctions on the country. Wealthy individuals and businesses gauge investment opportunities as many areas remain in need of reconstruction and development. The revolutionaries' vision for communal economies does not always match with demands on the ground, especially of members of the wealthier classes, who do not benefit from them. The example of Rojava shows that building just, sustainable, and independent economies is one of the greatest challenges of any revolutionary project, especially in conflict environments.

BRAIDING JUSTICE FROM BELOW: THE *MAL A JIN*

In the past, women who experienced violence were told 'You are a woman. This is your fate. You need to bear him'. With the revolution, we started building our own institutions. For the first time, we had physical spaces like the *mal a jin*, with women working in them, to solve our issues. In the first months of the revolution, we didn't have access to many vehicles, so women were walking to these spaces. Just looking at the streets, you could see that the women in our communities were flooding to institutions. Our town Kobanê saw with its own eyes how and why women were leaving their homes: they were walking to organize themselves! After so many years of 'honour killings', women were leaving their homes without people bothering them. No longer would they endure violence or remain servants of their family. Now, women had their autonomous structures. – Sara, Kobanê, 2018

In a world in which women's lived experiences of violence are often dismissed, the *mal a jin* (women's house) default position is to believe women. Operating in all cities, most towns and many villages of Rojava, these physical places represent an organized and institutionalized form of women's solidarity in society. Concretely, they help solve issues faced by women in their respective constituencies. In a broader sense, linked to the women's assemblies, and operating parallel to the *mal a gel* (people's house; mixed-gender), their grassroots conflict resolution, anti-violence work, and consciousness-raising efforts prefigure society's justice-seeking without the state.[14]

In the first instance in the self-organized structures in Rojava, conflicts in society are solved at the commune level through the *silh* (Arabic: reconciliation) committees, made up of people from the same neighbourhood. These committees are presented as updated forms of traditional community peace-making practices. They rotate, but volunteers are often elderly people, mainly women, who listen to all parties of a dispute and try to make sustainable social peace in a way that is acceptable to the people concerned. If the *silh* is unsuccessful, people can go to the *mal a gel* or *mal a jin*, where the problem gets taken up in a more formal manner. Only in the last instance, a people's tribunal gets activated.

When the first *mal a jin* were established at the beginning of the war, women found out that there were far more problems in society than they anticipated. One *mal a jin* worker told me about discovering a girl being chained by her family. Apart from domestic violence, the most common issues raised at the *mal a jin* are polygamy, divorce, forced or under-age marriage, and lack of access to education and work. The institutions generally suffer from a lack of capacity, especially since hundreds of thousands of IDPs arrived in the area. The workers, who visit women and their families and follow up on their issues, often experience intimidation and abuse, as well as smear campaigns, particularly around the question of divorce, and are therefore protected by local women's self-defence units.

Mal a jin workers receive trainings from the women's movement, but they are no 'professionals'. A minority may have gone to high school or even university, but most workers only went to primary or middle school, with many not having been able to go to school at all. Rather than establishing a bureaucratic system, workers claim that their aim is to establish socially useful, flexible, and generous structures to concretely solve people's daily issues. Their approach to justice is 'social', not normative or formal rights-based (although they draw part of their legitimacy from the women's laws). Everyone knows that the *mal a jin* are organized by local women in coordination with the women's movement Kongreya Star. Leyla, a 28-year-old coordinator in Tirbêspiyê (al-Qahtaniyah), told me that because their members are from the communities that they serve, their work was seen as genuine in the neighbourhood. In her eyes, the speedy, concrete work done by people for their own neighbours, legitimized and rendered their efforts lasting. It also established a sense of organized solidarity among women living in the same area:

> In the past, women did not feel that anyone has their back. Now, at the *mal a jin*, we resolve within days issues that people experienced for years. Every day, as you see with your own eyes, two or three different issues come in. Girls, who were married under-aged, married women, who have problems, young women, who escape violence at home … They see it as a place where their problems will be heard and solved on their own terms.

The act of solving social problems gives strength to the workers, who feel the positive impact of their emotional labour. Younger and older women work together on equal terms, not always without conflict. The older women are supposed to respect the young women's thoughts and decisions and are encouraged to remain open-minded for new perspectives, while the youth benefit from the former's life experience. One of the youngest *mal a jin* members I met was a 19-year old, who said that young women preferred speaking to her. I met her 'colleague' Ilham, a woman in her 60s at an education of the Women's Academy in Rimelan (see *Figure 4*). A strongly built woman, whose posture and speech radiate what the movement often calls 'natural authority', she explained that to transform mentalities, one had to make sure that proposed changes are understood and accepted by society:

> There is still a long way to go! But already homes are created in more egalitarian and democratic ways now. Families get influenced by our work. Today, women leave their homes early and come back late. For example, we have been here for one month at this academy, but nobody bothers us about it. Men at first rejected and resisted us. But they increasingly see that we do good things. We always explain that we are not against men, we want to be equal friends. Now men themselves even come to the *mal a jin*. Our aim is to educate our people to treat each other well, above all in the family.

I lived for two weeks in Ilham's house in Qamişlo and followed her around to get a sense of the work of the *mal a jin*, which she joined when it was first created in 2011. With her husband, who worked in the *mal a gel*, she exchanged experiences and events every night on their balcony over tea. They respected each other's work, which is of equal value. Sometimes, even late at night, Ilham would busy herself with resolving community disputes over the phone. When I, influenced by a capitalist organization of work/time, asked her if she ever got tired, she laughed: 'I am happier since I started this work. Because I can see my own impact, I can see what my labour achieves – a change in society for the better.'

Even with all the new possibilities available to them since 2012, activists I interviewed in Rojava were not as interested in bureaucratic protocols and legal formalities as they were keen on genuinely abolishing violence and domination in the communities' 'minds and hearts' forever. The women's struggle can only render itself lasting, they said, if it actually convinces and wins over society.

FIGHTING A CENTURY OF GENOCIDE-FEMINICIDE: SYRIAC WOMEN IN THE REVOLUTION

The mentality governing the Ottoman genocide and Daesh's terror campaigns, one hundred years apart, is the same. It's about eliminating the ancient peoples, cultures, and relations of this region. We believe that three things will protect us women from violence and massacre: organization, knowledge, and solidarity between peoples and faith groups.

ܣܝܦܐ – 'Seyfo' (the sword) – is the name given to the campaigns of mass murder, forced displacement, and systematic kidnapping of women and children against Syriacs, Chaldeans, and Assyrians in the late Ottoman Empire. The pogroms, which happened with Kurdish complicity parallel to genocide campaigns against Armenians and Greeks, took place almost exactly one century before Daesh terrorized the same geography. To many Christian women in the region, Daesh's systematic use of sexual violence, kidnapping, and forced marriage as a tool of war is based on a century-old legacy of genocide and feminicide.

We see Daesh as a project of terror, a Wahabist, Salafist organization that uses Islam for its own interest. It leads a war not only against Christians, but also against Êzîdîs and other Muslims. We understand that they don't represent Islam, but rather attempt to destroy ancient civilizations through a power-driven system of control and massacre. The basis for this was laid in

230

the Ottoman era. There is continuity in the method of using violence against women as a method of conquest.*

The French colonial mandate had used sectarianism for the purpose of dividing and controlling the diverse society in the new Syria in the aftermath of the Ottoman Empire. The pan-Arabist Ba'ath Party claimed to transcend religious divisions to an extent, but nonetheless disenfranchised and co-opted different ethnic and religious communities to consolidate its Arab nationalist rule. Like the Kurds, the Syriacs, Assyrians, Armenians, Chechens, Turkmens, or Circassians did not enjoy language rights in Syria. Christian communities enjoyed limited protection due to the church, which provided a degree of sanctuary through community, faith, and cultural identity. There is denomina-tional, linguistic, and political diversity among Christian communities in Syria. Moreover, there are differences in the socio-economic conditions of Christians living in cities like Damascus or on the coast and those living in the north. Among the latter, especially members of the Syriac community in Cizîrê (or *Gozarto* in Aramaic) in cities and towns like Qamişlo, Dêrîk, al-Hesekê, and Tirbêspiyê, and surrounding villages, actively and collectively participated in the co-construction of the evolving democratic federal system in North and East Syria.

The Syriac Union Party was from the beginning part of the various aspects of the self-administration's establishment, such as the drafting of the social contract. It organizes itself through committees for culture, women, youth, education, and language. The Syriac equivalent of the *asayîş* are the Sutoro, which are linked to the Syriac Military Council (Mawtbo Fulhoyo Suryoyo (MFS)). Mainly active in regions with sizeable Syriac populations, the MFS has been working in coordination with the YPG and YPJ since 2012 and became one of the founding components of the Syrian Democratic Forces (SDF).

The Syriac Women's Union was founded at the beginning of the revolution in Rojava. Affiliated to the Syriac Union Party, its membership currently amounts to several hundred Syriac women and affiliated associations inside Syria. Through cultural and educational activities as well as protest actions, alongside social organizing and economic initiatives, the organization addresses specific issues experienced by Syriac women in all towns and cities that they inhabit.

In the summer of 2015, I spoke to Hayat, Shamiran, and Sheza, coordinators of the Syriac Women's Union in Tirbêspiyê (al-Qahtaniyah). Their communal building was decorated with references to Syriac women's history and culture. Democratic co-existence between the peoples, they said, had been rendered unimaginable as a result of Ottoman era genocides, nationalist state-building

---

* I thank Alan Roj for his Arabic-Kurdish interpretation of this conversation and for his generous support during my time in Rojava.

in the twentieth century, and more recently, groups like al-Nusra and Daesh. From a women's perspective, they said, the methods and mentalities of these attacks resembled each other, especially in their systematic violence against Christian women. The protection of their endangered Christian identity is an important aspect of their work, but the Syriac Women's Union defines itself in secular terms.

According to these activists, expressions of their culture, public demands, and forms of organization could not transgress the limits set by the Syrian regime in the past. They blamed the regime's policies for divisions across Christian communities and described a sense of alienation from public life in an authoritarian system that was built on Arab nationalism: 'We saw nothing as ours.' They claimed that although the Christian community often tends to be less socially conservative compared to the neighbour communities, women also struggle specifically against the patriarchal structures of the church. At the time, their council in Jazeera consisted of 30 people, including a coordinating administration of eleven women, with delegates from the different cities. In each city, the structures worked through committees related to culture, economy, press, and education.

Among the Syriac Women's Union's practical work over the years has been the creation of nurseries, cooperatives, and work opportunities for women. A short-lived chocolate factory was their first economic initiative. Aramaic, which is believed to have been spoken by Jesus Christ, is considered to be an endangered language. The organized women of Gozarto, including the Syriac Women's Union, are actively reviving it through music, education, and media work. At the end of 2020, the Syriac Women's Union began publishing their first newspaper *The Voice of Syriac Women*, to be circulated in all parts within the autonomous administration. Parallel to pursuing their own work, including seminars on forced migration, self-defence, health and culture, Syriac women co-organize events and protest actions, and issue joint statements with Kongreya Star.

> None of our efforts are unchangeable. We are flexible in how we do things because many people remain afraid of self-organization despite the experience collectively gained so far. Our main objective is to develop sustainable and meaningful solutions to our communities' problems here and now. Peace between the peoples is at the heart of all our activities.

Repeatedly, the women stressed the importance of the co-authored nature of the social contract of the region, which in their eyes supported communities' ability to self-organize.

The 'democratic nation' system is designed to discourage one identity imposing itself on another. We see the space this opens for us as Syriac women. We never could have imagined seeing Syriacs become representatives in an administration here [with their own identity and demands], it would have been unthinkable to see a revival of our language. Previously, everything belonged to the regime. But we have been part of drafting the social contract and all the aspects of this system. Now, we are all able to represent ourselves based on specific needs, while we simultaneously lead efforts to democratize and advance our own communities.

Conscious of the fact that people may struggle with the public acclamation of Öcalan, I asked these activists about their views on his ideology. One of them mentioned patriarchal anxiety among men, who desperately cling on to their power in the public and private spheres, as she responded:

Öcalan advocates killing the traditional man. This is a universal claim. He doesn't make it in support of women of only one community, but for women in general. This is an opportunity for all of us. It's one reason why women from different communities take part in the organizations and the canton administration now. The system here is being built on the premise that there can be no free society without the freedom of women. We joyfully take part in this historic process and struggle alongside all those who fight for women's liberation.

A few months after this conversation in 2015, the Bethnarin Women's Protection Units were formed as an autonomous Syriac women's armed force. Previously, Syriac women, including elderly women, had already received training in self-defence, ideological and physical. Early on, they participated in the Sutoro structures before declaring their autonomous women's defence mechanisms.

The first Syriac women's house 'Asterut' was formed in al-Hasakah in 2017.[15] A second one was opened in late 2019 in Qamişlo, which the Syriacs call Zalin. The second conference of the Syriac Women's Union was held in 2018 with 200 delegates, where a new administrative council was formed. The resolution decided to increase relations with other women's organizations, political action groups, and other sections of the regional society, in addition to opening further educational, intellectual and justice-related institutions for women. The women acknowledged that they were at the very beginning of a long journey:

We are hopeful. We increase our struggle efforts daily against a system that wants to annihilate us. The women's struggle is our protection from concepts of honour and power that deny us the right to live freely. As we organize ourselves together with the women from other communities in this region, we create new colours.

RECLAIMING SECURITY FROM MEN AND THE STATE

During the battle of Kobanê, journalists often asked me where my experience as a commander is from. Well, I was not sitting at home when Daesh rose. How can I deny that my foundations, my philosophy, my consciousness are a product of decades of women organizing in the PKK? For decades, Kurdish women have been in the mountains, but there was an information embargo on them. This embargo broke with the YPJ. – Meysa Abdo, Rojava, 2015

In many ways, the YPJ presented a new stage in the decades-old history of Kurdish women's militancy. Its war against Daesh drew worldwide support across the political spectrum; in the context of feminicidal violence, the visibility of the YPJ also sparked transnational, cross-movement debates among feminists and women's movements around the question of women's self-defence. It revealed otherwise taboo-ized and silenced beliefs among many women on the necessity of organized, physical resistance for survival in a brutal patriarchal world. Thanks to the YPJ, today, the Kurdish women's movement's concept of self-defence has become one of the topics that other women's struggles are most interested in discussing with the Kurdish women's movement.

Herself having played a role in the Kurdistan freedom movement for more than two decades, YPJ commander Meryem Kobanê emphasized the importance of understanding the YPJ as a continuation of a longer history of Kurdish women's militancy:

The YPJ was built on the power of a 40-year-old movement and its experiences with autonomous women's units, battalions, and finally, a separate women's army. In other words, we had a Kurdish model to draw on: the women's army in Kurdistan's mountains. We have a wealth of experience of women commanders, Sakine Cansız, Azime, Zelal, Agirî, Berîtan, Ruken Türk. This is a history, an accumulation of women's labor. *Heval* Berçem, Peyman, Şîlan, Bêrîvan … Based on their legacy, we formed the YPJ as a women's army to defend the women's revolution. Creating an autonomous women's defence system requires faith, power, determination, self-confidence, and trust in women. All of this was possible also because of the trust that the Kurdish people's leader (Öcalan) put into the ability of women.

Figure 18 A group of wounded and disabled YPJ fighters being looked after by their comrades. Some women in this unit lost their lives afterwards. Amûdê. December 2014.

The first YPJ fighters I met in 2014 were mostly wounded women, who were recovering from battles with Daesh and Jabhat al-Nusra.[16] They, and the fighters I interviewed in the summer of 2015, insisted that more than just a fighting force, the YPJ was the defence mechanism of a revolutionary political and social system. One fighter named Zîlan stressed that they do not simply fight against Daesh and similar groups, but 'also against the state system and the male-dominated mentality, against the culture that looks down on women, uses violence, abuse, child marriage, and murder in the name of "honour"'. She also noted that education was essential to the success of the women's army in Rojava. Beyond military training, the fighter's academies organized discussions on women's history, women's participation in decision-making and the system-atization of autonomy.

The defence of Rojava always included women, many of whom were veteran guerrillas in the war against Turkey. Before the YPJ was formed as an autonomous women's army, women took part in the mixed YPG and its pre-decessor, the YXG (People's Self-Defence Units); they were in the formation of each unit and each unit formed its women's separate group. Already in 2012, when war broke out in Serêkaniyê (Ras al-Ain), women acted as commanders in the urban battles against al-Nusra and factions that operated under the name of the Free Syrian Army. Women first created platoons in every city, then

235

squads, and then battalions. After a large participation of women in the YPG's conference in January 2013, the women organized their own conference to declare the YPJ on 4 April, deliberately on Öcalan's birthday. Ever since, the autonomous women's army has been organizing itself in all regions, cities and towns with its programme and charter. Institutions such as the Şehîd Şîlan and Şehîd Bêrîvan academies in Afrîn and Aleppo were established to train new fighters and commanders.

Previously mentioned Nûda joined the revolutionary efforts first through the youth movement in 2011 and later educational work before participating in the establishment of the YPJ. She narrated the foundation of the women's army which she helped to build in the following way:

In 2011, when the Syrian protest movement began, we created self-defence committees because we believed that our efforts would be meaningless if we cannot protect our people and defend the values and system we want to build. When the regime was still here, people first organized in squads of perhaps eight to ten people in each neighbourhood. These were independent cells that did not know each other. It was the right choice. I was in Kobanê when we expelled the regime and declared revolution in 2012. There were many jihadist groups in the surrounding area at the time. Had we only focussed on the political and social struggle, Kobanê would have fallen in one day. Thanks to our defence preparation, we took Kobanê before extremist gangs did.

Before the YPJ's founding conference, first autonomous battalions were established in Afrîn. Şehîd Ruken battalion was followed by the Şehîd Adalet battalion in Qamişlo and the Şehîd Dîcle battalion in Kobanê. Then in Dirbêsiyê and Serêkaniyê, for example, Şehîd Berçem. Now we have autonomous battalions in all cities. The YPJ was not only a procedure as required by our ideology. It is really the case that no effort that excluded women succeeded in Rojava. Wherever women were missing, things failed, but the YPJ's morale could sometimes define an operation's success.

Although the YPJ could draw on the YJA Star's model and concept of women's self-defence to a large extent, the creation of a fighting force not in the mountains, but inside society presented many challenges, not least because some families opposed their daughters' wish to join the forces. Sometimes under-aged girls go to the YPJ to escape forced marriages. In turn, families sometimes accuse the fighters of 'kidnapping' their children. Such issues underline what Meryem Kobanê means by the need to take a comprehensive approach to the abolition of violence against women, beyond the battlefield:

It's not easy to establish a women's army in a community in which women are confined to the household. There are many social problems that need to be dealt with and the psychology of oppressed people is a particular one. Women are colonized and occupied by religion, tribalism, the family, a state-centric organization of political life. Our struggle is therefore against the colonization of women as a whole. This is why we don't just learn physical warfare – we analyze society, social relations, gender roles, we discuss how we create the conditions for hope in a different life.

The YPJ was created to live freely, to liberate our bodies, our personalities from all forms of slavery. In this sense, the YPJ is a movement of love in a geography where love was killed. It is a quest for true love in a place in which humanity, philosophy, human quest, and memory have been diminished. This is why our defence is not for a piece of land, but for the protection of life's ability to unfold itself.

Society in Rojava is militarized in many ways. Although many people voluntarily joined the YPJ and YPG, with time, the administration introduced a mainly male-only conscription system, the Erka Xweparastin ('duty of self-defence'). In part, this seems to have been established in response to ENKS-affiliated Kurdish political parties, who sought a power-share arrangement similar to the KRG, but without participating in the fight to defend Rojava. Prisons and security measures are seen as necessary in a region plagued by suicide bombings and assassinations carried out by Daesh sleeper cells. While military structures like the YPJ fight in the war at the frontlines, the towns and cities are internally secured by the asayîş (Kurdish for security or safety). Members of the asayîş often insist that they do not view themselves as 'police', as police protect the interests of the state using violence. The asayîş are mainly stationed in the places they are from, instead of being deployed to places they cannot relate to. The communities' often close-knit relations are an informal way of holding accountable the armed people. As a concept, the asayîş's conduct (speech, body language, etc.) is supposed to radiate calmness and discipline. Abusive behaviour is in principle monitored and can lead to withdrawal from duty.

The general Asayîş Academy in Rimelan was formed in 2013 to build up the internal security system. There, recruits cook, clean, and do other chores collectively alongside basic security training and political education. 'Democratic nation' and the women's struggle are core elements of the curriculum. In 2015, I spent a few days at the academy, where hundreds were training in martial arts, target shooting, and other basics. Kînem, a spokeswoman of the academy, explained to me that the most difficult part of the revolutionary process was overcoming the authoritarian personality created by the regime. In her eyes, both civilians and asayîş members struggled with the idea that security forces do not have to be intimidating and abusive. She believed that the Kurds' dispossession by the regime had led to the development of personalities that lie in the face of authority. Since people did not feel any sense of belonging to the system that governed them through surveillance and control, they had lost the ability to feel protective of each other and society:

Where does occupation begin? Rendering a population hungry by exploiting their lands, labour, and economies, initiates a process of assimilation through dependency. A person with no sense of responsibility cannot defend herself or others. Spirit, body, and lands are connected and together, they form our reflex to defend ourselves against danger. This is the case for all living beings. To create yourself, to exist, you must defend yourself. And only you can define your 'self', in relation to your autonomous will, your community and your lands. For historically oppressed people, it is difficult to understand the meaning of self-defence. We must prevent revenge from taking root. For example, there were new members, who refused to ensure Arab communities' security, due to historic grievances caused by the regime. We help turn these feelings into consciousness and a universal responsibility to defend society against attacks.

Women organize within the general *asayîş* forces, as well as autonomously. The *Asayîş a Jin* of Qamişlo, whose headquarters I visited in 2015, was formed in 2012 to intervene especially in cases of violence against women. There, Arab and Kurdish women explained the difficulties of legitimizing their presence as women in a traditionally hyper-masculine sphere. Their greatest problem at the beginning was a general lack of faith in women's abilities to manage chaotic situations and provide safety. When I asked about their detention facilities, one spokeswoman told me that they detained people for relatively short periods, viewing detention as a chance to discuss with people and rehabilitate them, while trying to understand reasons for their acts. Detained people are offered education and literature, alongside other activities. The vast majority of the high-risk prisoners in Rojava are Daesh members and their families, many of whom are foreign nationals, whose countries refuse to take them back. In recent years, several large-scale amnesties were issued for those who no longer seemed to pose threats to society.

In addition to the *asayîş*, the Civil Defence Forces (Hêzên Parastina Civakî – HPC) were formed in 2014 as a civilian voluntary community guard. These are civilians, often even elderly people, who rotate in taking turns to protect their own neighbourhoods, especially during protests, festivals, and funeral ceremonies. The autonomous HPC-Jin is empowered by the *Asayîş a Jin* to intervene in cases related to domestic violence.[17] As a grassroots body, the HPC and HPC-Jin further serve to develop a wider consciousness in society around the question of self-defence. The HPC represents what the movement views as society's self-defence reclaimed, one step towards the future abolition of militarizing and bureaucratic army and security structures.

*   *   *

With all hardships and shortcomings, the concrete institutions and structures built in the context of Rojava constituted a learning experience that showed that democratic self-governance is not a mechanical, procedure-driven undertaking. The many problems and issues faced in the process of setting up a new system in Rojava deepened people's understanding of democracy in practice at the same time as it alerted people to the danger of power, corruption, and authoritarianism within revolutionary contexts. It highlighted that different sites of the revolutionary struggle to abolish oppression are mutually reliant and constitutive. As such, organizers on the ground repeatedly stress that their political system is neither perfect nor final but that their revolution has only just begun.

To women, the revolution in Rojava opened new opportunities, lifestyles, choices, paths, and possibilities in an unprecedented manner. Women from different cultural backgrounds took steps to liberate themselves as individuals while simultaneously creating common vocabularies, cultures, and subjectivities in collective processes. They not only cultivated hope, but they also formed institutions and mechanisms to secure existential bases for their hopes. As later sections will discuss, protecting the solidarity and strength developed by women over the years became a central rallying point in the resistance of the Turkish state's military invasions and occupations.

*   *   *

After more than a decade of war, with war crimes committed by nearly everyone, one of the greatest challenges ahead will be the development of a sustainable political solution in Syria. Innocent people have died from thousands of bombs and airstrikes. Both US and Russian interests continue to undermine any form of justice for the millions of Syrians, who have seen their country collapse into ruins. In the particular context of Rojava, paradoxically, a NATO country's presence (US) in a historically anti-NATO state (Syria) is a lifeline in the shadow of attempts by another NATO country (Turkey) at ethnic cleansing and occupation. A commitment to a democratic, federal Syria is incompatible with the violent and authoritarian regime's culture, but US military presence in the region is neither sustainable nor desirable for the many ordinary Syrians, who view it as a colonial occupation. Parallel to its eventual military support for

239

Kurdish forces to fight Daesh three years into the war (following covert as well as open training and military aid to other armed factions fighting the regime), the US aimed to depoliticize (or de-revolutionize) Rojava in the hope of an arrangement similar to its relationship to the KRG. In many ways, a Turkish state/PKK stand-off is unfolding inside Syria with ideological-political characteristics similar to the two decades earlier phase inside Iraq (outlined in Part I of this book). Meanwhile, as a settlement without the Assad regime no longer seems to be on international agendas, Russian leverage over the Assad regime will play a key role in determining the future of Rojava.

In addition to the constant emergence of new challenges stemming from the growth of the self-governance system, violence, and geopolitical precarity implicate the AANES in the systems of power that revolutionaries claim to oppose. The space between a rock and a hard place can open room for lines of thinking that rely on external state-backing to temporarily protect gains – usually at great cost. Observing such trends and tensions, long-time revolutionaries in Rojava believe that the real revolutionary struggle is not the one in the geopolitical and military realms. Rather, long-term outcomes will be defined by the ideological struggles within revolutionary movements. To the extent to which ideological depth and organized autonomous action can decolonize politics, movements can resist being compromised and can continue to claim to present alternatives to the dominant world-system, even in times of genocidal wars. The movement's perspectives define moments of crisis as chaos intervals within which different forces compete; the most organized will become the subjects who can define outcomes, even eras. If the stability of states means chaos for peoples, peoples' self-organization should create and take advantage of moments of crises and chaos between states rather than seek shelter in one state or statist bloc or the other. Whenever hopelessness creeps in, victories like the ones in Kobanê and Şengal are evoked as reference points for the power of faith and resistance to change the course of history.

Currently, the existential basis of Rojava is being defended on multiple fronts. Parallel to the outward diplomatic engagement with representative institutions with the international community of states is the continuation of grassroots internationalist alliance-building against war and occupation, fascism, feminicide, ecocide, and the arms trade.

What next for Rojava's sustainability, at the intersections of revolutionary ideals and bare life? Could new forms of non-statist internationalism respond to such questions in the twenty-first century? And if so, what role will women play in the male-dominated world of geopolitics? The devastating tragedies that the peoples of Syria have seen in the past decade are too great to leave such questions unanswered.

27

Resistance or feminicide: Women against Daesh

In the summer of 2014, the so-called Islamic State, a terrorist group with origins in the Iraqi branch of al-Qaeda, entered world news headlines: blitzkrieg, slave trade, genocide. The many professionally curated videos of executions made Daesh the most spectacular, media-savvy terrorist organization until that point in history. Step by step, seemingly invincible, Daesh took over large areas across Syria and Iraq, and eventually occupied most of the border between them. For five years, people from around the world, including women, travelled to these countries, mainly through Turkey, to join the system of violence, rape, and control that Daesh presented as its glorious rule. According to some estimates, at least 10 million people lived under Daesh at the peak of its self-proclaimed caliphate, which enforced laws, taxes, and policing methods to 'govern' the population. Its sophisticated propaganda made use of modern media and social media platforms and drew tens of thousands of foreign nationals to Iraq and Syria. Children, including massacre survivors from religious minorities, were abducted and trained in indoctrination camps, sometimes even sent on suicide missions. The group's proud display of images of public executions and sexualized violence, and their slaughter and torture of minorities, normalized brutality in a region already traumatized by war and destruction. Daesh set the bar so high that other brutal Islamist groups were designated as 'moderate rebels' by pro-Western think tanks.

Systematic rape and sexual violence were at the heart of Daesh's regime. While any woman who resisted or was perceived to have violated their patriarchal codes faced violence, jail, torture, or death by beheading, shooting, or stoning, Daesh particularly focused on attacking women from religious groups it considers as infidels such as Êzîdîs, Kaka'is, and Christians, as well as non-Sunni Muslims like Shi'ites, 'Alawis, Isma'ilis, and Druze. Fighters were 'rewarded' for their brutality with women and girls 'gifted' to them. In its memos, Daesh offered instructions and guidelines for its followers on how and under what circum-stances they were allowed to rape women in captivity. Numerous women took their lives to escape this hell. Daesh also employed zealous women collaborators to aid the enslavement of the women in their fangs. Women resisted in many ways. Solidarity between women sometimes led to successful escapes.

Within a few years, Daesh's territorial grip collapsed, but its sleeper cells and ideology are very much alive. Attempts to explain the phenomenon of Daesh range from socio-psychological studies of individual motivations for joining Daesh to examinations of the group's political economy. However, beyond reports and investigations that expose the history of the group, its networks and inner workings, a comprehensive, historical-political analysis of the meaning of Daesh is fragmented in an atmosphere of Islamophobia and in light of the shadowy history of Western states' alliances with violent Islamist groups since the Cold War.

While understanding the specific context is crucial, one must be cautious not to exceptionalize the rapist traits of Daesh. Regional historical episodes like the Armenian genocide in many ways show that Daesh is merely one episode in a longue durée of feminicidal history in the region and beyond. Today, unprecedented amounts of funding are allocated to gender issues in the world of conflict and security. However, as feminists have pointed out for decades, gender is not something to 'also consider' during times of war and conflict. Since ancient times, gender has been a primary organizing principle of state, militarism, occupation, and political violence. The ruination of women's lives aims to tear the social fabric of communities. For example, under the guise of anti-communist counterinsurgency against the guerrillas in Guatemala, CIA-sponsored soldiers engaged in systematic rape and murders of Mayan women to destroy communal relations through regimes of terror, forced displacement, and disposession.[1] As noted by Rita Segato (2010), the symbolic power of sexual violence and its codes are legible in a near-universal manner, a lingua franca of patriarchy. By combining 'physical and moral subjugation in a single action', rape acquires meaning 'as a consequence of the function and role of sexuality in the world as we know it'. Across contexts, Segato claims, perpetrators 'share the collective gender imaginary. They speak the same language; they can be understood.' Genocide and occupation therefore rely on feminicide and other forms of violence (including but certainly not limited to rape) as the physical and symbolic degradation, capture and submission of women and, through them, society. In both war and peace, social and physical feminicide controls and disciplines society through violence.

At the moment, thousands of foreign Daesh fighters and supporters and their families are held within SDF-controlled camps inside Syria, as their governments refuse to repatriate them. At the time of writing, politically motivated international trials against individual Daesh members are underway. It is unlikely that such proceedings will offer complex answers to pressing questions around the many factors that led to the Daesh era. It is more realistic to think that such trials in fact help cover up the role played by state actors in fuelling the violence in the region, including the rise of Daesh.

The relationship between local fascisms and globally scaled systems of violence turns the question of justice into a conundrum. From the perspective of the hegemonic state system, it is relatively easy to put individuals on trial in Western courts or to execute them in the same prisons where political dissenters have been tortured and killed for decades. But isn't putting the Western state-led international world-system in charge of justice for genocides similar to expecting the patriarchal state for justice against feminicide? How should revolutionary feminists approach justice in the aftermath of genocide-feminicides? Is transformative justice possible? Could a feminist, anti-colonial, anti-capitalist, and anti-fascist definition of terrorism free itself from the imperialist and colonial system and in fact include that same system in its definition of terrorism and hold it, too, accountable? Meanwhile, how to defend oneself and society?

The Kurdish women's movement has over the years developed collective analyses of Daesh as a phenomenon and an episode in history. Autonomous women's media content proactively shaped the Kurdish discourse on Daesh. In these widely circulated ideological perspectives, justice is seen as something that can only come about with women's organized and autonomous efforts to develop new concepts of justice beyond the nation-state system and its liberal, legal frameworks. To put an end to the emergence of new forms of organized evil, the gaze of justice must be shifted from the individual to the patriarchal foundations of the world-system. When I asked women who witnessed Daesh's public executions, survived massacres, or got severely wounded in the fight about their interpretations and memories of Daesh, interestingly, many refrained from describing Daesh as a monstruous, irrational form of evil that attracted corrupt people. Instead of pathologizing individual recruits, these organized women repeatedly pointed to larger structures that govern global political life. Instead of focusing on its interpretation of Islam, they saw Daesh as a form of fascism, a product of a capitalist world-system. Many of the women described Daesh in terms of a full-on attack on Middle Eastern spiritual culture, as capitalist modernity's epitome, and as the most overt expression of a 5,000-year old legacy of patriarchal domination. The region needed a profound intellectual renaissance, they said, to fully expose all the spiritual and material aspects that made such an organization appealing to ordinary people. In their eyes, neither the regional nation-states nor the forces of imperialism, but only a native, women-led, revolutionary, non-statist, anti-fascist organization could develop the ideological and practical tools necessary to sustainably defeat the project that Daesh represents. If one dares to make sense of Daesh philosophically and in a long-term historical context, they believed, one will see that it is not a coincidence that organized, Mesopotamian women waged vendetta against patriarchy's logical conclusion.

Below are fragments of analyses at the height of the war, made by Kurdish women, culturally Sunni Muslim, Alevi, and Êzîdî, that took part in the struggles against Daesh in different regions. While the level of reflection in the words of these long-time revolutionaries does not represent all fighters and certainly not all victims, they give a sense of what sorts of collectively articulated thoughts and feelings were edited out when journalists craftily reduced a historic chapter of women's resistance to a 'badass' way of 'sending Daesh to hell because they are afraid of women'.

ROJAVA

Tell Mozan is the modern name for the ancient Hurrian city of Urkesh in northern Syria, estimated to have formed in the fourth millennium BC. In 2015, a YPJ academy was located close to the archaeological site, a few kilometres south of the border to Turkey. On that hill, I interviewed Meryem Kobanê, one of the commanders of the battle for Kobanê, the town that caused Daesh's first defeat. It was night, and so we could see the brightly shining lights of the city of Mêrdîn on the other side of the less than a century-old border. In Meryem's eyes, Daesh, as an idea and system of death, represented the opposite of all the human discoveries and values that had enabled complex social formations since Neolithic times:

In the Middle East, the non-material(ist) (Arabic: *al-ma'nawi*) is very important. Belief, faith, spirituality are at the heart of regional culture. The discovery of grains, observing the growth of fruit, understanding reproduction, using water – the history of human society is also about appreciating the mystery of mountains, feeling attracted to all that is magical and animate in life. In this sense, Daesh may refer to religion, but its attacks are against sacredness and belief, against the mental energy or faith in the possibility that something can be created, developed, built, grown. You need faith to appreciate the creativity of life. Daesh is against this faith. That is why we say that Daesh is attacking Middle East culture. Take Palmyra, an ancient city represented by a woman, Queen Zenobia, at some point, as Öcalan often points out. Daesh's destruction of Palmyra is an attack on the memory of women's leadership in this region. Daesh as a brutal men's organization is building a system in which men gift women to each other for pleasure. Study the ancient Mesopotamian story of Tiamat and Marduk – it is not simply a fairytale, it is a story about gender and power. Our struggle can be read in relation to it: even if our preference would be creation, not destruction, we need to defend ourselves. We can't become sacrificial lambs.

Daesh is a rapist force, an international mercenary that also serves to vilify Islam in the eyes of the world. Its project is not only about a state; it wants to establish an era. Male-dominated ideologies have a history of killing life while playing God on earth. It's the same mentality that caused the Holocaust. The authoritarian states in the region and beyond are not much different.

From around the world, people came to terrorize the people of this region, for money and power. All sorts of new weapons technologies were tested over the course of the wars in the region in the last years. Daesh attacked us with the tanks and bullets of the system: they took them from Iraq and from the armed opposition, which in turn had been armed by the UK, the USA, Libya, Turkey, and Gulf countries. The entire world was directly or indirectly implied in Daesh's military equipment. This is what we mean when we say Daesh is a product of the dominant system, even if it seems to be against it.

Daesh is simply an outcome of a system in which notions like friendship and love have been suffocated. Daesh is the drunken version of a power-based system that asserts itself all over the world. The people of this region can no longer bear this system and mentality. And this is what our struggle for a democratic nation solution represents. A new era, a renaissance is needed in the Middle East and we consider ourselves as its frontline defenders, not only in the physical sense, but also mentally, culturally, emotionally.

The struggle against Daesh became a rally cry for women around the world. It contributed to transnational discussions about women's autonomous self-defence beyond and against the state. Some internationalist women responded to Kurdish women's resistance against Daesh by making it their own cause. Ivana Hoffmann, a 19-year-old Black lesbian communist from Germany, was the first internationalist martyr of the Rojava Revolution. Familiar with the Kurdish freedom movement due to her involvement in Marxist-Leninist organizations in Germany, she took up the name Avaşîn Têkoşîn Güneş upon travelling to Rojava, where she died in the fight against Daesh in the majority Assyrian town of Tel Temir.

The YPJ led an active six-year long war against Daesh and lost several thousand women along the way. Women were commanders in some of the major battles. In 2019, around Newroz day, the SDF, which the YPJ co-founded, announced the end of Daesh's territorial claim to its self-proclaimed caliphate. Symbolic photos were published in the weeks leading up to the victory in the last stronghold, Baghouz, showing masses of surrendered or captured men, guarded by armed women.

MEXMÛR

As previously mentioned, residents of Mexmûr Refugee Camp often contrast their autonomous system to the UN's depoliticizing and pacifying approach to forced displacement. Many saw their view reinforced when Daesh attacked the camp in the summer of 2014 and the UNHCR did not assist the evacuation. In response to the collapse of the Iraqi army and the failure of the KDP to protect the communities in its sphere of control, the PKK sent reinforcements to the area. Despite its exposed location, Mexmûr's self-organized evacuation was a coordinated effort that involved the successful defence of the camp without civilian harm. During my September 2015 visit, a year after the big attack wave, residents were convinced that Daesh targeted the camp because of its proximity to the Kurdistan freedom movement. Sabriye of the Women's Assembly remembered the events vividly:

> We felt for all the women attacked by Daesh in Şengal. Based on our experience, we knew that the KDP would not protect us either. Daesh wanted to disperse our camp – this is a plan that others, especially Turkey, had in mind long before them. Aware of this, we gathered and armed ourselves when the camp was besieged. We were afraid but we didn't want to run away and leave our system behind. We decided to evacuate especially the children, elderly, wounded, and carers. The rest of us would stay and fight.
>
> When Daesh approached Mexmûr, the people from surrounding areas rallied around our camp. It was overwhelming and we couldn't let any strangers come in just like that. But we saw that they came because they didn't trust anyone else with protecting them; 300 Êzîdî families came here at some point. We were seen by all these strangers as a place capable of protecting them. Our camp always knew the importance of self-defence in a place like this, where we live under constant threat of genocide. From the first time we arrived here, everyone wanted to take the few weapons we had away from us. The UN[HCR], too. They neither protect us, nor do they allow us to protect ourselves. But when Daesh came here, we saw that we had been right all along. Once again, the PKK guerrillas died to protect our people. This is a warzone and this is our homeland Kurdistan, it is our right to defend ourselves. Nobody should tell us otherwise.

Residents drew parallels between the violent group and the nation-state system that forced Kurds and other communities into displacement. Some, such as Aryen from the Women's Academy, went as far as to link the situation to the UN system, which she described as a system designed to appease states:

> The system that causes violence, displacement, poverty and misery cannot claim to save us. Daesh and the nation-state share the same mentality. The nation-state system and the United Nations are fundamentally interlinked. If it hadn't been for our self-organization and self-defence, our people, after decades of forced displacement, would have fallen victim to Daesh, partly

also due to the UN's imposition of dependency on refugees. Our autonomy and the political consciousness guaranteed our survival, once again. We cannot surrender ourselves to the mercy of institutions that lack care. Instead, we develop self-organizing, self-defending communities with the willpower and political literacy to respond to events on their own terms, without dependency on anyone's goodwill.

Despite their claims to defend fundamental human rights, the UNHCR sometimes refrains from supporting the camp with basic needs because they see that it is not a camp that can be instrumentalized or integrated into their structures. Even if it wanted to, the UNHCR cannot interfere much with Mexmûr camp. The PKK, as a freedom movement, created a system here already. Even if instititions and governments laid hands on the camp, they can't make the people play by their rules. And because this place is ungovernable to them, they impose embargoes on the people, limit their access to education and health, and try everything to make self-organization impossible.

In designing and controlling refugee camps based on their top-down vision, the UN integrates refugees into an alien system. Mexmûr camp, on the contrary, is founded upon the principle of self-determination and autonomy. People, who are forced to flee, are displaced by power-driven nation-state policies and mentalities, which are based on denial, occupation, and anni-hilation. That same mentality created the UN. Even if it portrays itself as an institution with a neutral or balancing mission, the reality is far from that. It actively imposes a regime on the indigenous communities of our region, an agenda that serves the nation-state system. In a way, ours is a justice system. Against the dominant system's bureaucratically written-down, legalistic idea of justice, with our autonomous structures, we are building here an under-standing of how to struggle.

YJA Star commander Avesta Harun (Filiz Şaybak) from Wan, Bakur, was part of the guerrilla unit tasked with the defence of the camp. She was killed in the liberation of villages south of Mexmûr in 2014. Young reporter and revolutionary Deniz Firat provided first-hand footage of the Daesh attacks and the resistance against them. She was killed by Daesh while documenting the war from the area around Mexmûr. The camp holds an annual literature festival and short story and poetry competition in her honour, receiving submissions from different parts of Kurdistan and the diaspora, including writings from the mountains and the prisons.

KERKÛK

Gulan Gulveda (Eylem Kaplan) was one of the commanders of a YJA Star unit that arrived in Kerkûk in 2014. An Alevi woman from Malatya, whose warm eyes in her round, rosy face were framed by glasses, Gulan previously worked as a journalist in Turkey. As it was her kitchen duty that day, our conversation in Kerkûk in autumn 2015 was covered by the sound and smell of boiling rice and beans, one of the main guerrilla dishes. She explained that the guerrillas' presence in the region created a sense of Kurdish unity among the civilians and the pêşmerge, even though the latter's commanders and party-affiliated media outlets downplayed the PKK's fight in southern Kurdistan.

People might not be aware of this, but it is very difficult to leave the mountain to come to a place like this without a very strong rationale. There was high motivation among our ranks to fight this fascism, here in Kerkûk and everywhere. The pêşmerge commanders often asked for teams of our comrades to join their operations because our comrades' attitude 'We will win, no matter what' was a needed source of morale for the people here. After all, the pêşmerge had not seen active combat in decades. Many of the young pêşmerge had never been involved in fighting.

The guerrillas' style differs from formal armies and this was a great advantage in the fight against Daesh – militarily and psychologically. It is a fearless, sacrificial style of war. Our fighters don't receive salary and they don't have days off. Guerrillahood is also a culture of living, an ethical stance, a form of relating. Compared to other military forces in the region, we are approachable, open to be contacted by the ordinary people. We receive them respectfully and lend our ears to their stories. Some of these locals are extremely conservative but they are comfortable with women and girls from their communities visiting us. They see our women fearlessly fight and die alongside the men ... Recently, a battalion had to relocate. Families collectively visited the friends to try to change their minds. This kind of affection has to do with the fact that for decades, nobody developed actual politics for the people here. Nothing was done to specifically benefit the people in Kerkûk.

Similar to other fighters, Gulan described her movement's war on Daesh as a women-led effort against powers that want to suffocate alternatives. She linked the criminalization of the PKK's political works to a wider imperialist policy of legitimizing authoritarianism at the expense of liberationist social movements. In 2016, Gulan died in the clashes with the Turkish army in Şirnex.

We cannot see Daesh's worldview as totally different from more 'legitimate' violence on society. If the time of Middle Eastern dictatorships is over, what alternative will be able to respond to such a critical moment? In this period, which we more accurately call a 'Peoples' Spring', where the birth of alternatives, systems of governance based on genuine democracy, seemed possible,

Daesh appeared. A group so brutal that it almost makes people long for the times of dictatorship. It also makes the Western system, which is at the heart of our problems in the Middle East, look good. What is the difference between the imperialist wars that destroyed this region and the Daesh raids? Isn't American policy in the Middle East based on pitting communities against each other? Isn't this a cause for much of the hostility and violence here? Daesh does not wear a mask that would make its massacres look more civilized than those of the others. It terrorizes communities openly. We must analyze the mutually constitutive nature, the relations and connections between these things. Daesh is a perfect tool of controlling and pacifying the Middle East from the perspective of powerful forces, which sometimes fight each other. It forces people to settle for less than what they can have. No alternative remains in sight. As long as the US and Europe are imposed as the saviours of this region, there will be a lack of alternative solutions here. Women in other parts of the world are shown the things that happen to women in the Middle East, and are told: 'Look it is much worse over there. You don't have it as bad, so be content with your position'. I don't think this will continue to work. More women realize that oppression is not fate: neither on the monstrous scale of Daesh, nor in its more subtle, disguised forms in places like Europe.

QENDÎL

To the mountain-dwelling guerrillas, Daesh's ideology and methods exemplify the opposite of what the movement claims to stand for. In numerous statements, autonomous women's structures in the guerrilla explicitly framed the women's resistance against Daesh as a historic encounter between the forces of democratic civilization and the statist civilization. The battle for Şengal, described in the next chapter, is often described as a matter of fighting for the insistence of life, embodied by the ancient Êzîdî community, and death, represented by Daesh fascism. An Êzîdî woman herself, decades-old, leading PKK member Sozdar Avesta described Daesh to me in the following way:

Defeating Daesh requires the right approach to sociology and history. Just look at the areas that Daesh targeted within Iraq: Şengal, Kerkûk, Germiyan, Kalar, Tel Afar – these lands have historically been inhabited by Assyrians, Syriacs, Chaldeans, Shabaks, Kaka'is, and Êzîdîs. Lengthen that line, and you will reach the Azeri and Kalhuri, and many other communities. This diverse arch is under attack. Daesh is not only a military force, it's an ideological assault on this geography and its history of resistance and survival against empires and states. Daesh, its mentality, war tactics, strategy, the things it represents – they must be well-analyzed and understood. Its barbarism does not mean that it is not sophisticated. A spontaneous organization cannot lead the kind of war Daesh has.

Êzîdîs are among those who embody the most ancient cultures of the Middle East. This is evident in their reliance on faith, on ethics, a culture that is older than most religions. A life based on ethics and communality is the philosophical foundation of Ezdaism, Zoroastrianism, etc. It is an ecological worldview, very much connected to nature and the universe. The sun is a sacred entity. To welcome the day or to bid farewell to it, people wash their face with the rays of the sun, their prayers are in Kurdish. That is where we can find the unity of Ezdaism and Kurdishness. Even if written documents cannot support it, this is a lived reality. The sun, the soil, these are sacred to others as well, such as the Alevis. Like the Alevis, Êzîdîs do not put down fire with water. The Êzîdî faith is very much alive as a way of life in Şengal.

The more I analyze Şengal, the more I understand our leader's paradigm. For years, our leader had been saying: no matter what happens, ensure the safety of the Êzîdîs. On many occasions, from prison, he warned that the threat of genocide is looming over the Êzîdîs at all times. This is related to his analysis of Kurdish-ness, which, in his defence writings, he relates to the lives of Êzîdî and Alevi women. Protecting the Êzîdîs, as a community at the heart of Kurdish-ness, is therefore a duty for freedom-loving Kurdish people.

Figure 19   Billboard honouring Ivana Hoffmann, a Black German revolutionary from Germany and the first internationalist, who lost her life in the fight against Daesh in Rojava. Qamişlo. July 2015.

Daesh explicitly organizes against Öcalan's philosophy, against women's liberation, against the unity of all communities. On one hand, a movement that wants to revive and protect tens of thousands of years of human history, on the other, a group that assaults every single one of humanity's values. The more you think about the contradictions between the imposition of materialism on the wider region at the expense of its moral world, you understand just why such cultures and communities must continue to live at all costs.

28

Şengal: From feminicide
to women's autonomy

Thirsting, pregnant women, dead children left behind, slowly dying elderly people – we had to organize everything, from water to defence, just a handful of us. Anyone with a little bit of a conscience could not rest. We kept reassuring the survivors: 'Daesh will not reach this mountain, even if that means all of our fighters will die' ... We wanted to give everything to these people, but nothing would have been enough. We forgot about sleep, cold, heat, hunger – we did not sense anything anymore ... At some point, I didn't feel my body, I was wounded. People tell me about things I seem to have said or done in those days, and I honestly can't remember them. I once looked in the mirror and could not recognize myself. We lost ourselves amid the suffering of the people around us ... Our comrades from Kobanê, themselves besieged by Daesh, called us. Our friends are known for the kind of morale that no enemy can break. They said: 'Don't worry comrades, we are with you'. In the defence of Şengal, we were HPG, YJA Star, YBŞ, YPJ Şengal, YPG, and YPJ – one soul, united by the philosophy of Serok Apo. – Hedar Reşîd, Mount Şengal, 2015

On 3 August 2014, Daesh raided the majority Êzîdî city and surrounding villages of Şengal (Sinjar), murdering at least 5,000 men and kidnapping and enslaving 7,000 women and children according to UN estimates. While men were brutally murdered on the spot, thousands of women were kidnapped, sexually assaulted, and trafficked into slavery across Syria and Iraq. Tens of thousands of Êzîdîs managed to run to Mount Sinjar (Çiyayê Şengalê) to seek refuge, but the journey was fatal to many. Under the heat of the August sun, many children and elderly people died of thirst and exhaustion. In the aftermath of what would later be recognized by UN bodies as genocide, several mass graves were found in the region, sometimes multiple in single villages. Thousands of Êzîdîs remain missing to this day. Women, who have been able to escape captivity, have given testimony of life under a group that used rape not only as a systematic weapon of war, but also as part of its propaganda and government. The Êzîdîs refer to these catastrophic events as the 73rd or sometimes 74th *ferman* in their history.[1]

Despite efforts to cover up, it soon became public that the thousands of fighters of the KDP, who had been in charge of securing and protecting the area, were withdrawing from the region without a fight when Daesh attacked. Berfîn Hezil, a reporter working for RonahîTV at the time, caught the withdrawing units on the road, who told her that they were leaving for the city of Zakho (Zaxo) among other places. Her angry question: 'Çima Zaxo, çima?' (Why Zaxo, why?) was on many people's lips in Kurdistan at the time, who were shocked at the withdrawal. According to numerous reports, including testimonies I recorded myself, despite assuring the population that everything was under control, the KDP did not leave behind any weaponry for the Êzîdîs to defend themselves.

In the immediate aftermath of the massacre, tens of thousands of Êzîdîs, who had run to the mountain, were rescued by the coordinated effort of a small group of HPG and YJA Star guerrillas, who were soon reinforced by more arriving from the Qendîl mountains, as well as the YPG and YPJ from Rojava. These groups fought in coordination to open a 'corridor' to enable the Êzîdîs to cross into Rojava days later. The Jazeera canton of today's Autonomous Administration hosted them for years to come.

One year after the genocide, I spent two weeks on Mount Şengal from late July to early August 2015. At the time, Şengal City was still occupied by Daesh and approximately 2,000 families were residing on the mountain, mainly in makeshift tents. From some spots on the top of the mountain, one could see Daesh presence in the city with the naked eye. In my short stay, I spoke to survivors, civilian activists, and guerrillas, who were building democratic autonomy structures for Şengal in the aftermath of the genocide.

My impressions formed at a time that was particularly charged politically, and I cannot claim to represent the diverse emotions, politics, and visions within the Êzîdî community. Telling the stories that were marginalized in the mainstream humanitarian discourse is important, however: with time, as countless foreign-funded NGOs began charity work in Şengal and as news items and think tank reports increasingly framed the PKK's presence as a security liability, the guerrillas' contribution to the defence and political and spiritual reconstruction of Şengal was slowly written off, often to the benefit of the same political forces that many Êzîdîs blame for the genocide.

* * *

'Since the earth cooled down and the sky rested, Êzîdîs have existed', an elderly mother in a tent on Mount Şengal told me on the first anniversary of the genocide.[2] The Êzîdîs speak the Kurmancî dialect of the Kurdish language, which they often call 'Êzîdîkî'. The community, its lands, its sacred sites and practices are considered holy. Conversion into the Êzîdî faith is not possible. Their monotheistic religion, which involves many rituals and festivals, worships the Tawosî Melek (peacock angel) as the leader of the archangels and embodiment of the good, put in charge by God to look after the world. The pilgrimage site of Laleş, near Duhok is the most sacred place in the wider Êzîdî homeland, which they call 'Êzîdxan'.

The Êzîdîs have suffered from religiously driven pogroms, persecution, and discrimination for centuries and Kurdish groups often played a part in the violence and systematic stigmatization of this community. Violence campaigns against the Êzîdîs in the late Ottoman era led to large-scale forced migration to the Caucasus, Europe, and Russia. The Turkish army's war on rural Bakur in the 1980s and 1990s displaced much of the Êzîdî population indigenous to the areas around Wêranşar (Viranşehir) and Mêrdîn (Mardin). The second largest community of Êzîdîs, the largest being in Şengal, is believed to reside in Germany. In the 1970s, Saddam Hussein actively tried to drive a wedge between Êzîdîs and Sunni Kurdish groups in Iraq. Êzîdîs were made to register as Arabs and often conscripted into the army to help suppress Kurdish uprisings. After the fall of Saddam Hussein, Şengal's status remained ambiguous as part of the 'disputed territories' as per Article 140 of the post-war Iraqi constitution. As such, the KDP effectively took over on the ground, while the region was officially administered by the central Iraqi regime. This liminal status is a reason for systemic neglect, lack of accountability, and infrastructural underdevelopment in Şengal. For health emergencies, Êzîdîs were forced to travel to other cities. Only few could afford to send their children to university. Employment opportunities were limited and Êzîdîs are discriminated against in the job market in the nearby cities.

According to many Êzîdîs, the air of genocide hovered over Şengal long before Daesh seized territories in Iraq. In 2007, D'ua Khalil Aswad, a young Êzîdî girl, was stoned to death in Şengal, allegedly for being with a Muslim. The horrifying, video-recorded feminicide, committed amid a crowd of dozens of men, took place in front of the by-standing security forces. The video's circulation incited widespread anti-Êzîdî sentiments among Muslim groups in the region, who were weaponizing the killing of D'ua to attack the Êzîdîs. As a result, many Êzîdîs left Mosul for Şengal. On 14 August 2007, in Sîba Şêx Xidir and Tel Ezer, coordinated car bombs killed more than 700 Êzîdîs and wounded thousands more. Many seem to have disappeared under dubious circumstances in the attack that remains unclaimed. Theories abound. People I have spoken to acknowledged widespread violence against women but often mentioned that stoning is not an Êzîdî practice and believed that the massacre was a sinister pre-emption of the 2014 *ferman*. They believed that the genocide in Şengal came in handy for many of those to whom the Êzîdîs had been a thorn in the eye.

As much as their history is shaped by violence and persecution, it is at the same time a legacy of resistance, featuring powerful women such as Felek, Xatûna Fexra, or Sitiya Nisra. The Kurdish love story of Dewrêş and Edulê, orally recited in the tradition of *dengbêjî*, is centred around the courageous Êzîdî fighter Dewrêşê Evdî, who defeated the Ottoman army in a major battle. Êzîdîs are protective and proud of their culture and faith; their survival and resilience to this day is often narrated as a history of resistance against assimilation and annihilation. They often call Mount Şengal their 'shield' – a natural defence against violence and massacre. It was indeed the mountain that helped tens of thousands of Êzîdîs survive Daesh.

Years after the genocide, thousands of Êzîdî women continue to seek justice and truth in a variety of ways, from health projects and civil society work to revolutionary organizing. Hundreds of captured girls have been rescued and are being supported by their communities. Diasporic organizations have been helping the affected members of the community in their rehabilitation and healing. Many of the survivors use their experience to seek justice for the atrocities.

DYING FOR ŞENGAL

Years before the Daesh genocide, Öcalan had been issuing warnings, telling the PKK to send units to Şengal to protect the Êzîdîs from possible attacks. Following the fall of Mosul in June 2014, the PKK started preparations to establish a military plan for the defence of the Êzîdîs. When Mosul fell, the KCK issued several statements, calling on the need for a Kurdish joint defence force against the further spread of Daesh and for the defence of the communities in the region. These were largely ignored. In his meeting with the Imralı delegation in mid-August 2014, Öcalan expressed his devastation about the genocide and heavily criticized the guerrillas for short-sightedness, referring to the massacre as a repetition of the tragic story of Adulê and Dewrêş, a Kurdish love story in the area around Şengal, rendered impossible as a result of collaborationism, cowardice and lack of organized resistance against Ottoman assault.

Nobody had ever seen a catastrophe like this. The villagers said that the prettiest girls were singled out. The women with children were grouped together. The men were collectively massacred. Any possessions like gold were looted. Two wounded brothers came to us. Six of their brothers had been murdered, and they were only able to escape because Daesh believed them to be dead as well. There are many examples like this, especially from the village of Koço. They said that some young women gathered children around them to claim to be their mothers to evade capture.

The words belong to Hedar, a calm and serious-looking woman in her 30s. A PKK guerrilla from Rojava, she lost one eye while commanding the small group of fighters involved in the rescue operation to take tens of thousands of Êzîdîs across the Syrian-Iraqi border into Rojava on the other side of Mount Şengal. As one of the few guerrillas present in Şengal when the massacre began, she witnessed the misery of thirsting people on the run, the rapid withdrawal of the KDP forces, and the death of her comrades. One year after the massacre, on the same mountain, she was training young Êzîdî women in political ideology and armed struggle.

Before the massacre, I was first with another woman comrade, but after 15 days, twelve more comrades arrived here from the mountain, like the twelve cavaliers in the story of Dewrêşê Evdî. As soon as we arrived, we immediately saw that the KDP had not taken any precautions to defend the region. We immediately started setting up positions, but the KDP did not want our military presence there. Had we insisted more strongly, clashes could have erupted between us, and then they would have said that the *ferman* happened because the PKK caused chaos again. So, we operated secretly. At first, we started to warn people about the immediate threat of Daesh, but people had been assured by the KDP that they would be protected. Anyone, including the children, knew that Daesh would not spare the Êzîdîs because of their faith.

Three of our comrades and one villager were arrested in Xanêsor by the KDP. We received intelligence that they were asking families to invite our comrades to their homes to arrest them. Before the *ferman*, we wanted to train a group of 15 people, but it was risky. People had been told that we would take their children to Turkey, Iran, and Qendîl. The people didn't know us well, so barely anyone allowed their family members to be trained. Those who knew us better began convincing their own families until we finally had a group together for training. Afterwards people's sympathy and trust increased. We didn't have any guarantees to show people, but we encouraged them to prepare their houses in case of an attack, for example positions and spaces for women and children to hide.

Fact is, nobody would have believed that the KDP would withdraw without a fight, not even leaving behind any weapons for people to defend themselves. We appealed to the KDP, warning that Şengal's fall will eventually lead to the fall of Hewlêr and other regions. We asked for weapons, but the fighters could not do anything other than what their commanders had told them. The way they ran away was despicable, embarrassing. Some of them put on civilian clothes before leaving.

One of the arrested was Zerdeşt, an Ezîdî, who joined the PKK from Europe and was involved in the Youth Movement's activities in Şengal a year before the *ferman*. In our interview, Zerdeşt mentioned that in the months before the massacre, Tevda (Êzîdî Movement for Democracy and Freedom), an organization affiliated to the Kurdistan freedom movement that has been organizing Êzîdî families in the region since 2003 with limited capacity, had held its congress. Shortly after, the Êzîdî youth organized a relatively well-attended conference. Tevda's social work, which encompasses cultural activities as well as women's and youth organizing, was criminalized, as its members were intimidated, arrested, and assaulted by the security officials of the KDP. By the time of these congresses, nearby cities like Mosul and Tel Afar had already been attacked. Zerdeşt and his comrades were going from house to house to tell people that Şengal had already been surrounded by Daesh. Mere weeks before the Daesh attack, Zerdeşt and three others, including one civilian, were kidnapped by the KDP and interrogated about their mobilization of the Êzîdîs under torturous conditions. Shortly before the *ferman*, due to pressure by the PKK, they were released.

Before Daesh attacked, the guerrillas had prepared a secret quarter to use for training. Although the spot was never used for that purpose after all, the water and food supplies that had been prepared turned out to be life-saving when the *ferman* began. Sustaining the people on the mountain with basic needs proved to be as vital as the rescue operation itself. Hedar recounted:

We went to the mountain to organize the people on the run. We know our comrades, we know they would come here for sure, no matter where they are. But the people didn't know our friends' stance in war. Two civilians came with the four of us (guerrillas) in the car. I gave a flag of our leader to Martyr Canpolat to hoist on the vehicle. To give morale, we chanted slogans all the way until we reached the point of a Doshka that the pêşmerge had left behind but that the villagers did not know how to use. So much death, massacre, kidnapping, thirst, even car accidents had happened on the run – there was no hope left in people's eyes, so Canpolat did everything in his power to raise their morale, to bring back hope for survival. He shouted: 'The *heval* are with you, don't be afraid! You will live!' The people were shocked at this enthusiasm. We asked those who had weapons to come join us and told them that the guerrillas were on their way. We were only six people, who started building position, as more and more people arrived and we learned that Daesh had already taken around 3,000 people. That night, we stayed on that position. Daesh approached us by car the next morning to explore our presence. We immediately began shooting and saw that we had wounded two Daesh members, who ran away. We took their weapons, a BKC, a Doshka.

The civilians, who were with us, gained encouragement, as they saw that it was indeed possible to repel more attacks.

In the meantime, more guerrilla reinforcements arrived and Êzîdî youth were joining these efforts to hold position, as the YPG and YPJ were preparing to open the corridor from the Syrian side of the border. The survivors were brought to Hedar's hometown of Dêrîk, the north-easternmost corner of Syria, by Iraq and Turkey. Hedar continued:

We sent several comrades to different points in the hills in support of the YPG/YPJ's corridor operation, also for visibility, to decrease people's fear. That night, the corridor opened. First, pregnant women, the elderly, children, and disabled and wounded people were taken across. Civilians from Rojava, entire families, had come to the rescue by car with water and food. Our comrades kept sending us photos of the situation. They gave their lives just to give some water to these mothers, children, and elderly ... They sacrificed themselves. Some people stayed behind on the mountain to support the friends' resistance. Our reinforcements secured the area around the mountain. The guerrillas carried elderly people on their backs ... The youth that we had previously started training had no experience with fighting, but in that moment, anything helped, even carrying some water was vital ... There was just so much to do.

One of the Êzîdî civilians who participated in the operation to repel Daesh attacks on the mountain was Heso. Right before the genocide, he was in the area around Tel Afar, and learned from local Arabs that Daesh had already infiltrated villages in the region. He believed that people were being misled by security forces and stressed that authorities created obstacles for the community to organize itself by preventing people from spreading the news, supposedly to avoid panic.

I never would have believed that people can have such a will to resist. Only those twelve PKK fighters were there. One group with *heval* Merwan, one with *heval* Kawa, and one with *heval* Hedar. We didn't think anyone could fight Daesh, but together, we blocked some roads and saw that resistance, even with light weapons, makes a difference. On 7 August, a comrade named Soran arrived. They wanted to open a corridor. We wanted to fight but we didn't know how. All we knew is we did not want to die. It was scary, Daesh had heavy weapons. *Heval* Soran was trying to calm us down. He tried to contact the pêşmerge, but they kept retreating. For 12 days, I stayed with a group with Şehîd Viyan and Şehîd Genco. When the battle in Cezaa broke out, they said I could go with them or stay on the mountain. I said I will not leave Şengal. Many of us had taken an oath that we would rather die than leave Şengal.

Zerdeşt recounted how the guerrillas eventually had to withdraw from some villages to keep their positions. When the corridor was opened, fighters stayed in the village of Digurê for days without food. Several of them died, and more were wounded. They were among the first to be buried in the martyr's cemetery.

Full of images of peacocks, the pointy and white mausoleum, typical for Êzîdî sites, the martyr's cemetery in the mountain is maintained by the locals and oversees the tobacco fields, which are shaped like giant footprints in the hills.

Figure 20 Martyr's cemetery on Mount Şengal, partially still under construction at the time. Several young Êzîdî had cut off their hair and left it at their relatives' graves, with some joining the self-defence units themselves afterwards. Mount Şengal. July 2015.

Long, braided hair, belonging to Êzîdî women, was swinging on some of the gravestones during my visit.

Shortly after the attack, the YBŞ, the Şengal Resistance Units, were declared as an autonomous army for the defence of the Êzîdîs. Over time, the YBŞ grew into an army of young people, who know the area inside out.

For the guerrillas, it was of strategic importance to involve Êzîdî women in education and organization. According to Hedar, the first Êzîdî women to join the YBŞ mainly came from families who knew the movement. Admitting the difficulty of facing accusations that her movement was trying to introduce *bêehlaqî* (immorality) to Şengal, Hedar stressed that, in particular, negative representations through Turkish films and local news reports seem to have shaped people's perception of the guerrillas. Later, YPJ-Şengal was announced as an autonomous all-women's army. It later became the YJŞ (Şengal Women's Units).

DEMOCRATIC AUTONOMY IN ŞENGAL

Less than half a year after the massacre, with the help of the Kurdistan freedom movement, the Şengal Constituent Assembly (*Meclisa Avaker a Şengalê*) was formed on 14 January 2015 with the aim of organizing the rehabilitation and protection of the Êzîdî people, mainly on the mountain. Committees visited homes, telling people about the plan to form an umbrella organization. This was at the time seen as an outrageous attempt to separate Şengal from the Kurdistan Region. During my stay, I could occasionally see KDP officials distribute aid to the population, but many people were also boycotting the goods and expressed resentment over the fact that humanitarian organizations were handing aid to the same forces that had abandoned them. Xidir, spokesperson of the Constituent Assembly, explained the assembly's formation:

> In the first four months, before we founded the assembly, no government in charge, neither the central Iraqi state, nor the KRG took proper care of our people on the mountain. In that miserable period, we had to act, as the families, who had stayed behind. We had relations to Newroz Camp in Rojava and some camps in Başûr and decided to hold a conference. The main purpose was to support our people, to work with love for our land, culture, and religion – looking after and protecting our values, especially after the massacre. We wanted to show the world that we can do what nobody else did for us. Our assembly is an expression of an Êzîdî political willpower. It is a 'constituent assembly', because we do not claim to speak on behalf of all Êzîdîs. We need some sort of representative structure. If the central Iraqi state or the Kurdistan Region do not accept it, then we will organize ourselves through self-defence and political organization like the cantons in Rojava.

Mother Şîrîn, a strongly built elderly woman with sunburnt cheeks, was a co-founder of the assembly and a mother of a YBŞ martyr. Sitting on the floor of her tent in her light-coloured traditional attire, she was radiating a disarmingly positive authority, when I visited her. Despite a lack of formal education, she had remarkable analytical command over historical events prior to the *ferman*. She stressed that discrimination and persecution had a decades-old history in Şengal, when describing the destruction of Êzîdî villages by Saddam Hussein in the 1970s. According to her, at the time, there were ten women and twenty men in the general assembly, with committees for organization, defence, culture and art, and education. Together with women guerrillas, she made home visits to encourage women to participate.

We formed this assembly after the *ferman* to say 'It's enough. No to oppression, no to enslavement'. In these lands, with these waters, we will no longer accept oppression. For millennia, we protected our culture and faith, but now we will do that better. We are at the very beginning, our wounds are fresh, but we will never be safe without resistance.

We want the children of this land to return home, we don't want more people to be displaced and removed from Şengal. We don't want our people in Europe to forget their culture. Displacement is a continuation of the *ferman*, yet another assault on the Êzîdî. Tawosî Melek knows, the massacre happened to destroy our old history, culture, religion, way of life. We need to defend it, otherwise it will be forgotten.

When I asked her about the reaction of men regarding women's political organizing, she broke into hearty laughter. She was still giggling, when one of her male family members in the tent mentioned that there were indeed men who did not accept these developments. Men are oppressed, too, Mother Şîrîn responded empathetically, shrugging. She herself interpreted the movement's ideology through Êzîdî cosmology:

I believe Sitar (Ishtar) was an Êzîdî woman. We, the Êzîdîs are those who protect the land of water, fire, and the sun, and so did she. Xatûna Fexra. Sitiya Nisra – these are all heroic women in Êzîdî history. We need to learn lessons from their struggle. We need to know our own history, educate ourselves on it and rise up. Their stories raise our morale! Woman is life.

On 29 July 2015, mere days before the anniversary of the genocide, the Şengal Women's Assembly was formed with the slogan 'Êzîdî women's organization will be the answer to all *fermans*'. The congress took place on the mountain and was attended by around 80 delegates in addition to guests. Delegates included members of the Tirbêspiyê Êzîdî House and residents of the Newroz Camp, who had travelled together from Rojava, as well as activists from the Êzîdî Women's Assembly in Europe. Non-Êzîdî guest speakers, who had stood with the women of Şengal from day one, included politicians and women's movement represent-atives from Rojava. Hediye Yusuf, then Jazeera canton's co-president, greeted the conference hall on behalf of the resisting women in Rojava. She stressed that their struggle gained strength from Êzîdî women's determination and resistance against Daesh and all other forms of violence. Syriac politician and women's activist Elizabet Gawriya, at the time co-chair of the Executive Council of Jazeera, drew parallels between the histories of Syriac and Êzîdî women, calling for common struggle. Young Êzîdî women of YPJ-Şengal were applauded for giving political speeches, addressing the importance of taking the struggle for women's liberation beyond the fight against Daesh. Women, young and old, promised freeing women in captivity and rebuilding a free Şengal to return to.

A radical atmosphere that urged 'Never again!' was emerging from still open, traumatic wounds inflicted by genocide-feminicide. The entire conference, where small children sat next to grandmothers, was documented by women's cameras and pens, some more experienced than others. The place was protected by the YPJ, YPJ-Şengal, and YJA Star. The celebration at the end of the gathering

Figure 21   Founding conference of the Şengal Women's Assembly. One of the banners reads 'The organization of Êzîdî women of Şengal will be the response against all massacres'. The images mainly show Êzîdî women, who were 'martyred' in different parts of Kurdistan. Mount Şengal. July 2015.

was an unforgettable scene of women in different uniforms, from Muslim, Êzîdî, and Alevi backgrounds, speaking different Kurdish dialects, next to Êzîdî women in their traditional light-coloured attires, drinking tea, chanting slogans, and watching the circles of line dance to Soranî Kurdish music, away from the gaze of men, their violence and their states.

Days later, on 3 August 2015, the first anniversary of the genocide, I joined the powerful protest march on the mountain. Thousands of survivors were marching with slogans, flags, and determination in the same place that had been the site of killing, hunger, and thirst the year before. Fighters on hills were guarding the protest. One of them was Viyan Encü from Mako, Rojhelat (Iran), a woman in her early 20s. During our interview on another day, she told me that she had joined the PKK from a *welatparêz* family that became more explicitly politicized upon the capture of Öcalan in 1999. Her *nom de guerre* honours the Encü family, who lost dozens of family members, mainly teenagers, in a Turkish airstrike in Roboskî in 2011, which killed 34 civilians. Rojhelat is the only part of Kurdistan without an Êzîdî population. Viyan, who was among the group that arrived in Şengal shortly after the *ferman*, told me that she had never encountered the Êzîdî community and faith before her arrival. Since I had perceived her as calm and introverted throughout my stay, I was surprised at the anger in her voice during our interview. With horror in her eyes, she was clutching her weapon as she recounted the sight of dead corpses of families with children and still others dying of thirst.

Şengal is a sacred place, the Êzîdîs' faith is very special, pure. The people here are innocent. Before the *ferman*, our leader warned our movement about Şengal. He told us to protect the Êzîdîs. We fought and stayed on the mountain, thirsty and hungry like the survivors, because of his thinking. Really, we only had our Kalashnikovs, but we repelled Daesh and their heavy weapons ... We could listen into their conversations; they spoke of us like we were *jinns* in the mountains ...

For us, the option of defeat does not exist. There is only victory. The people who join Daesh don't know what exactly they are fighting for. What is their goal, their horizon, their purpose? It's sheer brutality. Violence for the sake of violence. This is the opposite of guerrilla life. We know what we want, we know how to achieve it and we know that we must win.

If anything, we want women in Şengal, but generally, all over Kurdistan and beyond, to know that our protection must never be in the hands of men. Without self-defence, we will always be at the mercy of others. I gain strength from seeing Êzîdî girls take up arms to avenge their community. We can't underestimate the historic meaning of this. The women started autonomously organizing a system for themselves and this is how we measure our victory: through these people's self-organization, in the aftermath of a genocide, nonetheless.

Another fighter at the protest was also from Mako, Eser Aras, who had joined the PKK in 2007. Eser, at the time 26, was in the first group of PKK fighters to arrive in Şengal. Şengal, in her words, became 'a matter of honour' to everyone. Defending it meant defending life itself. Her words were self-critical and even full of regret sometimes: 'Could we not have come sooner? What else could we have done to prevent the massacre altogether? What more could we do now? One wonders.' Like Hedar, she witnessed the devastation with her own eyes and saw the death of many of her comrades. Some of them detonated themselves to avoid falling into the hands of the enemy.

> Our leader says: 'Even if you have all the strength of all armies in the world, you must not attack the weak. But even if the entire world is against you, you must fight to win'. We always say that the use of weapons is a necessity in this atmosphere of violence. The PKK will always fight alongside our people. We don't recognize any borders in Kurdistan. Wherever we are, we will always fight on behalf of all the oppressed.

Figure 22 Protest commemorating the first anniversary of the genocide. Among the people in the crowd were women who had until recently been in Daesh captivity. Mount Şengal. August 2015.

Our paradigm addresses women everywhere in the world, not just Kurdistan. Our movement is based on the Women's Liberation Ideology, on women's self-defence and self-organization. In this sense, we understand our war as insistence on our truth against a group that represents 5,000 years of male-domination with an ideology that targets women specifically. Fighting Daesh means taking the struggle for women's liberation to the highest level.

When we arrived as YJA Star guerrillas, it sparked self-confidence and trust among women here. Their consciousness, participation, leadership, coordination, education, analysis – everything grows. They develop a mission for themselves, understand the importance of self-defence and political analysis. This would not have been the case if only the HPG had come here.

In 2019, Eser died in Hesekê, Syria, among the ranks of the YPJ.

Back at the protest, previously mentioned Heso, who is also a poet, expressed the rage of his community through art in assembly. A bearded young man with the traditional red-white checked *keffiyeh* on his head, Heso was a member of the youth committee of the Şengal Founding Assembly at the time and later became the deputy co-chair of the Şengal Democratic Autonomous Assembly. In our interview, I had asked him about what the struggle of women means to

Figure 23   A YPJ-Şengal fighter among the young women and men guarding the protest to mark the anniversary of the genocide. In the back, civilians taking a break during the rally. Şengal. August 2015.

men like him. He explained that he believed that Öcalan's ideas helped remove the fear in people that someone else's freedom poses a threat:

> I am proud to see the progress among my sisters and my mother. I want them to free themselves from the domination by men. Never before in the history of Şengal has there been a women's assembly. This is historic. The advancement of women is our greatest hope for the future. As Öcalan says: 'There can be no free society without the freedom of women.' Hence, if women in Şengal will not be free, then Şengal will not be free. The massacre has specifically targeted women, so women must be able to organize, defend, and educate themselves. We can build a canton-based system like Rojava – a progressive form of self-determination. We, too, can have a revolution in Şengal. We will never forget Rojava's role in rescuing our mothers, fathers, and children. Rojava is the legacy of women like Arîn Mîrkan. A sacred resistance.

One of the young Êzîdî women I interviewed had in fact taken up the *nom de guerre* Arîn, in honour of Kobanê's YPJ commander Arîn Mîrkan. Arîn, her parents, and seven siblings ran to the mountain when Daesh attacked. The guerrillas provided them with food and water. When we spoke, it was evident that Arîn had only recently become familiar with the concepts and ideas of the Kurdish women's liberation movement. In her words, she was developing an understanding of collective and individual experiences with violence as part of a system of oppression, rather than fate. Arîn was active in the practical activities, but shy in conversation. She often stopped in the middle of a sentence, seemingly thinking about how her words must have sounded. I asked whether she experienced new challenges in her personal life. Arîn mentioned that girls like her were disadvantaged in many ways, often prevented from going to school and burdened with a life of housework. Political education developed her self-confidence and ability to make sense of the traumatic events.

> Fighting Êzîdî women – it's like a dream. People did not think this was possible at first. I can see changes in my family, especially when it comes to women. They are proud of me being with the heval. They are relaxed about it, but they would not have been in the past. My (male) cousins told me that I could not become a fighter, but after education, I lost my fear that they could be right.
>
> I want our future to be free: together, strong, without oppression from anyone, but with organization and advancement for our women. We are very poor people. We never held assemblies before like this. We didn't know why we should get together as women to discuss important things. Now Êzîdîs everywhere, in Europe, too, are getting stronger than ever before. We learn that violence silences us and that we must organize and build our society in response.

REFUGE IN ROJAVA

The 'Newroz' refugee camp in Rojava's city of Dêrîk (al-Malikiyah), built within two weeks of the massacre, became the first home for the Êzîdîs of Şengal straight after the Daesh genocide in August 2014. While international institutions were still discussing possible response mechanisms, the administration of the Jazeera canton, aided by hundreds of civilian volunteers, took on the task of hosting and treating the tens of thousands of exhausted genocide survivors. Within a short period of time, the camp became part of the canton, participating in its political, social, cultural, and economic life. While work opportunities were created for the families, volunteer press workers, artists, and teachers began involving the refugees in their works. Early on, autonomous women's activities were introduced in a manner that would be sensitive to the experience of large-scale feminicide. A *mal a jin* (women's house) was established to take care of the issues of the women and girls.

I first visited the Newroz Camp at the end of November 2014, when around 10,000 people were inhabiting it. Under embargo itself, the self-administration was struggling with economic issues at the time, ahead of a cold winter. In the summer of 2015, I returned to the camp to conduct interviews with women, who had meanwhile set up communes, committees, and assemblies to organize themselves with the help of the women's movement and the canton. Nafiyah and Zehra, spokeswomen of the Newroz Camp's women's and youth committees, respectively, were among the thousands stranded on the mountain for days before being escorted to Rojava. Nafiyah, who is a mother of several children, recounted:

Dozens of the *heval* died until they managed to open the road. The people on this side of the border, in Rojava, had come by car with water, food, clothes. We could finally breathe … We saw humans, humanity. A few months after our arrival, we started educations and trainings, political and military. At our camp, we have specific educations for women, in addition to technical training for work and art. Of course, our Êzîdî assembly is represented here as well. Rojava is a special place. We have been introduced to new ideas that show a way and help us make sense of the things that happened to us.

Zehra, at the time 23, was in charge of the youth activities in the camp. She drew attention to the difficult situation of young women beyond the massacre:

Here, we say the 'red *ferman*' is over, but now we are facing a 'white *ferman*', one that is more subtle and invisible. It is a *ferman* that happens through displacement, assimilation, and politics. The YBŞ, especially Êzîdî girls, have

Figure 24 A makeshift living area at the Newroz Camp, Dêrîk (al-Malikiyah), Rojava. November 2014.

stopped the advancement of the red *ferman*, but the white *ferman* can only be prevented through autonomous self-organization.

Both women were highly critical of European government programmes that took women abroad to find medical solutions to individual cases of trauma.[3] They saw solutions for collective healing in local self-organization. After describing the horrifying scenes that she witnessed in the area around Xanêsor, Nafiyah, visibly angry, asserted that nobody should expect the Êzîdîs to return to how things were before the genocide.

Even if the men forget, women won't. Who is responsible for thousands of our girls being in captivity? The enemy wanted to destroy the roots of Êzîdaism, the roots of the world. They shake our leaves, make the earth tremble, until our roots break. But our leaves are greening again, our roots are back in place thanks to the resistance of our YBŞ.

I asked about her thoughts on the upcoming first anniversary of the catastrophic day.

Through organization and consciousness, we will put an end to all *ferman*. Some were upset about our assembly, but what have they ever done to benefit our people? Those who abandoned Şengal to Daesh have nothing to order. How do those who ran away have the audacity to decide who gets to stay on our land? Whoever has shed their blood for the Êzîdîs can stay with us. Our youth died alongside the PKK, defending our faith and lands. That is why we don't want the *heval* to leave the mountain. Abdullah Öcalan's ideas ensure that no *ferman* ever happens to us Êzîdîs again.

At the end of the month, I saw both women again, this time on Mount Şengal. Joyful, dressed in their traditional clothes, they had come to represent the women of the Newroz Camp at the founding congress of the previously described Şengal Women's Assembly. One month later, they helped form the autonomous women's assembly at Newroz Camp.

'NEVER AGAIN' AS AUTONOMY

Political commentators frequently claim that the PKK's presence in Şengal stems from its desire to secure another military base. PKK members themselves, however, stress that the rescue and post-genocide autonomy-building were a revolutionary *raison d'être*. KCK Executive Council member Sozdar Avesta, a decades-old Êzîdî member of the PKK, told me that the taste of autonomy in the aftermath of genocide had healing qualities. At all costs, she said, Şengal must live and do so on its own terms in a Middle East increasingly conquered by authoritarian nationalism, religious extremism, and capitalism:

The Êzîdîs saw that no state in the world protected them. As a movement, our paradigm's main aim is for all communities to self-govern, to create their own economy, to live with their own colours. These things are mutually constitutive. The PKK movement is a project to allow people to live on their terms. Even if we had truckloads of money, we would not give handouts to people. We would create academies, spend it on self-defence, on common, collective institutions.

To me, the autonomous organization of women in Şengal has revolution-ary quality. Now, an elderly woman in the Şengal mountains can easily get up in a meeting and analyze political developments, make suggestions to be discussed and implemented. Hundreds of women, young to old, show, through organizing, that they are not afraid. These people may not have theoretically engaged with our paradigm – some of them don't have any formal education, but this does not mean that they lack consciousness. They organize themselves from their deepest knowledge and feelings about life. This is meaningful and important. Such communal, ethical traditions won't end in these lands. Our leader says that 98 per cent of the dynamics of democratic civilization are invisible. The hope that this paradigm can give will be the power that spreads the struggle beyond borders. The ruling powers are digging their own grave when they say 'no bird shall fly without our permission'. But the birds do fly, and the peoples of this region see this.

Within five years of the genocide, the Şengal Democratic Autonomy Assembly established people's assemblies in the city of Şengal, as well as in several villages. In 2017, the autonomous women's army YJŞ participated in the operation to retake Raqqa from Daesh. The city was known as one of the main sites in which Êzîdî women had been held captive. I recognized some of the women I had met in Şengal on the media images from Raqqa.

Meanwhile, the PKK was militarily pressured by Turkey and the KDP to leave the area. At the time of my stay, the KRG's then prime minister Nêçîrvan Barzanî had already been issuing statements to suggest that the PKK is not welcome in the region. In the spring of 2018, after a series of threats and attacks by the Turkish state, which claimed that the PKK was turning Şengal into 'a second Qendîl', as well as shifting dynamics on the ground inside Iraq through the increasing

Figure 25   An HPG guerrilla with Mother Qadifa (mentioned in Chapter 16), an Êzîdî woman from Rojava and a community organizer at the *mal a jin* (women's house) in Tirbêspiyê (al-Qahtaniyah). Mother Qadifa had travelled across the temporarily eroded Syrian-Iraqi border to Mount Şengal to join the protest to mark the first anniversary of the genocide. Mount Şengal. August 2015.

power of the Iranian-backed al-Hashd ash-Sha'bi, the guerrillas left Şengal. The KCK statement published at the time stated that even though security had been established in the region, Öcalan's words on the need to protect the Êzîdîs everywhere would always be considered an order for the guerrilla. Footage of emotional scenes showed hundreds of people gathering and chanting slogans, crying as they embraced and bid farewell to units of guerrillas with whom they had been living for four years.

MEMORIES

One day, in the press centre on Mount Şengal, I saw a teenager, whom I could have sworn I had met about 300km away in Qendîl just a few months earlier. Her chubby face seemed oddly placed on her small body. Her thick, curly black hair was parted in the middle. Her dark eyes seemed to be giggling at everything around her and her voice sounded like a mouse. I had definitely seen a slightly bigger version of this Êzîdî girl hundreds of miles away. 'Do you have a sister in the mountains?', I asked. Her face beamed: 'Yes, Bêrîvan!'

I remembered Bêrîvan Şengal from a short visit in late spring to *Saziya Ziman*, the PKK's Kurdish language school in Qendîl. She had joined the guerrilla after the genocide on her people. Her *nom de guerre* was inspired by elsewhere mentioned Binevş Agal, who was one of the first Êzîdî women to join the PKK. At *Saziya Ziman*, internationalists from Latin America, Europe, and Africa, as well as Kurds, who did not speak their language, were learning Kurdish together in a camp next to a spring. That is also where I last saw Lêgerîn Çiya (Alina Sanchez), whom I had first met several years prior in Europe before she joined the Kurdistan revolution. Her Kurdish was better than that of the other internationalists, with whom she shared her experiences as a revolutionary from Argentina. Legerîn, who was trained as a medical doctor in Cuba, later helped set up the health system in Rojava. Mere days after another internationalist, Hêlîn Qereçox (Anna Campbell), a queer anti-fascist from the UK, died defending Afrîn against the Turkish occupation, Lêgerîn, whose name means 'quest', died in a car accident in March 2018 in Hesekê. The hospital in Tel Tamir was named after her.

At the language school, I was watching Bêrîvan stroll around, a teenager humming in her slightly big guerrilla uniform. During one lunch break, we sat together on a rock by the camouflaged bower that served as a living room, when I asked her about her journey to the mountains after the genocide and her new excitement about books. Bêrîvan, who was the youngest at the language school, fluently spoke Kurdish but could not read and write it properly. She was learning quickly with the help of fellow students, working herself arduously through the thick books available at the school. An Armenian-Kurdish woman

271

guerrilla, who was in the administration of the school, told me: 'The comrades have big plans for Bêrîvan. She can be a magnificent leading figure for Êzîdî women if she continues developing herself. The organization is dedicating a lot of time to her progress.'

Months after these brief moments with Bêrîvan, I unexpectedly met her mother, when a guerrilla named Özgür from the YJA Star representation took me around the camps on Mount Şengal. Özgür was from Maraş, a kind-hearted Alevi woman with an open-minded spirit. Another Alevi-Kurdish woman, who had come to stand with the Êzîdîs was Nurhak Boran Amanos, whose *nom de guerre* is a reference to mountain ranges around her native region, Elbistan, a district of Maraş. Once I told her the name of my father's family village, half an hour's drive from her home, she considered me family. Nurhak was part of organizing the Youth Movement on Mount Şengal and had many adventurous stories. Excitement was constantly spilling out of her big round eyes behind thick-framed glasses. Her anarchic spirit meant that she had no problem offering target practice to visitors. I learned that her civilian name was Döndü Gök, when she died in September 2017 in clashes with the Turkish army in Karakoçan, Elezîz (Elâzığ).

With Özgür, we were sitting outside Bêrîvan's mother Xensê's tent. The woman spoke of her now faraway daughter with immense pride. Xensê was a founding member of the Şengal Women's Assembly and among the hundreds of Êzîdî women who were now organizing with the '*heval*': 'PKK, YPJ, YJA Star, YPG, HPG – all these names, I confuse them. When we tell the story of who rescued us, we just say: *heval hatin* (the comrades arrived).' Like others, she believed that things could no longer continue as before:

> Before the *ferman*, too, Êzîdî lives were seen as cheap. They think we Êzîdî don't know anything. But we didn't run away out of fear; we were betrayed and had to save our children from death. What have states done for us until now? They only see us as a tool for their politics. Today, we organize ourselves. We want the children of this land to return. But to live in freedom in our own lands, we need to build a strong society. We don't want people to distribute aid and not listen to our demands.

Özgür helped me overcome my difficulty in understanding the Şengalî accent. Back in Qendîl, I had also struggled to understand Xensê's daughter Bêrîvan. Realizing my shortcoming, Bêrîvan grabbed my hand at once and held it tightly in her warm, soft palm. We sat serenely, hand in hand in silence for a minute. Bêrîvan – Dunya Zat Seid Hesen – was killed in a Turkish airstrike in the same year. Êzîdî women's assembly structures, education periods, and newborn girls have been named after her ever since.

In Şengal, months before Bêrîvan's death in Qendîl, her earlier mentioned younger sister was receiving media training from the '*heval*'. Located in one of the highest mountain tops, the press centre was a vibrant place of work and education. Here, the '*heval*' and volunteers from Rojava, Bakur, and Mexmûr Refugee Camp, were training young Êzîdîs in technical skills, news reporting, and politics. The centre was not cut off from the war at the skirt of the mountain. Guerrillas, who would take shifts in clashing with Daesh in the city, occasionally dropped by for tea and fruit. Everyone would try to help them overcome their visible exhaustion with music and laughter.

Based in Şengal since the early period after the genocide, Nujiyan Erhan, the main coordinator of the press centre, a young guerrilla and journalist from Wêranşar, a district of Riha (Urfa), had been documenting the ongoing war, geopolitical developments, and the newly forming autonomous structures in the aftermath of the genocide. In her journalistic work, published in Kurdish and Turkish, she described the self-organization and autonomous structures of the community with affection and hope. She made time for guests even though she was always working late. Occasionally, she disappeared behind rocks and came back with hand-picked grapes in her arms for everyone to eat.

Throughout the founding conference of the Şengal Women's Assembly, she had been coordinating the young reporters that she had trained, with care and seriousness. One image I remember vividly is the moment when otherwise disciplined Nujiyan put down her camera to join the joyful dance during the celebration. Less than two years later, in March 2017, she was injured by the fire of KDP-linked armed forces in Şengal. After several weeks of hospital treatment, Nujiyan (Tuba Akyılmaz), a witness and defender of Êzîdî women's autonomy after feminicide, died due to her injuries.

* * *

In early 2021, an agreement was reached between the Iraqi government and the KRG to expel the autonomous self-defence units and their affiliates from Şengal. Protests erupted by Êzîdîs, who once again saw their political will marginalized by powers that had previously either deliberately abandoned or actively neglected their formal responsibilities towards the Êzîdîs. At the time of writing, the people of Şengal continue to live in the shadow of power struggles within Iraq, the Iranian state's sectarian political and military activities, as well as Turkish drone strikes.

Writing about genocide and settler colonialism in the history of what are now the United States, indigenous feminist scholar Sandy Grande (2004) describes the quest for sovereignty also as a restorative process, a moral vision in competition with liberal notions around rights that often meant 'democratically

Figure 26 Xensê, co-founder of the Şengal Women's Assembly and mother of Bêrîvan Şengal, sitting next to her son while discussing something with YJA Star guerrilla fighter Özgür. Mount Şengal. August 2015.

induced' oppression and dispossession for entire nations. Similarly, statist frameworks around rights and democracy are used to deny the Êzîdîs not only any prospect of a self-determined sovereignty, but also the right to a life without constant threats of yet more genocides looming over them.

In the hours of interviews I conducted in Şengal, civilians and combatants told me that future genocides can only be prevented by forms of political autonomy that can defend people against the root causes of war, sectarian violence, and forced displacement. In their non-statist perspectives, the status of Şengal was not merely a juridicial matter of state power and local governance. What is at stake is a struggle between competing notions of justice and sovereignty for land and people – politically, ideologically, cosmologically, morally. What kind of peace and stability can there be for the region if the Êzîdîs are not safe and free in their sacred lands on their own terms?

29

Kobanê did not fall

Kobanê meant a new phase for the Kurdistan freedom movement. Kurds from Halabja, Amed, and Mako came and died there. The resistance embodied the spirit of the PKK, the ideology of Abdullah Öcalan. There, people around the world first saw the PKK's practice and reality. In Kobanê, everyone saw who the real terrorists are. – Meysa Abdo, Rojava, 2015

To many people, Kobanê, a small town by the Syrian-Turkish border, was their entrance point to the moral and aesthetic world of the Kurdish freedom struggle. It marked a turning point in Kurdish people's presence on global agendas: on one hand, the battle launched unprecedented international solidarity with revolutionary struggles in Kurdistan; on the other hand, it marked the beginning of the military cooperation with the US and allies, whose military, political, and economic policies continue to colonize and destroy meaningful prospects for freedom in the region and beyond.

To Kurdish women, the Kobanê battle and the meaning-making discourse around it presented powerful, in some ways even game-changing reference points for their identity and for their struggles: a new sense of self, collective and individual, emerged with the widely circulated representation of Kurdistan's women as courageous 'defenders of freedom'. Regardless of their relationship to the political movement and knowing the brutal realities of gendered violence in Kurdistan, many women felt so empowered by the images from the battle that the term 'the women in Kobanê' entered everyday vocabularies. As one young Kurdish woman, who grew up in Baghdad and who worked with different NGOs across Iraq, told me, many women around her began to negotiate with men in their families, saying: 'Have the women in Kobanê not proven what we women are capable of?'

The siege of Kobanê began in September 2014, a month after the Daesh genocide in Şengal. Daesh attacked with sophisticated weapons and vehicles it had exploited mainly from the collapsed Iraqi army. Residents of the small border town had collectively organized themselves ahead of the onslaught. Formed several years before the arrival of Daesh, the YPG and YPJ had already been clashing with Islamist groups such as Jabhat al-Nusra in the region. Months before the siege, even elderly women had received self-defence training and formed a 'Mothers' Battalion' of Kobane. The footage of these 'revolutionary grannies', some of whom had lost relatives in the war, were widely shared on social media. Even if such images remained symbolic, they psychologically helped prepare people for the popular mobilization that would be required in the face of imminent genocide. To prevent another Şengal, even grandmothers should at least know how to handle a gun – just in case.

As Daesh attacked with full force, a large-scale humanitarian disaster unfolded as hundreds of thousands of people were forced to flee across the border to Turkey. Before the siege, Kobanê had already been host to internally displaced people from within Syria. Local activists and workers of Suruç (Kurdish: *Pirsûs*) municipality, a majority Kurdish town on the other side of the border, organized the needs of the newly arrived. By the time of the siege, several international news outlets had already reported on the fact that Turkey was a lifeline for Daesh in terms of recruitment, money, and logistics. Yet, despite being part of the newly formed US-led coalition against Daesh, the AKP government remained deliberately inactive in the face of the major escalation at the border. Many believed that the de-population of majority Kurdish border areas was in the interest of the Turkish state, which had long insisted on establishing a pro-Turkish 'buffer zone' there. Since 2011, Turkey had been trying to use Syrian forced displacement for geostrategic interests. At the height of the siege, Erdoğan famously proclaimed, to a cheering crowd, that 'Kobanê is at the brink of falling.' Seeing that Daesh fighters were crossing into Syria with ease, activists set up a 'border vigil' to monitor the movement in the area. At protests, in community centres, family homes, and on social media, people increasingly began thinking about Daesh and the AKP interchangeably or at least as partners in a fascist coalition, as the Turkish army attacked and wounded the protesters at the border. Photos emerged of elderly people being dragged on the floor by authorities amid teargas. Young activist and graduate student Kader Ortakaya, who had joined the border solidarity, was killed with a shot to her head by Turkish soldiers. In this period, the Turkish state's reaction to the siege was interpreted by many people as endorsing Daesh, at the very least indirectly, against Rojava. Years later, 108 HDP politicians and members were put on trial in Turkey 'for supporting terrorism' for their activities in support of the resistance *against* Daesh in Kobanê.[1]

At the beginning of October 2014, violent riots spread across Bakur, resulting in dozens of deaths in clashes with security forces. On different points, protesters tore down border fences to cross into Syria to aid the resistance against Daesh. Videos circulated of Nisêbîn, where young people removed the Turkish flag on a border watch post and replaced it with a Kurdish one, after protesters had shooed the army vehicles away with rocks and Molotov cocktails. These images resembled the *serhildan* in the 1990s (see Chapter 5). In addition to protests in different cities of Turkey, Kurdish protests also took place within Iraq and Iran.

Hunger strikes and occupations in different parts of Europe pressured the media to report on the events. That autumn, many cities around the world were filled with revolutionary Kurdish songs, as hundreds of thousands of people occupied airports, parliaments, newspapers, train stations, motorways, universities, and human rights offices. Entire communities woke up and slept to Kobanê.

On 5 October young YPJ commander Arîn Mîrkan detonated herself during clashes and became the 'symbol of the Kobanê resistance'. Her action by the strategic Miştenur Hill to protect her unit and stop Daesh's advance is widely narrated as having contributed to turning the tide of the war. Throughout her participation in Kobanê's liberation, until her death, fighter Viyan Peyman from Rojhelat was singing about the battle through *dengbêjî* performance. Her videos were widely circulated and stood for the 'hevals' insistence on beauty and life in the face of fascism and death'. She also represented the phenomenon of women and men from all parts of Kurdistan fighting and dying in Kobanê together. And together, many more of such individual stories formed the collective face of the resistance.

Meanwhile, hundreds of internationalist activists had started camping at the border. When the Kurdistan freedom movement declared 1 November as 'World

Figure 27 Ruins from the battle of Kobanê, a short walking distance from the Turkish border. The Turkish state built a border wall only after Daesh was expelled from these areas. After demining, a chunk of this eastern part of town was intentionally left untouched by the community, with plans to turn it into a memorial site in honour of the resistance. Kobanê. May 2018.

Kobanê Day', actions took place from Latin America to Asia. In Afghanistan, women were at the forefront of organizing pro-Kobanê demos in multiple cities.

Soon, as a result of the resistance and the solidarity with it, Kobanê became a centre also of mainstream global attention, especially as the Obama administration – to Erdoğan's distress – took the decision to support the Kurdish fighters on the ground with airstrikes. The situation was seemingly paradoxical. The US was militarily aiding a group that its NATO ally considers as terrorist. In the end, not least due to the American airstrikes, Kobanê did not fall. At the end of January 2015, after five months of siege, on the first anniversary of Rojava's democratic autonomy declaration, Kobanê's victory became the symbol of the resistance against Daesh, as a small town that broke the myth of the group's invincibility. More than 400 fighters died in the defence of the town, which was 80 per cent destroyed.

The cooperation between Rojava's military structures and the US-led anti-Daesh coalition meant that the US government and army officials and their allies, the media, Western think tanks, as well as certain Kurdish individuals and organizations espoused a pro-American narrative of the events, using language reminiscent of the US-led war on terror paradigm. At the time of the battle, however, across different spheres of the resistance, the events were described in the movement's media, especially by women, in ideological, even mythological terms, as an epic historical encounter with the ugliness of capitalist modernity. Foreign journalists tend to edit out what they dismiss as partyspeak, but the movement's internal meaning-giving culture undeniably mattered greatly for the resistance, which was not just limited to the battlefield.

At the time, cadres and civilians involved in the mobilization, while emphasizing their Kurdish and revolutionary identity, often interpreted and narrated the battle not as a war against any religion or community, but in terms of a gendered struggle for democratic civilization against statist civilization, a 5,000-year-old feud, now playing out in a twenty-first century military clash between a women's liberationist front that defends the oppressed and 'rapist fascists' who want to wipe out everything that is 'other'. The discourse was spiritual. 'Defending humanity', as many defined their resistance at the time, was not an abstract idea, but a concrete socialist duty: in this case, real communities and the region's diverse social fabric were at stake. Therefore, they believed, it was only natural that Apoists, ideological, disciplined, and ready to sacrifice themselves 'for life', would be an organized front in a historic stand-off against those representing a meaningless 'cult of death'.

Despite receiving American aerial support, people continued to place the US in the 'statist civilization' camp. Fighters I interviewed consciously acknowledged the contradictions at hand, but (unlike official statements put out in their name) categorically refused to express gratefulness to the Obama administration. In their eyes, American imperialism, regardless of the tactical relief it can occasionally offer in times of desperation, was at the heart of the rise of groups like Daesh. Islamism, after all, had long been a useful tool in NATO's sinister destabilization and regime change policies in the region, while the so-called 'war on terror' served as a powerful paradigm of fear to cover up profit-driven interests and policies. Many veteran cadres, who had barely survived the fire on the ground, derived their knowledge of US warfare from their experience of being targeted by the Turkish army, using US intelligence and military technology, for many years. Offering aid to the Kurdish resistance against Daesh helped the US polish its well-deserved negative image in the region, they believed. Meanwhile, such tactical alliance with the US came in handy in the context of a real threat from Daesh, and from states like Turkey that seemed to benefit from the group's temporary existence. Moreover, many hoped, it could help them gain leverage, at least for a while, in a precarious conflict environment with no political solution in sight. Several months after the battle, one of the commanders, Meysa Abdo, shared with me her interpretation of Kobanê's meaning for world resistance history. She centred international solidarity in her narrative and mentioned the US airstrikes only in passing:

It was a universal war: Kurdistan against the capitalist system. It was the clash of two lines: the nationalist states against the democratic, ecological, women's liberationist society, on behalf of all nations. People were in Europe but were in Kobanê at heart. They were in Afghanistan, but in Kobanê in spirit. All democracy and freedom-loving peoples, not their states, stood with our resistance against fascism. It was like a historical referendum, to say yes or no to humanity. This truly mind-blowing resistance became a hope for women in the world, who could see themselves in this resistance against rapist patriarchal fascism.

Meryem Kobanê, another commander of the battle, similarly stressed that the fight was about more than just a piece of land. Having witnessed the death of many of her comrades, she claimed that military power alone could not defeat Daesh. Victory required above all a sacrificial, revolutionary morale and devotion to fight to death in order to protect innocent people, without expecting any reward, whether in this life or in whatever may come after.

For 25–30 days, we fought in Kobanê, as the world was watching the battle like a Hollywood film. Erdoğan openly said that he anticipates Kobanê's fall. The Americans, too, were waiting to watch it fall before they eventually decided to conduct airstrikes. Everyone watched the daughters and sons of this country fight to death. This is how one should understand Kobanê: between those who insist on enslaving others and those who insist on freedom. The people of Kobanê were willing to resist because they tasted the philosophy of Abdullah Öcalan. The Kurdistan freedom movement is an old culture here that cannot be easily destroyed. Beyond a struggle for territory, this is a war between defenders of a democratic system on one hand, and the mentality and system of capitalism on the other hand. As Diyar Bahoz, one of the commanders of Kobanê, said: 'If we cannot live freely in this land, then our philosophy must be resistance. And resistance creates freedom'. This was the last thing he said over his radio device.

* * *

Kobanê was not defended by armed fighters only. Sara and Adliyê are two women in their 40s, who were among the handful of civilians to stay behind for the entire duration of the siege. I met them when I visited Kobanê for the first time in 2018 together with the 'Women Rise Up for Afrîn' delegation I was accompanying. Together with their friend Semîra, these women, who had been organizing with Kongreya Star for many years, had worked day and night to sustain the fighters during the battle for their hometown.

The Serzorî resistance is considered to be the beginning of what people refer to as the 'epic of Kobanê'. Serzorî is a village not far from then Daesh-occupied Girê Spî (Tel Abyad). According to surviving commanders and fighters, thousands of civilian lives inhabiting the surrounding villages were at stake in this strategic battle. Surrender in Serzorî would have strengthened Daesh's ability to seize Kobanê. As Daesh was attacking with tanks and heavy artillery, 13 Kurdish fighters in a school building mainly had AK47s, with one BKC as their heaviest equipment. Rodî Afrîn, who commanded the battle alongside Peyman Tolhildan, prevented reinforcements from coming to their aid, when it appeared that it would be impossible to break the siege in the face of Daesh's superior weapons. After having fought to the last bullet, the fighters detonated themselves. According to Meryem Kobanê, the Serzorî resistance established a shared mindset among those who would participate in the protection of the city: Kobanê can only be defended through sacrifice.

Sara said the following about the Serzorî episode:

We once found the dead, tortured body of a YPG fighter. His body was almost completely burnt; they had beaten and abused him, rubbed gun powder on his open wounds to torture him. That's why those comrades in Serzorî collectively decided to detonate themselves when their ammunition finished. They shouted: 'Bijî Rêber Apo – Berxwedan jiyan e. We will never surrender!' With these slogans, they exploded themselves. After liberation, we found the remains of these *heval*. Hair on the floor, flesh on the wall … The food they were eating was still where they had left it … After this, Daesh stopped major attacks for a while. In the meantime, our *hevals* were preparing to defend the city. The people from the villages ran to the city centre.

Daesh's plan was to empty Kobanê, and the people who knew this remained at the border without crossing. They stayed there with their animals. They had to leave behind the homes and lands that they had been working for years. There were pregnant women, many children. People kept looking back as they left. Older people had to be carried in hand carriages. Some of them did not want to cross over, they preferred to die in their homes. People reached the border, but did not cross, so Daesh targeted an area around 3km from the border. Only when some lost limbs or died, people left Kobanê.

At that time, still 700 people were in Kobanê, many of them fighters and medical workers. We stayed behind to cook for them. We didn't sleep. The war was just too intense.

At the time, most of Sara's children were in different places in Bakur and Rojava, either with family or somehow involved in organizing. One of her sons was looking after wounded people in Suruç. Adliyê reiterated that the resistance of Kobanê was a result of incessant organization inside Kobanê, coordinated with people across Rojava and Bakur. The woman spoke proudly of the role they collectively played for the reproduction of the resistance.

We are not talking about a few battles here. There were nonstop clashes for months. We were like living dead in a long dark night. The enemy was just across the street. At some point, the enemy and our *heval* were chest-to-chest. They were only metres away from each other. And yet, our morale was high. We healed the wounded, washed the dead. We washed their clothes and gave them to others. There was no water, no electricity at some point, which meant we could not prepare food properly. We were making tonnes of bread until the city's main bakery oven was attacked.

Although these two women did not physically fight, they witnessed death from up close. Repeatedly, they stressed that it was not possible to put into words the trauma they lived through.

Sara: Daesh knows that we honour our dead, that we respect our martyrs and that the recovery of bodies and burial are important. Many fighters here died or got wounded when they re-entered the battle zones just to retrieve the bodies of comrades. Because we honour our dead through burial and ceremony, because these martyrs are sacred to us, they abuse the bodies.

Daesh has no war ethics. They sometimes even removed the bones from our comrades' bodies. Some of the captured Daesh youth confessed that they were taking drugs. This added more stress for the *hevals*. Daesh had indoctrinated and abused these kids and was sending them everywhere.

Adliyê: One old man, who did not want to leave his home, was beheaded … They hated the YPJ. They put the head of a YPJ fighter on a pole and circulated the image. They especially wanted Arabs in surrounding areas to see their atrocities so that they would not support the YPG/YPJ. They slaughtered the animals senselessly. They did not allow any living being to survive.

Sara and Adliyê know the stories of nearly all martyrs of Kobanê. In their own words, some fighters died within moments of speaking to them. They spoke fondly of all those who had come from faraway places to support the resistance:

Heval Viyan from Wan was a Kurdish language teacher. Thanks to her and others, our kids were learning in their mother tongue for the first time. All her students were heartbroken when she died. With her, *heval* Dilovan, Mahmut and Rustem lost their lives. After that, the war didn't stop anymore.

The attacks started from the east and south with heavy weapons. *Heval* Zozan and Êrîş were with a group of *heval*, who said: 'If the Daesh gangs enter Kobanê, they will have to go over our dead bodies.' And that is what happened. Daesh actually ran over their bodies so many times that only their clothes remained intact.

Kader Ortakaya, a young woman from Istanbul, was murdered by the Turkish army when she tried to enter the city. Others died within moments of crossing the border. It was cruel. I remember how some of our *hevals* cried as they mourned them, saying: 'Had they at least drank some water in Kobanê before dying.' There is blood. Everywhere you walk in Kobanê is blood.

After the war, Sara's husband was among the more than 200 people, who died in the Daesh revenge attacks launched on Kobanê from within Turkey in late June 2015. Despite the horrors they witnessed, Sara and Adliyê remember the time as an atmosphere of comradeship and courage. According to Adliyê:

Every single one of these human beings, every single *heval* was worth an entire world. Many of them had stayed in the mountains for so many years. They entered Kobanê with their great ideals and visions. It was their resistance that turned every place in the world into Kobanê. All over the world, people launched a state of emergency for Kobanê. Meanwhile, Erdoğan said 'Kobanê

Figure 28   A street sign named after fighters who died
fighting against Daesh on this spot. Kobanê. May 2018.

is falling, it is about to fall', but with their 'tilili' and revolutionary slogans, our
girls in the trenches proved that Kobanê will never fall.

It would be an injustice to try and describe the destruction and rebuilding of
Kobanê as someone who watched it from afar. With immense collective labour,
much of the city was reconstructed through the efforts of the community and
the local administration, with the support of the Jazeera canton and several
local, regional, and progressive international organizations. During my visit, the
east of the city, which had seen the greatest damage, was left untouched, with
plans to turn the site into an open-air museum in memory of the resistance.
With explosives largely cleared, children were playing hide-and-seek among
damaged tanks and walls that look like swiss cheese, a big playground of rubble,
burnt metal and dust. Writings and makeshift signs in random spots – on trees,
in the streets, by crumbling buildings – indicated that the places were named
after the fighters who had died there. This is what anti-fascist history apparently
looks like.

283

Figure 29   Members of a women's commune in Kobanê. The woman in the middle is Adliyê, one of the handful of civilians who stayed behind in Kobanê during the Daesh siege to support the fighters logistically. Kobanê. May 2018.

30

Life after Daesh:
Women's solidarity in Manbij

Manbij, a northern Syrian town just west of the Euphrates river, has a millennia-old, erased history of women's leadership. The name is Aramaic in origin and means 'site of spring'. The ancient Greeks referred to it as a 'holy city', the residence of the fertility goddess Atargatis, who is often portrayed as half-woman, half-fish. Historians view Atargatis as versions or counterparts of Phoenician, Mesopotamian, Greek, or Anatolian goddesses like Astarte, Ishtar, Aphrodite, or Cybele. In the third century BCE, Stratonice of Syria, queen of the Seleucid Empire, rebuilt a temple in Atargatis' honour. Anti-woman iconoclasm however erased much of the memory of women's historical role and leadership in the region. Few of the goddess temples and shrines in the region survived over the course of millennia of male-dominated empire and conquest. In the summer of 2015, images circulated of Daesh in Manbij publicly destroying archaeological artefacts from the ancient site of Palmyra. Daesh had established an 'Archaeological Administration' in Manbij to give its looting of a formal face. Long before that, much of the heritage, including ancient figurines and statues of women, had been stolen by European colonialists.

Nearly two millennia before Daesh was enslaving women in these lands, Queen Zenobia of Palmyra, praised for creating a vibrant intellectual and pluralistic culture in her court, was reigning over a territory stretching from modern day Turkey to Egypt. In 2021, mere years after Daesh's defeat, the Zenobia Women's Collective was formed in Manbij and other majority Arab regions such as Raqqa, Deir ez-Zor, and Tabqa.

Manbij is a majority Arab city with Turkmen, Kurdish, and Circassian communities. It changed hands several times over the course of the Syrian war. Before Daesh took over in January 2014, it was controlled by factions of the FSA and governed by oppositional organizers. Several mass graves were found in the outskirts of Manbij in the aftermath of Daesh's years-long terror regime.

In May 2018, months after Turkey launched 'Operation Olive Branch', I visited Manbij together with the previously mentioned women's solidarity delegation. The population had lived under Daesh for several years; as such, the city was less secure than other areas in the region at the time. The presence of sleeper cells caused a suspenseful, rushed vibe in the city. Suicide attacks and explosions had marked Manbij since 2016. Traffic was dense, markets were open, children were playing outside, but many buildings of the city had been destroyed by airstrikes or pierced by bullets.[1] A Turkmen teacher in her 50s told me about public executions that she had witnessed with her own eyes. Her matter-of-fact tone when recounting atrocities was haunting. A young Arab woman told the group:

> We could no longer breathe, when Daesh was here. Women were absolutely nothing in their system. Many women, myself included, tried to struggle and protect ourselves individually. We all resisted in our own ways, from our homes. It was so oppressive, and I would have been grateful to whoever would liberate us. In the end, the women in the SDF embraced us in freedom.

In August 2016, the SDF, aided by the US-led coalition forces, had taken Manbij and its surroundings from Daesh. Moving images were widely circulated from Manbij at the time, of women burning their black veils, ululating with joy. Videos showed civilian women, formerly held hostage, hugging and kissing the women who freed them from captivity. Elderly women making victory signs were filmed freely smoking cigarettes for the first time after years, while men were cutting their beards in public to celebrate regained liberties.

The Manbij Civilian Council, the predecessor of the later administrations, was established in April 2016, months before the liberation from Daesh, in a nearby town. After Daesh was expelled, the Democratic Civilian Administration of Manbij and its surroundings was founded in early 2017 with Arab, Turkmen, Kurdish, Armenian, Chechen, and Circassian members. The coalition airstrikes had led to many civilian deaths and destroyed many homes. Demining, reconstruction, and infrastructure works began in five municipalities early on. Healthcare and humanitarian assistance were among the key concerns of the administration, especially as tens of thousands of displaced people were arriving in Manbij from areas like Raqqa, Tabqa, and later Idlib. Culture and arts committees offered training courses, alongside curating art and book exhibitions, lectures, poetry readings, theatre plays, and music festivals. The youth and sports committee was put in charge of (re)building facilities for recreational activities and organizing training and athletic matches. For the first time, Turkmen and Circassian children began cultural activities such as dance classes and education in their own language.

Manbij's many unsolved economic and social problems, including poverty and displacement, affect women in particular. Brutalization through years of war and Daesh rule further normalized violence against women. Domestic abuse, child marriage, and so-called honour killings are widespread. The Women's Assembly of Manbij and Surrounding Villages was established on 8

March, International Women's Day, in 2017. The assembly, made up of Arab, Circassian, Turkmen, and Kurdish women, regularly meets with women in the security forces, political structures, and other spheres to report about their respective work and develop shared practices and plans. The first autonomous women's cooperative, *Beyt al-Baraka* (House of Blessing), was formed in autumn 2017, shortly before the Women's Economy Centre was opened to create work opportunities for women, including restaurants, food cooperatives, poultries, textile workshops, and bakeries.

Following a series of discussions and consultations, people had come to the conclusion that a sudden imposition of Rojava's women's laws could have amounted to rejection or hostility by local communities against a system perceived as Kurdish (and sometimes, 'communist', so therefore 'atheist'). While this presented a set of difficulties, it also rendered the activists more flexible and spontaneous in their work. As one of them stressed: 'We are at the very beginning of everything. That's the beauty of it. Everything is new. We are only starting to get to know the communities here, to understand people and identify their needs. Our efforts will be shaped accordingly. There is no standard way of proceeding.' Another coordinator at the assembly explained that it was neither realistic nor sustainable to expect entire communities, who lived under different regimes and occupations, to genuinely embrace new policies and organizational principles without preparation.

> The necessary groundwork for women's laws has not been done yet. We do present our perspective and stance in different ways. Take for instance polygamy, a widespread practice. We can't just say we will ban it and punish those who do it. But we don't let polygamous men lead in our self-organized structures. We educate people about issues like violence, help women file divorces and support them in lifting obstacles to their lives.

In the absence of a clearly spelled out social contract in Manbij's difficult social and political context, emotional intelligence and cultural and social sensitivity shaped activists' decisions. In the words of a Kurdish member of the assembly:

> After years of living under different groups, people are suspicious of anyone that wants to establish yet another rule. Our work requires sensitivity. People here suffered unimaginable terror in a short period. As the women's movement, we made sure to let people know we came to hear their pains. We slowly entered homes, listened to experiences. We didn't speak about politics, because people have come to fear political projects. They perceive them as threats. Instead, we talked to people about their family lives, about women's problems. This way, we saw the scale of all the things that women endured

under Daesh. Many people here, not just the women, are totally traumatized. There are so many things that people are not even ready to speak about yet.

Committees in charge of home visits divide the city among themselves to regularly follow up on their previously established contacts. Not rarely do they experience backlash and hostility, even violence. Patience, they said, was key to overcome Manbij's post-Daesh psychology. In the words of an Arab member:

In home visits, we discuss with everyone, not just the women. We recognize that women's issues are connected to the family and society as a whole. Let's not forget that men were targeted by Daesh, too. Of course, women suffered in a specific way, but men relate to their experiences of violence, because Daesh was brutal to all. People have not yet left behind the psychological mindset that Daesh is around and ready to harm them. It's not easy to forget. We try, though not everyone is willing to open up.

One younger Arab member of the council mentioned that she left for Rojava when Daesh took over her family's home. There, she witnessed the works of Kongreya Star and decided to help take this work to Manbij.

There are many women, who have great ideas and are keen on participating in public work, but they are afraid of their husbands. Sometimes, the families fear for the women as well. At least, we let women know, house by house, that the women's assembly has their back. Women in Manbij should know that the assembly will stand for them from now on. They look at Rojava and see that organized women's struggle is indeed possible … and they invite us again! 'Come back', they say. People clearly have a lot to share.

Only two months after Daesh, the first *mal a jin* was opened in Manbij. At the time of my visit, there were three *mal a jin* in Manbij, one in the city, two in the countryside. A women's economic committee was at the time struggling to develop economic opportunities through cooperatives. Educations were offered to counter domestic abuse and child marriage. The Manbij Jineolojî Centre was founded in 2018 and started offering week-long retreats for groups of women. Among their main areas of work are public discussions and education sessions, fieldwork-based sociological research among communities, and campaigns against under-aged marriage.

Following the establishment of the AANES later in 2018, representatives from the different regions including Manbij, that collectively make up the Women's Assembly of the self-administration, launched efforts to draft region-specific women's bylaws. With the help of the Syrian Women's Council, the first women's conference in Manbij was held in December that year, with the slogan 'Organized woman is the guarantee for democratic Syria's future'. In April 2019, the young women's movement held its first conference in Manbij. It began establishing its own coordination and decision-making mechanisms, protest actions, and awareness-raising campaigns on issues like child marriage and domestic violence.

For the moment, these efforts remain limited to a small section of women. The implementation of AANES laws relating to issues such as polygamy and inheritance, modified in consultation with women's organizations, tribes, and others, to adapt to local cultural sensitivities, is often misrepresented as being hostile to religion. Political participation has turned women into targets of violence by different actors. For instance, in early 2021, Hind Latif al-Khadir and Sa'da Faysal al-Hermas, two Arab women involved in structures of the self-administration, were abducted and murdered through beheading in Shaddade. This double feminicide was claimed by Daesh the next day.

The city's location and its multi-ethnic make-up gives it strategic importance for a variety of state and non-state actors. Following the Turkish military invasion of 2019, the SDF struck an agreement with the Syrian regime forces to secure the border. In light of this precarious situation, the AANES continues to be perceived as temporary by many residents in Manbij and in other areas still recovering from Daesh rule. Populations routinely complain and protest about forced conscription, arbitrary arrests, detention conditions, housing issues, confiscation of papers and property, censorship, fuel and gas prices, and inadequate access to needs. The AANES has taken steps to address these legitimate demands and criticisms, while noting that discontent is often weaponized or actively incited by external actors with agendas to destabilize Manbij, in particular the Syrian state and groups with connection to the Turkish state and intelligence.[2] On TV programmes and in protests, residents frequently mention that the solidarity between communities like Arabs and Kurds and the wider democratic autonomous self-governance model that Manbij represents are among the main reasons for various actors' 'special warfare' on the city. While acknowledging that multiple factors are at play, it is worth mentioning that there is plenty of footage of women vibrantly participating in women-organized or mixed protests and rallies led by structures loosely or directly affiliated with the AANES system (e.g. against gendered violence and occupation, etc.), but women are notably absent in the protests that resist it.

In many ways, despite ongoing challenges arising from a combination of factors (such as ethnic and religious tensions, Ba'ath Party and Daesh legacies, the administration's shortcomings, etc.), Manbij came to symbolize an example of the possibility of organizing society along the 'democratic nation' model, albeit in the context of war. As challenges continue to prevail, the fate of places like Manbij remains a litmus test for the AANES' claims to uphold its emancipatory promise.

31

War and peace

In the run-up to the June 2015 general elections in Turkey, I was in the Qendîl mountains. Parties of the Kurdish tradition had historically run with independent candidates to avoid the 10 per cent electoral threshold. This time, the Peoples' Democratic Party (HDP) was going all in. For weeks, I followed the election campaigns with the guerrillas, who took turns cheering for their hometown rallies. Young women from places like Colemêrg (Hakkari), Êlih (Batman), and Wan (Van) were scanning TV screens for their extended family members, shrieking with joy at faces they recognized. Themselves unable to vote, having broken with electoral politics when they had gone to the mountains, they commented on the rallies' aesthetics, the politicians' speeches, the crowds' sizes – but why did guerrillas care about elections?

One day, as we watched a multilingual pro-HDP election song made by the guerrillas, previously mentioned Heja from the Black Sea region, explained this apparent paradox in the following way.

The HDP represents the solidary spirit of the joint life of all peoples in the Middle East, with all their diverse colours and identities. It is a form of organizing a mentality to enable common life. The election campaign is an opportunity to communicate this desire to friends and foes alike.

The 10 per cent election threshold is in reality the state's way of saying: No matter if you are Kurd, Turk, Alevi, Sunni, Assyrian, or Armenian, you must live within the limits of the state. It's an absurd, anti-democratic threshold from the time of the coup. Passing the threshold is only one formal way of resisting the statist mentality. It's part of the struggle to force the state to acknowledge democracy. The struggle for democracy must be led in all spheres if we truly believe in putting an end to the bloodshed. If the HDP enters parliament, it can add another voice to peoples' demands to put an end to the war through political solution.

When Daesh exploded a bomb in June 2015 at the HDP rally in Amed, killing five and wounding many dozens, anger and grief took over the camps. The explosion was outrageous, but not entirely surprising to the guerrillas, who were used to fighting both Daesh and the AKP, two groups they saw as being allied.

Despite everything, the HDP smoothly passed the threshold with 13 per cent of the vote, achieving a record number of MPs. Three of my interlocutors were elected to parliament. One of them, Edibe Şahin, became the first woman to represent the Alevi-Kurdish city of Dêrsim in parliament.

The moment the results were announced it seemed as though each guerrilla unit was throwing a party in Qendîl. The local Soranî-speaking Qendîl villagers joined the guerrillas in dances around the fire in Newroz-like celebrations. Guerrillas and villagers formed convoys of pick-up trucks, racing through the starlit night, which is chilly in the mountain, even in the summer. Different Kurdish slogans, flags, dances were united especially by the children, who got carried away by this rare moment of ecstasy. Everyone had hope. My only worry in that moment were the children next to me, who were recklessly climbing around the back of the trucks that raced around, for once, just for fun. Not long after these scenes, civilians like myself were asked to leave, as combat jets threateningly increased their visibility. War was announcing itself. Shortly after, the mountains were bombed.

*   *   *

The collapse of the peace process between the Turkish state and the PKK in 2015 led to the most violent episode in the decades-old conflict, leaving at least

Figure 30   Guerrillas visited by a Peace Mother, watching an HDP rally ahead of the general elections in Turkey. Qendîl. June 2015.

6,000 people dead. The end of this two-and-a-half-year period of hope was accompanied by several Daesh massacres inside Turkey's borders. In July, 33 mostly young socialists were massacred in Suruç, where they had been waiting to cross into Kobanê to help with the reconstruction. In October, an HDP rally for the snap elections was targeted in the Turkish capital of Ankara by a Daesh suicide attack – 102 people were murdered on the spot, with hundreds wounded. Horrifying videos showed people dancing and singing revolutionary songs moments before the explosion. Like in Amed and Ankara, seen as capitals of Bakur and Turkey, respectively, colourful flags and banners proclaiming peace and democracy were on blood-covered floors in Suruç, the town that had summoned internationalists around the world. People commented that the attacks targeted the solidarity of peoples, which had been flourishing in the context of the peace process and support for the Rojava Revolution. Earlier that year, major newspapers had broken the news about the police and gendarmerie intercepting trucks in which the Turkish intelligence had been delivering heavy weapons and supplies across the border to Islamists in 2014. International media reported the scandal, which exposed claims that local civilians and Kurdish news agencies had been making all along. Can Dündar, editor-in-chief of *Cumhuriyet*, one of Turkey's major daily newspapers, was arrested and later exiled for the story.[1] Several of the people involved in attacks within Turkey had been known to the state as having links to Daesh cells in Turkey.[2] Why, after losing a battle in Kobanê for the first time, was Daesh targeting the AKP's enemies inside Turkey? YouTube videos broadcasted in the late spring of 2021 by infamous mafia leader Sedat Peker further substantiated the long-suspected military, logistical, and financial support of the AKP for radical Islamist terrorist groups in Syria.[3]

Before the snap elections in November 2015, violence had already escalated. The 'stone-throwing children' in the largely poor neighbourhoods, whose images of street-based resistance against the state's armoured vehicles had proliferated since the 1990s, had become an organized armed urban youth movement that dug trenches to defend their areas from the state's attacks.[4] Following the end of the peace process, people's assemblies across Kurdish towns and provinces declared 'democratic autonomy'. The state imposed military lockdowns on more than two dozen towns, at times placing more than 1 million people under army siege. In Amed's Sur district, the armed resistance of the youth, later reinforced by the guerrilla, defied the siege for 106 days.[5] In the months and years to come, the Turkish army besieged places like Nisêbîn, Sur, Silopî, and Cizîr, committing massacres on civilians during military lockdowns. In Cizîr, hundreds of civilians, including well-known, respected leaders, were entrapped in basements during the military lockdown and many were burned alive by Turkish forces. Special forces units left behind seemingly used condoms and racist graffiti with rape threats, formulated as jokes, in the ruins of people's homes.[6] In analyses, leading PKK members self-critically declared that they had underestimated the brutality of the state in the urban war. The escalation into violence forced many activists to withdraw or halt their activites. Thousands were jailed or forced into exile.

Patriarchal symbolism had permeated the peace process between the PKK and the state from the start. As noted in the 'İmralı meeting notes', at the end of the first meeting with a political delegation on 3 January 2013 on the prison island İmralı after a period of isolation, Abdullah Öcalan said: 'Send my wishes to the woman comrades. I celebrate the new year on this basis.' Six days later, Sakine Cansız, Fidan Doğan, and Leyla Şaylemez were assassinated by a Turkish intelligence operative in Paris. Despite this clear attempt to sabotage the developments, Öcalan announced the peace process via a letter that was read out at the Newroz celebration in Amed.

A few months into the process, in November 2013, Erdoğan staged a 'historic' gathering in the same city, with then KRG president Mesûd Barzanî and famous Kurdish artists and politicians. The event featured a wedding ceremony of 400 young couples, shortly after a government announcement that those marrying at young age will receive a start-up credit, along with other economic benefits, especially in case of childbirth in the first few years. The special guests were given the role of marriage witnesses to symbolically seal the life commitments of the young couples at the same time as the peace process. Kurdish women's activists interpreted this orchestration as an ideological attack signalling that the peace process would be based on the terms of the conservative sections of Kurdistan, who traditionally sided with the Turkish state. This patriarchal marriage would reveal its abusive colours on multiple fronts in the years to come.

In retrospect, the brutalized naked body of killed guerrilla fighter Ekin Wan (Kevser Eltürk), laying bare in the streets in Varto district of Muş province (another area that had declared autonomy), circulated widely on social media in early August 2015, shortly after the collapse of the peace process, appears like a symbol of what was to come in the following years: the feminicidal face of the Turkish state's war concept on the Kurdish people and their resistance movements. On 4 January 2016 in Silopî, three (civilian) Kurdish women activists of the Free Women's Congress KJA, Sêvê Demir, Pakize Nayır, and Fatma Uyar were murdered by the army during the curfew. Their deaths came mere days before the third anniversary of the killing of three other Kurdish women, Sakine Cansız, Fidan Doğan, and Leyla Şaylemez in Paris.[7]

The coup d'état attempt in the summer of 2016, believed to have been incited by the former partner of the AKP, the infamous Islamist Fethullah Gülen movement, which had long tried to sabotage the peace process, led to a series of unprecedented purges. With the governmental decrees, the activities of dozens of women's organizations were frozen or banned, their buildings and programmes co-opted or repurposed by authorities.[8] The government mass arrested politicians, journalists, academics, lawyers, and civil society workers it charged with 'terrorism'. The homes of elected politicians were raided and some were taken to detention facilities by plane, followed by several weeks or months of isolation. Many remain in prison at the time of writing.[9] Government-appointed trustees (*kayyum*) abolished co-presidency in the municipalities.[10] Numerous municipal workers were sacked, jailed, or forced to exile.

After the relaunch of war in Bakur and immense crackdowns on domestic oppositions, the Turkish state expanded its policies to Rojava and Başûr, invading, occupying, and bombarding even civilian settlements in Mexmûr and Şengal with impunity. In the months before the publication of this book, the Turkish army targeted Mexmûr Refugee Camp with drone strikes. Between 2018 and 2022, Turkey launched several military operations or missions in Syria, Iraq, Libya, and Artsakh, in the quest to become a regional power by using Islamist mercenaries recruited from remnants of Daesh and al-Qaeda-linked groups in Syria.

In January 2018, Turkey launched 'Operation Olive Branch' against the majority Kurdish region of Afrîn in north-western Syria. As Turkey bombed civilian settlement areas, its mercenaries on the ground, whose slogans, looks, and methods appeared like copies of Daesh, engaged in systematic war crimes, including assassinating civilians, attacking Syria's few Êzîdîs and Alevis, sexually assaulting women, torturing people, looting homes, and destroying natural and historical heritage.[11] The settlers cut down thousands of Afrîn's olive trees and exported them to Turkey. A Turkish airstrike destroyed the 3,000-year-old

Figure 31 View overlooking Sur district of Diyarbakır (Amed), one of the places besieged by the Turkish army during the urban wars that started after the peace process collapsed in mid-2015. Sur, Amed. January 2015.

Hittite era Ain Dara temple in Afrîn, believed to have been devoted to the goddess Ishtar. After two months of fighting, the Kurdish fighters withdrew and organized the evacuation of civilians, hundreds of thousands of whom remain displaced at the time of writing, four years on. Turkey's blackmailing of the EU with the refugee crisis meant that its militarist policies were largely tolerated, including settling populations not native to the region in Afrîn. This suited Turkey's years-old plans to change the demographics of Rojava by replacing the Kurds with pro-Turkish Islamist groups. Turkey installed a puppet 'self-government' in de facto annexed Afrîn, removing all references to Kurdish culture and language that had appeared since 2012, and replacing them with symbolism glorifying Ottomanism and Erdoğan's version of Turkish nationalism. In the media, Turkey presents its annexation as an act of charity by handing out aid, offering infrastructure, education, and economic opportunities. Children are made to learn Turkish in schools, which, like many public buildings, display Turkish flags.

All women's structures were destroyed. Afrîn's vibrant streets, decorated with symbols of the women's struggle, turned into a sea of men. During the operation, Turkish-backed forces circulated a video in which they insulted and stepped on the dead and mutilated body of young YPJ fighter Barîn Kobanê. Stripping and assaulting the corpses of Kurdish women fighters is not an invention of Daesh or Turkey's new allies, but a decades-old tradition of the Turkish state.

Shortly after the formation of the joint Syriac-Assyrian Military Council by the Khabour Guards and the Syriac Military Council in July 2019, Syriacs and Assyrians were among the first victims of the Turkish state's Peace Spring Operation starting on 9 October 2019.[12] Peace Spring, launched in the area between Serêkaniyê (Ras al-Ain) and Girê Spî (Tel Abyad) following the sudden withdrawal of US troops on the order of Donald Trump, resembled the Olive Branch operation in many ways, as documented by the UN and various human rights organizations (see Bibliography). Hevrîn Xelef, a women's activist and leader of the Syrian Future Party was brutally assassinated by the Turkish-backed Islamist group Ahrar al-Sharqiya a few days into the invasion.[13] Similar to Barîn Kobanê in Afrîn, the dead body of YPJ fighter Amara Renas was abused and filmed by the Turkish proxy forces. Jinwar Women's Village had to be temporarily evacuated.

Like a phallus, the Turkish flag was erected in the occupied territories by mercenaries, who systematically destroyed the women's movement's institutions and symbols. Wherever the flag appeared, women disappeared from public view. The state's expansionist ideology was boldly illustrated in the abduction of YPJ fighter Çiçek Kobanê during Operation Peace Spring. In widely circulated footage filmed by Turkey's mercenaries, the small-framed and visibly disoriented woman is insulted, harassed, and abused by a group of armed men.[14]

Although Çiçek Kobanê is a Syrian citizen captured within Syrian borders by Turkish-affiliated mercenary fighters of the so-called Syrian National Army, the Turkish court ruled that she had violated the unity and integrity of the Turkish state. Her case is just one of many instances in which Turkish-backed militias handed over Syrian citizens to Turkish authorities for prosecution – as legal experts point out, in breach of international law. Numerous reports have been published about the abuses during these operations and the occupation regimes that were subsequently established. Yet, other than local resistance and internationalist solidarity, there is no effort that challenges Turkey's illegal invasions and annexations of land. In the summer of 2020, once again, like the triple feminicides in Paris and Silopî, three Kurdish women activists, Zehra Berkel, Hebûn Mele Xelîl, and Amîna Waysî, were killed by the Turkish state, this time in a cross-border drone strike on a gathering in a house in Kobanê.

In post-Daesh northern Syria, struggling against the Turkish state became a central cause unifying women. In several interviews, Syriac women compared the Turkish operation to previous genocide campaigns in the region, just as they had compared Daesh to Ottoman pogroms during my interviews in 2015. At the time of my 2018 visit, Erdoğan was eyeing Manbij. According to the Manbij women's assembly members, who had been protesting the invasion of Afrîn, the same forces that incite conflict between the communities were united in their suppression of women. As one Turkmen woman pointed out: 'We will never accept a Turkish invasion. If Turkey enters Manbij, it will take us back in time, back to an era of darkness. This is clear in Erdoğan's language. We want to face a free future; we don't want to go back again.' In the years that followed, women organized large protests in previously Daesh-occupied cities and towns like Manbij, Raqqa, Deir ez-Zor, and Tabqa. Across the region, Syriac, Assyrian, Kurdish, Arab, and Turkmen women co-organized 25 November International Day against Violence against Women rallies with slogans like 'Occupation is Violence'. Kongreya Star launched the Women Defend Rojava campaign as a call for women around the world to protect the women's revolution from feminicidal occupation. In many statements, the YPJ expressed their determination to fight occupation by the second largest NATO army, just as they had fought Daesh.

The attacks on Rojava were accompanied by numerous other developments that led organized women to speak of the Turkish state as pursuing a 'genocide-feminicide' war and occupation. Inside Turkey, thousands of women and LGBTQI+ people resisted police violence in the streets as they protested with slogans that connected the attacks on the women's revolution in Rojava to Turkey's withdrawal from the Istanbul Convention. Inside Başûr, several Kurdish and Iraqi women's activists and organizations joined forces to condemn the Turkish army's military operations and territorial invasions, facilitated by the KDP and to a great extent tolerated by the Iraqi state. In Şengal, Êzîdî women routinely protested Turkish airstrikes as a 'continuation' of the Daesh genocide. At Mexmûr Refugee Camp, women made similar comparisons and condemned the UNHCR and other institutions for their silence on drone strikes on a refugee camp.

In the summer of 2021, a Turkish nationalist named Onur Gencer launched an armed attack on the Izmir headquarters of the Peoples' Democratic Party (HDP). His plan was to commit a massacre in a planned gathering. The meeting was cancelled, and he murdered only one person in the building: a young Kurdish woman named Deniz Poyraz. Though Poyraz was not the killer's primary target, the Kurdistan freedom movement, together with women's movements in the region and beyond, immediately labelled the attack as a feminicide. As it turned out, Gencer had spent time training inside Turkish-occupied parts of Syria.

These developments across borders deepened the Kurdish women's movement's analysis of patriarchal violence and its relationship to state, ecocide, and capitalism. In the same years, the struggle against feminicide became a global feminist rallying point. In Latin America, where feminists had long pointed to the role of the state in the reproduction of feminicide, transnational movements like *Ni una menos* (not one [woman] less) were at the forefront of exposing the extent of feminicide in the lives of especially poor, racialized, and colonized women.[15] During the Covid-19 pandemic, evidence emerged about a global surge of patriarchal violence, including feminicide. While building common fronts against feminicide, war, and occupation among Kurdish, Arab, Turkish, Syriac, Armenian, and other women in the region, the movement accelerated its global alliance-building work on such issues in this period.

Against the compartmentalization of gendered violence into different 'types', a commonplace practice in mainstream anti-violence campaigns, new platforms were created on the local and international levels to expose the links between different manifestations of patriarchal violence. As stated by the 100 Reasons campaign, launched by the Kurdish Women's Movement in Europe (TJK-E) to prosecute Erdoğan for feminicide and to build internationalist women's bridges against violence: 'As the Kurdish women's movement, we speak of feminicide as a comprehensive, structurally anchored war against women – both in armed conflicts and in everyday life. This war takes place on a physical, military level as well as on an ideological and psychological level …' Moreover, in various publications, the term 'political feminicide' was introduced to refer to the specific targeted killing of politically engaged women as a method to kill society's alternative political futures. As the campaign notes: 'Women are not (only) attacked as biological bodies, but as potential representatives of a society based on cooperation and care, justice and peace, community and sustainability, love and diversity.' In other words, the assassination of struggling women is an attack on women's individual and collective leadership, a war on women's resistance, autonomy, organization and revolutionary politics from below.

In the past, the term 'martyrs of the women's struggle' usually described militant women, who died while consciously participating in political resistance. Civilian women's mass involvement in politics in places like Rojava, and their indiscriminate targeting under the occupation, blurred such categories and thereby expanded the use of the term. Today, the movement honours historical figures like Rosa Luxemburg and the Sisters Mirabal, alongside more recently assassinated activist women such as Hevrîn Xelef, Marielle Franco, Berta Cáceres, Karima Baloch, and Frozan Safi, at the same time as exposing the 'everyday' occurrences of feminicide. As explicitly expressed in the movement's statements from recent years in solidarity with women in Afghanistan, Palestine, Poland, and Argentina and Black women around the world in the aftermath of the killing of George Floyd, whether protesting political feminicide or any other form of patriarchal violence, including so-called 'honour killings', the Kurdish women's movement now weaves stories together in its pledge to abolish all mentalities that destroy life in the personage of women – from patriarchy in the family and in the movement, all the way to the global arms trade.

To mark International Day against Violence against Women in 2021, hundreds of men staged several demonstrations against patriarchal violence and feminicide in different towns and cities across northern Syria, stating their respect and commitment to the women's liberation struggle.

PART IV

Empowerment or revolution?

Everywhere, nature is under attack. Weapons sales, economic projects in the hands of states are responsible for this. Look at the powers that produce and sell the arms for wars in Kurdistan. Who divided these lands? Who gave chemicals to Saddam Hussein? Who condemns our children to early death? Why are so many armed groups terrorizing communities here? What drives people from countries far away to join Daesh here? People in places like Europe that are believed to be free should think about these questions very hard. They must understand their governments' complicity in the wars here. – Kanî, Silêmanî, 2015

32

Two rivers, two freedom agendas?

In 2017, Hollywood actress and UNHCR Special Envoy Angelina Jolie and NATO Secretary General Jens Stoltenberg (2017) co-authored a *Guardian* article to declare that they would cooperate 'to identify ways in which NATO can strengthen its contribution to women's protection and participation in all aspects of conflict-prevention and resolution'. Outlining their plan to render the Western military alliance more sensitive to gender issues, they stated:

> We believe that NATO has the responsibility and opportunity to be a leading protector of women's rights. In particular, we believe NATO can become the global military leader in how to prevent and respond to sexual violence in conflict, drawing on the strengths and capabilities of its member states and working with its many partner countries.

This collaboration between a multimillionaire celebrated as a 'feminist icon' and the head of the biggest militarist organization in the world is an example of how in recent years issues around social justice increasingly entered the dominant system's discourse. More governments, universities, and corporations, including institutions at the core of perpetuating war, forced displacement, sexism, racism, ecocide, poverty, censorship, and authoritarianism, are pressured to react to growing demands for equality and justice. 'Women, peace and security' has become a well-funded research complex.[1] The first female foreign minister of Germany, a country that is one of Turkey's main arms suppliers, claims to work on developing a 'feminist foreign policy', following the example of Sweden and Canada. The previous section gave an overview of NATO's 'gender-sensitivity' track record in Kurdistan.

In early 2021, former US Secretary of State Hillary Clinton announced that she and her daughter will work on a TV series about female Kurdish fighters. The YPJ, the most 'hyped' army of Kurdish women became an ally of the US-led coalition as the outcome of an unlikely temporary and tactical alliance in the context of the war against Daesh. But, as we have established by now, its members view it as an army of women whose sisters have for decades fought and died in the mountains against NATO member Turkey. Clinton's move, in line with her signature soft power foreign policy doctrine, came after several years of Western media coverage that ideologically distorted the meaning and nature of the militant Kurdish women's struggle. Years into the war in Syria, a photograph of YPJ fighter Asia Ramazan Antar (Viyan Qamişlo) in her uniform with a rifle on her shoulder widely circulated, with titles referring to her as the 'Kurdish Angelina Jolie'. Viyan was a young woman from Qamişlo, who lost several family members in the Daesh war. Following her death in the summer of 2016 in a battle in Manbij, media outlets once again reported about her, again with headlines nicknaming her after the Hollywood actress. Another story that made the rounds was that of a young YPJ fighter named Rehana, whose photo was posted by a journalist on social media, along with the claim that she had single-handedly killed more than one hundred Daesh fighters. Other than a viral social media post by a white male reporter, it is not clear if there is any evidence that the woman in the photo had ever claimed such a thing.

In both of these illustrative cases, the headlines were not written or disseminated by Kurdish fighters themselves, who had no say in the erotic framing, content, or circulation made by (often male) journalists and outlets that used machoistic language to glorify the women's ability to kill. 'Counting kills' would in fact be considered a shameful patriarchal practice by most of these fighters. Through clickbait framings, the sentence 'Daesh is afraid of being killed by women, because that means they won't go to heaven' became a hackneyed cliché in reports on Kurdish women's battles. The male and Western-centric gaze of these portrayals sometimes contrasted the Kurdish YPJ to other women in the region as an exceptional group of liberated women in an otherwise misogynistic region. Such representations undermined the YPJ's own self-understanding as an army for all women in the region and beyond. An opportunity for Middle Eastern women to develop radical, but grounded cultural critiques of ultra-patriarchal worldviews was emptied of its meaning and turned into a joke to mock Daesh for the entertainment of Western audiences. Ironically, even Kurdish parties that reject the PKK's ideology and that are known for excluding women from decision-making capitalized on this positive image for their own interests.[2] Feature films and theatre plays (sometimes with non-Kurdish or even white actresses playing the lead roles), often produced without meaningful consultation with actual Kurdish women fighters, also distorted historical events in favour of apolitical narratives. Conservative political talk shows whitewashed US interventionism in the region by conflating the war against Daesh with a US commitment to freedom, justice, and democracy (a discourse that is painfully familiar from the wars in Afghanistan and Iraq), strategically omitting Kurdish women's explicit criticisms of patriarchy, capitalism, and imperialism. These framings also drew unnatural wedges along war on terror discourses between the YPJ and YJA Star.

Fighters themselves did not usually decline interviews but they did pay more attention to photos of solidarity demonstrations than to mainstream media coverage of their battle. As several fighters told me, they wished to see women around the world take a proactive role in countering the sexist, simplistic portrayals of an army that claims to fight against patriarchal domination on behalf of all women. Near the Daesh frontline in Kerkûk, YJA Star guerrilla Tavîn commented:

> Whenever the capitalist system is unable to deny something that challenges it, it aims to empty its meaning by portraying it in a different manner. So, when Kurdish women appear as revolutionaries, instead of understanding or appreciating us for what we are, they reduce us to meaningless aesthetic and rhetorical devices. It is an attempt to re-attribute to us the same forms that we struggle to rid ourselves from.

Through the power of discourse and propaganda, the Kurdish women's movement was made digestible for liberal, global mainstreams. For activists in the Kurdish women's movement, this continues a decades-old attempt to sway the Öcalan-affiliated Kurds away from revolution, towards alliance with American interests in the region.

While the US and its allies increasingly amplified male Kurdish military commanders as their interlocutors in the war, in 2017, the YPJ gifted the liberation of Raqqa, the former 'capital' of Daesh in Syria, to all women of the world – at a press conference held in front of a gigantic photo of Öcalan.

Beyond theories around media sensationalism and Orientalism, how should one make sense of the Hollywoodization of Kurdish women fighters?

The story of the image of the Kurdish woman fighter is an important example of the ideological co-optation of freedom utopias in the region and beyond. The politics of the very same women that became symbols of the victory against Daesh is criminalized by the 'war on terror'. This is not a surprise when considering a much older strategic agenda in US history: namely, the suppression of the idea of socialism through both violence and perception management.

TWO RIVERS, TWO FREEDOM AGENDAS?

𒂼� or *Ama(r)gi* is believed to be the oldest written historical record for the concept of freedom. The Sumerian word seems to have emerged around 2400 BCE in an ancient Mesopotamian city-state at a time in which the first institutionalized forms of human unfreedom arose. *Amargi* means freedom from debt, as well as return to the mother or return to the origin.

A decade ago, the so-called Arab Spring seemed to bring a wave of hope and freedom to the Middle East and North Africa. Today, war and violence rage over many parts of the region, with mercenaries jumping from country to country.

The death of people fleeing these conflicts and issues related to them has over time been normalized as a fact of life.

In late 2003, on the twentieth anniversary of the National Endowment for Democracy, thousands of years after the first emergence of the word 'freedom' in Mesopotamia, US president George W. Bush announced a 'Forward Strategy of Freedom' for the region. Within this and subsequent frameworks, billions of dollars were spent on numerous civil society organizations, conferences, training and scholarship schemes, with particular focus on women's and youth empowerment. Seemingly incapable of adapting to the norms of modern civilization, the Middle East had to learn the values championed by the 'free' world. Such language, of course, served to avert the gaze from the decades-old legacies of colonialism in the region, as well as the United States' own atrocities and support of anti-democratic dictatorships around the world throughout the twentieth century. With the so-called 'war on terror', the term 'freedom' framed civilizational discourses that helped cover up decades of occupation, war crimes, torture, civilian massacres, and large-scale environmental destruction in the region. Twenty years later, the Biden administration's rapid withdrawal brought the Taliban back to power in Afghanistan.

Over a period of two decades, soft power policies of the US and European countries created a whole class of pro-Western civil societies in other countries. On the surface, the Euro-American 'pro-democracy' works may seem benign, but what are their long-term implications? What theory of change underlies them? And what methods are used to induce forms of change that are compatible with capital and external states' interests? To what extent have programmes in the name of democracy promotion, development, and counter-extremism con-tributed to the erasure of alternative horizons? In what ways have organizations, often funded by the same Western institutions and foundations, produced new elites who are less critical of capitalism and foreign intervention? The extent to which this political knowledge economy has shaped and continues to shape people's – especially women's – ability to act politically will be something for historians to assess in the future. However, decades of critical scholarship on other parts of the world help understand their depoliticizing effect.

Activists and scholars have long argued that governments and states have for decades promoted 'NGO-ization' in the South as a neo-colonial form of social and ideological engineering in reaction to the emergence of revolutionary, popular mass movements against imperialist wars, neoliberal policies, and state authoritarianism in the twentieth century.[3] Filling vacuums caused by state neglect and competing with social movements that demand profound system change and redistribution, NGOs often function as state-backed agents of 'civil society'. The coloniality of the development discourse, as argued by globali-zation critics, aggressively fetishizes capitalist trajectories as universal human strife.⁴ Deflecting from systemic inequalities and injustices on a global scale, NGO-ist discourses compartmentalize interrelated systems and structures of violence, exploitation, and oppression into separate spheres of concern, as Aziz Choudry (2010) explains. Even as they appropriate the radical language of social movements, NGOs generally lack serious critical or political perspectives and address social problems only in a managerial way and to the extent to which they serve the business models and agendas of funders. With catchy phrases like 'holistic approach', 'comprehensive strategy', and 'lasting impact', NGOs brand as unique what are in reality standardized, top-down procedures with little accountability. In Arundhati Roy's words (2004),

> Eventually – on a smaller scale, but more insidiously – the capital available to NGOs plays the same role in alternative politics as the speculative capital that flows in and out of the economies of poor countries. It begins to dictate the agenda. It turns confrontation into negotiation. It depoliticizes resistance. It interferes with local peoples' movements that have traditionally been self-reliant. NGOs have funds that can employ local people who might otherwise be activists in resistance movements, but now can feel they are doing some immediate, creative good (and earning a living while they're at it).

As activists across grassroots women's movements have observed, the glossy image of this industry is gendered. It particularly incentivizes passionate young women to leave their provinciality behind and join the global elite world of Westernized NGOs. Reflecting on the NGO-ization of Arab women's activism, Islah Jad (2004) writes that the qualities of Palestinian cadres whose labour had sustained the intifadas, including building communities and long-term revolutionary strategies, were replaced over time by resourceful NGOs that could co-opt women into their world. From Morocco to Afghanistan, women's activists repeatedly point out that the 'women's empowerment' promoted by foreign (mostly Western) NGOs is often weaker than women's resistance struggles on the ground. In fact, superficial and patronizing approaches to the many complex issues experienced by women is tolerated by conservative states and establishments, as this helps pacify and marginalize more radical demands for system change. As Shahrzad Mojab argued in 2007:

> Women NGOs that I have studied in northern Iraq manifest the same symptoms as other NGOs studied in Latin America, Palestine and Europe. They have a short-term agenda, and their contribution is often piecemeal, curative, limited and dependent on the agenda of donors. By contrast, women's movements pursue long-term goals such as reform or radical change of patriarchal relations in both civil society and the state. While the two should not

be seen as mutually exclusive, states in the Middle East are more tolerant of women's NGOs than women's movements, and the imperialist powers under the US leadership encourage that.

The promotion of a particular managerial and funding-dependent model for change is a strategic tool of foreign policy. It is a way of organizing the political and ideological future of entire regions. For instance, the State Department-funded Middle East Partnership Initiative (MEPI), announced in December 2002, mere months before the Iraq invasion, is self-described as 'one of the many tools that advance US foreign policy by responding to the changing dynamics in the region, which are expected to last for years'. Drawing on her fieldwork on foreign-funded women's empowerment projects in Morocco, sociologist Zakia Salime wrote as early as 2010 that MEPI serves as a pacifying discourse of power that shapes 'the very way dissent is branded and dealt with by local governments. Beyond rhetoric, the fight against terror continues to materialize under MEPI's various programmes that aim at shaping the fabric of the MENA [Middle East and North Africa] politics and societies.'

Understanding the links between this depoliticizing 'change' agenda and the emergence of new expressions of fascism in the region and around the world today is an important matter especially for women, not least because their plight is often used to justify further violence and occupation. As liberal feminism becomes increasingly more compatible with systems of power and domination, revolutionaries face urgent questions about the political economy of women's liberation today. What memories of resistance are erased when places with powerful legacies of anti-colonial women's organizing are now full of workshops teaching women how to sew? Who is empowered and who is disciplined by 'inspiring' stories of young and ambitious individual women from poor or conflict-ridden regions, while women's collective anti-system rage in poverty-stricken squares is met with state violence? What are the conditions for autonomous politics when funding for organizing comes with neoliberal strings attached? Can projects imposed from the top down ever achieve the profoundly transformative effect necessary to abolish the deep roots of patriarchy in society?

On a more sinister level, 'democracy promotion', conflict resolution, and think tank activities are the continuation of a wider decades-old practice of states to recruit, gather intelligence, and advocate their interests by less direct means. Leaked emails of former Secretary of State Hillary Clinton, widely seen as an architect of such policies since the time of Bill Clinton's administration, reveal much about the entanglement of 'democracy promotion', intelligence, foreign policy, and the tech industry.

In times of political polarization, and especially in the age of social media, critical effort is needed to expose the propaganda of major political actors. The developments of the 2010s show that Turkish-style pro-NATO Islamism was one model of change sponsored by the same powers that fund the neoliberal, pro-Western NGO complex that undermines radical demands for system change, climate justice, women's liberation, and anti-militarism. That is why we see more women of colour CEOs and more political violence, but few tangible prospects for hope and justice. This marriage between Western empire and fascistic organizations that deploy anti-Western rhetoric depends on ideologically confusing and sometimes conflicting narratives. Moving beyond images and words, and instead examining material relations and shared strategic interests offers more insight. Clinton may well be a progressive in the context of US domestic politics. However, her impact on women's lives should be measured not by the superficial rhetoric of 'women's empowerment', but by her relationship to the military and political decisions, technologies, and alliances that kill women in the Middle East and beyond. Turkey and other regimes and actors in the region play specfic roles for the advancement of imperialist agendas, and they increasingly do so by using superficial anti-colonial rhetoric for propaganda.

A nuanced and informed understanding of such matters is crucial in order to avoid falling into simplistic sectarian and highly masculinist narratives that blame all evil on 'the US empire'. Valid criticism of foreign intervention often plays into the hands of authoritarian governments that opportunistically stigmatize all dissent as foreign conspiracy. In this way, democratic alternatives are suppressed, either softly through ideology or harshly through violence. It goes without saying that the self-interested policies of countries like Russia, Iran, and China are no 'anti-imperialist' alternatives or safeguards of 'stability'. These states are active players in the wars, violence, and oppression in the Middle East and beyond. The status quo is not sustainable. The more we know about the circumstances, events, and agendas that helped fuel violence in the region over the past decades – especially Western involvement with radical Islamist groups in parallel to its wars in the name of anti-terrorism – the more people will be able to challenge imperialism and authoritarian regimes and build free alternatives, beyond the hegemonic frameworks defined by Western liberal democracies, without dependence on external state forces. The real axis of resistance lies within the struggles of those who refuse to position themselves on either side of the coin of state power, and develop alternative horizons instead. The future of anti-imperialism increasingly looks anti-patriarchal, non-statist, and ecological.

The depoliticizing discourse on the Kurdish woman fighter should be seen behind this wider global backdrop – it can be read as a form of special warfare. The news reports on the anti-Daesh war often featured highly ideological claims by senior journalists and politicians that the 'Kurds share our Western values'. [5] This helped reinforce a decades-old regional racist trope that Kurds serve imperialists to divide the Middle East. After years of devastating the lives of women abroad, the US seemed to have found a poster child for American interests in the region. Unfortunately to them, it was an anti-capitalist revolutionary movement, and so, capitalism had to do what it does best: brand and sell. Seemingly at odds with the Turkish state's claim that the local Kurdish forces in Syria are no different from Daesh, the US tried to cover the contradictions between its interests and those of its military allies on the ground. For example, during the Aspen Institute Security Forum in 2017, commander of the US Army Special Operations, General Raymond Thomas, claimed that the Americans urged the YPG to 'rebrand' itself to keep Turkey at bay. Claiming that the group came up with the name 'Syrian Democratic Forces' within days after this communication, Thomas made the audience laugh when he joked: 'I thought it was a stroke of brilliance to put "democracy" in there somewhere.' In reality, long before the US decided to cooperate with Rojava's fighting forces, the movement on the ground already had thousands of revolutionary institutions, including a social contract, with 'democracy in there somewhere'. Unlike the many USAID-sponsored schemes in the region and beyond, these 'Apoist' institutions never had anything to do with the world of US soft power. There was no need for the white man to 'encourage the Kurds to include Arabs', another popular talking point of US officials and analysts. The solidarity of peoples was enshrined in the first documents of the self-administration, based on the movement's stated commitment to 'democratic nation', embedded in its decades-old commitment to internationalism, which first developed through relations with Arab, Armenian, and Turkish anti-imperialist revolutionaries in the region.

Despite its military support for the SDF and its good relations with the KRG, the US strategy towards the Kurdish question is marked by a carrot-and-stick approach. In its effort to dominate and control regional politics in the Middle East, the US sometimes goes as far as to signal support for Kurdish demands for autonomy or independence, while making sure that these never materialize. In any case, the US has consistently been clear about what sort of Kurdistan concept is compatible with its interests – a domesticated, neoliberal, 'Housewifized' one. On one hand, Kurdish communities are sometimes portrayed in essentialist ways as inherently progressive to serve as rhetorical devices to amplify the positive impact of US policy in the region. On the other hand, actual Kurdish political alternatives and progressive movements are terror-labelled, stigmatized, and destroyed by regional and global powers. This leads to a situation in which even as the US supplies the Turkish state, its closest ally in the region after Israel, with intelligence, drone technologies, and means to bomb Kurdish women fighters, US policy-makers can produce movies about the same women's heroism in their battles against Daesh on the other side of the border. This approach to the Kurdish question also serves to control regional powers through discipline and reward. It turns Kurdish liberation into a tool to divide and rule the region, driving wedges between the peoples of the Middle East. Similar concepts are applied by European governments, where Kurdish communities organizing along Öcalan's ideas are routinely demonized, criminalized, surveilled, and sometimes imprisoned and deported. Platforms, scholarships, and resources are provided by European state-affiliated think tanks, NGOs, and institutes to system-friendly Kurdish individuals and groups in a time in which radical Kurdish politics drew attraction from other social movements. This is particularly the case in Germany – a country that has a strategic relationship with Turkey and that is at the forefront of ideological demobilization and sustained co-optation of refugees and migrants through civil society sponsorship. The criminalization of the Kurdistan freedom movement, undoubtedly one of the most radical, community-rooted, and well-organized social movements in Europe, is something that all those resisting authoritarian state policies, police violence, securitization, and criminalization should worry about.[6] On a daily basis, Kurdish women defend themselves against a NATO member state's drones and terrorist mercenaries directly trained and paid by it – Turkey, an EU membership candidate that has received billions from the EU to cope with the so-called refugee crisis, itself in part caused by Turkish and European policies in the conflict in Syria. The Turkish state is able to loot, ethnically cleanse, and rebrand as Turkish entire regions beyond Turkey's own borders, with the help of both Islamist mercenaries and the otherwise Islamophobic 'war on terror' discourse whose foundations were laid by its Western allies. As I write, the state once again imposes isolation on Öcalan to prevent a political dialogue, while engaging in a series of political and military operations to annihilate the movement organizing around his ideas. European governments, increasingly more inclusive of women in leadership, actively criminalize Kurdish activists who try to forge alliances with women's struggles around the world. The French state continues its silence about the Paris murders. These issues are reasons for why the Kurdistan freedom movement views the so-called Kurdish issue as pivotal vis-à-vis the Gordian knots that sustain crisis in the region: Kurdistan can be used by regional and global powers to divide and rule and deepen existing tensions, or it can be one site of a new internationalism against the nation-statist world-system, a local nourishing soil for regional democratization and a new planetary politics towards peace, justice, and liberation.

More than one hundred years ago, Rosa Luxemburg, a revolutionary socialist Jewish Polish woman, who was assassinated by fascist paramilitary death squads unleashed by the social democratic government in Germany, argued that the question 'reform or revolution?' required urgent answers if humanity was to choose socialism over the barbarism of capitalism. Today, when feminicide is taking place on an unprecedented scale at the same time as gender equality has become a daily agenda item for institutions that reproduce power and violence on a global scale, women's struggles might want to ask: 'empowerment or revolution?'

Explicit cheerleadings of imperialist war and violence aside, even seemingly less harmful incarnations of liberal feminism do not represent the feminist politics of the majority of those on the streets. Its proximity to power – whether tactical or strategic – is not only colonial and racial in nature. It also does little to change the conditions of white lower-class women in the North. Its approaches overinvest in institutional reform and therefore implicitly lack faith in wider social transformation. They are conservative and open the door to opportunism, collaborating with the system and celebrating minor improvements as landmark achievements. They adopt social justice language without challenging or abolishing institutions of power. The neoliberal model of feminism – or 'girl boss feminism' – writes Lola Olufemi (2020),

> argues that 'inequality' is a state that can be overcome in corporate environments without over-hauling the system, centralizes the individual and their personal choices, misguidedly imagines that the state can grant liberation, seeks above all to protect the free market and fails to question the connection between capitalism, race and gendered oppression.

What others would antagonistically describe as 'the system', liberal feminism views as the real world, a world that just needs to carve out a bit more space for women. Its realm of activity is defined by political and epistemic borders; its solutions are carceral, capitalist, statist, hopeless. Its ability to engage in transnational feminist solidarity is limited to elite circles within academia, politics, and legal practice.

Feminist agendas emerging from within the system follow a longer history of bourgeois, liberal, and imperial agenda-setting. The essentially statist and status quo-maintaining UN system has played a key role in colonizing and bureaucratizing movements for gender equality. In her essay 'Going to Beijing: How the United Nations Colonized the Feminist Movement' (Federici 1997 [2020]), Silvia Federici powerfully outlines the ways in which the UN created a specific global elite state feminism and how that countered decades-old feminist agendas such as struggles against neo-colonial structural adjustment schemes imposed by the IMF and World Bank or internationalist resistance against war and occupation:

> The feminist movement owes no debt to the United Nations for its acquired international consciousness, especially since the UN has gone a long way in

promoting politics that are a blatant denial of that internationalism, as they have not only supported all the U.S. calls for war but also, in the name of equality, enlisted women to fight them.

Efforts for peace, justice, and equality within the UN system will always be limited by the fact that the Security Council's five permanent members are among the top arms dealers in the world and all have nuclear weapons.

Radiating around such institutions, system feminisms become a tool to tame, discipline, and marginalize liberation struggles. They drain feminist energy by focusing on monitoring the slow implementation of conservative agendas of governments and international institutions. This creates, on a global level, a new, docile femininity, whose imagination is impaired by a quest to seek technical solutions within existing systems of violence and power.

The recent rise in global feminist rhetoric can be misleading especially for younger generations. Moves towards equality are not inevitable progress; they are outcomes of struggles. More importantly, visibility and awareness alone do not bring about liberation. Being feminist must not be an identity label. Claiming to be feminist cannot protect you, me, and our loved ones from patriarchy. Feminism is a decision to organize and fight back, to struggle for oneself and for others simultaneously. Differentiating between feminist reform, feminist rebellion, and feminist revolution, revolutionary Black feminist thinker bell hooks stressed the importance of refusing a politics of settling for breadcrumbs and instead envisioning another, freer world for all. Revolution is an all-pervading spiritual war, a matter of conscience, belief, morality, self-criticism. People both dance and die for revolution.

We are past the stage of acknowledging that women, too, can 'do it'. For our survival, against physical, social, and political deaths, we need to actively resist the false sense of security offered by scams like 'feminist foreign policy' advanced by arms trading countries. It is important that feminists in the capitalist core learn from women's struggles at the margins of the nation-state system and meanwhile develop autonomous political analyses and strategies to confront the ways in which their own states reproduce feminicide on an international scale. Feminist individuals, organizers, and movements do not need to agree on everything in order to recognize the urgency of building system-critical feminist alliances for peace and justice and concretely, not just symbolically, defending liberationist alternatives around the world. The Kurdish women's liberation movement is one well-organized and popular front that is keen on building bridges. It encourages women and women's movements around the world to organize in autonomous political structures and to form transnational alliances, not for solidarity, but for 'common struggle'. Its theory and praxis, which constantly evolves, does not limit itself to the decolonization of Kurdistan, but seeks methods and frameworks to decolonize life from systems of power. In its efforts to reach out to other social movements, it shares its perspectives and experiences for wider discussion and to learn from other contexts. World Democratic Women's Confederalism aspires to be a non-statist, revolutionary, autonomy-based counter-force to the status quo politics of the UN system and its agendas. In any case, as members of the movement always stress, just as society will not be free without the liberation of women, Kurdistan will not be free without the liberation of the Middle East and the world. Even as it attributes a historical mission to itself in this process, the Kurdistan freedom movement is aware that its project depends on its ability to join with other anti-system movements on a global level. The return of the Taliban in Afghanistan two decades after the US launched the so-called war on terror, the Russian state's invasion of Ukraine, and other escalations in the run-up to this publication demonstrate the urgent need to dismantle the war machine worldwide.

In times of ecological catastrophe, the ability of movements to join forces and decolonize their imaginations from the positivist and liberal underpinning of capitalist modernity will be a factor that will determine the course of much of human and non-human life in the near future. Radical transformative feminist movements divorce themselves totally from the ideologies that created the world-system to begin with. When genocide, ecocide, and feminicide are

Figure 32   Street art in Rojava, portraying YPJ martyrs Avesta Xabûr, Barîn Kobanê, and Arîn Mîrkan. Near Qamişlo. May 2018.

entangled on a planetary level, anti-capitalist, anti-war, anti-fascist feminisms from the periphery promise to be the revolutionary force of the twenty-first century. With love and respect, I leave the last word to the rebellious Zapatista women:

> The system would prefer that we limit ourselves to screaming our pain, desperation, anxiety, and impotence. It's time to scream together, but now out of rage and indignation. And not each of us on our own, scattered and alone which is how they rape, kill, and disappear us, but together, from our own times, places, and ways. What if, compañera and sister, we learn not only to scream out of pain, but to find the way, place, and time to scream a new world into being? Just think, sister and compañera, things are so bad that in order to stay alive we have to create another world. That's how bad the system actually is, that in order to live we have to kill it off – not fix it up a little, or give it a new face, or ask that it be a little more considerate and not so mean. No. We have to destroy it, disappear it, kill it until there is nothing left, not even ashes. That's how we see the situation, compañera and sister, it's either the system or us.[7]

Notes

PREFACE

1. Much of this work has historically taken place outside of the English-speaking realm. One early social scientific account of the role of women in the PKK was written by Genç (2002).
2. See Mahmoud (2021).

INTRODUCTION

1. I have preferred 'feminicide' over 'femicide' throughout the book. Using the term 'feminicide' acknowledges the work of Latin American feminists that have pointed to the role of the state in the reproduction of patriarchal violence. Publications of the Kurdish women's movement on the topic usually refer to this legacy. See, for example, Fregoso and Bejarano (2010).
2. Such approaches are not novel. For a perspective for studying the history the Palestinian left, see Qato (2019).
3. The autobiography of Sakine Cansız has been published in English by Pluto Press (see Bibliography).
4. For a detailed account of the autonomous projects built up in Bakur since the late 2000s, see Tatort Kurdistan (2013).
5. I have written methodological reflections on the issue of conducting research in the shadow of the so-called 'war on terror'. See Dirik (2021) and Dirik (2022, forthcoming).
6. For one anti-fascist critique, see Gelderloos (2020).
7. The fieldwork took place in 2014/15 in three parts of Kurdistan (Bakur, Başûr, Rojava). In 2018, I accompanied a feminist delegation to Rojava in the aftermath of the Turkish army's 'Olive Branch' operation, and I was able to follow up with some previous contacts. My main fieldwork sites in the different regions included, among others, guerrilla-held territories, civilian community spheres, and refugee camps. In addition to attending protests, assembly meetings, seminars, celebrations, and conferences of the movement, I conducted around 150 recorded interviews with individuals and focus groups in Kurdish and Turkish (and in rare instances in German and English) and received support for interviews in Arabic. Due to the crackdowns in Turkey after my fieldwork, I have changed the names of some of the people I interviewed, even if at the time of our meeting they had agreed for their names to be published. In two cases, Sarya and Kanî (mentioned in Chapters 21 and 25), who both seem to have left the movement ever since, I also changed *noms de guerre* to protect their identity. Unless otherwise noted, all translations in this book are mine.

CHAPTER 1

1. In the weeks after the murder, I received a copy of six double-sided, handwritten pages from Sakine Cansız; the delayed answers that she had written in response to

my questions on the role of women in the PKK for my by then already submitted Master's thesis. Unless noted otherwise, the quotes provided in the book are from her handwritten notes to me.

2. See Galip (2016).
3. For an account of the sexualized violence against Armenian women during the genocide, see Ekmekçioğlu (2013).
4. The Kurdish political movement Xoybûn (Independence) was founded in Lebanon and contributed to the Ararat uprisings in Bakur in 1927 and 1930.
5. A recent comprehensive volume was edited by Bozarslan, Güneş, and Yadırgı (2021).
6. For an overview of the state of Kurdish politics inside Iranian borders, see Saadi (2020).
7. Elif Genç, Gülay Kılıçaslan, and Berivan Kutlay Sarıkaya (2019) reflect on their encounter of recurrent forms of erasure of Kurdish women, which happen even in academic spaces curated to debate revolutionary feminisms in the Middle East and North Africa region.
8. For more detail on the Dêrsim genocide, see Göner (2017).
9. For an ethnography of *dengbêj* music as practised by Kurdish women in Turkey, see Schäfers (forthcoming).
10. In her research on Kurdish women in the late nineteenth and early twentieth centuries, Rojda Yıldız writes (in the Turkish language) that knowledge on Kurdish women has historically been filtered through the words of Kurdish men at a time in which Eurocentric ideas about modernism and nationalism represented the hegemonic concepts for thinking about identity and self-determination (see, for example, Yıldız, 2020). For further discussion on Kurdish women's political involvements in the late Ottoman period, see Rohat Alakom and Janet Klein's chapters in Mojab (2001): 'Kurdish Women in Constantinople at the Beginning of the Twentieth Century' and 'En-gendering Nationalism: The "Woman Question" in Kurdish Nationalist Discourse of the Late Ottoman Period', respectively.
11. For a detailed account of women in the Republic of Kurdistan, see Shahrzad Mojab's book chapter, 'Women and Nationalism in the Kurdish Republic of 1946', in Mojab (2001).

CHAPTER 2

1. Turkish sociologist Ismail Beşikçi's book, *International Colony Kurdistan*, was a milestone academic work which developed this thesis. This conceptualization framed Kurdistan as an internal colony of Turkey and as an international colony.
2. The first volume of the autobiography of Sakine Cansız (2018) provides an insider account of the group's early formation.
3. Other than Sakine Cansız, the only other woman present at the meeting was Kesire Yıldırım (*nom de guerre* Fatma), married to Öcalan at the time. Kesire Yıldırım broke away from the party and is believed to have evaded execution by party members due to Öcalan's intervention.
4. Akkaya and Jongerden (2012) place the PKK in the historical context of the revolutionary left. They detail the role of leftist internationalism in the PKK through the story of Haki Karer.
5. Excerpt from the 1978 manifesto (my translation):

Creating an independent Kurdistan is possible through the decolonization from the economic colonization of Kurdistan's underground and overground resources, labour, agriculture, trade, financial and industrial sphere, and from the military

316

occupation and cultural and political colonization of language, history, culture, the social and political spheres. Once colonization in these spheres has been abolished, the path to the development of Kurdistan's independence in the political, economic, cultural, and social spheres will be possible. Creating a democratic Kurdistan on the other hand is linked to the abolition of the heavy feudal-comprador pressures on Kurdistan's societal make-up. The abolition of the oppression and exploitation by the feudal-comprador class will secure the liberation of women, peasants, minorities, and the social make-up.

CHAPTER 3

1. For a reading of the significance of Mazlum Doğan's political defence and of the ways in which court materials from Diyarbakır Prison present an archive for Kurdish revolutionary aspirations, see Hakyemez (2017).

CHAPTER 4

1. For a brief history on the dynamics between the Palestinian and Kurdish struggles, see Genç (2020).
2. As argued by Behlül Özkan (2019), diplomatic tensions between the two countries would for decades be marked by the presence of the PKK in Syria and the Muslim Brotherhood in Turkey.

CHAPTER 5

1. For some insight into the difficulties of establishing accountability for atrocities committed against Kurdish civilians, see, for example, the Human Rights Watch (2012) report on the historic trial of former Turkish colonel Cemal Temizöz, who later became the mayor of Cizîr. He was the highest-ranking member of a counter-terrorism unit charged with the murder and disappearance of 21 people. Temizöz and other security forces members were cleared of charges in 2015.
2. On several occasions, UN Special rapporteurs, the Parliamentary Assembly of the Council of Europe, and European Court of Human Rights have called on the Turkish state to abolish the village guard system.
3. For more detail on the Kurdish movement's use of Newroz for mobilization purposes, see Aydın (2014).
4. For decades, Germany has been one of the biggest arms suppliers to Turkey, despite evidence that the military equipment is used for war crimes in Kurdistan. The protest slogan *Deutsche Panzer, raus aus Kurdistan!* (German tanks, out of Kurdistan!) still used today was born in the 1990s.
5. For one ethnographic account of the PKK's Newroz tradition, see Rudi (2018).

CHAPTER 6

1. I have taken this translation of the term 'army-fication' for *artêşbûyîn* (Kurdish)/ *ordulaşma* (Turkish) from Can Evren's translation of Çağlayan (2012).
2. According to some (unconfirmable) PKK accounts, the pêşmerge were promising her a good life in marriage if she surrendered.
3. A selection of Öcalan's analyses between 1993 and 1998 on women's liberation were compiled into the book: *The March Towards Equality and Freedom: Towards Women's Armyfication* (YAJK 1999a).
4. For martyr profiles (in the German language), see Cenî (2012).
5. See, for example, Flach (2003).

317

6. Her *nom de guerre* is the name of a valley in which the Turkish army committed a massacre against participants in the Ararat rebellion of 1930.

CHAPTER 7

1. For more detail on Abdullah Öcalan's abduction, visit the International Initiative 'Freedom for Abdullah Öcalan – Peace in Kurdistan' website: freeocalan.com. See also Miley and Venturini (2018).
2. The congress resolution stated that: 'The democratic civilisation will be an era of freedom for women. It is obvious that the democratic transformation, which will free the society as a whole, will be a revolution of women's liberation' (see PKK 2002).
3. One of the most cited books, Aliza Marcus' 2007 *Blood and Belief*, is a journalistic account almost exclusively based on the testimonies of men who left and often turned against the PKK. As noted in a critical book review by Reimar Heider (2008), some of Marcus' interlocutors are people who worked for intelligence services or committed atrocities that they omit. With the exception of former MP Leyla Zana, women are marginal to Marcus' account and mainly invoked as victims.

CHAPTER 8

1. In this period, new legislation encouraged PKK members to defect and repent their actions. Defectors were promised protection and milder sentences for informing on the organization. This 'Reinstatement into Society Law' was dismissed as 'Returning Home Law' by the Kurdish movement. See Biner (2006).

CHAPTER 9

1. For example, KODAR is the umbrella movement to organize society in Rojhelat (eastern Kurdistan) with KJAR as the corresponding women's movement. These take ideological perspective from the Kurdistan Free Life Party (PJAK), the PKK's Iran-focused affiliate based in the mountains. Since these are unable to operate freely within Rojhelat's society, campaigning for the freedom of political prisoners and against feminicide and state violence, as well as educational and cultural work, including media, are among their primary efforts.
2. The Women's Defence/Protection Units (YPJ) emerged in the context of the Syrian war in 2011 and formally later as an autonomous army parallel to the People's Defence/Protection Units (YPG). The Women's Defence/Protection Forces (HPJ) are the armed structure for women of eastern Kurdistan, organizing under the umbrella of the Society of Free Women of Eastern Kurdistan (KJAR), alongside the Eastern Kurdistan Units (YRK). The YJŞ are the all-Êzîdî Şengal Women's Units based in Şengal (Sinjar), organizing parallel to the YBŞ (Şengal Resistance Units). In 2016, in the context of the urban wars between the Turkish army and Kurdish fighters, young Kurdish women founded the YPS-Jin in districts, towns, and cities like Nisêbîn, Gewer (Yüksekova), Sur, and in various districts of Amed and Şirnex (Şırnak), after their involvement in the YPS (Civil Defence Units), previously known as the Homeland-loving Revolutionary Youth Movement (YDG-H).

PART II

1. See Graeber and Wengrow (2021).
2. See, for example, Rita Segato's work on the 'village world' (Segato 2016).

CHAPTER 11

1. See von Werlhof, Mies, and Bennholdt-Thomsen (1991).
2. The Democratic Islam Congress, for instance, was formed, among others, to counter the AKP government's use of Islam for its authoritarian and Islamist agenda.

CHAPTER 12

1. See, for example, Jineolojî.org (2021).
2. Numerous Jineolojî publications, workshops, and media programmes by women who collectively develop this realm provide a wealth of resources in different languages.
3. For a critical response to an academic journal article written about Jineolojî, see Jineolojî Collective in Europe (2021).

CHAPTER 14

1. Öcalan seems to prefer 'rêber' or 'rêbertî' over serok. The words contain rê, meaning 'way' or 'path', thus evoking the idea of leader/leadership as a form of 'opening the path'.
2. Since he is not able to communicate or clarify his ideas or follow their journey due to isolation, the International Initiative for the Freedom of Abdullah Öcalan – Peace in Kurdistan put together the book *Building Free Life: Dialogues with Abdullah Öcalan* (2020), in which renowned critical thinkers engage with Öcalan's work. See, for example, Graeber (2020). For an in-depth discussion of his thought, see Güneşer (2021).
3. For example, see Barkey (2018) or van Bruinessen (2001).
4. As the former lawyer of Mandela, Judge Essa Moosa, who led the international delegation to Imralı Prison Island to support the peace process when governments did not, said in the years before his death: 'In my lifetime, I have seen the freedom of Nelson Mandela. I hope that I can also see in my lifetime the freedom of Abdullah Öcalan.' See Miley and Venturini (2018) for a detailed account of the delegation's efforts.
5. For a recent publication, see Davis, Dent, Meiners, and Richie (2022).
6. One of Öcalan's lawyers, Faik Özgür Erol (2019) draws on the work of legal philosophers like Giorgio Agamben and Carl Schmitt to describe the state of exception inside the Imralı Prison complex.

CHAPTER 15

1. From 'Marriage and Love', in *Anarchism and Other Essays* (Goldman 1911).
2. From *The Will to Change: Men, Masculinity, and Love* (hooks 2004).

CHAPTER 16

1. See also Çetinkaya (2020).

CHAPTER 18

1. One of the most popular guerrilla-made movies is titled *Berîtan*, dedicated to Gülnaz Karataş (see Chapter 6).

CHAPTER 19

1. There is no official number of female political prisoners in Turkey. However, data provided by World Prison Brief on female prisoners in Turkey (general) gives an indicative sense: between 2000 and 2021, the number of female prisoners quadrupled (from 2,591 to 11,392). Within that timeframe, the number nearly doubled from 2015 to 2021 (i.e. since the breakdown of the peace process).
2. Among the prisoners was 32-year-old teacher, poet, and human rights defender Farzad Kamangar. In 2013, the Farzad Kamangar Kurdish Language and Literature Academy was opened in Rojava. In recent years, political refugees from Iran and Turkey opened a language school for migrants and refugees in Greece, naming it after Kamangar. In 2013, the Bağlar municipality in Amed opened a Kurdish language school named after Farzad Kamangar. The school was later deemed 'illegal' and forcibly closed by the governor.
3. For an analysis of the role of Turkey's judicial system in the criminalization of Kurdish politics, see Bayır (2014).
4. In an interview with *Yeni Yaşam* newspaper in January 2022, prominent human rights lawyer and Human Rights Association (IHD) co-chair Eren Keskin estimated 1,605 ill prisoners in Turkish jails.

CHAPTER 20

1. Since many Kurds, including some of the founding PKK members, did not speak Kurdish well enough, much of this work was done in Turkish. The predominance of Turkish as the movement's intellectual language has been criticized and challenged over time. The Kurdish language (kurmancî dialect) experienced a historic revival with the Rojava Revolution, which also influenced the movement's own knowledge production.

CHAPTER 21

1. See Shahrzad Mojab's book chapter, 'Women and Nationalism in the Kurdish Republic of 1946', in Mojab (2001).
2. For a discussion on some of these publications, see Açık (2013).
3. It is possible to watch *JinTV* on its YouTube channel.
4. Sarya seems to have left the movement ever since.

CHAPTER 22

1. See Bookchin (2005) and Bookchin, Bookchin, and Taylor (2015).
2. For example, the philosophy of the Alevi community does not encompass an afterlife in the Abrahamic sense but holds that the divine is embodied in all living beings. The Turkish state routinely burns forests in the Alevi area of Dêrsim, under the pretext that they host guerrilla fighters. See Ayboğa (2018) on the fires.
3. See Kadıoğlu Polat (2016).
4. See Sen (2016).
5. For more background on the Mesopotamia Ecology Movement, see Tatort Kurdistan (2013).
6. The Bağlar Women's Cooperative, founded in 2005, is an interesting case. See Varlı (2017).

7. For a detailed overview of the campaign's perspective and works, see Internationalist Commune (2018).

CHAPTER 23

1. Accounts by the older generation claim that the UNHCR initially resisted the idea of establishing a school at the camp, due to the lack of professionally trained teachers and because Kurdish is not an official language.
2. For background on Ferhat Kurtay, see Chapter 3.

CHAPTER 24

1. See Tuncel in Kışanak (2018).
2. In 1991, HEP allied with the Social Democratic People's Party (SHP) to pass the 10 per cent electoral threshold to enter parliament. The party was banned by the state in 1993, as were other pro-Kurdish political parties that were formed subsequently in response to more bans. Elected representatives of the closed parties were frequently imprisoned: Democracy Party (DEP, 1993–94), People's Democracy Party (HADEP, 1994–2003), and Democratic Society Party (DTP, 2005–09). Founded in 1997, the Democratic People's Party (DEHAP) dissolved itself to merge with the DTP.
3. The number of seats has ever since risen to 600.
4. Before her political career, Aysel Tuğluk, for instance, was a practising lawyer, who defended political prisoners that she had met as revolutionaries in her teenage years. For years, Tuğluk worked on documenting human rights abuses, including torture. Before her election as MP for Muş province, Burcu Çelik Özkan was working for the rights of political prisoners. Both eventually became political prisoners themselves. Former or current MPs such as Selma Irmak, Pero Dündar, Gültan Kışanak, Leyla Güven, Gülser Yıldırım, Sebahat Tuncel, and Besime Konca entered parliament after years of resistance as political prisoners.
5. See Tuncel in Kışanak (2018).
6. For a more detailed account of the HDK's mission and work, see Anya Briy (2019).
7. This number decreased in the snap elections in the same year: the overall number of HDP MPs fell to 59, of which 23 were women (38.9 per cent).
8. See Şahin in Kışanak (2018).
9. See Yüksekdağ in Kışanak (2018).
10. See Davutoğlu (2010). For an analysis of the expansionist, pan-Islamist foreign policy strategy envisioned by Ahmet Davutoğlu, see Özkan (2014).
11. For more on the history of LGBTQI+ organizations in Turkey and their relationship to struggles in Kurdistan, see Sandal-Wilson (2021).
12. See Sandal (2016).
13. See Bor, Daşlı, and Alıcı (2021).
14. See Irmak in Kışanak (2018).
15. See Bor, Daşlı, and Alıcı (2021).
16. This number fell to 43, when Gülcan Kaçmaz Sayyiğit (Van Edremit) and Leyla Atsak (Van Çaldıran) were not handed their certificate of election due to charges pressed against them within the state of emergency statutory decree.
17. See Kubilay in Kışanak (2018).
18. See Güven in Kışanak (2018).
19. Mere months after assuming office as mayor, she was jailed for nearly five years.
20. For one overview of these initiatives, see Tatort Kurdistan (2013).
21. See Keskin in Kışanak (2018).

22. The KCK formalized the practice at its ninth congress in 2013. The de facto application of co-leadership in Kurdish politics since the mid-2000s eventually resulted in an amendment in Turkey's political parties' law.
23. See Yüksekdağ in Kışanak (2018).
24. See Tuğluk Kışanak (2018).
25. See Kaya in Kışanak (2018).

CHAPTER 25

1. For accounts of women's activism in post-2003 Iraq, with focus on NGO-ization, see Mojab (2007), al-Ali and Pratt (2009), Hardi (2013), and Ali (2018).
2. For a period, 'The Other Iraq' PR-campaign showcased the people of the Kurdistan Region as a pro-American, secular community that embraces neoliberalism and Western values. For more details, see Glastonbury (2018).
3. Using a snowball method, following introductions from Europe and Kurdistan-based journalists and writers, I interviewed politicians from the Gorran Movement, the PUK, and the Kurdistan Islamic Union. I made several attempts to secure interviews with women in the KDP, but I only managed to meet one leader of the KDP's women's wing very briefly. My identity and disclosed proximity to institutions of the Kurdistan freedom movement likely influenced participation in my research. After several brief interrogations by authorities, my safety concerns eventually led me to abandon the idea of interviewing people in the party.
4. Kanî seems to have left the movement.
5. This satirical text was written by Sardasht Osman, a young journalist, who was kidnapped and assassinated by gunmen in 2010 after receiving death threats for criticizing the regional government.
6. At the time, the KRG president Mesûd Barzanî was refusing to step down after his extended presidency.

CHAPTER 26

1. See Knapp, Flach, and Ayboğa (2016), Tejel (2009) and Schmidinger (2018).
2. One overview, which mainly focuses on the traditional Syrian Kurdish parties, is offered in Allsopp (2015).
3. For different perspectives on debates about the disputed question of (in)evitability of the escalation into violence by Syrian intellectuals and former political prisoners, see Rateb Sha'bo (2016) and Yassin Al-Haj Saleh (2017).
4. As early as 2012, al-Qaeda leader Ayman al-Zawahiri had made a call to join the fight against the Syrian state. For accounts of these trajectories, see ICG (2012) and Abouzeid (2018).
5. See Amnesty International (2017).
6. The International Crisis Group (ICG 2011) provided one early account of the role of the Jisr al-Shughour massacre.
7. Journalist Fehim Taştekin (2017) outlines these dynamics in detail in his 2015 Turkish-language book *Suriye: Yıkıl Git, Diren Kal!* Journalist Rania Abouzeid (2018), who circulated the initial story of Harmoush in her reporting for *TIME*, reflects on this episode in her book *No Turning Back: Life, Loss, and Hope in Wartime Syria*. See also Glioti (2012).
8. For an ethnographic account of border encounters, see Can (2017).
9. See also ICG (2013).
10. For overviews closer to the time, see Knapp, Flach, and Ayboğa (2016), Altuğ (2013) and ICG (2013).

11. The HDP's meeting notes with Öcalan on Imralı Island during the peace process have been published as a book in Turkish (Öcalan, 2015a).
12. One example is this translated article by Syrian thinker Jad Karim al-Jiba'i (2016).
13. For more information on the economic exploitation of Rojava, see Knapp, Flach, and Ayboğa (2016) or Internationalist Commune (2018).
14. I gave a broader overview of the justice system in Rojava elsewhere. See Dirik (2020).
15. Asterut/Ashtarut is a name for the Phoenician-Canaanite goddess Astarte, who is considered the counterpart of Ishtar and Inanna.
16. In recent years, the thousands of *gazî*, people wounded during the war, began forming democratic associations to organize themselves through committees especially in the sphere of education, culture, media, and health.
17. Kurdish academic and poet Hawzhin Azeez (2020), who spent several years in Rojava, describes her observations in the following way: 'Nothing restores and empowers the soul of a traumatized, war-torn community more than seeing the matriarchs of a neighborhood stand confidently at street corners wielding AK-47 rifles for the people's protection. These images do not inspire fear and terror; they inspire communal confidence, pride, dignity, self-respect, and belonging.'

CHAPTER 27

1. See Cumes (2021).

CHAPTER 28

1. The word *'ferman'* is often translated as edict, order, or decree, issued by Ottoman authorities. It is the word used by the community to describe the genocides and massacres that they survived over the centuries.
2. The question of whether or not Êzîdîs are Kurds is a highly contested one within the community. Out of respect to the Êzîdîs' self-determination, I refrain from imposing a definition.
3. For a critique of one German programme for survivors of the genocide, see McGee (2018).

CHAPTER 29

1. See McKernan (2021).

CHAPTER 30

1. That the civilian toll of the US airstrikes against Daesh is much higher than expected and that there is little transparency in the often 'faulty' and 'rushed' decision-making in this form of warfare has been revealed in an investigative report in the *New York Times* (see Khan 2021).
2. See RIC (2021).

CHAPTER 31

1. See Letsch (2016).
2. In her book, Turkish journalist Ezgi Başaran (2017), former editor-in-chief of liberal daily *Radikal*, reflects on her paper's reporting at the time.

3. See Pamuk and Tattersall (2015) and Taştekin (2021).
4. See Darıcı (2016).
5. For one analysis of the resistance in Sur and the symbolic meanings attributed to the district in different Kurdish imaginations (especially along class lines), see Hakyemez (2018).
6. Journalist Nurcan Baysal (2016), among others, reported from the scene. For a detailed report on women's experiences of violence during the curfews, see the Migration Monitoring Association (2019).
7. Rosa Burç (2019) reads the Turkish state's authoritarianism and violence against the Kurdish movement as an effort to reinstate the male hegemony that informed the very foundations of the republic: 'The more strongly national unity along the lines of Turkishness is constructed, the more sexualized violence is committed publicly by state authorities against those who are considered outside the boundaries of Turkishness, mostly Kurdish people.'
8. For a report on the state's ban of women's and LGBTQI+ organizations in the aftermath of the peace process collapse, see Bor, Daşlı and Alıcı (2021).
9. To name some of the women mentioned in this book: Edibe Şahin was sentenced to eight years and nine months in prison on terrorism charges. A month later, Çağlar Demirel was arrested and later sentenced to seven and a half years for 'membership in a terrorist organization' and for 'spreading terrorist propaganda'. In 2016, the AKP appointed a trustee to Kocaköy municipality, removing co-mayor Bêrîvan Elif Kılıç. One year and a half into office, Diba Keskin was initially given 13 years and nine months in prison on terrorism charges for speeches advocating democratic self-administration as co-mayor of Erdîş but was released after four years. Aysel Tuğluk is denied treatment for her early onset dementia.
10. With reference to the seizure of the HDP-held municipalities, the term *kayyum* has ever since been adapted across different struggle sites, for instance, by students and academic staff against Melih Bulu, an AKP politician, who was appointed as rector of Boğazçi University in Istanbul by presidential decree in 2021. See Üstündağ (2021).
11. These war crimes have been documented in reports prepared by the United Nations, Amnesty International, and Human Rights Watch (see Bibliography).
12. Symbolically, the day marked the 29th anniversary of Öcalan's exodus from Syria.
13. See Azize Aslan's (2019) interview with Hevrîn Xelef on her involvement in autonomous women's economy work on Rojava.
14. Among the men identified in the video is Yasser Abdul Rahim, commander of Faylaq al-Majd. He participated in the Astana negotiations.
15. For more background, see Fregoso and Bejarano (2010).

CHAPTER 32

1. See Meger (2016).
2. For example, after decades of vilifying the PKK and portraying women guerrillas as victims of exploitation, German news agencies dedicated programmes to women in the ranks of other Kurdish parties. Around the same time, the German government had decided to deliver arms to the Kurdistan Democratic Party (KDP), at the time still one of the only Kurdish parties without women among its armed ranks. In response to the media attention on the YPJ and YJA Star, the KDP began to recruit women. Although images of these uniformed women were circulated, their actual inclusion in combat duties is questionable.
3. See, for example, Kamat (2004).
4. See Arif Dirlik (2014).

5. A representative example is a 2014 CNN article by Frida Ghitis, who, while claiming that 'the Kurds are comparatively more modern than many of their neighbors', omitted the socialist identity of the movement that she described as fighting against Daesh while giving women rights in Syria. In her version of history, this was 'also a message to the West. The Kurds are tacitly saying "Look at us. We are the ones who share your ideas about human rights and equality. We are the ones in this many-sided conflict that deserves your support."'
6. See Sarıcan and Matheou (2020).
7. Coordinators of the Zapatista Women for the Second International Gathering of Women Who Struggle (2019).

Bibliography

Abouzeid, R. (2018) *No Turning Back: Life, Loss, and Hope in Wartime Syria*. New York: W.W. Norton and Company.

Açık, N. (2013) 'Re-defining the Role of Women within the Kurdish National Movement in Turkey in the 1990s', in Zeydanlıoğlu, W. and C. Güneş (eds), *The Kurdish Question in Turkey: New Perspectives on Conflict, Representation and Reconciliation*, London: Routledge, pp. 114–36.

Akkaya, A. H., and Jongerden, J. (2012) 'The Kurdistan Workers Party and a New Left in Turkey: Analysis of the Revolutionary Movement in Turkey through the PKK's Memorial Text on Haki Karer', *European Journal of Turkish Studies*, 14.

Al-Ali, N., and Pratt, N. (2009) *What Kind of Liberation? Women and the Occupation of Iraq*. Berkeley: University of California Press.

Ali, Z. (2018) 'Women's Political Activism in Iraq: Caught between NGOization and the Struggle for a Civil State', *International Journal of Contemporary Iraqi Studies*, 12(1), 35–51

Alakom, R. (2019) *Kürd Kadınları Teâli Cemiyeti (1919)*. Istanbul: Avesta.

Al-Haj Saleh, Y. (2017) *The Impossible Revolution: Making Sense of the Syrian Tragedy*. London: Hurst.

al-Jiba'i, J. K. (2016) 'Symptoms of Flawed Pluralism: The Debate on Federalism', *Syria Untold*, 10 June. https://syriauntold.com/2016/06/10/symptoms-of-flawed-pluralism-the-debate-on-federalism/ (last accessed January 2022).

Alinia, M. (2013) *Honor and Violence against Women in Iraqi Kurdistan*. Basingstoke: Palgrave Macmillan.

Allsopp, H. (2015) *The Kurds in Syria: Political Parties and Identity in the Middle East*. London: I.B. Tauris & Co.

Altuğ, S. (2013) 'The Syrian Uprising and Turkey's Ordeal with the Kurds', *Dialectical Anthropology*, 37(1), 123–30.

Amnesty International (2017) 'Human Slaughterhouse: Mass Hangings and Extermination at Saydnaya Prison, Syria', February.

—— (2019) 'Syria: Damning Evidence of War Crimes and Other Violations by Turkish Forces and Their Allies', October.

Aslan, A. (2016) 'Economic Self-governance in Democratic Autonomy: The Example of Bakur (Turkish Kurdistan)', *Cooperation in Mesopotamia*. https://mesopotamia.coop/economic-self-governance-in-democratic-autonomy-the-example-of-bakur/ (last accessed June 2021).

—— (2019) 'Hevrin Khalaf and the Spirit of the Democratic Nation', *Roar Magazine*, 24 October. https://roarmag.org/essays/hevrin-khalaf-interview/ (last accessed June 2021).

Ayata, M. (2011) *Yaşam Geçidinde Yirmi Yil* [Twenty Years in the Passage of Life]. Neuss: Mezopotamien Verlag.

——(2015) 'Sara: Aufrecht wie die Berge', in S. Cansız, *Mein ganzes Leben war ein Kampf, Band 1: Jugendjahre* [German version of Cansız 2018]. Neuss: Mezopotamien Verlag, pp. 13–19.

Ayboğa, E. (2018) 'Where Is the Outrage about Turkey's War on Kurdistan's Forests?', *Komun Academy*, 17 December. https://komun-academy. com/2018/12/17/where-is-the-outrage-about-turkeys-war-on-kurdistans-forests/ (last accessed June 2021).

—— (2021) 'Ecology Structures of the Kurdish Freedom Movement', in Stephen E. Hunt (ed.), *Ecological Solidarity and the Kurdish Freedom Movement: Thought, Practice, Challenges, and Opportunities*. Lanham: Lexington Books, pp. 77–96.

Aydın , D. (2014) 'Mobilising the Kurds in Turkey: Newroz as a Myth', in C. Güneş and W. Zeydanlıoğlu (eds), *The Kurdish Question in Turkey: New Perspectives on Violence, Representation and Reconciliation*. London: Routledge, pp 68–88

Azeez, H. (2020) 'Police Abolition and Other Revolutionary Lessons from Rojava', *Roar Magazine*, 6 June. https://roarmag.org/essays/police-abolition-and-other-revolutionary-lessons-from-rojava/ (last accessed June 2021).

Aziz, A., Mahmoud, H., Rauf, R., and Tahir, S. (2020) 'A Response: In Defence of Kurdish Diaspora Feminism', *LSE Women, Peace and Security blog*, 7 October. https://blogs.lse.ac.uk/wps/2020/10/07/a-response-in-defence-of-kurdish-diaspora-feminism/ (last accessed June 2021).

Barkey, H. J. (2018) 'The Making of a Kurdish Mandela', *Foreign Policy*, 10 May. https://foreignpolicy.com/2018/05/10/the-making-of-a-kurdish-mandela/ (last accessed June 2021).

Başaran, E. (2017) *Frontline Turkey: The Conflict at the Heart of the Middle East*. London: I.B. Tauris & Co.

Bayır, D. (2014) 'The Role of the Judicial System in the Politicide of the Kurdish Opposition', in C. Güneş and W. Zeydanlıoğlu (eds), *The Kurdish Question in Turkey: New Perspectives on Violence, Representation and Reconciliation*. London: Routledge, pp. 21–46.

Baysal, N. (2016) '*Cizre'deki evlerin içinden: "Kızlar biz geldik siz yoktunuz" yazıları, yerlerde sergilenen kadın çamaşırları!*' ['From the Inside of the Houses in Cizre: "Girls We Were Here But You Weren't" Writings, Women's Underwear Exhibited on Floors!'] *T24*, 7 March. https://t24.com.tr/yazarlar/nurcan-baysal/cizrenin-gorunmeyenleri,14049 (last accessed June 2021).

Beşikçi, I. (2015) *International Colony Kurdistan*. London: Gomidas Institute.

Bhattacharya, T. (ed.) (2017) *Social Reproduction Theory: Remapping Class, Recentering Oppression*. London: Pluto Press.

Biner, Z. Ö. (2006) 'From Terrorist to Repentant: Who Is the Victim?' *History and Anthropology*, 17(4), 339–53.

Boochani, B. (2018) *No Friend But the Mountains: Writing from Manus Prison*. London: Picador.

Bookchin, M. (2005) *The Ecology of Freedom: The Emergence and Dissolution of Hierarchy*. Oakland: AK Press.

Bookchin, M., Bookchin, D., and Taylor, B. (2015) *The Next Revolution: Popular Assemblies and the Promise of Direct Democracy*. London and New York: Verso.

Bor, G., Daşlı, G., and Alıcı, N. (2021) 'From Converging Roads to Narrowing Grounds: The Struggle for Peace by LGBTI+ and Women's Organizations in Turkey', *DEMOS*.

Bozarslan, H., Güneş, C., and Yadırgı, V. (2021) *The Cambridge History of the Kurds*. Cambridge: Cambridge University Press.

Briy, A. (2019) 'Interview: Peoples' Democratic Congress (HDK) in Turkey – a New Model for Organizing?', *Jadaliyya*, 12 February. www.jadaliyya.com/Details/38362 (last accessed June 2021).

Burç, R. (2019) 'One State, One Nation, One Flag – One Gender? HDP as a Challenger of the Turkish Nation State and Its Gendered Perspectives', *Journal of Balkan and Near Eastern Studies*, 21(3), 319–34.

Cabnal, L. (2015) 'Without Being Consulted: The Commodification of Our Body-land territory', in Urgent Action Fund of Latin America (ed.), *Women Defending the*

Territory: Experiences of Participation in Latin America. Bogota: Fundación cultural Javeriana de artes gráficas – JAVEGRAF, pp. 43–55.

Çağlayan, H. (2007) *Analar, Yoldaşlar, Tanrıçalar: Kürt Hareketinde Kadınlar ve Kadın Kimliğinin Oluşumu.* Istanbul: İletişim Yayınları [English translation 2020].

—— (2012) 'From Kawa the Blacksmith to Ishtar the Goddess: Gender Constructions in Ideological-Political Discourses of the Kurdish Movement in post-1980 Turkey: Possibilities and limits', *European Journal of Turkish Studies*, 14.

—— (2013) *Kürt Kadınların Penceresinden: Resmî Kimlik Politikaları, Milliyetçilik, Barış Mücadelesi.* Istanbul: İletişim Yayınları.

Can, Ş. (2017) 'The Syrian Civil War, Sectarianism and Political Change at the Turkish–Syrian border', *Social Anthropology*, 25(2), 174–89.

Cansız, S. (2018) *Sara: My Whole Life Was a Struggle – the Memoirs of a Kurdish Revolutionary.* London: Pluto Press.

—— (2019) *Prison Memoir of a Revolutionary.* London: Pluto Press.

Cenî – Kurdisches Frauenbüro für Frieden (2012) *Widerstand & Gelebte Utopien. Frauenguerilla, Frauenbefreiung und Demokratischer Konföderalismus in Kurdistan* [Resistance and Lived Utopias. Women's Guerrilla, Women's Liberation and Democratic Confederalism in Kurdistan]. Neuss: Mezopotamien Verlag.

Çetinkaya, H. (2020) 'Mothers as the Middle-ground between the Mountain and the State', *Journal of International Women's Studies*, 21(7), 207–24.

Choudry, A. (2010) 'Global Justice? Contesting NGOization: Knowledge Politics and Containment in Antiglobalization Networks', in A. Choudry and D. Kapoor (eds), *Learning from the Ground Up: Global Perspectives on Social Movements and Knowledge Production.* New York: Palgrave Macmillan, pp. 17–34.

Çiçek, M. (2018) 'Serhildan: The Story of Bakur's First People's Uprising', *Komun Academy*, 11 December. https://komun-academy.com/2018/12/11/serhildan-the-story-of-bakurs-first-peoples-uprising/ (last accessed June 2021).

—— (2020) 'For a New Internationalism of Women: Democratic World Women's Confederalism', *Komun Academy*, 27 May. https://komun-academy.com/2020/05/27/for-a-new-internationalism-of-women-democratic-world-womens-confederalism/ (last accessed June 2021).

Colville, R. (1996) 'More Turmoil in Northern Iraq', *Refugees Magazine* Issue 106 (1996). https://unhcr.org/uk/publications/refugeemag/3b5832451/refugees-magazine-issue-106-focus-1996-review-turmoil-northern-iraq. html (last accessed June 2021).

Coordinators of the Zapatista Women for the Second International Gathering of Women Who Struggle (2019) 'Invitation to the Second International Gathering of Women Who Struggle', *Enlace Zapatista*, 21 September. https://enlacezapatista.ezln.org.mx/2019/09/21/invitation-to-the-second-international-gathering-ofwomen-who-struggle/ (last accessed February 2022)

Cumes, A. E. (2021) 'Sexual Violence in the Genocide of the Mayan People in Guatemala', in S. Federici, L. Mason-Deese, and S. Draper (eds), *Feminicide and Global Accumulation: Frontline Struggles to Resist the Violence of Patriarchy and Capitalism.* New York: Common Notions, pp. 74–88.

Darıcı, H. (2016) 'Of Kurdish Youth and Ditches', *Theory & Event*, 19(1).

Davis, A. Y. (2003) *Are Prisons Obsolete?* New York: Seven Stories Press.

—— (2019) 'Turkey, Free Leyla Guven, Hunger Striker', *New York Times*, 16 January. www.nytimes.com/2019/01/16/opinion/letters/angela-davis-turkey-leyla-guven.html (last accessed June 2021).

Davis, A. Y., Dent, G., Meiners, E. R., and Richie, B. (2022) *Abolition. Feminism. Now.* London: Penguin Books.

Davutoğlu, A. (2010) 'Turkey's Zero-problems Foreign Policy', *Foreign Policy*, 20 May. https://foreignpolicy.com/2010/05/20/turkeys-zero-problems-foreign-policy/ (last accessed September 2021).

Dîle, A. (2017) *2005–2015 Türkiye-PKK görüşmeleri: Kürt sorununun çözümüne 'çözümsüreci' operasyonu* [2005–2015 Turkey-PKK Meetings: The 'Solution Process' Operation on the Solution to the Kurdish Issue]. Neuss: Mezopotamien Verlag.

Dirik, D. (2020) 'Only with You This Broom Will Fly: Rojava, Magic, and Sweeping Away the State Inside of Us', in C. Milstein (ed.), *Deciding for Ourselves: The Promise of Direct Democracy*. Chicago: AK Press, pp. 199–229.

—— (2021) 'Understanding the Resistance: Researching Kurdish Movements in Europe – While Doing No Harm', *The Sociological Review Magazine*. https://thesociologicalreview.org/magazine/november-2021/methods-and-methodology/understanding-the-resistance/.

—— (2022, forthcoming) 'Mekap – a Social History of the "Terrorist Shoe" That Fought ISIS', in B. Abrams and P. Gardner (eds), *Symbolic Objects in Contentious Politics*. Ann Arbor: University of Michigan Press.

Dirik, H. (2021) 'Kette der Gewalt', *Missy Magazine*, 24 June. https://missy-magazine.de/blog/2021/06/24/kette-der-gewalt/ (last accessed February 2022).

Dirlik, A. (2014) 'Developmentalism: A Critique', *Interventions*, 16(1), 30–48.

Ekmekçioğlu, L. (2013) 'A Climate for Abduction, a Climate for Redemption: The Politics of Inclusion during and after the Armenian Genocide', *Comparative Studies in Society and History*, 55(3), 522–53.

Erol, F. O. (2019) 'Institutionalizing the State of Exception: The Imrali Isolation Regime', *Komun Academy*, 15 March. https://komun-academy. com/2019/03/15/institutional-izing-the-state-of-exception-the-imrali-isolation-regime/ (last accessed June 2021).

Federici, S. (1997 [2020]) 'Going to Beijing: How the United Nations Colonized the Feminist Movement', Essay in *Revolution at Point Zero: Housework, Reproduction, and Feminist Struggle, Second Edition*. Oakland: PM Press.

—— (2004) *Caliban and the Witch: Women, the Body and Primitive Accumulation*. New York: Autonomedia.

—— (2020) *Revolution at Point Zero: Housework, Reproduction, and Feminist Struggle, Second Edition*. Oakland: PM Press.

Flach, A. (2003) *Jiyanekê din – Ein anderes Leben: Zwei Jahre bei der kurdischen Frauenarmee* [Another Life: Two Years with the Kurdish Women's Army]. Neuss: Mezopotamien Verlag.

—— (2007) *Frauen in der kurdischen Guerrilla: Motivation, Identität und Geschlechterver-hältnis in der Frauenarmee der PKK* [Women in the Kurdish Guerrilla: Motivation, Identity and Gender Relations in the PKK's Women's Army]. Cologne: PapyRossa.

Fregoso, R., and Bejarano, C. (2010) *Terrorizing Women: Feminicide in the Américas*. Durham, NC: Duke University Press.

Freire, P. (1970 [1968]) *Pedagogy of the Oppressed*. New York: Herder and Herder.

Galip, Ö. B. (2016) 'The Politics of Remembering: Representation of the Armenian Genocide in Kurdish Novels', *Holocaust and Genocide Studies*, 30(3), 458–87.

Gelderloos, P. (2020) 'Debunking the Myths around Nonviolent Resistance', *Roar Magazine*, 22 August. https://roarmag.org/essays/chenoweth-stephan-nonviolence-myth/ (last accessed March 2022).

Genç, E. (2020) 'The Kurdish Movement's Relationship with the Palestinian Struggle', *Middle East Report* 295 (Summer 2020). https://merip.org/2020/08/the-kurdish-movements-relationship-with-the-palestinian-struggle/ (last accessed February 2022).

Genç, E., Kılıçaslan, G., and Kutlay Sarıkaya, S. (2019) 'A Reflection of Kurdish Women on Revolutionary Feminism(s) and Solidarity in the MENA| Kurdistan', *Kohl: A Journal for Body and Gender Research*, 5(3). https://kohljournal.press/A-Reflection-of-Kurdish-Women (last accessed June 2021).

Genç, Y. (2002) *PKK'de Kadının Dönüşüm Anatomisi*. Weşanên Jina Serbilind.

Glastonbury, N. S. (2018) 'Building Brand Kurdistan: Helly Luv, the Gender of Nationhood, and the War on Terror', *Kurdish Studies Journal*, 6(1), 111–32.

Glioti, A. (2012) 'Secrets from Jisr Al-Shughour'. *Majalla*, 5 April. https://eng.majalla.com/2012/04/article55230561/secrets-from-jisr-al-shughour (last accessed November 2021).

Göksel, N. (2018) 'Losing the One, Caring for the All: The Activism of the Peace Mothers in Turkey', *Social Sciences*, 7(10), 174.

Goldman, E. (1911). *Anarchism and Other Essays*. New York: Mother Earth Publishing Association.

Göner, Ö. (2017) *Turkish National Identity and Its Outsiders: Memories of State Violence in Dersim*. London: Routledge.

Graeber, D. (2020) 'Öcalan as Thinker: On the Unity of Theory and Practice as Form of Writing', in International Initiative 'Freedom for Abdullah Öcalan – Peace in Kurdistan' (ed.), *Building Free Life: Dialogues with Öcalan*. Oakland: PM Press, pp. 167–90.

Graeber, D., and Wengrow, D. (2021) *The Dawn of Everything: A New History of Humanity*. London: Allen Lane (Penguin).

Grande, S. (2004) *Red Pedagogy: Native American Social and Political Thought*. Lanham, MD: Rowman & Littlefield.

Güneşer, H. (2015) 'Öcalan: 40 Years of Struggle and Resistance', *New Compass Press*. http://new-compass.net/articles/%C3%B6calan-40-years-struggle-and-resistance (last accessed June 2021).

—— (2021) *The Art of Freedom: A Brief History of the Kurdish Liberation Struggle*. Oakland: PM Press.

Hakyemez, S. (2017) 'Margins of the Archive: Torture, Heroism, and the Ordinary in Prison No. 5, Turkey', *Anthropological Quarterly*, 90(1), 107–38.

—— (2018) 'Sur: A City of Imagination, a City under Occupation', *Middle East Report 287* (Summer 2018). https://merip.org/2018/10/sur/ (last accessed January 2022).

Hardi, C. (2011) *Gendered Experiences of Genocide: Anfal Survivors in Kurdis- tan-Iraq*. Farnham: Ashgate Publishing.

—— (2013) 'Women's Activism in Iraqi Kurdistan: Achievements, Short- comings and Obstacles', *Kurdish Studies Journal*, 1(1), 44–64.

Heider, R. (2008) 'Review of "Aliza Marcus: Blood and Belief. The PKK and the Kurdish Fight for Independence"', *Kleine Kurdistan Kolumne* (blog), 31 May. http://kurdistan-kolumne.blogspot.com/2008/07/review-of-aliza-marcus-blood-and-belief.html (last accessed June 2021).

Hilal, M. T. (2013 [1963]) *Studie über die Provinz Al-Jazeera in nationaler, sozialer und politischer Hinsicht* [A Study about the National, Social, and Political Aspects of Al-Jazeera Province]. Berlin: HAN Verlag.

hooks, bell (1984) *Feminist Theory: From Margin to Center*. Boston: South End Press.

—— (1991) 'Theory as Liberatory Practice', *Yale Journal of Law and Feminism* 4(1), 1–13.

—— (2004) *The Will to Change: Men, Masculinity, and Love*. New York: Atria Books.

Human Rights Watch (2009) 'Group Denial Repression of Kurdish Political and Cultural Rights in Syria', November.

—— (2012) 'Time for Justice: Ending Impunity for Killings and Disappearances in 1990s Turkey', September.

—— (2019) 'Syria: Civilians Abused in "Safe Zones": Summary Executions, Blocked Returns by Turkish-backed Armed Groups', November.

ICG (International Crisis Group) (2011) 'Popular Protest in North Africa and the Middle East (VII): The Syrian Regime's Slow-motion Suicide', *Middle East/North Africa Report 109*, 13 July.

—— (2012) 'Tentative Jihad: Syria's Fundamentalist Opposition', *Middle East Report 131*, 12 October.

—— (2013) 'Syria's Kurds: A Struggle within a Struggle', *Middle East Report 136*, 22 January.

Internationalist Commune of Rojava (2018) *Make Rojava Green Again*. London: Dog Section Press.

International Initiative 'Freedom for Abdullah Öcalan – Peace in Kurdistan' (ed.) (2020) *Building Free Life: Dialogues with Öcalan*. Oakland: PM Press.

Jad, I. (2004) 'The NGO-isation of Arab Women's Movements', *IDS Bulletin*, 35(4), 34–42.

Jineolojî Akademisi (2015) *Jineolojiye giriş* [Introduction to Jineolojî]. Neuss: Mezopotamien Verlag.

Jineolojî Collective in Europe (2021) 'Open Letter to the Public about the Article "Beyond Feminism? Jineolojî and the Kurdish Women's Freedom Movement"', *Jadaliyya*, 24 May. www.jadaliyya.com/Details/42819 (last accessed June 2021).

Jineolojî.org (2021) 'The uprising of the oldest colony: Feminism', *Jineoloji.org*, 2 January. https://jineoloji.org/en/2020/04/22/the-uprising-of-the-oldest-colony-feminism/ (last accessed April 2022).

Kadıoğlu Polat, D. (2016) 'Sur: Urban Renewal in the Southeast Anatolian War Zone', *OpenDemocracy*, 21 January. https://opendemocracy.net/en/sur- urban-renewal-in-southeast-anatolian-war-zone/ (last accessed June 2021).

Kamat, S. (2004) 'The Privatization of Public Interest: Theorizing NGO Discourse in a Neoliberal Era', *Review of International Political Economy*, 11(1), 155–76.

Kav, F. (2008) *Mavi Ring*. Neuss: Mezopotamien Verlag.

—— (2018) 'Einige Worte über Sakine' ['A Few Words on Sakine'], in S. Cansız, *Mein ganzes Leben war ein Kampf – 3: Guerrilla*. Neuss: Mezopotamien Verlag, pp. 7–13.

Khan, A. (2021) 'The Civilian Casualty Files: Hidden Pentagon Records Reveal Patterns of Failure in Deadly Airstrikes', *New York Times*, 18 December. www.nytimes.com/interactive/2021/12/18/us/airstrikes-pentagon-records-civilian-deaths.html.

Kışanak, G. (ed.) (2018) *Kürt Siyasetinin Mor Rengi* [The Purple Colour of Kurdish Politics]. Ankara: Dipnot Yayınları.

Knapp, M., Flach, A., and Ayboğa, E. (2016). *Revolution in Rojava: Democratic Autonomy and Women's Liberation in Syrian Kurdistan*. London: Pluto Press.

Kolmasova, S., and Krulisova, K. (2019) 'Legitimizing Military Action through "Rape-as-a-Weapon" Discourse in Libya: Critical Feminist Analysis', *Politics & Gender*, 15(1), 130–50.

Lerner, G. (1986) *The Creation of Patriarchy*. Oxford: Oxford University Press.

Lorde, A. (1984) *Sister Outsider: Essays and Speeches*. Trumansburg, NY: Crossing Press.

Letsch, C. (2016) 'Turkish Journalists Face Secret Trial for Revealing Arms Deliveries to Syria', *Guardian*, 25 March. www.theguardian.com/world/2016/mar/25/turkish-journalists-can-dundar-erdem-gul-secret-trial-revealing-arms-deliveries-syria.

Mahmoud, H. (ed.) (2021) *Kurdish Women's Stories*. London: Pluto Press.

Marcus, A. (2007) *Blood and Belief: The PKK and the Kurdish Fight for Independence*. New York: NYU Press.

McGee, T. (2018) 'Saving the Survivors: Yezidi Women, Islamic State and the German Admissions Program', *Kurdish Studies Journal*, 6 (1), 85–109.

McKernan, B. (2021) 'Turkey Puts 108 Kurdish Politicians on Trial over 2014 Kobani Protests', *Guardian*, 26 April. www.theguardian.com/world/2021/apr/26/turkey-puts-108-kurdish-politicians-on-trial-over-2014-kobani-protests.

Meger, S. (2016) 'The Fetishization of Sexual Violence in International Security', *International Studies Quarterly*, 60(1), 149–59.

Merchant, C. (1980) *The Death of Nature: Women, Ecology and the Scientific Revolution*. San Francisco: Harper & Row.

Mies, M. (1986) *Patriarchy and Accumulation on a World Scale: Women in the International Division of Labour*. London: Zed Books.

Mies, M., and Shiva, V. (1993) *Ecofeminism*. London and New York: Zed Books.

Migration Monitoring Association (GÖÇ-İZ-DER) (2019) 'Report on Human Rights Violations against Women and Their Experiences during the Curfews and Forced Migration, 30 January. https://gocizlemedernegi.org/en/i/report_on_human_rights_violations_against_women_and_their_experiences_during_the_curfews_and_forced_migration (last accessed June 2021).

Miley, T. J., and Venturini, F. (eds) (2018) *Your freedom and Mine: Abdullah* Öcalan *and the Kurdish Question in Erdoğan's Turkey*. Montréal: Black Rose Books.

Mohanty, C. T. (2003) '"Under Western Eyes" Revisited: Feminist Solidarity through Anticapitalist Struggles', *Signs* 28(2), 499–535.

Mojab, S. (ed.) (2001) *Women of a Non-State Nation: The Kurds*. Costa Mesa: Mazda Publishers.

—— (2007) 'Women's NGOs under Conditions of Occupation and War', *Solidarity*. https://solidarity-us.org/atc/129/p576/ (last accessed June 2021).

Öcalan, A. (2000) *Dönüşüm Süreci Üzerine Perspektifler: Politik Rapor* [Perspectives on the Transformation Phase: Political Report]. Cologne: Weşanên Serxwebûn.

—— (2010) *Jenseits von Staat, Macht und Gewalt* [Beyond State, Power and Violence]. Cologne: Mezopotamien Verlag.

—— (2010a) *Demokratik Uygarlık Manifestosu IV: Ortadoğu'da Uygarlık Krizi ve Demokratik Uygarlık Çözümü* [Manifesto for a Democratic Civilization IV: The Civilization Crisis in the Middle East and the Democratic Civilization Solution]. Neuss: Mezopotamien Verlag.

—— (2011) *Prison Writings: The PKK and the Kurdish Question in the 21st Century*. London: Transmedia Publishing.

—— (2013) *Demokratik Uygarlık Manifestosu V: Kürt Sorunu ve Demokratik Ulus Çözümü: Kültürel Soykırım Kıskacındaki Kürtleri Savunmak* [Manifesto for a Democratic Civilization IV: The Kurdish Issue and the Democratic Nation Solution: Defending the Kurds from Cultural Genocide]. Azadi Matbaasi.

—— (2015) *Manifesto for a Democratic Civilization Volume I: Civilization – the Age of Masked Gods and Disguised Kings*. Porsgrunn: New Compass Press.

—— (2015a) *Demokratik Kurtuluş ve Özgür Yaşami İnşa (Imralı notları)* [Democratic Liberation and Building Free Life (Imralı Notes)]. Neuss: Mezopotamien Verlag.

—— (2017) *Manifesto for a Democratic Civilisation, Volume II: Capitalism – the Age of Unmasked Gods and Naked Kings*. Porsgrunn: New Compass Press.

—— (2020) *Manifesto for a Democratic Civilization, Volume III: The Sociology of Freedom*. Oakland: PM Press.

Olufemi, L. (2020) *Feminism Interrupted: Disrupting Power*. London: Pluto Press.

Özkan, B. (2014) 'Turkey, Davutoglu and the Idea of Pan-Islamism', *Survival*, 56(4), 119–40.

—— (2019) 'Relations between Turkey and Syria in the 1980's and 1990's: Political Islam, Muslim Brotherhood and Intelligence Wars', *Uluslararası İlişkiler Dergisi*, 16(62), 5–25.

Pamuk, H., and Tattersall, N. (2015) 'Exclusive: Turkish Intelligence Helped Ship Arms to Syrian Islamist Rebel Areas', *Reuters*, 21 May. www.reuters.com/article/us-mideast-crisis-turkey-arms/exclusive-turkish-intelligence-helped-ship-arms-to-syrian-islamist-rebel-areas-idUKKBN0O61L220150521.

Qato, M. (2019) 'Forms of Retrieval: Social Scale, Citation, and the Archive on the Palestinian Left'. *International Journal of Middle East Studies*, 51(2), 312–15.

RIC (2019) 'Beyond the Frontlines: The Building of the Democratic System in North and East Syria', Rojava Information Center. https:// rojavainformationcenter.com/storage/2019/12/Beyond-the-frontlines-The-building-of-the-democratic-system-in-North-and-East-Syria-Report-Rojava-Information-Center-December-2019-V4.pdf (last accessed June 2021).

—— (2021) 'Explainer: What Is Happening in Manbij?', *Rojava Information Center*, 1 July. https://rojavainformationcenter.com/2021/07/explainer-what-is-happening-in-manbij/ (last accessed February 2022).

Roy, A. (2004) 'Tide? Or Ivory Snow? Public Power in the Age of Empire', transcript of full speech by Arundhati Roy in San Francisco, California, on 16 August 2004. *Democracy Now!* https://democracynow.org/2004/8/23/public_power_in_the_age_of (last accessed June 2021).

Rudi, A. (2018) 'The PKK's Newroz: Death and Moving Towards Freedom for Kurdistan'. *Zanj: The Journal of Critical Global South Studies*, 2(1), 92–114.

Saadi, S. (2020) 'The New Wave of Politics in the Struggle for Self-determination in Rojhelat', *Middle East Report 295* (Summer 2020). https://merip.org/2020/08/the-new-wave-of-politics-in-the-struggle-for-self-determination-in-rojhelat/ (last accessed February 2022).

Salime, Z. (2010) 'Securing the Market, Pacifying Civil Society, Empowering Women: The Middle East Partnership Initiative', *Sociological Forum*, 25(4), 725–45.

Sama, S. (2015) 'A Periphery Becomes a Center? Shopping Malls as Symbols of Modernity in Iraqi Kurdistan', *Middle East – Topics & Arguments*, 5, 89–98.

Sandal, H. (2016) 'The Turkish State of Emergency and LGBTI+ Kurds', *Jadaliyya*. www.jadaliyya.com/Details/33867 (last accessed June 2021).

Sandal-Wilson, H. (2021) 'Social Justice, Conflict, and Protest in Turkey: The Kurdish Issue and LGBTI+ Activism', *Social Research: An International Quarterly*, 88(2), 561–86.

Sarıcan, E., and Matheou, N. (2020) 'Criminalising the Kurdish Struggle', *Tribune Magazine*, 13 February. https://tribunemag.co.uk/2020/02/criminalising-the-kurdish-struggle (last accessed March 2022).

Schäfers, M. (forthcoming) *Voices That Matter: Kurdish Women at the Limits of Representation in Contemporary Turkey*. Chicago: University of Chicago Press.

Schmidinger, T. (2018) *Rojava: Revolution, War and the Future of Syria's Kurds*. London: Pluto Press.

Scott, J. C. (2009) *The Art of Not Being Governed: An Anarchist History of Upland Southeast Asia*. New Haven: Yale University Press.

Segato, R. L. (2010) 'Territory, Sovereignty, and Crimes of the Second State: The Writing on the Body of Murdered Women', in R. L. Fregoso and C. L. Bejarano (eds), *Terrorizing Women: Feminicide in the Américas*, Durham: Duke University Press.

—— (2016) 'Patriarchy from Margin to Center: Discipline, Territoriality, and Cruelty in the Apocalyptic Phase of Capital', *The South Atlantic Quarterly*, 115(3), 615–24.

Sen, B. (2016) 'The Ethnic Limits of Gentrification: The Kurds and Battle in Kurdistan', *Contested Cities*. http://contested-cities.net/working-papers/wp-content/uploads/sites/8/2016/07/WPCC-164008-SenBesime-EthnicLimitsGentrification.pdf (last accessed June 2021).

Sha'bo, R. (2016) 'On the Inevitability of Militarization in the Syrian Uprising', *Syria Untold*, 14 November. https://syriauntold.com/2016/11/14/inevitability-militarization-syrian-uprising/ (last accessed February 2022).

Sima, Z. (2018) 'Being Beautiful', *Komun Academy*. https://komun-academy.com/2018/10/30/being-beautiful/ (last accessed June 2021).

Smith, L. T. (1999) *Decolonizing Methodologies: Research and Indigenous Peoples*. London and New York: Zed Books.

Stoltenberg, J., and Jolie, A. (2017) 'Why NATO Must Defend Women's Rights', *Guardian*, 10 December. https://theguardian.com/commentisfree/2017/dec/10/why-nato-must-defend-womens-rights (last accessed June 2021).

Taştekin, F. (2017) *Suriye: Yıkıl Git, Diren Kal!* Istanbul: İletişim Yayınları.

—— (2021) 'Turkish Mobster's Revelations Extend to Arms Shipments to Syria', *Al-Monitor*, 2 June. www.al-monitor.com/originals/2021/06/turkish-mobsters-revelations-extend-arms-shipments-syria.

Tatort Kurdistan (2013) *Democratic Autonomy in North Kurdistan: The Council Movement, Gender Liberation, and Ecology in Practice*. Porsgrunn: New Compass Press.

Tejel, J. (2009) *Syria's Kurds: History, Politics and Society*. London: Routledge.

UN Special Rapporteur on the situation of human rights in the Islamic Republic of Iran (2019), 'Report of the Special Rapporteur on the Situation of Human Rights in the Islamic Republic of Iran: Situation of Human Rights in the Islamic Republic of Iran', July.

Üstündağ, N. (2016) 'Self-defense as a Revolutionary Practice in Rojava, or How to Unmake the State', *The South Atlantic Quarterly*, 11, 197–210.

—— (2017) 'Power Relations: State and Family', in Network for an Alternative Quest (ed.)., *Challenging Capitalist Modernity II: Dissecting Capitalist Modernity – Building Democratic Confederalism (Conference 3–5 April 2015, University of Hamburg)*. Neuss: Mezopotamien Verlag, pp. 205–11.

—— (2019) 'Mother, Politician, and Guerilla: The Emergence of a New Political Imagination in Kurdistan through Women's Bodies and Speech', *Differences*, 30(2), 15–45.

—— (2021) 'Quick Thoughts: Nazan Üstündağ on the Protests at Turkey's Boğaziçi University', *Jadaliyya*, 11 Feburary. www.jadaliyya.com/Details/42372/Quick-ThoughtsAnonymous-on-the-Protests-at-Turkey's-Boğaziçi-University.

van Bruinessen, M. (2001) 'From Adela Khanum to Leyla Zana: Women as Political Leaders in Kurdish History', in S. Mojab (ed.), *Women of a Non-State Nation: The Kurds*. Costa Mesa: Mazda Publishers, pp. 95–112.

Varlı, S. (2017) 'The Experience of Bağlar Women's Cooperative', in Network for an Alternative Quest (ed.), *Challenging Capitalist Modernity II: Dissecting Capitalist Modernity – Building Democratic Confederalism (Conference 3–5 April 2015, University of Hamburg)*. Neuss: Mezopotamien Verlag, pp. 135–40.

von Werlhof, C., Mies, M., and Bennholdt-Thomsen, V. (1991) *Frauen die letzte Kolonie* [Women the Last Colony]. Zurich: Rotpunktverlag.

Walia, H. (2021) *Border and Rule: Global Migration, Capitalism, and the Rise of Racist Nationalism*. Chicago: Haymarket Books.

Westrheim, K. (2008) 'Prison as Site for Political Education: Educational Experiences from Prison Narrated by Members and Sympathisers of the PKK', *Journal for Critical Education Policy Studies*, 6(1), 1.

Yıldız, R. (2020) 'Tarihe bir itiraz: Kürt Kadınları Teali Cemiyeti', *Gazete Karınca*, 8 March. https://gazetekarinca.com/tarihe-bir-itiraz-kurt-kadinlari-teali-cemiyeti-rojda-yildiz/ (last accessed March 2022).

Yıldız, Y.Y. (2016) 'Forced Confession as a Ritual of Sovereignty: The Case of Diyarbakır Military Prison in Turkey', *Asia-Pacific Journal on Human Rights and the Law*, 17(2), 185–98.

ARCHIVAL MATERIAL REFERENCED (CHRONOLOGICAL ORDER)

PKK (1993 [1978]) *Kürdistan Devrimin Yolu (Manifesto)* [The Way of the Kurdistan Revolution], 5th edition. Cologne: Weşanên Serxwebun. Agri Verlag.

—— (1995) *PKK 5. Kongre Kararları* [PKK 5th Congress Resolution]. Cologne: Weşanên Serxwebûn – Agri Verlag.

YAJK (1999) Özgürlük Manifestosu Zilan [Freedom Manifesto Zilan]. Weşanên Jina Serbilind.

—— (1999a) *Eşitliğe ve Özgürlüğe Yürüyüş: Kadın ordulaşmasına doğru* [The March Towards Equality and Freedom: Towards Women's Armyfication].

PJKK (2000) *PJKK olağanüstü 3. kongresi'ne sunulan merkez raporu ve kararlar* [Central Report and Decisions Proposed at the PJKK 3rd Extraordinary Congress]. Weşanên Jina Serbilind.

PJA (2000) *PJA Program ve Tüzüğü* [PJA Programme and Charter]. Weşanên Jina Serbilind.

—— (2001) *Insanlık Özgür Kadınla Yeniden Doğacaktır – PJA III. Kadın Konferansi Belgeleri* [Humanity Will be Reborn with the Free Woman – PJA Third Women's Conference Documents]. Weşanên Jina Serbilind.

PKK (2002) Final Resolution on the Eighth Congress of the PKK. https:// freeocalan. org/news/english/final-resolution-on-the-8th-congress-of-the-pkk (last accessed May 2021).

PJA (2003 [2002]) *The Social Contract Declaration*. Cologne: Mezopotamien Verlag.

—— (2004) *4. Konferans Tartışmaları* [Fourth Conference Discussions]. Weşanên Jina Serbilind.

—— (2004a) *Kadın Ordulaşması – I & II* [Women's Armyfication I & II]. Weşanên Jina Serbilind.

Cenî Kurdisches Frauenbüro für Frieden (2011) *Eine junge und sagenhafte Geschichte – Die Kurdische Frauenbewegung: Vom ersten Frauentreffen zum komplexen Modell des demokratischen Konföderalsimus*, unpublished material, retrieved from the authors.

FURTHER ENGLISH-LANGUAGE RESOURCES

Academy of Democratic Modernity. https://democraticmodernity.com/

International Initiative Freedom for Abdullah Öcalan – Peace in Kurdistan. www. freeocalan.org/

Jineoloji. https://jineoloji.org/

Kurdistan Women's Communities (KJK). www.kjkonline.net/en/

Women Defend Rojava. https://womendefendrojava.net/en/

Index

8 March (International Women's Day)
10, 49, 93, 95, 114, 144, 180,
189–91, 217

AANES (Autonomous Administration
of North and East Syria) 22, 2010,
222–7, 240, 253, 288–9
Abdo, Meysa 234, 275, 279
Abdil, Songül Erol 175–7
abolitionism 2, 91, 101, 129
abortion 4, 129, 187
abstinence 100–101
academies 108, 136–40, 145, 151,
166–7, 180, 201, 224, 229, 237,
244, 320; women's academies 10,
62, 104–8, 135, 138–9, 151, 156,
167, 201, 220, 223–4, 229, 246–7;
Jineolojî xvi, 67, 79
see Şehîd Zîlan Academy; Şehîd
Jiyan Academy; Ishtar Women's
Academy; Mesopotamia Academy
for Social Sciences; Abdullah
Öcalan Academy for Social
Sciences
Adliyê 280–4
aesthetics 5, 43, 66–67, 73, 78, 85, 90,
106, 142, 153, 172, 201, 223, 290
Afghanistan 177, 278, 279, 298, 302,
304, 305, 312 war: 177, 302;
women's solidarity: 278, 279, 298
see Taliban
Africa xx, 25, 27, 271; North: 303, 306,
316
see South Africa
Afrîn 58, 97, 208, 213, 219, 222, 236,
271, 280, 294–6
see Operation Olive Branch
Agal, Binevş (Bêrîvan) 34, 39–41, 271
Ahrar al-Sharqiyah 295
airstrikes 239, 278–9, 286, 297, 323
AK47 (Kalashnikov) 121, 208, 263, 280

Akkuş, Nermin (Hêlîn Çerkez) 46
AKP Adalet ve Kalkınma Partisi
(Justice and Development Party)
38, 52–3, 57, 117, 172, 174, 177–9,
185, 197, 205–6, 214, 276, 290,
292–4
Akşener, Meral 172
Alamhouli, Şirîn 130
'Alawis 241
Alevi 9, 19, 20, 23, 27, 34, 35, 44, 73, 85,
131–2, 175–7, 244, 247, 250, 263,
272, 290–1, 294,320
Algeria 2, 45, 65
Alkan, Zekiye 40
Altun, Nurhayat 172–3, 177
Amara village (Ömerli) 25
amargi 303
Amed – Diyarbakır 26, 30, 40, 44,
84, 107, 114, 116, 118, 131, 139,
153, 171, 174, 176–7, 180–2, 186,
189–90, 206, 275, 290, 292–4, 318,
320; Bağlar 176, 186, 320; Kocaköy
181–3, 189, 324; Sur 62, 104, 107,
118, 139, 153, 186, 292, 294, 318,
324
Amnesty International 93, 131, 324
anarchism 2, 12, 62, 71, 99, 134
al-Anfal 192–3
Angola 25, 27
Ankara 25, 49, 116, 140, 182, 185, 292
anti-capitalism xviii, xxi, 12, 71, 136,
142,149, 153–4, 174, 209, 227, 243,
308, 313
anti-colonialism xxi, 2, 7, 24–26, 29–30,
56, 63, 104, 113, 128, 134–6, 149,
211, 243, 306–7
anti-fascism 2, 12, 30, 41, 46, 74, 209,
243, 271, 283, 313, 315
anti-imperialism 26, 30, 307–8
anti-racism 2, 125
see race, racism

Anuş, Besê 35
Anyık, Eşref 29
apartheid 2, 91, 93
Apo(ism) xviii, 10, 25, 55, 83–90, 95–8,
    196, 212–14, 224, 252, 278–80, 308
  see Öcalan, Abdullah
Arabic 15, 79, 144, 222, 228, 231, 244,
    315
Arab Spring 10, 178, 215, 220, 303
Aramaic 226, 231–2, 285
Aras, Eser 264–5
ARGK Artêşa Rizgariya Gelê Kurdistan
    (People's Liberation Army of
    Kurdistan) 35
Arjîn 122–3
armed struggle xviii, 23, 42, 52, 55,
    120–3, 190, 256
Armenians 33, 141, 211, 230–1, 271,
    286, 290, 297, 308
  see genocide: Armenian
arms trade 89, 240, 298, 311
army 15, 122, 123, 239, 260, 278, 296,
    303, 308, 318; Turkish army: 36–8,
    40–1, 46–8, 50, 112, 118, 121, 133,
    145, 161, 191, 198, 248, 254, 272,
    276, 279, 282, 292–7, 315, 318;
    Iraqi army: 204–5, 246, 254, 275;
    Syrian army: 217; Free Syrian
    Army: 215, 216, 220; Ottoman
    army: 23, 255; women's army:
    44–6, 51, 54, 57–8, 65, 120, 234–7,
    260, 270, 301–3, 318; women's
    army-fication: 44–6, 51, 65, 120,
    317
Aryen 151–2, 156, 167, 246–7
asayîş 97, 231, 237–8
Asia 19, 25, 27, 39, 278
Aslan, Azize 151, 154, 324
Aslan, Özgecan 182
Aslan, Yusuf 25
al-Assad, Bashar 33, 209, 214–8, 221,
    240
al-Assad, Hafez 33, 212
assassination 9, 22, 24, 37, 47, 126, 192,
    237, 293–5, 297–8, 309, 322
Assata Shakur 129

assimilation xix, 19, 22, 34, 39, 66, 73,
    80, 84, 121, 133, 134, 141, 198, 238,
    255, 267
Assyrians 20, 23, 47, 123, 204, 211,
    230–1, 245, 249, 290, 295
Astarte 232, 285, 323
Atargatis 285
authoritarianism xx, 5, 8, 12, 71, 74, 90,
    104, 105, 135, 136, 155, 170, 178,
    186, 194, 211, 212, 215, 218, 220,
    221, 223, 232, 237, 239, 245, 248,
    269, 301, 304, 307, 309, 319, 324
Ayata, Muzaffer 29, 31

Ba'ath Party (Iraq) 24, 192–93, 204
Ba'ath Party (Syria) 209–18, 224–26,
    231, 289
Baghdad 275
Bağrıyanık, Ceylan 180
Bakurê Kurdistan (Bakur) – northern-
    Kurdistan/Turkey 10, 33–5, 38–40,
    42, 43, 78, 114, 130, 134, 136, 139,
    144, 153, 154, 158, 160, 164, 169,
    170–91, 221, 247, 254, 273, 276,
    281, 292, 294, 315, 316
Baloch, Karima 298
Barzanî family 22, 194, 197, 218;
    Mesûd: 196, 198, 205, 293, 322;
    Mullah Mistefa 20; Nêçîrvan 270
Basque Country 45, 65
Başûrê Kurdistan (Başûr) – southern
    Kurdistan/Iraq 10, 24, 48, 54,
    78, 114, 136, 143, 146–7, 157,
    192–207, 260, 294, 296, 315
Batman – Êlih 34, 39, 173, 290
BDP Barış ve Demokrasi Partisi (Peace
    and Democracy Party) 174, 182
Bekaa Valley 33–5
Berîtan (Gülnaz Karataş) 44, 118, 234,
    319
Berkel, Zehra 296
Besê 93–5, 100–3
Bethnarin Women's Protection Units
    233
Beyt al-Baraka 287
Biden administration 304

Black Panther Party for Self-Defense 134

Black Sea 26, 30, 47, 290

Boochani, Behrouz 156

Bookchin, Murray 70, 150–1

Boran Amanos, Nurhak (Döndü Gök) 272

borders 19, 27, 33, 40, 96, 118–19, 156–61, 190–1, 197–8, 206–7, 16–18, 227, 241, 244, 256, 267, 270, 275–7, 281–2, 289, 292, 296, 308, 322

Botan (Nizamettin Taş) 53–4, 105

Botan region 39–41

Brazil 89, 91, 134

bride 114; child bride 181; bride exchange 184; bride price 167, 184

Britain 20, 23, 54

Bruno, Giordano 127

Bush George W. Jr. 53, 177, 195, 304; Sr. 193

Cáceres, Berta 149, 298

cadre 7, 9, 10, 27–9, 33–4, 50, 52, 54–5, 56, 66–7, 73, 85–9, 93, 95, 101, 105–6, 123, 134, 141, 198, 209, 213–4, 219, 278–9, 305

Çağırga family 118

Çağlayan, Handan 112, 172

Campbell, Anna (Hêlîn Qereçox) 271

Cansız, Sakine (Sara) 1, 9, 10, 15, 19, 24, 25, 29–31, 85, 87, 120, 180, 213, 220, 224, 234, 293, 315–6

capitalism xx, xxi, 1, 2, 4, 7, 8, 12, 25, 59, 66, 67, 70, 71–2, 76, 79, 91, 94, 96, 99, 100, 103, 106, 109, 113, 121, 124, 134–41, 143, 149–51, 152, 154–5, 156–7, 195, 198, 200, 201, 203, 209, 227, 230, 243, 269, 279, 280, 297, 302, 303, 304, 308–11

see anti-capitalism; capitalist modernity

capitalist modernity 8, 54, 66–7, 70–2, 80, 92, 94, 127, 138, 152, 157, 243, 278, 312

carceral 101, 124, 310

Çayan, Mahir 25–6

cemetery 41, 127, 259

censorship xix, 21, 131, 147, 289, 301

Chaldeans 20, 23, 47, 211, 230, 249

chauvinism 26, 36, 141, 171, 211, 225

Chechens 231, 286

chemical weapons 192–3, 300

children 2, 13, 25, 31, 34, 41, 42, 67, 87, 90, 93, 97, 100, 102, 104, 107, 109, 110, 112–5, 117, 118, 121, 126, 128, 131, 134–5, 139, 148, 159, 160, 162, 164–5, 177–8, 181, 187, 190–3, 194, 199, 211–2, 223, 227, 230, 236, 241, 246, 252, 254, 255–6, 258, 261, 262, 263, 266, 267, 276, 281, 283, 286, 288, 291, 292, 293, 295, 300
see marriage, child

Choudry, Aziz 305

CHP Republican People's Party 171

Christian 19, 20, 225, 230–3, 241

CIA (Central Intelligence Agency) 37, 242

Çiçek, Ali 30

Çiçek, Meral 40, 58

Circassians 46–7, 231, 285–7

citizenship 59, 211–2, 217, 222, 223

civilization 63, 69, 212, 304; statist civilization (mainstream civilization): 70, 72, 128, 249, 278; democratic civilization 51, 70, 249, 278; Manifesto for a Democratic Civilization (title): 76, 92

civil society 58, 72, 140, 159, 172–74, 185, 193–5, 198, 223–4, 255, 294, 304–9

Cizîr – Cizre (Jazeera) (Bakur) 40–1, 118, 292, 317; (Rojava) 203, 211, 222, 227, 231
see Jazeera Canton

Cizîrî, Bêrîvan 41, 213

class xviii, 1–2, 4, 7, 12, 14, 25, 27, 34, 36, 42, 45, 48, 63, 67, 70, 80, 83–4, 115, 125, 146, 129, 135, 138, 146, 151, 156, 195, 200–5, 213, 225, 227, 304, 317, 324; working class xix-, 11, 14, 27, 42, 47 83–4

Clinton, Hillary 301, 306–07

co-chairing 92, 163, 165, 172, 183, 187–89, 262, 265, 320
  see co-presidency; (co-)mayor
Colemêrg – Hakkâri 34, 290
Colombia 2
colonial(ism) xx, xxi, 1, 2, 19, 23, 25, 27, 29, 45, 63, 66–7, 70–2, 76, 91, 99, 104, 113, 121, 135, 143, 149, 150, 152, 153, 156, 192, 195, 225, 231, 239, 243, 273, 285, 304, 310; post-colonial 25, 198; neo-colonial 53, 157, 304, 310
  see settler colonialism
colonization xxi, 2, 5, 6, 8, 9, 12, 13, 26, 33, 40, 56, 66, 78, 79, 83, 87, 100, 104–6, 117, 124, 128, 135, 140, 149–51, 198, 210, 221, 237, 240, 275, 297, 310, 316
  see decolonization
(co-)mayor 30, 92, 130, 170–9, 181–7
  see co-chairing; co-presidency
commodification 150–1, 201, 204
commune xviii, 7, 67, 71–2, 98, 110, 126, 135, 155, 158, 162–3, 167–8, 187, 215, 221–4, 227, 228, 267, 284
  see Paris Commune; Internationalist Commune of Rojava
communism 24, 37, 176, 202, 242, 245, 287
comradeship 14, 51, 75, 84, 87–8, 94–6, 101, 106, 121, 126, 139, 257, 282
  see heval
conscription 237, 254, 289
conservative 4, 5, 26, 30, 36, 37, 41, 42, 53, 66, 90, 100–2, 147, 153, 167, 171, 173, 175, 177, 185, 192, 194, 195, 202, 213, 223, 225, 226, 232, 248, 293, 302, 305, 310–11; gender roles 54, 112, 132, 178
constitution 24, 25, 27, 53, 173, 194, 204, 219, 254
cooperatives xviii, 7, 126, 139, 153–5, 163, 183, 186, 190, 215, 221, 223, 226–7, 232, 287–8, 320
co-presidency 57, 110, 162, 172–4, 176, 187–9, 202, 203, 219, 222, 224, 262, 294
  see co-chairing; (co-)mayor

Council of Europe Committee for the Prevention of Torture (CPT) 91
coup 70; d'état 20, 25, 27, 28, 37, 130, 172, 175, 192, 211, 290; regime 9, 132; attempt 92, 130, 144, 293
Covid-19 pandemic 131, 297
criminalization xviii, xix, 11–12, 14, 39, 62, 85, 86, 90, 99, 112, 124, 129, 134, 136, 143, 158, 174, 177, 198, 217, 248, 257, 303, 309, 320
Cuba 25, 27, 30, 65, 271
curfew 41, 293, 324

Daesh – ISIS/ISIL ad-Dawlah al-Islāmi-yah (Islamic State (of Iraq & Syria/Levante) xviii, xix, 6, 9, 10–11, 15, 58, 67, 90, 98, 109, 118, 121–3, 162, 190, 196, 204–5, 209–10, 220, 224, 230–8, 240–73, 275–84, 285–9, 290–7, 300–3, 307–8, 323, 325
Davis, Angela Y. 91, 92, 129
Davutoğlu, Ahmet 321
defection 38, 54, 202, 214, 216
decolonization 3, 4, 9, 13, 48, 62–3, 72, 85, 116, 128, 135, 149 151, 154, 210, 240, 311–3, 316
  see colonization
deep state 37–8
DEHAP Demokratik Halk Partisi (Democratic People's Party) 172–3, 183, 321
Deir ez-Zor 222, 225, 285, 296
Demilitarization 130, 149
Demir, Sêvê 190, 293
Demirel, Afitap (Ruken Çiya) 46
Demirel, Çağlar 176–7, 179, 186–9, 324
Demirel, Rahşan 40
Demirtaş, Azime 35, 234
demonstrations 125, 298, 302
  see protest
Democratic Confederalism 7, 22, 55–9, 71–5, 122, 151, 153, 156, 158, 166, 167, 214, 221, 223; World Democratic Women's Confederalism: 7, 57–8, 312
democratic modernity 69, 71–3, 186, 335

democratic nation 72–5, 88, 108, 141, 164, 174, 186, 204, 224, 233, 237, 245, 289, 308
demographic change 295
dengbêjî 23, 255, 277, 323
Dêrîk – al-Malikiyah 176, 179, 183, 186, 231, 258, 267, 268
Dêrsim – Tunceli 20, 23, 25, 34, 44, 47, 172, 175–7, 291, 316, 320
Derya 58, 198–9
Devrim 82, 142–6
Dewrêş and Edulê 106, 255
diaspora xviii–xxi, 7, 9, 11, 14, 41, 42, 77, 78, 89, 110, 121, 135, 143, 210, 247
diplomacy 10, 20, 21, 41, 58, 164, 195, 197, 200, 206, 216, 240, 317
Dirbêsiyê –al-Darbasiyah 155, 236
Dirik, Hêlîn 124–5
dissent 37, 129, 139, 194, 197, 212, 243, 306–7
Diyarbakır Prison 9, 24, 28–32, 317
Doğan, Fidan 9–10, 15, 24, 220, 293
Doğan, Mazlum 29, 48, 126, 317
Doğan, Zehra 133
DÖKH Demokratik Özgür Kadın Hareketi (Democratic Free Women's Movement) 173, 179–80
Dolmabahçe Agreement 180–1
domestic violence/abuse 4, 107, 110, 124, 167, 168, 171, 185, 190, 194, 228, 238, 286, 288, 289, 294
dress, traditional 39, 112, 118, 190, 269
drones xx, 78, 309; strikes 273, 294, 296, 297; technologies 308
Druze 241
DTP Demokratik Toplum Partisi (Democratic Society Party) 172–5, 187, 321
Dündar, Can 292
Durmuş, Hayri 30

ecocide xxi, 2, 149–50, 155, 240, 297, 301, 312
eco-feminism 150
ecology 3, 6, 7, 11, 48, 56, 62, 66, 67, 70–1, 72, 78, 108, 139, 144, 149, 155, 163, 164–5, 167, 175, 176, 179, 183, 185, 209, 250, 279, 307, 312, 320
economy xix, 4, 5, 8, 51, 58, 63, 69, 70, 71, 73, 76, 78, 79, 99, 199, 108, 110, 114, 121, 124, 124, 142, 144, 146, 149–55, 157, 159, 162, 163–4, 166, 168–9, 177, 183, 190, 194–5, 201, 203, 206, 210, 212, 221, 224–7, 231–2, 238, 242, 267, 269, 275, 286–8, 293, 295, 300, 304–6
education xxi, 1, 4, 8, 23, 24, 29, 31, 33, 35, 48, 51, 65, 73, 78, 85, 86, 88, 89, 96–7, 101, 104–110, 126, 130, 132, 134–41, 142, 154, 159, 162–7, 170, 173, 176, 185, 186, 195, 196, 201–2, 204, 219, 223, 224, 228, 229, 231–3, 235–8, 247, 260–61, 265–7, 269, 272, 273, 286, 288, 295, 318, 323
Egypt 218, 285
elections, electoral politics 4, 73, 90–1, 92, 118, 130–1, 166, 170–91, 222, 290–2, 294, 321
El Saadawi, Nawal 1
Encü family 263, Viyan 263
Engîn, Rotînda 54, 95
English Channel 157
ENKS Encûmena Niştimanî ya Kurdî li Sûriyê – Kurdish National Council in Syria – KNC) 218, 221, 237
Erdem, Zeynep (Jiyan) 167
Erdîş – Erciş 185, 324
Erdoğan, Recep Tayyip 53, 112, 116, 177–8, 276, 279, 282–3, 293–7
Erhan, Nujiyan (Tuba Akyılmaz) 273
Eritrea 27
ERNK Eniya Rizgariya Netewa Kurdistan (National Liberation Front of Kurdistan) 35
Ersöz, Gurbetelli (Zeynep Agir) 144–5
Esma 93, 95, 101–3
Eurocentricism xx, 3, 13, 14, 21, 23, 76, 80, 157, 201, 316
Europe xix, 2, 9, 10, 11, 14, 19, 20, 22, 23, 35, 41, 42, 45, 50, 51, 63, 70, 74, 76, 78, 79, 86, 88, 89, 91–2, 93, 98, 114, 117, 118, 120–1, 124, 135, 136,

137, 143, 148, 150, 156, 157, 158, 160, 187, 194, 211, 249, 254, 257, 261, 262, 266, 268, 271, 277, 279, 285, 297, 300, 304, 305, 309, 317, 319, 322

European Union 50, 157, 177, 295, 309

Evren, Kenan 27

executions 20, 24, 25, 26, 27, 38, 43, 122, 130, 175, 193, 241, 243, 286, 316

extra-judicial killings 27, 38, 41, 114

Êzîdî 19, 34, 39, 41, 73, 102, 118, 230, 241, 244, 246, 249–50, 252–74, 294, 296, 318, 323

families xix, 2, 3, 7, 10, 23, 24, 25, 28, 29, 35, 36, 39, 40, 42, 44, 50, 83, 84, 86, 88, 90, 92, 96, 97, 100, 101, 103–08, 110, 112, 113, 115, 117, 126, 127, 132, 133, 139, 142, 143, 147, 159, 160, 162–64, 168, 171, 178, 179, 194, 196, 197, 198, 200, 203, 204, 213, 214, 228–29, 236, 237, 238, 242, 246, 248, 253, 256–58, 260, 261, 263, 266, 267, 272, 275, 276, 281, 287, 288, 290, 298, 302; family relations 36, 137; martyrs' families 161, 162, 166

Fanon, Frantz 104

federalism 222; federal Syria 218, 225, 231, 239

Federici, Silvia 76, 100, 113, 150, 310

female genital mutilation (FGM) 4, 194

feminicide 2–5, 10, 14, 20, 23, 76, 124, 135, 142, 149, 182, 186, 230, 240, 241–51, 252–4, 262, 267, 273, 289, 296–8, 309, 311–2, 315, 318

femininity 23, 43, 45, 94, 132, 311

feminism liberal 14, 306, 310–11; Black xxi, 2, 101, 311

ferman 252–74, 323

feudalism 4, 38, 90, 100, 317

Feyli 23

Firat, Deniz 247

flag 72, 75, 88, 112, 174, 196, 206, 257, 263, 291, 292; false flag 38; Turkish flag 47, 50, 153, 276, 295

forced displacement/migration 4, 7, 20, 152, 157, 160, 179, 230, 232, 242, 246, 254, 274, 276, 301

forced marriage 23, 36, 104, 178, 230, 236

forests 75, 150; deforestation 153; fires 320

France 9, 10, 20, 309; French mandate 33, 211, 231

Franco, Marielle 120, 298

Freire, Paulo 134, 137

FSA al-Jaysh as-Sūrī al-H.urr (Free Syrian Army) 215–6, 220, 235, 285

Gawriya, Elizabet 262

Gencer, Onur 297

genocide xviii, 4, 19, 20, 23, 25, 47, 63, 66, 73, 85, 120, 149, 192, 195, 197, 199–200, 230–4, 241, 242–3, 246, 250, 252–274, 276, 296–7, 312, 323; Armenian 20, 23, 47, 230, 242, 316; al-Anfal 160, 192–3, 195; Sengal 102, 118, 252–274, 275, 323; Dersim 23, 25, 85, 316; Seyfo 20, 23, 47, 230–4; Greeks 20, 47

Georges-Picot, François 20

Germany 39, 41, 42, 45–6, 78, 245, 250, 254, 301, 309, 317, 323, 324

Germiyan 203, 249

Gewer –Yüksekova 318

Gezi Park 83, 178

Gezmiş, Deniz 25–6

Gilgamesh, Epic of 76

Girê Spî – Tel Abyad 222, 280, 295

goddess 117, 285, 295, 323

Goldman, Emma 99

Gozarto 226, 231–32

Gramsci, Antonio 137

Grande, Sandy 273–4

graves 84, 127, 216, 252, 259–60, 270, 285

Greek 20, 47, 50, 77, 201, 230, 285

Grey Wolves 27, 38

Gulabi Gang 144

Gülen, Fethullah 177, 293

Gulveda, Gulan (Eylem Kaplan) 205, 247–49

Güneşer, Havîn xvi, 91, 319
Güven, Leyla 92–3, 184–5, 321

HADEP Halkın Demokrasi Partisi
(People's Democracy Party)
Halabja 193, 275
see al-Anfal
Halfeti 25, 33
al-Hallaj, Mansour 127
Hanife 212–3
harassment 1, 3, 4, 28, 29, 99, 112, 124,
132, 133, 148, 161, 170, 182, 187,
194–6, 295
Harmoush, Hussein 216, 322
Harun, Avesta (Filiz Şaybak) 247
Hasankeyf 153
Hatay 33, 216
HDP Halkların Demokratik Partisi
(Peoples' Democratic Party) 90, 92,
171, 174–80, 183, 185–9, 197, 276,
290–2, 297, 321, 323, 324
Heja 26, 47, 74–5, 290
Hesekê – al-Hasakah 211, 222, 231, 233,
265, 271
Heso 258–8, 265–6
heval 13, 34, 83, 208, 257, 266, 267, 269,
272–3, 277, 281, 282; hevaltî 15, 83
Hêvîdar 164–5
hevjiyana azad (free co-life) 68, 78, 102,
106, 188
Hewlêr – Erbil/Arbil 58, 196, 198, 206,
256
Hezil, Berfîn 253
Hikmet, Nâzım 75
Hilal, Muhammad Talab 211–2
Hittite 294
Hizbullah 38
Hoffmann, Ivana (Avaşîn Têkoşîn
Güneş) 245, 250
Hollywood(ization) 11, 279, 301–3
Holocaust 245
home-maker xx, 80, 96, 104, 110, 144,
213
homophobia 2, 178
'honour killings' 4, 104, 194, 286, 298
hooks, bell 62, 99, 311
Housewifization 9, 71, 308

HPC Hêzên Parastina Civakî (Civil
Defence Forces) 238–9
HPG Hêzên Parastina Gel (People's
Defence/Protection Forces) 57, 58,
205, 252–3, 265, 270, 272
HPJ Hêzên Parastina Jinê (The
Women's Defence/Protection
Forces) 318
HRK Hêzên Rizgariya Kurdistan
(Kurdistan Liberation Forces) 35
hunger strike 9, 90–3, 126, 132, 160,
277
Husen Mihamad, Tara 203–4
Hussein, Saddam 53, 116, 146, 160–3,
192–3, 196–8, 214, 254, 261, 300

Ilham 97, 229–30
Ilisu Dam 153
IMF 157, 310
imperialism xx, 1, 11, 24, 25, 27, 29, 48,
53, 56, 66, 70, 72, 123, 150, 210,
212, 214, 218, 243, 248–9, 279, 302,
304, 306–8, 310
see anti-imperialism
Imralı Prison 6, 50, 56, 91–2, 180, 218,
93, 319, 323; delegation 255, 180;
meeting notes 293
Inan, Hüseyin 25
India 2, 144, 202
indigenous xxi, 3, 13, 63, 113, 134, 149,
151, 209, 210, 247, 254, 273
industrialism 70, 150–2
International Initiative for the Freedom
of Abdullah Ocalan - Peace in
Kurdistan 90–1, 318–9, 335
internationalism xviii, 7, 13, 24, 26–7,
46, 51, 57–8, 66, 74, 78, 89, 91, 136,
157, 209, 240, 245, 250, 271, 277–8,
292, 296, 297, 308–311, 316
Internationalist Commune of Rojava
154–5, 321, 323
Iran, Islamic Republic of xviii-xix, 4,
19–24, 78, 121, 130, 134, 156, 157,
193, 194, 198, 204–6, 256, 263,
271, 273, 276, 307, 316, 318, 320;
Iran-Iraq war 198

Iraq xviii, 4, 10, 19–24, 33, 44, 52, 53, 57, 96, 118, 119, 121, 146, 156, 158–162, 177, 192–207, 211, 214, 226, 240, 241, 245, 246, 249, 252, 254, 256, 258, 260, 270, 273, 275, 276, 294, 296, 302, 305, 306, 322; Iran-Iraq war 198
Ishtar (goddess) 261, 285, 295, 323
Ishtar Women's Academy 220, 224
Ishtar Women's Assembly 162–4, 166–9, 246
Islam 73, 177–8, 185, 230, 243, 244, 319
Islamism 22, 37, 38, 131, 132, 172, 177–8, 194, 215–6, 218–9, 241–2, 275, 279, 292–5, 307, 309, 319, 321
Islamophobia 11, 242, 309
Isma'ilis 241
Israel 33, 34, 39, 50, 177, 206, 14, 308
Istanbul Convention 296
İYİ Parti (Good Party) 172

Jabhat al-Nusra 10, 219, 235, 275
Jalalian, Zeynab 130
Jazeera Canton 208, 211, 218–19, 222, 224, 226, 232, 253, 262, 267, 283
Jesus Christ 127, 232
Jewish 19, 309
Jina Serbilind 143
Jînda 62, 104, 107–8, 139–41
Jineolojî xvi, 62, 67, 76–80, 108, 110, 133, 139, 144, 149, 155, 164, 288, 319
JinHa 144, 147–8
JinNews 144
JinTV 144, 320
Jinwar Women's Village 76, 155, 295
Jisr al-Shughour 216, 322
JITEM Jandarma İstihbarat ve Terörle Mücadele (Gendarmerie Intelligence and Counter-Terrorism Organization) 38
Jolie, Angelina 216, 301–2
journalism xix, 11, 14, 37, 38, 40, 41, 91, 98, 109, 121, 130, 133, 144–5, 148, 156, 178, 195, 198, 216, 234, 244, 248, 273, 278, 294, 302, 307, 322, 324

junta 27, 30
  see coup

KADEK Kongreya Azadî û Demokrasiya Kurdistanê (Kurdistan Freedom and Democracy Congress) 51–3
Kahraman, Rahime 34
Kaka'i 19, 241, 249
Kamangar, Farzad 320
Kanî 198–200, 300, 315, 322
Kapakkaya, Ibrahim 26
Karadağ, Ayşe 183
Karer, Haki 26, 29, 316
Karyo, Siham 226–7
Kav, Fuat 29
Kaya, Sara 190–1
kayyum 294, 324
KCD/DTK Kongreya Civaka Demokratîk (Turkish: Demokratik Toplum Kongresi) (Democratic Society Congress) 92, 174
KCK Koma Civakên Kurdistan (Kurdistan Communities Union) 54, 57, 131, 174, 187, 197, 255, 269, 271, 322
KDP Partiya Demokrat a Kurdistanê (Kurdistan Democratic Party) 22, 24, 44, 54, 145, 159, 161–2, 167, 194, 197–9, 204–06, 221, 227, 246, 253–7, 260, 270, 273, 296, 322, 324
KDP-I Kurdistan Democratic Party-Iran 21, 24
Kemal, Musafata 20, 23
  see Kemalism
Kemalism 25, 29, 47, 112, 171, 177, 178
Kerkûk 86, 196, 204–6, 247–9, 303
Keskin, Diba 185, 324
Khaled, Leila 92
Khalil Aswad, D'ua 254
Kılıç, Bêrîvan Elif 181–3, 189–90
killing, the man 45, 103–111, 233
Kınacı, Zeynep (Zîlan) 47–8, 126
  see Şehîd Zîlan Academy
Kînem 237–8
Kışanak, Gültan 30, 171, 176, 321, 322

KJA Kongreya Jinên Azad (Free
Women's Congress) 179–181, 190,
293
see TJA
KJAR Komelgeya Jinên Azad ên
Rojhilatê Kurdistanê (Society of
Free Women of Eastern Kurdistan)
130, 318
KJB Koma Jinên Bilind (High Women's
Council/Union) 57
KJK Komalên Jinên Kurdistan
(Kurdistan Women's Communi-
ties) 57, 82, 93, 101, 142, 145, 335
knowledge production xviii, xx, 3, 4, 6,
13–15, 22, 62, 73, 76–7, 79, 80, 132,
164, 198, 208, 210, 320
Kobanê – Ain al-Arab xvii, 10, 33,
90, 96, 144, 208, 213, 219, 222,
228, 234, 236, 240, 244, 252, 266,
275–84, 292, 295, 296
Kobanê, Barîn 295, 312
Kobanê, Çiçek 295–6
Kobanê, Meryem xvii, 10, 234, 236, 244,
279, 280
see YPJ; Kobanê
Koç, Nilüfer xvi, 13
KODAR Komelgeya Demokratîk û
Azad a Rojhilatê Kurdistanê (Free
and Democratic Society of Eastern
Kurdistan) 318
Kolbar xix
Komala 21, 24
Konca, Besime 131–3, 321
Kongra Gel (People's Congress) 53, 57
Kongreya Star - Congress of Star
(Ishtar) xvi, 97, 208, 215, 225, 229,
232, 280, 288, 296
Korkmaz, Mahsum 34–5
KRG Hikûmeta Herêma Kurdistanê
(Kurdistan Regional Government)
22, 57, 153, 158, 163, 164, 194–205,
237, 240, 260, 270, 273, 293, 203,
322
Kubilay, Mukaddes 183
Kurdi, Alan 156

Kurdish language 19, 22, 73–4, 88, 116,
120, 134–5, 143–4, 164 177, 184,
253, 271, 282, 295, 320, 321
Kurdish Women's Association 23
Kurdistan Region (of Iraq) 146, 194–6,
260, 322
Kurdistan Revolutionaries 25–7, 85
Kurtay, Ferhat 29, 166, 321

land 3, 4, 21, 27, 48, 58, 66–7, 69, 70, 83,
86, 88, 112, 116, 118, 124, 151, 154,
156, 193, 203–4, 207, 220, 225–7,
237–8, 246, 249, 253–4, 260–1,
269, 272–4, 279–81, 285, 296, 300;
homeland love 58, 66, 83, 86, 88,
204
see welatparêzî
Latin America 27, 45, 79, 91, 121, 144,
271, 278, 297, 305, 315
Lausanne, Treaty of (1923) 20, 199
League of Nations 21
Lebanon 10, 33–5, 38, 74, 96, 316
left Turkish left: 25–26, 47, 174–75;
Palestinian left 33, 315; Syrian left
209–10, 217
Lerner, Gerda 69
lesbian 100, 245
Leyla 24; (Rojava) 229
see Güven, Leyla; Khaled, Leila;
Qasim, Leyla; Şaylemez, Leyla;
Zana, Leyla
LGBTQI+ (people, organizations) 131,
174–5, 179, 296, 321, 324
see queer
liberalism 13, 54, 66, 70–1, 87, 103,
200
see neoliberalism; feminism, liberal
Libya 216, 245, 294
local governance 181–7, 274
see municipality; municipalism
looting 116, 255, 285, 294, 309
love 13, 30, 31, 58, 66, 76, 94, 96,
99–111, 113, 116, 117, 118, 151–2,
164, 182, 198, 204, 237, 245, 255,
260, 297, 313
Luxemburg, Rosa 126, 150, 220, 224,
298, 309

al-ma'anawi 79, 244
Madimak Hotel 132
Mahabad 23
Mahir, Atakan 106
Al-Majid, Ali Hassan (Chemical Ali) 192
Mako 263, 264, 275
mal a jin 79, 97, 227–30, 267, 270, 288
Malatya 47, 247
Malik 108–9
Manbij 222, 225, 285–89, 296, 302
Mandela, Nelson 50, 91, 319
Maoism 85, 121
Maraş 27, 35, 131, 272
marriage 94, 99, 104, 107, 178, 181, 192, 213, 228, 293, 307, 317; child marriage 4, 135, 167, 171, 184, 228, 235–6, 286, 288–9; forced 4, 23, 36, 104, 178, 228, 230
martyrs 10, 32, 35, 44, 46, 65, 84, 96, 98, 126–8, 139, 158, 161–2, 166, 201, 213–4, 245, 257, 259, 261–2, 281–2, 298, 312, 317
see şehîd
Marxism 71, 99; Marxism-Leninism 6, 85, 212, 245; Marxism-Feminism 71, 150
masculinity 4, 6, 8, 43, 45–6, 94, 102–111, 122, 193, 213–4, 307
media xx, 1, 8, 11–2, 28, 54, 66, 104, 106, 135, 141, 142–8, 162, 166, 170, 176, 181, 189, 197, 202, 205, 210–12, 216, 232, 241, 243, 248, 270, 273, 277, 278, 292, 295, 301–3, 318, 319, 323, 324
see social media
MedTV 143
Mele Xelîl, Hebûn 296
Mem and Zîn 106
menstruation 79
Merchant, Carolyn 150
Mêrdîn – Mardin 40, 144, 176, 179, 183, 186, 190, 244, 254
Mesopotamia 19, 69, 108–9, 192, 207, 243–4, 285, 303–4; Ecology Movement 152–3, 175, 320; Academy for Social Sciences 108

Mexmûr (Refugee Camp) 10, 122, 128, 151, 156–69, 221, 245–7, 273, 294, 297
see refugees; forced displacement
MFS Mawtbo Fulh.oyo Suryoyo (Syriac Military Council) 231
MGRK Meclîsa Gel a Rojavayê Kurdistanê (People's Council of Western Kurdistan) 219
MHP (Nationalist Movement Party) 172
Middle East Partnership Initiative (MEPI) 306
Mies, Maria 9, 71, 150
Mihemed, Qazî 20, 23
Mihemed, Ramziya 227
militarism xx, 1, 2, 11, 24, 45, 66, 122, 157, 171, 178, 242, 295, 301, 307
military lockdown 118, 133, 292
see curfew
Mîrkan, Arîn 266, 277, 312
misogyny 30, 76, 124, 136, 147, 185, 302
Mohammadi, Zara 134
Mojab, Shahrzad 36, 305–6, 316, 320, 322
Moosa, Essa 319
Morales de Cortiñas, Nora 92
see Plaza de Mayo Mothers
motherhood 112–8
mountain
see Qendil; Şengal; Zagros; Taurus
Mozambique 27
MP 92, 118, 130, 170–1, 173–6, 179, 184, 291
municipalism 221
municipality 30, 98, 153, 154, 163, 171–6, 181–7, 189, 190, 276, 286, 294, 320, 324
Muslim Brotherhood 33, 215, 218, 317
mythology 78, 80, 109

Nafiyah (Êzîdî) 267–9; (Rojava) 97–8
Narîn 87–8, 106, 123, 138–9
National Endowment for Democracy 304
national liberation xxi, 2, 25, 45, 51, 56–7, 71

nation-state 2, 4, 5, 7, 13, 20–3, 56, 63, 70, 72, 90, 92, 113, 117, 122, 123, 128, 143, 156, 160, 201, 209, 221, 243, 246–7, 309, 311

NATO (North Atlantic Treaty Organization) xviii, 6, 11, 15, 33, 37, 50, 53, 121, 177, 208, 214–5, 218, 239, 278–9, 296, 301, 307, 309

Nayır, Pakize 293

neoliberalism 2, 6, 59, 121, 151–53, 158, 163, 172, 177, 193, 195, 198, 200, 203, 304, 306–8, 310, 322

Newaya Jin 143–4

Newroz 29, 39–41, 49, 55, 84, 89, 115, 131, 217, 245, 291, 293, 317

Newroz Camp 260, 262, 267–9

NGO 59, 153, 195, 304–6, 322; NGO-ization 107, 178, 195, 201–2, 211, 253, 275, 309

Nicaragua 2, 65

Nisêbîn – Nusaybin 40, 133, 190–1, 276, 292, 318

Ni una menos 144, 297

No-Fly Zone 160, 193

nom de guerre 9, 34, 39, 46, 47, 126, 144, 167, 263, 266, 271, 272, 316, 318

non-state/non-statist 6, 10, 63, 72, 123, 240, 243, 274, 289, 307, 312

nuclear family 101, 107, 110, 113

nuclear weapons 311

Nûda 221, 223, 236

Obama, Barack 177, 278–9

Öcalan, Osman (Ferhat) 53–5, 105

Öcalan, Abdullah xviii, xix, 6,7, 9–11, 24–7, 33, 35, 38, 44–9, 50–5, 56–7, 62–3, 65, 60–76, 83, 86, 90–8, 104, 106, 107, 110, 123, 127, 130, 134–7, 139–40, 151, 154, 173–4, 180–1, 196–7, 209, 212, 213, 214, 218, 233, 234, 236, 244, 251, 255, 263, 266, 269, 271, 275, 280, 293, 303, 309, 316, 317, 318, 319, 323; Abdullah Öcalan Academy for Social Sciences 136–41

occupation xx, 2, 37, 39, 66, 93, 106, 115, 120, 125, 152, 153, 192, 238–40, 242, 247, 271, 277, 287, 289, 296–8, 304, 306, 310, 316

Olufemi, Lola 310

Önen, Necmi 29

Operation Olive Brach 285, 294–5, 315

Operation Peace Spring 155, 295–6

Orientalism 72, 80, 90, 157, 303

Ortakaya, Kader 180, 276, 282

Osê, Amina 218–9

Oslo process (2009) 177

Özgür 272–4

Özsökmenler, Yurdusev 176

Pahlavi, Mohammad Reza 21

PAJK Partiya Azadiya Jin a Kurdistan (Kurdistan Women's Freedom/ Liberation Party) 48, 55–7, 65, 106, 138, 192, 200

Palestine 2, 13, 26, 27, 30, 32, 33, 34, 45, 65, 91, 92, 157, 298, 305, 315, 317; intifadas 39, 305
    see PLO; Leila Khaled

Palmyra 244, 285

Pan-Arabism 192, 211, 231

Pan-Turkism 206

paradigm xviii, 7, 8, 41, 51, 55, 56–7, 63, 121, 123, 135, 143, 150, 173, 179, 201, 209, 250, 265, 269–70, 278–9

Paris Commune 209

Paris murders 9, 10, 24, 144, 293, 296, 309

parliament 22, 27, 52, 93, 104, 118, 131, 170, 174–5, 179, 184, 203, 209, 277, 290, 291, 317, 321

patriarchy xviii–xxi, 1–6, 7–8, 13, 36, 44–46, 48–9, 51, 54–5, 58, 65–8, 69, 73, 76–9, 82, 85, 87, 89, 90, 95, 99–111, 112–3, 117–19, 124, 129, 135–7, 143, 146, 149, 150, 151, 167, 170–1, 176, 178–9, 187–8, 194, 194, 203, 209, 209, 213–14, 232–3, 234, 241–3, 279, 293, 287, 298, 302, 303, 305–7, 311, 315

Peace Mothers 93, 112–9, 166, 179

peace process 9, 41, 91, 93, 108, 114, 115, 130, 139, 179, 181, 190, 197, 200, 291–4, 319, 320, 323–4

Peker, Sedat 292

perception management 12, 303

Perwîn 201–2

pêşmerge 24, 44, 120, 193, 196, 198, 204–5, 248, 257–8, 317

Philippines 2, 78, 89

Pir, Kemal 30–2

PJA Partiya Jina Azad (Free Women's Party) 51, 55, 65

PJAK Partiya Jiyana Azad a Kurdistanê – Kurdistan Free Life Party 318

PJKK Partiya Jinên Karker ên Kurdistanê (Kurdistan Working Women's Party/Kurdistan Women Worker's Party) 50–1

Plaza de Mayo Mothers 92, 114

PLO (Palestine Liberation Organization) 33, 34, 39

Poetry 99, 132, 144, 247, 286; poet 23, 39, 100, 120, 148, 192, 193, 265, 320, 323; poem 39, 85

political prisoners xviii, xx, 9, 28–32, 46, 49, 50, 63, 78, 83, 90–93, 114, 129–33, 170, 179, 318, 320–22
see Diyarbakir Prison

politicians xviii, xx, 104, 109, 130, 133, 170, 171, 179, 193, 196, 226, 262, 276, 290, 293–94, 307, 322, 324

polygamy 167, 173, 184–5, 192, 228, 287, 289

Popular Mobilization Forces; al-Hashd ash-Sha'bi 204–5, 271

positivism 14, 62–63, 70, 76, 80, 210, 312

Poyraz, Deniz 297

prisons 28–32, 129–33; F-type 133; prison-industrial complex 91, 93, 101, 129
see Diyarbakır prison; Imralı Prison Island; political prisoners

proletariat 30, 56, 175, 213; proletarian revolution 27

propaganda 11, 12, 36, 113, 122, 241, 252, 303, 306, 307, 324

protest xix, xxi, 5, 8, 12, 24, 29, 30, 35, 40–41, 48, 50, 83–84, 90, 92, 93, 102, 104, 107, 114, 118, 124, 127, 129, 133, 136, 144, 160, 164, 167, 170, 178, 194, 198, 200, 206, 209, 214, 215–18, 219, 231, 232, 236, 238, 263–5, 270, 273, 276, 289, 296–7, 298, 315, 317
see demonstration

PUK/YNK Yekîtiya Nîştîmanî ya Kurdistanê (Patriotic Union of Kurdistan) 44, 194, 197, 204, 322

PYD Partiya Yekîtiya Demokrat (Democratic Union Party) 209, 214, 217–8, 221

Qadifa 118, 270

al-Qaeda 216, 219, 241, 294, 322

Qamişlo – al-Qamishly 97, 108, 190–1, 214, 222, 226, 230–1, 233, 236, 238, 250, 302, 312
see Zalin

Qasim, Leyla 24

Qasr-e Shirin Treaty 19

Qatar 209, 215

Qendîl 26, 35, 42, 82, 93, 100, 101, 119, 140, 142, 145, 196, 213, 249–51, 253, 256, 270, 271–3, 290–91

Qoçgirî Uprising 23

queer 2, 12, 80, 150, 178–9, 271
see LGBTQI+ (people, organizations)

race, racism: xxi, 2, 11, 34, 89, 125, 135–6, 211–2, 214, 292, 301, 307
see anti-racism

radical democracy 11, 13, 56–7, 62, 87, 90, 135, 153, 170–1, 179, 181, 185, 202, 224

ragihandina azad 143

RAJIN 145–6

Raparîn Uprising 193

rape 3, 4, 9, 23, 28, 99, 124, 178, 182, 187, 198–9, 241–2, 252, 292, 313; rape culture: 2, 101, 124, 171, 186, 198–9

Raqqa 222, 225, 270, 285–6, 296, 303

rebellion 8, 20, 23, 29, 37, 70, 192, 198, 209, 211, 311, 318
referendum 91, 117, 204, 205, 279
refugees xviii, xx, 10, 42, 63, 90, 122, 126, 128, 151, 156–69, 174, 194, 216–7, 221, 226, 245–7, 267–8, 273, 294, 295–7, 309, 315, 320
Reinstatement into Society Law 54, 318
religion 1, 4, 7, 42, 69, 72, 75, 78–80, 126, 178, 237, 244, 250, 254, 260–1, 278, 289
Renas, Amara 295
reparations 129, 149
Republic of Kurdistan 20, 22–4, 316
Reş, Fatê (Black Fatma) 23
Reşîd, Hedar 252, 255–60, 264
Riha – Urfa 25, 33, 34, 90, 94, 185, 273
Rimelan 220, 224, 229, 237
RJAK - Rêxistina Jinên Azad a Kurdistanê (Free Women's Organization of Kurdistan) 201–2
Rojavayê Kurdistan (Rojava) – western Kurdistan/Syria 10–11, 22, 40, 43, 46, 74, 76, 78–9, 87, 96–8, 108, 109, 110, 114, 118, 126, 136, 139, 154—6, 164, 178, 179, 187–8, 189, 190, 197, 206, 208–240, 244–5, 250, 253, 256, 258, 260–2, 255, 267–9, 270, 271, 273, 275–84, 287–88, 292, 294–8, 308, 312, 315, 320, 323, 324–5
Rojgar 192, 200
Rojhelat a Kurdistan (Rojhelat) – eastern Kurdistan/Iran xix, 24, 130, 156, 198, 263, 277, 318
Ronahî, Elif 35, 42, 46, 56, 66, 105
Roy, Arundhati 305
Russia 23, 30, 50, 56, 216, 239–40, 254, 307, 312

Safi, Frozan 298
Şahmaran 76–7
Şahin, Edibe 175–6, 291, 324
Sakık, Şemdin 38, 42–3
Şakir, Şîlan 202–3
Sanchez, Alina (Lêgerîn Çiya) 271

Sara (Sakine Cansız) 9, 15, 220; (Kobanê) 208, 228, 280–3
Sarya 147–8, 315, 320
Saturday Mothers 114
Saudi Arabia 209, 215
Save the Tigris 153
Şaylemez, Leyla 9–10, 24, 220, 293
Saziya Ziman 271
SDF Hêzên Sûriya Demokratîk (Syrian Democratic Forces) 215, 225, 227, 231, 242, 245, 286, 289, 308
sectarianism 123, 183, 192–3, 196, 206, 211, 216–7, 231, 273–4, 307
Segato, Rita 3, 242, 318
şehîd 126–8
see martyrs
Şehîd Jiyan Women's Academy 151, 156, 167
see Zeynep Erdem
Şehîd Zîlan Academy 87, 106, 138
see Zeynep Kınacı
self-criticism xxi, 45, 54, 56, 73, 85, 138–9, 165, 168, 188, 204, 264, 293, 311
self-defence xviii, 7, 13, 57–8, 65, 66, 68, 71, 73, 78, 120–5, 126, 129, 136, 143, 144, 166, 167, 181, 217, 219, 228, 232, 233, 234–9, 245, 246–7, 259, 260, 263–5, 269, 273, 275
self-determination 6, 20, 24, 26, 48, 58, 67, 74, 88, 94, 100, 117, 153–4, 156, 158–9, 186, 196, 247, 266, 316, 323
self-immolation 29, 90, 126, 194
self-sacrifice 126–7
Seljuk Empire 19
Semalka/ Faysh Khabour crossing 206, 227
Şemzînan – Şemdinli 34
Şengal – Sinjar 90, 102, 118, 204, 240, 246, 249–50, 252–74, 275–6, 294, 296–7, 318
Şengal Women's Assembly 261–3, 266, 269, 272–4
Serêkaniyê – Ras al-Ain 235–6, 295
serhildan 39–41, 44, 213, 276
settler colonialism 150, 273–4; settlers 294
see colonialism

Sèvres, Treaty of (1920) 20
sex 101; sex work 85, 129; sexual health 167, 186
sexism 2, 36, 49, 66, 70–2, 76, 78, 79, 105, 109, 110, 136, 139, 152, 164, 167, 170, 171, 178, 183, 184, 186, 198, 212–3, 301–3
Şêx Mehmûd Berzencî (Sheikh Mahmoud Barzanji) 20
Şêx Seîd (Sheikh Said) 20
Seyfo 230
Seyit Riza 20, 175
Shi'ite 19, 204, 205, 241
    see Islam
Shiva, Vandana 150
Şikak, Simko 23
Silêmanî – as-Sulaimaniyah 23, 196, 200, 202, 204, 206, 300
Silopi killings
Sincar, Cihan 183
Sipçik, Zeynep 176
Şîrîn 261
Şîrîn and Ferhad 106
Şirnex – Şırnak 160, 248, 318
Sisters Mirabal 126, 298
Sivas massacre 132
    see Alevis; Madimak Hotel
slavery 1, 2, 98, 237, 241, 252; women's enslavement: 27, 46, 48, 104, 113, 188, 237, 241, 261
Smith, Linda Tuhiwai 3
SNC al-Majlis al-Wat.anī as-Sūri (Syrian National Council) 218, 222
social contract 49, 51, 59, 65, 74, 102, 167–8, 185, 219, 222, 224, 231–3, 287, 308
social ecology 150–53
social history xx, 1–15, 66, 72, 128
socialism xviii, xx, xxi, 2, 7, 8, 12, 13, 22, 24, 25–7, 33, 42, 45–48, 51, 53–4, 56, 62, 71–72, 85, 96, 99, 107, 122, 134, 151, 175, 177, 183, 202, 212, 278, 292, 303, 309, 325
social media 5, 11, 113, 134, 147–8, 241, 276, 293, 302
social work xxi, 45, 80, 107, 146, 198, 257

Society for the Advancement of Kurdish Women 23
Soleimani, Qasem 205
solidarity xvi, 2, 5, 12, 14, 26, 30, 31, 51, 74, 80, 100, 107, 110, 122, 124, 130, 132, 133, 136, 152, 154, 156, 158, 164, 171, 175–6, 181, 190, 208, 217, 218, 224, 228, 229, 230, 239, 241, 275, 276, 278, 279, 285, 289, 292, 296, 298, 302, 308, 310, 311
South Africa 2, 50, 78, 91, 93
Southeastern Anatolia Project (GAP) 33, 153
sovereignty 2, 20, 70, 117, 149, 151, 154–5, 160, 210, 273–74
Soviet Union 21, 25, 33, 37, 65
special war(fare) 37, 145, 210, 214, 289, 307
Sri Lanka 2
students 24, 42, 85, 108, 134, 136, 163–5, 172, 182, 271, 282; university 25, 40, 93, 213, 276, 324
subsistence 38, 152; perspective 150; economies 152, 195, 203, 225
Sujîn 144
Sumerian 65, 69, 70, 78, 109, 303
Sunni 19, 34, 178, 244, 254, 290
    see Islam
Suruç (Pirsûs) 276, 281, 292
surveillance 89, 114, 124, 129, 158, 212, 238
Susurluk 37
Sykes, Mark 20
Sykes-Picot Agreement 20
Syria xviii, 4, 10, 11, 19, 20–2, 27, 33–6, 42, 46, 47–9, 50, 74, 76, 78, 96, 98, 108, 127, 141, 153, 156, 157, 190, 208–240, 241–5, 249, 252, 258, 265, 276, 285–9, 292, 294–7, 298, 302, 303, 308–9, 317, 318, 322–4, 325
Syriacs 20, 23, 47, 123, 141, 211, 226, 230–34, 249, 262, 295–7; Syriac Union Party 231; Syriac Women's Union 230–34
Syrian Democratic Council 224–5
Syrian National Army 296

Tabqa 222, 225, 285–6, 296
TAJK Tevgera Azadiya Jinên Kurdistan
    (Kurdistan Women's Freedom
    Movement) 44
Talabanî 194
Taliban 304, 312
    see Afghanistan
'Tamil solution' 178
Taş, Bedriye (Ronahî) 41
Taurus 19
Tavîn 86, 303
Tawosî Melek 254, 261
teachers 23, 38, 98, 108, 109, 130,
    134–36, 163–5, 167, 267, 282, 286,
    320, 321
Tel Afar 249, 257, 258
television (TV) 80, 110, 112, 116, 132,
    135, 143–8, 182, 198, 219, 253, 289,
    290, 301, 320
Tell Mozan 244
terror(ism) 1, 29, 36, 112, 118, 230, 242,
    243, 275, 276, 278, 285, 287, 294,
    307, 309, 323, 324; terrorist group/
    organization 11, 24, 83, 197, 241;
    state terror xxi, 2, 66, 101; war on
    terror(ism) 11, 53, 220, 278, 279,
    302–4, 306, 309, 312, 315
Tevda Tevgera Demokratîk û Azad a
    Êzîdiyan (Êzîdî Movement for
    Democracy and Freedom) 257
Tev-Dem Tevgera Cîvaka Demokratîk
    (Movement for a Democratic
    Society) 212, 214–15, 219, 223
Tevgerî Azadî Komelgey Kurdistan
    (Kurdistan Free Society
    Movement) 202–4
think tanks 11, 210, 241, 278, 309
Thomas, Raymond 308
Tirbêspiyê – al-Qahtaniyah 118, 229,
    231, 262, 270
TJA Tevgera Jinên Azad (Free Women's
    Movement) 179
    see KJA
torture xix, xx, 3, 24, 27, 28–32, 37–8,
    40, 41, 46, 76, 91–2, 112, 129–32,
    175, 192, 193, 212, 215, 216, 241,
    243, 257, 280, 294, 304, 321

Tosun, Remziye 118
transphobia 2, 178
tribes, tribalism 4, 20–2, 23, 34–5, 36,
    37, 42, 58, 72, 84, 88, 95, 104, 117,
    120, 162, 122,185, 187, 193, 203,
    213, 221, 237, 289
Trump, Donald 295
Truske 146–7
Tuğluk, Aysel 321, 322, 324, 174, 187,
    189
Tuncel, Sebahat 170, 173, 321
Tunisia 218
Turkey xviii, xix, 4, 6, 9, 10, 11, 19–21,
    22–23, 24, 25–7, 33–6, 37–41,
    44–7, 50–2, 53–7, 74, 78, 83, 85,
    90, 91, 93, 112, 114, 121, 130–1,
    144, 153, 155, 156, 157, 159, 160,
    161, 162, 170–91, 193, 194, 197,
    205–6, 209, 211, 214–9, 221, 222,
    235, 239, 241, 244, 245, 246, 248,
    256, 258, 270, 276, 279, 282, 285,
    290–7, 301, 307–9, 315, 316, 317,
    320, 321, 322, 323
    see army, Turkish
Turkmen 204, 206, 231, 285–7, 296

Uğraş, Sultan 171
UKO National Liberation Army –
    Ulusal Kurtuluş Ordusu 25
Ukraine 312
United Nations 246, 310–11,
    312, 324; Security Council
    311; United Nations Revised
    Standard Minimum Rules for the
    Treatment of Prisoners (Mandela
    Rules) 91; United Nations High
    Commissioner for Refugees
    UNHCR 159–64, 246–7, 297, 301,
    321; United Nations Rules for the
    Treatment of Women Prisoners
    and Non-custodial Measures
    for Women Offenders (Bangkok
    Rules) 129
United States of America US(A) 11, 13,
    14, 50, 52, 53–4, 57, 58, 93, 130,
    177, 193, 195, 197, 206, 209–10,
    214, 222, 227, 240, 249, 275, 278–9,

286, 301, 303, 304, 306, 307–9, 312, 322, 323
urban war 292–4, 318
Urkesh 241
Üstündağ, Nazan 117, 181, 223, 324
utopia(nism) 1, 5, 71, 87, 94, 96, 101, 124, 213, 303
Uyar, Fatma 293

Vietnam 25, 27, 45, 65
village destructions 26, 172, 193
village guards (korucu) 37–8, 116, 160, 317

Walia, Harsha 156, 208
Wan – Van 46, 114, 185, 247, 282, 290
Wan, Ekin (Kevser Eltürk)293
Waysî, Amîna 296
welatparêzî 66–7, 83, 86–8, 107, 213, 263
Wêranşar – Viranşehir 185, 254, 273
witch-hunt 76, 150
Wolf, Andrea (Ronahî) 46, 78
womanhood 9, 43, 79, 104, 112, 201
womenandchildren 113
Women Defend Rojava 296
women's empowerment xix, 2, 195, 305–07
Women's Liberation Ideology 48–9, 54, 65–8, 265
women's revolution xviii, 1, 5, 10, 13, 45, 49, 96, 179, 208, 211, 234, 296, 299–313
Women Rise Up for Afrîn 280
World Bank 157, 310
World Women's March 144, 190
WWI 20
WWII 209

Xabûr, Avêsta 312
Xan-î Neqeb, Hepse 23
Xelef, Hevrîn 295, 298, 324
Xensê 272–4
Xeyr, Qedem 23
Xidir 260

YAJK Yekîtiya Azadiya Jinên Kurdistan (Kurdistan Women's Freedom Union) 45, 48, 50, 197

Yarsan 19
Yaverkaya, Hanım 34
Yavuz, Sultan 35
YBŞ Yekîneyên Berxwedana Şengalê (Şengal Resistance Units) 252, 260–1, 267–8, 318
YDG-H Tevgera Ciwanên Welatparêzên Şoreşger (Turkish: Yurtsever Devrimci Gençlik Hareketi) (Homeland-loving Revolutionary Youth Movement 318
    see youth; YPS; YPS-Jin
Yıldıran, Esat Oktay 30–32
Yıldırım, Kesire 94, 104, 135, 316
Yıldırım, Nilgün (Bêrîvan) 41
Yılmaz, Akif 30
YJA - Yekîtiya Jinên Azad (Union of Free Women) 57
YJA Star Yekîneyên Jinên Azad ên Star (Star (Ishtar) Free Women's Units) 43, 57–59, 102, 122, 144, 205, 236, 247–48, 252–53, 262, 265, 272, 274, 302–03, 324
YJŞ Yekîneyên Jinên Şengalê (Şengal Women's Units) 260, 270, 318
    see YPJ- Şengal
YJWK Yêkitîya Jinên Welatparêzên Kurdistanê (Union of Home-land-loving Women of Kurdistan) 35, 42
young women 10, 41, 67, 73, 83, 86, 104, 110, 141, 146, 166, 179, 182, 195, 197, 198, 206, 208, 226, 229, 255, 265, 267, 282, 289, 290, 302, 305
youth xviii, 5, 7, 10, 25, 27, 34, 39, 42, 57, 58, 70, 71, 85, 90, 126, 131, 136, 138, 139, 147, 163, 164, 172, 174, 196, 198, 213, 219, 229, 231, 257, 258, 265, 267, 269, 282, 286, 292, 304; youth movement 25, 40, 74, 126, 158, 165, 166, 174, 236, 257, 272, 292, 318; assembly 162, 163, 166, 224
    see YPS, YPS-Jin, YDG-H
YPG Yekîneyên Parastina Gel (People's Protection/Defence Units) 97, 209,

215, 231, 235–7, 252–3, 258, 272, 275, 280, 282, 308, 318
YPJ Yekîneyên Parastina Jin (Women's Protection/Defence Units) 58, 144, 209, 215, 231, 234–7, 244–5, 252–3, 258, 262, 265–6, 272, 275–7, 282, 295–6, 301–3, 312, 318, 324
YPJ-Şengal 252, 260, 262, 265
   see YJŞ
YPS Yekîneyên Parastina Sivîl/ (Civil Defence Units) 318
YPS-Jin Yekîneyên Parastina Sivîl a Jin (Civil Defence Units – Women) 318
YRK Yekîneyên Rojhelatê Kurdistanê (Eastern Kurdistan Units) 318
Yüce, Sema 49

Yüksekdağ, Figen 176, 188
Yusuf, Hediye 219–20, 262
YXG Yekîneyên Xweparastina Gel (People's Self-Defence Units) 219

Zagros 19
Zalin 233
   see Qamişlo
Zana, Leyla 170, 318
Zapatistas 74, 134, 209, 313, 325
Zarife 23
Zaxo (city) 202, 253; (name) 213–14
Zehra (Êzîdî) 267–9
Zelal 136–8, 141
Zengin, Mahmut 29
Zenobia 225, 244, 285
Zerdeşt 257, 259
Zetkin, Clara 220, 224

Thanks to our Patreon subscribers:

Andrew Perry
Ciaran Kane

Who have shown generosity and
comradeship in support of our publishing.

Check out the other perks you get by subscribing
to our Patreon – visit patreon.com/plutopress.
Subscriptions start from £3 a month.